THE NEW GLOBAL UNIVERSITIES

The New Global Universities

Reinventing Education in the 21st Century

Bryan Penprase

Noah Pickus

PRINCETON UNIVERSITY PRESS

PRINCETON AND OXFORD

Published by Princeton University Press
41 William Street, Princeton, New Jersey 08540
99 Banbury Road, Oxford OX2 6JX

press.princeton.edu

All Rights Reserved
ISBN 978-0-691-23149-5
ISBN (e-book) 978-0-691-23148-8

British Library Cataloging-in-Publication Data is available

Editorial: Bridget Flannery-McCoy and Alena Chekanov
Production Editorial: Jenny Wolkowicki
Jacket design: Chris Ferrante
Production: Erin Suydam
Publicity: Alyssa Sanford and Kathryn Stevens
Copyeditor: Maia Vaswani

Jacket image: Maisei Raman / Shutterstock

This book has been composed in Adobe Text Pro & Gotham

Printed on acid-free paper. ∞

Printed in the United States of America

10 9 8 7 6 5 4 3 2 1

CONTENTS

ACKNOWLEDGMENTS

As part of our research for this book, we interviewed the founders of all of eight of the universities whose stories we tell, as well as members of their founding teams and others. Unless otherwise cited, all quotations in this book come from these interviews. We thank all our interviewees for their time and for their support. Their stories inspired us and made this book possible.

We would also like to thank our research team, including Linda Zhang, Duke University undergraduates Amiya Mehrotra and Blair Spencer, and Takako Mino, who joined from Ghana and Uganda and brought special insight to new universities in Africa. Linda Zhang led the team of student researchers, and Amiya Mehrotra was especially helpful in her work on multiple chapters. We are grateful to Matthew Rascoff for his wise and encouraging comments in the early stages of the project and to Stacia Pelletier for her sage advice and expert editorial eye in the latter stages.

During the preparation of the book, we were helped by the staff of Princeton University Press, including Peter Dougherty, who offered excellent insights into how best to structure the book for a wide audience and guided us through the final stages of review. Others from Princeton University Press include our new editor, Bridget Flannery-McCoy, Alena Chekanov, and Jen Hill. We thank our anonymous reviewers for their careful review of the manuscript and for many helpful suggestions to improve the accuracy and clarity of our presentation.

Our greatest debt is to our families for their patient and unstinting support. We benefitted greatly from multiple writing retreats where we would ramble through hours of conversation and debate as we navigated through complex issues and sometimes conflicting viewpoints. Josh Pickus provided helpful perspective on the book and he and Carey Pickus were gracious hosts during one of our retreats in Utah. Our families also supported us throughout the years of preparing the book as well as in our global travels that led up to it. Bryan would like to thank his wife, Bidushi Bhattacharya, for her love and support and humor and her deep insights into the true meaning of education as a way for providing a deeper humanity. Noah would like to thank Trudi Abel for her love, faith, and unfaltering partnership, and Micah and Mira, whose own educational journeys have given shape and meaning to this book.

December 21, 2022
Alisa Viejo, California and Durham, North Carolina

ABBREVIATIONS

ALA African Leadership Academy

ALG African Leadership Group

ALU African Leadership University

ALX African Leadership Experience

ASU Arizona State University

BJP Bharatiya Janata Party

DKU Duke Kunshan University

EHU European Humanities University

ELM experiential learning module

FETP Fulbright Economics Teaching Program

FUV Fulbright University Vietnam

HBCUS historically Black colleges and universities

HCs Habits and Concepts

IDS Institute for Development Studies

IIE Institute of International Education

IIT Indian Institute of Technology

ISB Indian School of Business

KGI Keck Graduate Institute

KIC Kigali's Innovation City

KNUST Kwame Nkrumah University of Science and Technology

MENA Middle East/North Africa

MIT Massachusetts Institute of Technology

MOOC massive open online course

NAB National Accreditation Board

NAE National Academy of Engineering

NEET New Engineering Education Transformation

NUS National University of Singapore

NYU New York University

NYUAD NYU Abu Dhabi

SPS Special Project in Science

STEM science, technology, engineering, and mathematics

UAE United Arab Emirates

UC University of California

UCL University College London

USC University of Southern California

USFQ Universidad San Francisco de Quito

USP University Scholars Program

WASC Western Association of Schools and Colleges

WEIRD Western, educated, industrialized, rich, and democratic

YIF Young India Fellowship

THE NEW GLOBAL UNIVERSITIES

1

Introduction

START-UP U

As the last century wound to an end, Patrick Awuah, a former software engineer and program manager at Microsoft, and Nina Marini, his fellow MBA student at the University of California, Berkeley, created a business plan for a new kind of liberal arts college in Awuah's native Ghana. Twenty years later, their vision became Ashesi University, designed to educate the next generation of African leaders. Around the same time, the F. W. Olin Foundation asked Richard Miller, an engineering dean based in Iowa, to bring its vision for an innovative engineering school to be based in Massachusetts to reality. That germ of an idea became Olin College of Engineering, which today rivals MIT in the rankings of engineering education.

Just over a decade later, in 2010, John Sexton, the president of New York University, met in Abu Dhabi with Sheikh Mohamed bin Zayed, and the two agreed to launch a new campus for NYU in the Middle East that would come to be known as NYU Abu Dhabi. Soon after Sexton and Sheik Mohamed shook hands, Dam Bich Thuy, the chief executive officer of ANZ Bank in Vietnam, sat in her office with Thomas Vallely, a former marine who had served in Vietnam and was then the head of Harvard's Vietnam Program; together, they imagined building a kind of university unknown in the region—one that would combine public policy, business and management, engineering, and the liberal arts. This vision became a reality in the form of Fulbright University Vietnam.

Meanwhile, in India, four first-generation entrepreneurs—Pramath Sinha, Ashish Dhawan, Sanjeev Bikhchandani, and Vineet Gupta—began meeting in the Oberoi Hotel in New Delhi. By 2010, they had decided to pool their resources to launch a liberal arts school to compete with the most prestigious institutions in the world and attract the best students from across India and beyond, which became Ashoka University. At the same time, Tan Chorh Chuan, the president of the National University of Singapore, and Richard Levin, the president of Yale University, began negotiating a partnership to build a new global liberal arts college in Singapore, which became Yale-NUS College.

During these same years, in California, the Silicon Valley entrepreneur Ben Nelson secured a $25 million dollar investment from Benchmark Capital to create a university that would be named Minerva, which promised to revolutionize the teaching enterprise while radically cutting costs. And in a 2014 TED talk, Fred Swaniker, a former McKinsey consultant, would articulate a vision for building twenty-five university campuses across Africa that would educate three million new leaders by 2035. This network, now known as African Leadership University, is part of a larger ecosystem of institutions that has raised almost a billion dollars, built two campuses, created a set of cost-efficient regional hubs, and launched a virtual career accelerator and a global talent matching system.

All this activity might strike many as odd, given the ways in which higher education observers routinely predict the demise of the university and question the value of a liberal arts education. Critics in the United States point to a series of interlocking problems facing contemporary higher education: increasing costs and a perceived lack of return on investment, a monochrome political culture that stifles wide-ranging debate on controversial topics, and a growing perception of the liberal arts as outmoded and irrelevant to the challenges of the twenty-first century. Yet even as these storm clouds hover over traditional forms of higher education in the United States, the sun is shining brightly on new institutions that are redefining and reinventing liberal arts in every corner of the world.

Since the turn of the century, new schools devoted to liberal education have sprung up in Asia, Africa, Europe, and the Middle East, as well as in North and South America. Student demand for entry to these schools is unprecedented, and some of them are more selective than the far more established schools in the Ivy League. After the excitement of launching the new schools, the high-quality results of this type of education have kept observers interested—and made parents, governments, and employers enthusiastic supporters. Despite the global pandemic and fraying international relations, we are witnessing ever-greater interest across the world in new global liberal arts universities, as nations seek to build their own incubators for creativity and innovation.

This book tells the inside story of the who, what, why, when, and especially the how behind the launch and development of eight of these new colleges and universities. We provide a detailed assessment of these schools, and the lessons learned from the dramatic history of their founding can guide anyone aspiring to start up a new college or university. We also aim to spur the imagination of those seeking to reinvent established institutions. Two of the schools in this book are global ventures of established universities: Yale-NUS College in Singapore and NYU Abu Dhabi in the UAE (United Arab Emirates). The other six schools—the Olin College of Engineering and Minerva University in the United States, Ashoka University in India, Fulbright University Vietnam, the African Leadership University in Mauritius and Rwanda, and Ashesi University in Ghana—are entrepreneurial ventures built from the ground up.

Some of these new colleges and universities seek to recover and reimagine ancient traditions of learning in countries that previously offered only more colonial forms of education. Others concentrate on creating modular and integrated curricula that draw on advances in our understanding of how students learn. Still others focus on the complexity and richness of education that can arise from a truly global student population. All of these schools offer new learning environments focused on achieving the highest quality of undergraduate education, advancing the most cross-cutting forms of inquiry and experiential education, and cultivating the dispositions and skills needed to navigate a turbulent world. They exemplify practices that have a high impact on student learning, including a strong emphasis on writing and research, first year and capstone seminars, common intellectual experiences and collaborative assignments, and internships and civic engagement.[1]

We follow each of these schools through its history to date, with a special focus on the founding era, when the complexities and difficulties of the enterprise rise to their greatest levels. By studying this wave of new institutions, we preview the future possibilities for an educational enterprise unhindered by preexisting structures and legacy curricula: these are laboratories for innovation. The schools we examine aspire both to curate the knowledge and accomplishments of a wide range of global cultures and to transform their own societies to meet the profound challenges of the twenty-first century. Their formation, evolution, and setbacks tell dramatic stories of how academic entrepreneurs have overcome the constraints on innovation that pervade much of higher education. How the founders of these universities have navigated these constraints offers important lessons in leadership and intellectual courage.

We have visited most of these institutions in person, though the COVID-19 pandemic meant that we conducted our formal interviews online. And while you will hear the voices of students and faculty in each chapter, our attention in this book primarily falls on the founders and other leading architects of these schools. Building from interviews with nearly thirty university founders and current leaders, we offer vivid portraits of individuals who have taken the risk of starting up an entirely new institution, often forgoing the safety and security of successful careers in industry and academia. Pramath Sinha, for instance, trained in metallurgical engineering at the Indian Institute of Technology and the University of Pennsylvania, built a successful consulting career in North America and India, and then cofounded Ashoka University. Ben Nelson pivoted from the private sector, where he had spent ten years building Snapfish, a technology company, to found Minerva University.

Other leading innovators came from inside higher education. Sidee Dlamini, born in South Africa and educated at Texas Christian University and the University of California at Berkeley, left her home to help build the new African Leadership University in Mauritius. Canadian Pericles Lewis, an expert in modernism and digital humanities and professor in Yale's English Department, gave up his life in New Haven to begin a new chapter as the founding president of Singapore's first liberal arts college. And as Olin College entered its twentieth year—it is the oldest of the start-ups we studied—Gilda Barabino left the City College of New York to take Olin's helm and complete the transfer of leadership from its founding president, Richard Miller.

We hope our interviews with university founders and leaders capture the drama and heroism of their quest to create new institutions and entirely new academic cultures. We trace what they sought to preserve, what they wanted to change, and how they pursued strategies to foster innovation. Diving deeper, we explore the transition of each new university from its inception to the emergence of distinctive characteristics influenced by location, local culture, and institutional partners—as well as by fiscal, political, and academic considerations. The stories of these universities are multifaceted, and offer lessons on multiple dimensions, while eluding simple categories and storylines. We found them continuously inspiring.

Your Guides to the Future of the University

We came to this study after thirty years of teaching, research, and academic leadership in American colleges and universities. We approach this book primarily as practitioners in higher education. Both of us have been deeply involved in launching new ventures similar to the start-ups we analyze in this book, having played key roles in the founding of Yale-NUS College in Singapore and Duke Kunshan University in China. (Noah also became so intrigued by one of our case studies, Minerva, that he ended up doing a stint as part of it.) Both of us have studied and taught at liberal arts colleges and research universities. We come from the fields of astrophysics and politics, and together our perspectives help bridge the cultures of science and the humanities. With decades of experience in academic research and administration, we know all too well the barriers to change in academic life, yet we recognize the necessity of new academic programs for renewing and sustaining higher education.

How did our collaboration come about? We met in 2012 when we were going in different directions. After a long career at Pomona College, Bryan left for a fellowship at Yale University, where he would help design the curriculum and work with the inaugural faculty and leaders of the nascent Yale-NUS College. Noah, who had been teaching ethics and public policy at Duke University for fifteen years, was spending his fellowship year working with the president of Franklin and Marshall College in Pennsylvania, as that school adapted to significant demographic, financial, and educational pressures. We made common cause, and, jointly and individually, we visited over fifty schools in the United States and abroad. At every stop, we sought to understand how university leaders were dealing with the waves of change washing over their institutions.

Despite our disparate academic backgrounds and trajectories, we share two core beliefs. First, we are both devoted to the transformative value of high-quality, meaningful liberal arts and sciences education. As students and as teachers, we know firsthand how a college community can cultivate deep learning that goes beyond narrow areas of specialization. We appreciate the ways in which a liberal arts college is optimized for undergraduate learning and how faculty are incentivized both for their prowess as scholars and for their effectiveness as educators and contributors to the commonweal. This teacher-scholar model provides opportunities for frequent interaction and deep mentoring between faculty and students and is combined with a more open-ended pathway through the curriculum, enabling students to explore unexpected interests and engage in a process of self-discovery. By receiving opportunities to discover new talents and interests before specializing, students can maximize their learning engagement and also make connections between different forms of knowledge that equip them to better analyze and address complex problems in their own communities.

At the same time, we also share a deep frustration with the inability of both liberal arts colleges and liberal-arts-oriented research universities to embrace change. Narrow, specialized forms of expertise are still the primary form of knowledge recognized and rewarded in most of higher education, and especially among the top-ranked schools. Majors still largely reflect traditional, disciplinary-based knowledge, as if ten courses in English or political science are the only or best ways to prepare students for a world in which deep habits of writing and reading and crucial skills as leaders will be required. While we value students gaining some measure of depth and expertise in a field of study, we see siloed and increasingly narrow forms of research and teaching as barriers to cultivating adaptable, creative, and truly wise students.

This narrowness is exacerbated by the demise of any commitment to ensuring that students share enough knowledge and experience in common, so that, as Columbia University's Andrew Delbanco puts it, "no one student is a complete stranger to any other."[2] Instead, faculty offer students vague distribution requirements, as if a course in chemistry here and literature there amounts to any kind of coherent exposure to core ideas or ways of knowing. The highest quality of teaching is also insufficiently prioritized, even at some of our best schools. When tenure largely rewards scholarship, great teachers remain the exception rather than the rule. And even when a school does prioritize the highest-quality teaching in thoughtfully designed curriculums, the cost of attendance is beyond the means of many. Those few schools that can afford to provide significant financial aid move mountains to meet the needs of as many students as they can. But the very cost of the education and the unwillingness of most institutions to think differently about ways to offer more flexible and affordable ways of learning mean that most elite schools remain overwhelmingly populated by students who come from the wealthiest backgrounds. As we began to talk about these issues, we realized how frustrated we both felt by these seemingly intractable barriers to a genuinely outstanding education.

The reasons for these constraints are not hard to find. Too often, colleges and universities are driven to conformity by their desire to maintain or to achieve prestige. Indeed, far more than creativity, cost control, or innovation, the world of higher education is defined by rankings based on research productivity and by popularity based on how difficult it is for students to be admitted. These twin metrics—research productivity and student exclusivity—cause colleges and universities to emulate one another, replicating practices that maximize research scholarship and curriculums that imitate highly ranked peer institutions. In the most prominent institutions, the historic accretion of wealth and prestige has paralyzed the academic culture into a state of stasis, leaving leaders unable to muster the energy to fix something that many faculty do not think is broken. While serving as founts of creative thinking inside the laboratory or by the solitary thinker, universities paradoxically lack all but the most superficial forms of differentiation.[3] Richard Brodhead, former president of Duke University, calls this "the inertia of excellence."[4] This lack of differentiation also reflects the cultures and structures of higher education, which were designed internally to support institutional longevity and to encourage mimicry owing to external regulation; over time, these forces converge to reduce dynamism in the market. This risk aversion is further supported by a system of shared governance that fragments decision-making authority and often requires a high degree of consensus to try something new or even just to stop doing something old.

As Bryan was working to launch what became Yale-NUS College in Singapore, Noah was invited to help create a new university in China, today known as Duke Kunshan University. As we pursued our respective work, we met many others around the world who were also founding new institutions, and we became inspired by the possibilities to push at the boundaries of the constraints on innovation in higher education. Both of us began our explorations by leaving our own institutional culture to learn about other cultures; and, to our happy surprise, we were indeed discovering fresh perspectives about the value of the liberal arts. Traveling in India to visit new universities and living and working in Singapore and China gave us the chance to see the exhilarating new ways in which Asian countries were embracing the liberal arts as a way to invigorate and accelerate economic growth. They saw a direct linkage between higher education and their national success, an understanding that seems notably absent today in the United States.

It was bracing and refreshing to see how important the educational enterprise was for the future of these countries. Our travels also gave us insights into what a start-up in education looks like on the ground. Start-up universities embody the youthful energy, the utopian spirit, and the open-ended possibilities that match the mind-set and energies of their students. While traditions and culture strongly shape what's possible at well-established schools, start-ups create their own cultures and new ways of thinking, often cocreated by faculty, students, and staff in real time. This process of cocreation was another wonderful surprise from our journey across the higher-education landscape and is shared in the pages of this book. Across all these institutions, we found a truly compelling level of engagement in the creation of the institutional fabric—and a sense of shared ownership of the school's vital importance. We came away wanting to share those institutional stories with readers who might also find them inspiring.

Thorny Questions

Our journey also made plain the many thorny questions that founders of new universities must confront. Higher education is a complex environment in which simple solutions often end up dashed on the rocks. Some of the problems arise in the planning process, such as how to communicate the vision behind a new venture to attract supporters, faculty, and students. Essential to this quest is the elusive quality of prestige and the accompanying question: *How do you start a new university and create an appealing brand when nobody knows who you are?*

Another problem, much lamented by the popular press and by parents paying for tuition in the United States, involves higher education's astronomical cost. Paradoxically, the best weapon for reducing these costs is a massive institutional endowment, which allows for expenses to be reduced through financial aid. At most of the wealthiest private universities, these endowments are built over centuries and amount to billions of dollars. They are supplemented by gifts from generations of alumni and well-wishers, allowing the established university to bank on the accumulated social capital of many generations. A new university enjoys none of these benefits. Yet it somehow must build a new campus, pay faculty, and provide financial aid and a reasonable price point for students. This raises the question: *Where in the world do you get the money needed to build a top-ranked university from scratch and keep it financially viable?*

Even if the university founder has somehow navigated past these daunting obstacles, the new institution needs to attract high-quality faculty, who in coming to the new university are taking giant risks for their career, and almost certainly will be saddled with Herculean challenges in designing the curriculum, starting new research programs, and establishing the institution, sometimes in an unfamiliar country thousands of miles from their home.

This raises another difficult question: *How do you attract faculty to commit their careers to an institution that does not yet exist, and then convince students and families to invest in the unproven institution?*

Once the initial capital, campus, and founding faculty are in place, the next steps involve building the new curriculum and earning accreditation from agencies that often favor familiar and time-tested approaches to teaching and learning. While faculty and supporters are often motivated by the challenge to innovate and provide something entirely new, their energy and enthusiasm can collide head on with the harsh reality of creating classes that work and that accreditors are willing to validate, while finding faculty who understand how to teach in new ways. Hence another thorny question: *How does one design a new curriculum that is innovative and distinctive, that is responsive to the demands of the new century, and yet is recognizable to accreditors and employers?*

As a new university begins to mature and rapidly outgrows its initial location, its physical and virtual infrastructure simultaneously needs to grow with it to support the many new programs, classes, and research projects underway. The process is a bit like building a railroad track right in front of the locomotive as it moves ahead at full steam. Somehow the campus needs to be built out even as the programs are being initiated. *How does one acquire land, build a new campus, and expand the physical and virtual presence of the new university, even while the institution is being launched?*

As daunting as these questions are, they are only the most tangible challenges in building a new institution. Still knottier challenges arise in creating a workable system of governance and forging an academic ethos that can help the new institution's leaders collectively make intelligent decisions and respond to the needs of the country and region where their college or university is located. These challenges can be summarized as follows: *How does a founding team build an effective governance structure and an authentic shared culture in a brand new institution, without any of the shared assumptions or traditions that most universities enjoy?*

Another set of especially difficult questions arises from the tensions between an explicit or implicit commitment to preparing students to function in a democratic society within a world in which they might live under radically different forms of governance. The nature of both the questions and the answers here varies, but they are shaped by the location, the local culture and community, legacy practices imported by faculty, and the energetic influence of the student body. All these forces shape an institution and its emerging cultures and values. Yet this process raises additional thorny questions. *To what degree are these new start-ups reflections of a distinctly American approach to the liberal arts, and to what degree do they reflect local traditions and aspirations? What are the different and sometimes hidden meanings embedded in aspirations to offer a globalized form of education and to create "global citizens"?*

Some of the schools we survey in this book have had to navigate explicit and implicit challenges to their commitment to *ars liberalis*, or the "art of freedom," when operating in different cultural and political contexts. *How, then, can one create a university that protects academic inquiry and free expression in societies that don't share democratic values?* The chapters that follow offer observations and lessons learned—sometimes lessons still in process—from the institutions we examined.

A Pluralist View of Impact

Higher education has paid much attention in recent days to the tasks of increasing access and lowering costs. The primary strategies for addressing these vital concerns have involved building larger institutions and deploying technology to reach even more students. These strategies have begun to have a significant impact. Schools such as Arizona State University (which in 2022 enrolled over 70,000 students on campus and more than 60,000 students online, with 13,000 international students on campus and 29,000 graduate students) and Southern New Hampshire University (with 3,000 students on campus and 175,000 online as of 2022) have led the way in inventing new and improved ways to deliver higher education to more students.

By way of contrast, the institutions we profile in this book have all started small, usually with well under a thousand students, and even the ones that imagine scaling their size aspire to reach no more than a few thousand students, though a couple aspire to reach ten to twenty thousand students. We focus on these smaller schools for several reasons. As important as it is to lower costs and increase access, some of the larger institutions are simply scaling up existing models of higher education. While these larger institutions are indeed refining efficiency and improving delivery mechanisms to reach larger and larger audiences of students, their Achilles' heel can be the quality of the education they offer. In too many cases wider access, whether in person or online, offers poorly defined curricula and outdated modes of teaching often delivered either by faculty focused primarily on research or by adjunct instructors cobbling together classes at different colleges or universities. These larger-scale institutions, with only a few notable exceptions, do very little to ensure that their students actually receive a meaningful education. For this reason, we concentrate on smaller institutions with a more innovative bent that have set their sights on reimagining ways to offer the highest-quality education. These schools also face the challenge of increasing access and reducing cost, and so we spotlight several that have taken on this challenge in exciting new ways. Even for those institutions that intend to remain relatively small—and some of them are also expensive—we see enormous value in examining what innovations are possible when the quality of education constitutes the highest priority.

Not all these innovations will be adaptable by larger institutions, of course. But we think much can still be learned from the opportunity to loosen the constraints on the imagination and by the process of design. As with any sort of monoculture, a lack of diversity and experimentation poses a long-term threat to higher education. Certainly, the COVID-19 pandemic gave us all a shared personal experience of how our human species is threatened, and it reminds us of how ecosystems are at risk without the ability to learn from differentiation. For this among other reasons, we see our start-up universities as vibrant green shoots of change, of innovation and experimentation, traits that can be notably lacking in the larger or older institutions, including many well-established liberal arts colleges. Ultimately, we are pluralists in the educational arena: we think that having more schools worldwide in which participants and planners get under the hood and tinker with the engine, or even reimagine the chassis, drives impact. A thousand smaller to medium schools that offer high-quality education should complement the current preoccupation with a few schools gaining increasing market share.

Our start-up universities have employed a spectrum of strategies for developing greater impact beyond their walls. Ashesi University in Ghana is an example of a school that seeks to stay small, form partnerships with others, and to accomplish its mission of nurturing a new generation of entrepreneurial and ethical leaders for Africa. By seeking to educate a new vanguard, Ashesi aims no less than to foster a new African renaissance and allow African countries to fully enter the global stage. By contrast, another of the institutions we study, African Leadership University (ALU), aspires to operate on a completely different scale of student enrollment and refuses to limit itself to one country or even one continent. Some of the institutions we study, such as ALU and Minerva University, are pushing the boundaries to find more efficient ways to develop the highest-quality learning environments, while others, such as Yale-NUS College and NYU Abu Dhabi, instead prioritize maximizing quality, with few cost constraints.

Still other institutions, such as Ashoka University and Fulbright University Vietnam, have had a direct impact on higher-education law in their regions—here India and Vietnam, respectively. Fulbright leaders successfully pushed to revise regulations in their country so that the measure of independence they gained from government oversight could be claimed by other universities as well. Ashoka's imprint can be seen in the National Education Policy issued by the government in 2020 and in subsequent government promulgations. The 2020 policy document validated the liberal arts approach within Indian education and urged its broader implementation across the country.

The influence of these start-up institutions doesn't end there. We can also observe their demonstration effect—that is, the ways in which their new organizational forms and pedagogical cultures have become a reference point for broader transformations in higher education. For Ashoka, these transformations are apparent in the spread of similar kinds of ventures across India, as hundreds of new privately funded universities have opened their doors since 2015, including prominent entrants that offer Ashoka-like interdisciplinary and liberal arts forms of education. Olin College of Engineering sits at the top of the rankings for engineering education, a remarkable level of recognition that has enabled it to achieve a worldwide impact: leaders of engineering schools around the world regularly visit and establish connections to emulate the unique ingredients of success that Olin has found. Minerva University, too, is regularly recognized within the top ranks of innovative universities; and the for-profit Minerva Project now partners with a growing number of new and established universities across four continents, which seek to adopt Minerva's approach to curricular design, teaching pedagogy, and systematic assessment for their own regions.

Who This Book Is for and How It Unfolds

There are three different audiences for this book. First, our colleagues in higher education will find value in the courage and intellectual chutzpah that it takes to start a new college or university from scratch. Leaders of future start-up institutions as well as established universities can learn valuable lessons about fostering innovation and change. Second, the growing legion of entrepreneurs who come from outside the academic tradition can also gain from reading this book: we hope it will help them see more clearly how academic culture and priorities within a start-up university share certain characteristics with industrial start-ups but also have substantive differences—and why these differences matter. Finally, we would like to help the general public, both in the United States and globally, better understand the value of a liberal education for unleashing creative capacities and building collective understanding both in the humanities and social sciences and in the STEM (science, technology, engineering, and mathematics) and entrepreneurial fields.

As participants in start-up ventures ourselves, we are painfully aware of how hard it is to create something truly new and valuable in academic life. As such, our inquiry has been driven by an appreciation of the intellectual challenges and practical trade-offs involved in founding new colleges and universities. We haven't looked for scandals, written an exposé, or sought to discredit what the various founders have aspired to achieve. Where warranted, however, we have brought an appropriate measure of skepticism, because we wanted to test claims and dig deeper than a public relations exercise. One of the greatest ills in academia occurs when critics shift from skepticism to cynicism, and we've worked to avoid that in these pages. Instead, we've sought to question superficial claims made by both supporters and detractors, and we want in our inquiry to understand deeply and fully how these institutions have come to life. As a result, our narrative offers few easy solutions; instead, it seeks to inspire others by showing how our founders have, for the most part, successfully completed inordinately difficult journeys, while also revealing tensions that they have navigated along the way.

This chapter has provided a brief introduction to us as authors and our journey through the landscape of higher education. The following chapter provides an overview of the global landscape of higher education and some of the emerging trends that affect universities around the world, and that have set the scene for a wave of exciting new start-up universities. The subsequent eight chapters provide deep dives into the founding stories of eight of the most exciting twenty-first-century global start-up universities. Our stories focus on the founders, their vision, and the struggles and achievements that arose within the first years of starting their new university. These stories constitute chapters 2 through 9, the main body of this book. In each chapter-length case study, we create a portrait of the founding team members, their environment, and the unique factors that shaped the design solutions they developed.

Our first two case-study chapters follow the founding of two new institutions built in Asia by well-established parent institutions: NYU Abu Dhabi in the UAE (chapter 3), and Yale-NUS College in Singapore, built by Yale University and the National University of Singapore (chapter 4). The next two chapters follow the development of new institutions that made use of a codesign process where students and faculty worked together to build the curriculum: Olin College of Engineering in the United States (chapter 5) and Fulbright University Vietnam (chapter 6). The subsequent chapters consider the adoption of a largely American-style liberal arts model to new contexts, founded by leaders who were making a return to their home countries after experiencing the US liberal arts model in their own education: Ashoka University in India (chapter 7) and Ashesi University in Ghana (chapter 8). The final two case-study chapters explore the founding of two unique models for a new kind of university that offers holistic reform and promises to lower costs and leverage new technologies as a central design feature. These institutions also are both heavily influenced by corporate entrepreneurial culture and arise from founders with extensive experience within the Silicon Valley start-up environment: African Leadership University in Mauritius and Rwanda (chapter 9) and Minerva University in the United States (chapter 10).

After our journey through the stories of each of these schools, we conclude with three chapters that synthesize and analyze what we have observed. While the geography and personalities are indeed distinct, all the new universities share common properties shaped by similar forces and constraints within higher education. In chapter 11 we explore the visible dimensions of building a new university, which can be thought of as the artifacts and espoused values of the emerging culture, to use the terminology of organizational theorist Edgar Schein. These artifacts and values include the development of institutional prestige and a sustainable business model, the mechanics of the build and launch (including hiring faculty and recruiting students), developing a new curriculum, and achieving accreditation. The development of both a physical and a virtual presence is also explored in this chapter, and the ways in which the resulting community and campus foster a new institutional culture and the interactions needed for a vibrant intellectual learning environment. Chapter 12 dives into the complexities that arise within the newly established academic community, including the thorny issues of governance, the conflicts that can arise from competing interests in the new university, and strategies for resolving these tensions. Among these complexities are the ways in which the new university interacts with multiple stakeholders, especially local governments, and manages competing political interests within its country and region.

In chapter 13 we reflect on several underlying patterns. We include in this final chapter a set of takeaway lessons for the diverse audiences for this book and for higher education as a larger shared enterprise within human civilization. This chapter includes lessons for future founders of new universities and participants in established colleges and universities (current faculty, students, academic leaders, and boards), as well as all who care about preserving what's special about a liberal arts education, while creating new ways for this type of learning to flourish in the world. Lastly, we conclude with a set of personal reflections on our journey together, on what most inspired us, what we found most surprising, and what questions continue to consume us. We thank all the founders, faculty, critics, and supporters who have made a high-quality liberal education accessible to their students and to future generations. We hope you enjoy this journey as much as we did in taking it.

2

The Liberal Arts Go Global

To understand how our start-ups have gone about answering the thorny questions we outlined in the last chapter, it will help if we first define what we mean by the liberal arts and briefly trace the term's evolution. A liberal education is a comprehensive and holistic approach to the purpose of education. Its aim is to prepare workers and citizens who can think broadly and learn independently. It includes a set of common courses or classes in a breadth of disciplines as well as the development of intellectual competencies that go beyond specific disciplinary content. The liberal arts purposefully inculcate problem-solving and analytical skills, the ability to listen and to communicate, and the capacity to integrate and make meaning out of contending intellectual and cultural perspectives. Graduates develop both qualitative and quantitative acumen, as well as what the educational researchers Gerard Postiglione, Ying Ma, and Alice Te call "a deep understanding of complex connections between issues of profound importance."[1] Liberal arts and sciences education strives to prepare graduates to make wise contributions to technologically dynamic and culturally diverse societies. This approach contrasts most directly with the dominant method of education globally, which is highly specialized or technical and explicitly vocational in orientation.

Historians in the West often trace the idea of a liberal education to ancient Greece and Rome. As higher-education scholars Philip Altbach and Kara Godwin write, "it stems from two Western traditions: Socrates' belief in the value of 'the examined life,' and Aristotle's conviction for 'reflective citizenship.'" To free the mind from mere tradition or habit, a liberal education "requires its students to study beyond a single subject or within one family of disciplines (and beyond the humanities). . . . [I]t lays the foundation for learning how to interpret, interrogate, or to make new knowledge framed in the constructs of various fields."[2] From the beginning, and contrary to popular assumption, the "liberal arts" does not mean the humanities and the fine arts alone. It is a frequent misunderstanding that the arts and humanities are antithetical or unrelated to the science, technology, engineering, and medicine fields, when in fact they are vital counterparts. Within the liberal arts, science is an equally indispensable element for fostering adaptability and creativity as part of a holistic education. In the modern knowledge economy, skills associated with STEM graduates (for example, quantitative literacy) are necessary in the arts and humanities as well as in society and politics. In this book, we use "liberal education," "liberal arts," and "the liberal arts and sciences" interchangeably to mean a broad, interdisciplinary curriculum and comprehensive higher-education philosophy.

This liberal arts approach has proven itself highly effective in preparing students for careers in the sciences, technology, politics, business, and culture. One point of evidence is that twelve of the fifty-three Nobel Prize winners between 1999 and 2008 who received their undergraduate education at a US college or university received it at a liberal arts college, amounting to 23 percent of Nobelists educated in the United States.[3] This is all the more remarkable given that less than 2 percent of US undergraduates study at a liberal arts college. The top ten institutions per capita for producing Nobel Prizes include two US liberal arts colleges, Swarthmore and Amherst. Liberal arts colleges account for twenty-seven of the top fifty sources of science and engineering doctorates per hundred bachelor's degrees and produce a larger percentage of the tech workforce than that made up by technical graduates.[4] And while these statistics are impressive for stand-alone liberal arts colleges, almost all large American research universities have colleges of liberal arts and sciences as well as a general education program in the liberal arts and sciences. So the impact of liberal arts education is also felt in larger research universities, making this form of education central to the success of US and many global universities.

The small liberal arts college has also outperformed its size in producing leaders in politics and culture. Twenty-seven percent of US presidents attended liberal arts colleges and thirty-five percent of US Supreme Court chief justices.[5] Fourteen percent of US-educated MacArthur "genius" fellows have come from liberal arts institutions. The CEOs of major companies are disproportionately graduates with liberal arts degrees, including at Disney, Starbucks, HBO, Hewlett Packard, Whole Foods, YouTube, and Alibaba.[6] Liberal arts graduates are frequently found among the ranks of Pulitzer Prize winners.[7] In one of the few extended analyses comparing liberal arts college alumni and other college graduates, Richard Detweiler found that adults with liberal arts backgrounds were far more likely to exercise leadership and to volunteer and give to charity and that these students were significantly more likely to report that they were generally satisfied with their lives and viewed their professional and family lives as meaningful.[8] While students who graduate with preprofessional degrees tend to secure higher salaries upon graduation, in some fields their earnings curve often flattens out in contrast to liberal arts majors, whose earnings rise over time.[9]

Liberal arts education has also been surprisingly effective at training the top inventors of advanced technologies. The connections between human factors and engineering, most notably embodied in a wave of "design thinking" that is revolutionizing engineering programs, is well suited to liberal arts education. Steve Jobs often cited his time at Reed College as instrumental in his inspiration for the many Apple computer products. Jobs described himself as "a humanities person as a kid, but I liked electronics." Through his liberal arts training he was able to develop himself as one "who could stand at the intersection of humanities and sciences."[10] Another tech entrepreneur with liberal arts training is Robert Noyce, coinventor of the integrated circuit and cofounder of Intel Corporation, who went to Grinnell College. These outcomes have inspired many new engineering curricula based in the liberal arts, blurring the lines between traditional liberal arts and technology.[11]

In 2015, the World Economic Forum surveyed 370 top executives from nine global industry sectors representing over thirteen million employees to inquire about drivers of change in the workplace and to provide insights on the needed characteristics of future employees. The resulting study, "The Future of Jobs," highlighted the need for skills that remain central to a liberal arts education. The report notes that "social skills—such as persuasion, emotional intelligence, and teaching others—will be in higher demand across industries than narrow technical skills."[12] Other skills needed by future graduates include complex problem-solving, critical thinking, creativity, people management, coordinating with others, judgment and decision-making, service orientation, negotiation skills, and cognitive flexibility, all of which are developed extensively within most liberal arts programs.[13]

Waves of Change

Historically, the idea of a liberal education found its most prominent expression in the United States. Hundreds of liberal arts colleges founded by competing religious denominations began this most distinctively American form of education. The influence of this tradition can also be seen in the near-universal requirement in the United States and commonly in global universities that students receive some form of general education before they narrow their focus of study. In the United States, start-up universities have come in waves, and we can see several groups of new colleges and universities that were founded in the past two centuries that incorporate a broadly liberal arts approach.

The first US universities were variations of the British model adapted for the new American world. These schools introduced a new living and learning environment in which education would take place both inside and outside the classroom, and in what Andrew Delbanco calls "lateral learning" and today we call "peer learning." The core philosophical approach derived from the Protestant-inflected idea that we are not here simply to understand the divine but to learn the truth. This education was primarily there for those who would go into the ministry or teaching and character building was viewed as an important part of educational experience.[14]

A large number of small liberal arts institutions were founded soon after the establishment of the Ivy League schools in the late seventeenth and early eighteenth centuries. These new liberal arts colleges were often led by faculty who emerged from Harvard and Yale and who wanted to pioneer a more personal and more progressive form of liberal arts education. Williams College was founded by former Yale faculty and alumni in 1793, as was Middlebury College in 1800, and Amherst College in 1821. The pace of institutional creation soon accelerated, with dozens of new liberal arts colleges founded at a rate of one every eight months in the 1820s. By 1860 more than ten colleges were being founded each year. By the end of the nineteenth century, over 150 liberal arts colleges had been founded, sometimes with an agenda that included the education of women and of African American students.[15]

By the mid-nineteenth century, dozens of new public universities had popped up, largely in the American West and Midwest, sparked by the Morrill Act of 1865. Some of the first start-up universities of this period are now leading world universities. These include Cornell (1865), Massachusetts Institute of Technology (MIT) (1865), the University of California (1868), and the University of Wisconsin (1866). These schools focused on teaching practical applications of knowledge in response to changes wrought by the Industrial Revolution. In an era of increasing mass production, teaching came to resemble a one-way transmission from professor to student with standardized examinations as the metric for assessing retention. (Letter grades, departments, electives, majors, and the credit hour also all emerged in this period, as Steven Mintz points out.) This ethos reflected an egalitarian push to offer education to "the sons of toil," and increasing emphasis was placed on scaling institutions to reach more students.[16] Under the influence of German universities, faculty research became more specialized and narrowly disciplinary, as well as more applied.

By the end of the nineteenth century, a hybrid model of education emerged that combined the first wave's emphasis on undergraduate education and the second wave's focus on the finest and most specialized forms of disciplinary research, often integrating the German model of graduate education into the institution. Johns Hopkins University (1876), Stanford University (1885), and the University of Chicago (1890) all exemplify this new wave of institutions. Over time, writes the sociologist Jonathan Cole, "a robust value system was put in place on which great 'steeples of excellence' could be built—organized around transmitting knowledge to both undergraduates and advanced and professional school students."[17]

The number of bachelor's-degree-granting institutions in the United States grew steadily through the twentieth century and beyond, reaching nearly three thousand by 2015. Attendance at American colleges and universities rose even faster—increasing by 400 percent in the first half of the century and accelerating further after World War II, with a corresponding increase in the diversity of student populations and increasing social mobility for graduates who benefitted from their education.[18] Generous state and federal funding shaped the twentieth-century higher-education landscape, including the new indirect cost model, in which the government funded individual researchers conducting specialized investigation at universities. These ample funding sources further developed the emphasis on disciplinary research, even as the GI Bill and federal student aid vastly expanded who could attend college. The result was a vast growth of the largest universities, while the small liberal arts colleges remained largely unchanged in size, typically capped between one thousand and two thousand students. By the end of the twentieth century, these liberal arts colleges were enrolling a tiny proportion of US college students and yet wielded a disproportionate impact, thanks to the achievements of their graduates.

Different phases of innovation in higher education continue to profoundly shape colleges and universities today: the intense, handcrafted approach seen most often in the small liberal arts colleges, the mass-production model of education pioneered in the nineteenth century, and the powerful focus on ever more specialized research that came to dominate the most prestigious research universities in the twentieth century. These three trends have left a blended legacy, with most schools today seeking a delicate balance among goals for increased access and social mobility, reduced costs, and high-quality education and research.[19]

As these three waves formed and left their imprint on the shores of higher education, innovation among the smaller liberal arts colleges also kept pace. Women's colleges and historically Black colleges and universities (HBCUs) carved out room for students excluded by mainstream institutions. Between 1836 and 1875, fifty women's colleges opened. The majority of HBCUs launched between 1865 and 1900, with most starting in 1867, two years after the Emancipation Proclamation.[20] And in the era following World War I and the Great Pandemic of 1918, academic entrepreneurs initiated a series of new ventures. "In the 'hour of experiment' that ensued," the historian Emily Levine and education reformer Matthew Rascoff observe, "innovators developed alternative models of higher learning that eschewed research for authentic learning." These models included: "the Socratic method (Deep Springs College, 1917), adult education (the New School, 1919), the Oxbridge tutorial system (Sarah Lawrence College, 1926), euthenics—an early self-improvement movement (Bennington College, 1932), and the experimental arts (Black Mountain College, 1933, deemed by John Dewey a 'living example of democracy in action')." Levine and Rascoff describe these new schools as part of a pattern "that would be repeated many times over: when institutions fail, academic entrepreneurs establish new spaces for learning outside existing structures."[21] This pattern reappeared later in the twentieth century. In the 1950s and 1960s, a small group of experimental colleges was founded, including private schools such as Pitzer College, Harvey Mudd College, and Hampshire College, and public schools including the University of California at Santa Cruz, Stockton State, and Ramapo College of New Jersey. Many of these institutions pioneered new interdisciplinary curriculum and teaching methods; and some schools, such as Harvey Mudd, have influenced more recent waves of change.

The Liberal Arts Go Global

Our book documents the most recent wave of innovation in the liberal arts, beginning in the late twentieth century and accelerating in the years since. Like previous surges of higher-ed innovation that responded to epoch-making changes in technology and society, the new institutions whose stories we tell are responding to seismic changes in information technology, intellectual life, and social affairs. What is most distinctive about this newest wave is its global dimension.[22]

While various forms of American schools have long existed abroad, such as the American University in Cairo and Franklin University Switzerland (an outgrowth of the American School in Switzerland), the last two decades have seen significant growth in liberal arts schools and affiliated modes of learning that are far more than branch campuses of US institutions: these are new independent ventures.[23] Kara Godwin has documented over two hundred such programs in fifty-eight countries outside of the United States, including in Asia, Africa, Latin America, the Middle East, Europe, and Russia, a significant uptick from the 1980s, when only about sixty such ventures existed.[24]

Some start-ups have focused on realigning academic units and degree programs away from traditional fields and toward interdisciplinary problems. Examples include Leiden University College in the Netherlands, with its Global Challenges curriculum and immersive engagement with the international agencies and courts of law in The Hague, and University College London's new Arts and Sciences BASc program, which includes an interdisciplinary core curriculum emphasizing connections between disciplines while integrating arts and sciences within individually developed degree programs. These programs at UCL, Leiden, and the many "university colleges" in the Netherlands exemplify the experimentation underway within centuries-old universities—and serve as a reminder that older institutions, too, can initiate new ventures.

Quest University in Squamish, British Columbia, was founded as a standalone liberal arts university to help solve problems identified in larger Canadian universities—neglect of undergraduates, increasing academic specialization, and a sense that graduates were ill prepared to face the modern world. The university's unique academic curriculum includes a block system calendar, where students take a single course for three and a half weeks; students also organize their studies around a self-generated question rather than a traditional major.[25] Despite this innovative approach and a decade of successful operations, Quest is struggling owing to financial problems, a reminder that fresh approaches often are vulnerable to fiscal realities.

Within Latin America, bold new universities have been founded to fill in much-needed niches for innovation in science and technology and provide liberal arts approaches to education. Examples include Tec de Monterey, a private university that includes twenty-six campuses across Mexico, and which in 2019 developed a new undergraduate curriculum known as Tec21 that is based on innovative new pedagogy, such as team-based learning, problem-based learning, and interdisciplinary approaches to grand challenges.[26] In Ecuador, the top-ranked university is Universidad San Francisco de Quito (USFQ), founded in 1988 as the first private nonprofit university, which prides itself on its liberal arts education.[27] A new STEM university, Yachay Tech, was founded in 2014, and in the past five years has finished first in the Nature index for science research among universities in Ecuador.[28]

Other new start-up institutions are dedicated to opening opportunities for women. Founded in 2005, the Asian University for Women in Chittagong, Bangladesh, offers an American-style liberal arts and sciences curriculum and is the first independent institution in Asia primarily dedicated to women's education and leadership development. It currently educates more than a thousand students from eighteen countries, including many from Afghanistan, Myanmar, and Syria, who receive refuge and education safely away from their war-torn countries.[29] Another example is the Akilah Women's Center, which was founded in 2008 and is the first and only all-female higher-education institution in Rwanda. It has subsequently expanded to offer a coeducational option called Davis College Rwanda.[30]

Still other start-ups courageously offer students a learning environment free from the political constraints that limit discourse in their countries. In doing so, they also demonstrate the fraught nature of their ventures, especially as authoritarian governments have become more prominent in recent years. In the aftermath of the Soviet Union's collapse, new institutions like the European Humanities University (EHU) were founded to emphasize "the basic roots of European civilization" through liberal arts instruction.[31] EHU was founded in 1992 in Belarus to create a new type of university that would be "untainted by the old ideology and the sudden idolatry of capitalism," in the words of inaugural rector Anatoli Mikhailov.[32] In 2003, Belarusian authorities nearly forced the school to close until the Lithuanian government offered to host it, and it operates in Lithuania today "in exile." Smolny College in Russia has faced an even more difficult path. Established in 1997 as a partnership between Saint Petersburg University and Bard College in the United States, the college has offered self-designed majors to develop creative and unconventional thinkers. In 2019, however, the Russian government declared Bard "a threat to the foundations of Russia's constitutional order" and effectively ended the unique dual degree program, although Smolny may still survive as an independent school.[33]

Many of the new start-up institutions also draw inspiration from their local regions and cultures. One example is Habib University, unique within Pakistan. It offers a liberal arts education that arises from its South Asian context and heritage and invokes the Islamic notion of *Yohsin*, which emphasizes the need for applying knowledge for both "personal self-cultivation and perfecting the world." In the United States, Zaytuna College, headquartered in Berkeley, California, has made its mark as the first accredited Muslim liberal arts college in the country. Founded in 2009, its mission is to "ground students in Islamic scholarly tradition as well as in the cultural currents and critical ideas shaping modern society."[34]

Although a liberal education emerged historically most prominently in the United States, many of the new liberal arts schools are drawing on their own indigenous traditions. Across Asia, Confucian thinking offers deep literary and philosophical traditions oriented around humanism and self-reflection and promoting personal exploration rather than passive learning. Hindu and Buddhist traditions have also emphasized self-reflection and self-realization, which were fostered in universities founded centuries before the oldest European universities. Nalanda University in India, founded in 427 CE, was a residential university hosting a global community of scholars, and helped foster intellectual connections across the world. In Cairo, Al-Azhar University, founded in 975 CE, supplemented theological studies with philosophy, mathematics, and astronomy.[35]

Nonetheless, today the vast majority of countries shaped by Confucian, Hindu, Buddhist, and Islamic traditions offer highly utilitarian and ideological forms of education. Some nations have inherited educational systems from their former Western colonial overseers that are narrowly vocational, bureaucratic, and hardly designed to cultivate citizens and knowledge workers. Others have struggled to emerge from the Soviet emphasis on science and engineering at the expense of the humanities, even as the heavy hand of the state seeks to impose new forms of ideological conformity in countries like China.[36]

Yet even in China, leading research universities have started new and experimental residential liberal arts colleges within their boundaries. In 2014, for example, Tsinghua University established Xinya College as a reform program to further advance liberal education. *Xin* (new) *ya* (beautiful cultivation) focuses on integrated, interdisciplinary learning and self-cultivation.[37] Students are exposed to classical and contemporary literature, linear algebra, and quantum mechanics and can major in fifteen concentrations ranging from philosophy, politics, and economics to creative design and intelligence engineering.[38] China is also the site of several multinational start-up universities in partnership with US and European universities. Prominent examples include NYU Shanghai, established in 2011 in partnership between New York University and East China Normal University, and Duke Kunshan University, established in 2013 in partnership between Duke University and Wuhan University. Both of these two new institutions offer broad-based interdisciplinary liberal arts education, with US degrees.

What accounts for this new global wave of liberal arts innovation and institution building? Scholars point to three main factors driving the growth of liberal arts education outside the United States, which emerge from the economic, social, and human currents roiling the waters of modern life. Marjik van der Wende, the founding dean of Amsterdam University College, characterizes these three factors as economic and utilitarian when it comes to student outcomes, epistemological in the growing convergence of knowledge especially in the sciences, and social and moral with regard to personal development and social responsibility.[39]

The first factor arises from the changing nature of work and the economy. Globalization, rapidly changing technology, and the evolution of the knowledge economy all require fresh thinking—the hallmark of a liberal arts and sciences education. As technological advances render many jobs obsolete, success will be defined by those who can adapt to quickly changing markets and learn new skills throughout their careers. In a future with unscripted, difficult-to-predict problems, more important than what one learns will be *how* one learns—the central focus of a liberal arts and sciences education. Ingenuity and inventiveness are essential in a knowledge economy.[40]

A second factor emerges from the increasing complexity of national and global challenges and the parallel emergence of new forms of cross-disciplinary knowledge. Problems like environmental sustainability, inadequate public health, social inequality, and natural disasters all require integrated solutions that span multiple fields of knowledge and necessitate open inquiry.[41] The organization of knowledge itself has also changed, with the increasing convergence of fields that cross traditional disciplinary boundaries. In the United States, the National Academies of Sciences and Engineering and the Institute of Medicine have identified four key drivers of interdisciplinary research: "the inherent complexity of nature and society, the desire to explore problems and questions that are not confined to a single discipline, the need to solve societal problems, and the power of new technologies."[42] It's important to note that the need for interdisciplinary work is not confined to the natural sciences, engineering, and medicine: it is also evident within efforts to solve broader societal problems, where it is necessary to fully incorporate the human dimensions of industrialization, technological change, and globalization.[43]

The third and final factor is driven by the decline in shared religious norms, the growth in hyperindividualism, and increased group conflict. These trends have required colleges and universities to give greater attention to building a deeper sense of purpose among students and strengthening the social compact. Economic innovation and a newfound emphasis on material prosperity in many countries has raised concerns about the spread of Western values that prioritize personal success at the expense of the well-being of others.[44] At the same time, the resurgence of ethnic, religious, and national conflicts has drawn attention to the need for certain kinds of citizens—those who are capable of making wise judgments, caring for the least protected in society, and navigating the complex welter of local, national, and global identities and interests that make up our twenty-first century reality.

These three traits can all be cultivated by a truly liberal arts education, though other scholars warn that current trends within the American academy threaten to undercut this opportunity. As elite colleges and universities have become more narrowly focused on fields of study seen as gateways to financial success, some argue that these institutions are now more likely to produce conformists than independent thinkers, more beholden to the individual and the global over the local and the communal.[45] Set amid a broader range of cultures and communities, the new wave of global institutions offers an opportunity to counterbalance these tendencies.

Innovation and Tradition

Given our focus on start-ups, a reader might well think that we are captivated by innovation and change in higher education. Yet that would be an incomplete or even inaccurate assessment. As much as we are taken by the stories of the new schools we tell in this book, we are both marked by our long experience within the heart of academia. We value the way universities promote deliberation over dispatch, the central role accorded to faculty and the contemplative life, and the dual commitment both to preserving cultural memories and to pushing the frontiers of discovery. We know that while companies and governments come and go, colleges and universities have been designed to produce long-term value; their resistance to public fads and private-sector nostrums is one of their greatest virtues. As Clark Kerr, former president of the University of California, observed in 1963, of the eighty-five institutions in the Western world established in 1520 that still exist in recognizable form, seventy of them are universities "in the same locations, with some of the same buildings, with professors and students doing much the same things." (The other fifteen institutions include the parliaments of the Isle of Man and of Iceland and several Swiss cantons). Colleges and universities are among the most long-standing of social institutions, and we prize our connection to venerated historical traditions.[46]

If this track record means that it is hard to do new things in academic life, that's not all to the bad. Innovation for innovation's sake serves no one. New kinds of education, like advances in medicine or surgery, must be judged based on their effectiveness in meeting the appropriate goals. To be worth the time and effort, educational innovation must improve how students learn and how their education serves society. Breathless calls for "disruptive innovation" and wholesale change across the higher-education sector too often undervalue the remarkable achievements of our colleges and universities.

Innovation is one of those words that can be hard to pin down. It is most simply described as a new product or a new process. In this book, we do not advance a single concept of innovation or offer a detailed innovation checklist. We see valuable instances of change within existing parameters of educational practice as well as examples of change that push out those parameters. To our mind, innovation can range from rapid incrementalism to radical transformation.[47] We are most interested in what Michael Crow and William Dabars call pedagogical and curricular innovation (new forms of teaching and learning), as well as design innovation (novel institutional frameworks); where relevant, we note instances of epistemic innovation (new approaches to discovery and knowledge production).[48]

We know that a wide variety of innovation and experimentation is actively underway within long-established liberal arts colleges and universities in the United States and elsewhere. In the ten-plus years preceding the pandemic, new innovations were emerging across higher education, from the access and impact focus at upstarts like Arizona State University to the educational and degree innovation at the venerable Georgetown University. ASU's Michael Crow has written powerfully about the importance, as one title has it, of "designing the new American University," and he has spearheaded the launch of the University Innovation Alliance, a coalition of public research universities committed to increasing the number and diversity of college graduates in the United States. In her work leading the Futures Initiative at the City University of New York and in her book *The New Education*, literary scholar Cathy Davidson has identified evolutionary strategies that, over time, can fundamentally transform an institution—such as programs that offer more support for first-generation students. In his work transforming Northeastern University and in his book *Robot-Proof*, Joseph Aoun has placed the advent of intelligent machines at the center of his educational vision to "make people more agile, adaptable, and creative, and inspire us to be fully human."[49]

Small liberal arts colleges have also seen an uptick in experimentation and innovation, as is evident from the titles of several recent books: *Redesigning Liberal Education: Innovative Design for a Twenty-First-Century Undergraduate Education, Remaking College: Innovation and the Liberal Arts*, and *The Undergraduate Experience: Focusing Institutions on What Matters Most*.[50] In an indication of increasing ferment, the former president of St. Johns College, a "great books" school founded in 1696, and a host of academics and intellectuals, dispirited by what they saw as the growing illiberalism on American campuses, announced the launch of the University of Austin. This new school, they said, would dedicate itself to "the right to think the unthinkable, discuss the unmentionable, and challenge the unchallengeable."[51]

Meanwhile, historians and futurists have been assessing the drivers of change in the modern world and plumbing their imaginations for what these shifts might mean for learning. In *Academia Next*, Bryan Alexander forecasts a series of alternative scenarios for the future of higher education that range from technology-driven open education and personalized tutoring to a "retro" campus that rebuffs the encroachment of the digital world. In *Alternative Universities: Speculative Design for Innovation in Higher Education*, historian David Staley imagines ten different kinds of new universities, ranging from "Interface University," which would focus on the intersection of human and artificial intelligence, to "Polymath University," which would require students to major in three unrelated disciplines, to "Nomad University," in which the physical location would shift from course to course and year to year.

We embrace the aspirations and experiences of the schools in our book as worthy for consideration in the context of all these varied efforts at speculative design and actual reform. "In order for any of the designs proposed in this book to be actualized," Staley writes, "I suspect we would very likely need to create a new institution, rather than expect to redesign or reorganize an existing organization, since resistance to change is endemic in higher education."[52] In that same spirit, we offer eight stories of what happens when dreamers and designers take up Staley's challenge and create a real, live, new university. In doing so, we see more clearly the possibilities and the constraints in imagining a new world and then doing the hard work to bring it into being. We join these writers and reformers in believing it is imperative to launch new experiments as a way of meeting the needs of our students and the challenges of the world that awaits them. We depart from and expand on some of our writerly peers by drawing as much as possible from the real-world specifics of actual start-ups.

3

The World's Honors College

NYU ABU DHABI

On December 7, 2009, New York University celebrated the opening of the new NYU Abu Dhabi "Downtown Campus." Gathered that day were NYU president John Sexton and the newly appointed NYU Abu Dhabi leadership, which included Alfred Bloom, vice-chancellor; Carol Brandt, director of international programs; and Mariët Westermann, provost. The group also included Mohamed bin Zayed Al Nahyan, crown prince of Abu Dhabi, and Khaldoon Al Mubarak, chairman of the Abu Dhabi Executive Affairs Authority. The school's first class of students was scheduled to arrive in August 2010. Bloom told the assembled group that NYU Abu Dhabi's location at the "heart of the city" was a "perfect symbol of our goal to become an essential thread of the fabric of Abu Dhabi."

For Sexton, the new university in Abu Dhabi was more than just "playing another octave on the piano," his metaphor for having the courage to try new things. The idea for the new campus had arisen after Bill Clinton had urged Sexton to speak with Sheikh Mohamed in 2006. The NYU team rushed to board a plane to meet the sheikh in Abu Dhabi, recognizing the potential value of the city for a new NYU campus. Despite the length of the flight and the possibility that they'd be given no more than a fifteen-minute audience with the sheikh, they didn't hesitate. Their decision paid off: Sexton wound up in a multi-hour conversation with Sheikh Mohamed that he described as "magical." According to Sexton, Sheikh Mohamed said, "I made my decision in that first meeting. The decision that brought us here. I come from a society that judges people through their eyes, and it's been fun over the last year and a half finding out the guys from Brooklyn do the same thing."

Before he became NYU's president in 2002, Sexton had propelled the university's law school into the top ten in national rankings while he was dean from 1988 to 2001. His presidential vision was similarly ambitious. He wanted to build NYU into a new kind of global university, and a proposed campus in Abu Dhabi was central to that strategy. The idea had generated controversy from his home campus faculty, some of whom decried the development as cultural imperialism, and others who worried that the liberal arts could not flourish in an illiberal society. Sexton held fast. He characterizes his overall approach as mirroring the "attitudinal endowment" of New York City, which he describes as "a city of immigrants" who "had little to lose." Sexton wanted to carry this approach to NYU because "we're first movers, which carries with it inherent risks."[1]

Sexton's background included a PhD in religious studies prior to his Harvard Law School degree, and he brought some of the terminology from his previous life as a theologian into his administrative roles. In his vision, the campus becomes a "sacred space for dialogue," which serves as an

> incubator for a secular ecumenism that not only rejects secular dogmatism but also seeks to create a community of interlocking communities, a whole that is greater than the sum of its parts—a world that today is only a dream. The contours of such a university are already developing; and there is substantial evidence that talented faculty, students, and staff want to be part of it. For many of our great universities, this is the future, and a source of hope.[2]

Sexton dreamed of creating a set of interconnected campuses—not satellite campuses but equally valuable components of a truly global network university. In contrast to traditional universities like Oxford and Cambridge, this networked university would not be tied to any one location. It would serve the "97 percent of the high school graduates in the world [who] graduate from outside the United States."[3] As he said at the campus opening celebration:

> Preparing the next generation of global leaders requires a new approach to higher education. The vibrant connection between NYU Abu Dhabi and NYU New York will provide the foundation for the world's first truly global university and is perfectly aligned with Abu Dhabi's vision for becoming one of the world's next great idea capitals. History has shown that great universities have proven indispensable in that evolution.[4]

Both Sexton and Sheikh Mohamed wanted to make Abu Dhabi one of the "idea capitals" of the world, along with New York, drawing the world's best talent from the combination of "intellectual, cultural and educational assets that help turn a metropolis into a center of ideas."[5] To train global leaders, Sexton argued, "we have to have the most diverse student body in the world," not only "diverse at the surface level" but also "drawn from every sector of every society." To accomplish such an ambitious goal would require significant resources. "We have to be like a guy that's trying to jump on a motorcycle across the Grand Canyon," says Sexton, "because you don't want to be ten feet short. You'd rather be twenty feet too far." New fundraising and partners such as Sheikh Mohamed would provide abundant resources to build and operate the new campus: Sexton also raised $3 billion for NYU during his Campaign for NYU, which ended in 2008 and was then the most lucrative fundraising campaign in the history of higher education.[6] As the NYU Abu Dhabi downtown campus was opening, planning was simultaneously underway for building the much larger "island campus" on Saadiyat Island, a location that would include extensive research laboratories and integrate with a major cultural center with four new museums, including the Louvre Abu Dhabi, constructed between 2013 and 2017, a new Guggenheim Abu Dhabi Museum, the Zayed National Museum, and the Natural History Museum, all planned for an opening in 2025.

A Provost without a University

In 2007, two years before the campus dedication, NYU appointed Mariët Westermann as NYU Abu Dhabi's first provost. She arrived with her husband and children in 2008, as what one 2019 article described as "a provost without a university."[7] Westermann was a former director of NYU's Institute of Fine Arts, a former dean at NYU, and a distinguished art historian. As NYU's first senior staff member and "employee number one" in Abu Dhabi, she began to hire faculty and staff in the midst of numerous other administrative duties. She understood that these hires could make or break the new university, saying in a 2010 interview that "the quality of this institution will stand or fall by its faculty." Crucial to recruiting faculty was the assurance of academic freedom. Sexton and Westermann had made it clear that academic freedom was a "walk away issue for us" and that "if we are going to be some kind of positive change agent, which the Emirates understand us to be, they understand that we come with that risk."[8] Westermann later reflected on her work in those first days of NYU Abu Dhabi: "When we started in 2007, John Sexton used to say, the Polaroid picture is still developing. . . . We were going to establish a really strong, small liberal arts college that we called the honors college for the world." Westermann knew that this new institution had the potential to grow to be much more than just a liberal arts college for undergraduates by pairing with its parent institution of NYU. Westermann later described how this unique arrangement "would envelop it in the plenitude of this increasingly global research university that NYU was becoming."

Sexton, too, had high hopes for NYU Abu Dhabi as an "ecumenical university" capable of pioneering new levels of intercultural engagement. The new campus was to go well beyond the mere "toleration" of difference found on many campuses, which Sexton calls "intellectual indifferentism." This ecumenical university, instead, would foster a "genuine embrace of difference" and engage in "dialogical dialogue," a concept developed by the Spanish theologian Raimon Panikkar, who pioneered new forms of intercultural education and worked to foster deeper understanding between Christianity, Hinduism, and Buddhism.[9] In Sexton's words, the dialogical approach would "allow for us to see ourselves as others see us," pushing the community to "get into that partner's place . . . and see the world without giving up my own place." Going even further, he believes that this form of dialogue can help bring about what he terms the "Second Axial Age," where humans will develop a convergence of cultures and a new consciousness that he has called "planetization."[10] He derives this term from the Jesuit theologian Pierre Teilhard de Chardin, who described a sequence of social evolution in which human beings transcend tribal orientations and move toward a convergence in a planetary community, or a global civil society.

Soon after Sexton and Westermann had negotiated the terms of the new campus and NYU's relationship both with the city of Abu Dhabi and with NYU Abu Dhabi, they confronted challenges. Principal among these was the task of keeping the interests of NYU and Abu Dhabi aligned and informing the various stakeholders. These diplomatic duties often fell to Westermann, who worked tirelessly to navigate between the two countries, campuses, and cultures. She found herself playing the role of "diplomat plenipotentiary" embarked on a "mutual education project."

One of the first of the mutual education efforts was to launch the NYU Abu Dhabi Institute, based at the NYU campus, and the Sheikh Mohamed Scholars program, based in Abu Dhabi. Both programs were led by women: Westermann and Diane Yu from the NYU main campus. Bringing these women into key leadership roles sent a message about the values of the NYU community and the importance of empowering women in the UAE.

A 2007 press release described how the NYU Abu Dhabi Institute will host "conferences, research workshops, short courses and seminars involving scholars and students from NYU and the Middle East." The goal for the institute, according to the release, was to "promote academic and intellectual connections between NYU in Washington Square and NYU Abu Dhabi while the campus is being developed."[11]

Sexton was enthusiastic about how the Scholars program provided a preview of the new university, as it would "give students an NYU Abu Dhabi experience" and "expose them to the ideas NYU will be bringing to the Emirates." The program additionally would provide "academic learning, leadership activities, and cross-cultural experience," according to Sexton. Both programs gave NYU and the UAE an extended exposure to each other and demonstrated the value of the partnership to a wide range of stakeholders before the campus had admitted its first student.

In its early days, the partnership also required developing a clear understanding of each side's expectations. Sexton describes the discussions with the head representative from the UAE, Khaldoon Al Mubarak, as "not so much a pull and push negotiation" but rather a discussion to make sure "we fully understand each other." The UAE representatives told him, "We just want the NYU that's in New York," he says, to which Sexton would respond:

> Neither we nor you want the NYU in New York. Why the heck would we go halfway around the world to create the same thing we have in New York? The whole point is to create something which at its core is faithful to the core in essence of what NYU is, but which manifests itself and is experienced by those in it differently, because it's in a different place that gives it a different look.

Both men agreed, however, that they wanted the new university to attain the highest educational quality and to fully respect academic freedom. Sexton describes them agreeing on the principle that "whatever academic freedom is in New York, it should be in Abu Dhabi, and whatever the academic standards are in New York, they should be in Abu Dhabi."

Beyond hiring faculty and establishing shared expectations with their Abu Dhabi partners, Westermann and Sexton needed to find an inaugural vice-chancellor. In 2008, they recruited Al Bloom to take on the role. Bloom was finishing up his eighteenth year as president of Swarthmore College. Since his inauguration as Swarthmore's president in 1992, Bloom had urged students to "address the needs of a society and a world in need"—and to do so with "ethical intelligence."[12] In 2008, he had just announced his decision to retire from Swarthmore when the call came from New York. According to Bloom, Sexton said to him, "I've just been talking to Sheikh Mohamed of the UAE and he wants to join NYU in creating a really fine liberal arts college." The school "would be a place for teaching for global leadership and experiencing a global world intensely." Sexton offered Bloom the chance to visit and meet about the job opportunity over dinner. Soon after, Bloom accepted the invitation. "I had written seventeen graduation talks already," he says of his time at Swarthmore. It was time to move into something new.

Creating the World's Honors College

With temporary campus facilities in place, Bloom and Westermann faced yet another challenge: how to convince the best and brightest students from around the world to join NYU Abu Dhabi for its inaugural year. They found their answer in Carol Brandt, who arrived in Abu Dhabi in 2009 as a key early staff member tasked with shaping the student recruitment and orientation programs. Brandt had spent twenty-five years at the Claremont Colleges, working as vice-president for international and special programs and serving as a member of the faculty of modern languages, literature, and culture at Pitzer College. An expert in linguistics and second-language acquisition, Brandt had helped Pitzer develop unique study-abroad programs known as "cultural immersions" in Botswana, China, Ecuador, Wales, Nepal, Japan, Turkey, Italy, and Zimbabwe, as well as a establishing a biological field station in Costa Rica.[13] Her diverse global experience had trained her well for the new campus in Abu Dhabi—and for the ambitious task of creating the most internationally diverse group of students for any entering class in higher education.

The NYU Abu Dhabi mission appealed to students and faculty alike. As Westermann says, "What you needed in a globalizing world was an ability for students really to connect across lines of difference." NYU Abu Dhabi offered this chance for students to engage one another across "national difference, gender, ethnicity, and race." This immersive form of learning through relationships and collaboration would prepare students for the rest of their lives, enabling them to work with "people from all regions, countries and linguistic communities, religious communities and backgrounds."

With these aspirations in mind, the new admissions team would seek to craft an incoming class like no group of students ever assembled before, with applicants coming from over one hundred countries and students competing to attend with full financial aid. Sexton told the team that "the quality of a school, really, is going to turn on the quality of the students."

To attract the best students, NYU Abu Dhabi recruited from the top nine hundred high schools in the world as identified by the Fulbright commission and also partnered with the Institute of International Education (IIE). Some of the students were "diamonds in the rough." One student had lived on the streets of Addis Ababa from the age of seven for some years until he received a scholarship from the Ethiopian Educational Foundation. The IIE had a branch office in Addis Ababa, and staff members there had learned about this incredibly bright young man and nominated him for admission to NYU Abu Dhabi. The student later graduated with a degree in social research and public policy and is now employed as a senior administrator for the UAE government.

To help convince students to come to a newly established university in an unfamiliar country and region, NYU Abu Dhabi flew in the top four hundred candidates (from nearly ten thousand applications) for Candidate Weekend in the UAE. These events include attending sample classes, tours of Abu Dhabi, and, perhaps most importantly, a chance to meet students from all over the world and to begin making friends before attending NYU Abu Dhabi. The visit was thus both an interview (candidates participated in sample classes where they were observed for their ability to interact) and a travel adventure (students toured the desert under the stars, went on camel rides, and visited the Grand Mosque). In the process of selecting the first students, admissions officers asked prospective students to create a research proposal and to submit a piece of reflective writing. In the end, NYU Abu Dhabi selected just 2.1 percent of the over nine thousand applicants, a group so distinctive and global in scope that NYU began describing itself as the "world's honors college." Two hundred students were selected for admission to fill 150 slots, making up the first class of students.

The inaugural class included sixty-three women and eighty-seven men, with 75 percent of the students receiving SAT scores above 770 in reading and 780 in math. These students fully embodied the "global" portal aspirations of NYU Abu Dhabi: as a cohort, they spoke forty-three languages and came from thirty-nine countries. A generous financial aid package was included for all students who needed it.

How would they live together? Although NYU Abu Dhabi offered a lofty vision for a unique residential community, making this vision a reality required practical adjustments on the ground since no arrangements had yet been made for housing. As Bloom recounted in a 2018 interview, "We had no idea of where we would house students or faculty. And then, an apartment building grew called Sama Tower, and we said to the government, 'Can we have that?' And, a miracle, they said yes."[14] The forty-six-story building was the tallest and most luxurious building at the time in the heart of Abu Dhabi and became the residential hub of the new university for both students and faculty until 2014, when construction of the Saadiyat campus and residences was completed. The students loved the luxury that the Sama Tower provided: the apartments were far superior to the typical accommodations in New York that regular NYU students would occupy. One student blog entry from 2010 gushed about the living quarters:

> Hello my cynical, fellow NYU student. If you aren't cynical, from what I've heard you soon will be. As one of the 151 students selected to be flown across the planet on the dime of a monarch, I have the privilege of starting something of a new NYU culture here in Abu Dhabi. And, for now, it is anything but cynical.

The student then described the dorm room:

> Each room has a kitchenette, complete with a refrigerator and microwave. Every person in the dorm has the standard desk, dresser and nightstand, but the desks are accompanied by surprisingly comfortable swivel chairs (that are in NYU purple, of course). Also included in the apartments are a couch and armchair. Hard wood door frames are accompanied by marble windowsills. Every single bathroom has a bidet (considered standard in the UAE). Some of the students have nice views. Administration and their families are in the very top floors, though, so they probably have the true vistas.[15]

Abu Dhabi as the Middle East Ideas Capital

NYU was not the only American university expanding into the Middle East during these years. New campuses were sprouting up in UAE, Qatar, and other Middle Eastern countries, a phenomenon the *New York Times* termed an "educational gold rush."[16] In 1995, Qatar established what it called Education City, which by 2012 included the Weill Medical College from Cornell, a computer science and business campus from Carnegie Mellon University, an engineering campus from Texas A&M University, and a journalism school from Northwestern. Gulf states such as Qatar and UAE realized that high technology and knowledge industries were key to their long-term economic

survival. UAE, for example, despite holding 7 percent of the world's oil supply, will need new industries to maintain the wealth of the country as the
oil reserves are depleted. A recent listing of higher-education institutions
in the Arabian Peninsula shows the UAE as hosting seventy-nine academic
institutions by 2016, well above the number in neighboring countries. Many
top world universities were placing branch campuses in the UAE, such as
the New York Institute of Technology, Australia's University of Wollongong,
and Canada's University of Waterloo. By 2012, of the 162 branch campuses
in the world, half were located in the Persian Gulf, and 25 percent were in
the UAE. The region was becoming crowded with higher-education entrepreneurs and visionaries.

All of the countries within the Middle East/North Africa (MENA) region
had burgeoning populations, and in the case of UAE the native-born population was joined by millions of immigrants and expatriate workers, who
composed 88 percent of the UAE population in 2022.[17] The new NYU Abu
Dhabi campus stood out from the other institutions, which focused primarily on vocational training in engineering and other professional fields. NYU
Abu Dhabi described itself as a "research university with a fully integrated
liberal arts and science college."

As in many countries, the exact meaning of "liberal arts" in the UAE
could be a source of confusion since both words—liberal and arts—do not
translate exactly to Arabic. In Arabic, "liberal" (*liberali*) often has associa-
tions with political notions of liberal progressivism, and the "arts" belies the
strong emphasis on science and engineering within NYU Abu Dhabi. Dale
Eikelman, former president of the Middle East Studies Association and professor at Dartmouth College, suggested that liberal arts is better expressed
with the Arabic term *al-fikr al-naqdi*, which roughly translates to "critical
thinking." Eikelman explains that this term also connotes a combination of
attributes like "local cultural knowledge, skills, discernment, good judgment" that Muslim societies have long valued.[18]

Westermann agrees that the term "liberal arts" often was misunderstood
in the UAE. She would explain to audiences of potential students and their
parents that "liberal did not mean a lifestyle disposition or a political ideology," and those in attendance would find that explanation "very reassuring."
She would go on to share what the liberal arts meant to her and to NYU:
"It's about the mind being one of the great gifts that we have, that we are
endowed with. It needs to be given free rein to develop itself. To develop
thought and especially to maximize your own potential, especially in your
early years when you can study at a university." Westermann also clarified to

Abu Dhabi audiences that the "arts" in "liberal arts" comes from Latin and could mean "any sort of deeply honed skill over time." She would continue to stress that this definition did not just mean an artisanal skill but instead could take a variety of forms, including mathematical, political, scientific, and social skills. With this messaging, NYU Abu Dhabi was able to stress that it brings together two ingredients not often found together in universities outside the United States: a research mission and a liberal arts approach. This combination stands in contrast to the "technocratic university" more frequently found in developing countries, which serves "the interests of agriculture, industry and government through applied research and work-force training."[19]

When the downtown campus opened to its first students in 2010, that first cohort created a unique community. The global diversity of the NYU Abu Dhabi students (approximately 23 percent from the United States, 15 percent from the UAE, and the rest from thirty-seven other countries) was combined with unprecedented socioeconomic diversity, since students from impoverished backgrounds could attend with full scholarships and travel funding. This mix of students created a distinctively rich learning environment but also created challenges from the wide ranges of life experiences and cultures among the students. To help bring these disparate cohorts of students into a cohesive group, NYU Abu Dhabi faculty created a unique ritual—the *Marhaba* (welcome) week.

The first Marhaba in 2010 began in an improvised manner, with students asked to introduce themselves. The heady beginnings of NYU Abu Dhabi were described in a 2010 newspaper article:

> Each one stood and took the microphone to address the room in ringingly confident tones: Americans and Russians; Chinese and South Asians and eastern Europeans; a smattering of Middle Easterners, a few Africans, a small Latin American contingent. So many home countries, yet they all spoke the same language of unreserved enthusiasm. It was unique, they said, a dream, brilliant, an honour. It was a reality, an adventure. It was the future.[20]

Unlike an orientation session on an existing campus, this Marhaba introduced the students both to each other and to the new university. As the article described, "no one was coming back to the Abu Dhabi campus; it had sprung up overnight, fully formed, like a magic castle. Hundreds of people flowed in from the four corners of the earth, negotiating visa problems and lost luggage and the thousand administrative obstacles to travel."[21] The Marhaba included discussions of the book *Cosmopolitanism: Ethics in a World of Strangers* by NYU philosopher Kwame Anthony Appiah (who regularly teaches at NYU Abu Dhabi); a variety show where students showcased their talents; a trip to the top of the world's tallest building, the Burj Kalifa; a welcoming dinner; and many other improvised and fun activities.

NYU Abu Dhabi offered three living options in the dorms: a co-ed hall that housed both men and women, a single-gender hall that allowed students of other genders to visit, and a single-gender hall where other genders could not visit. In this third option, a student who wears the hijab could feel comfortable removing it in the company of other women (gender-fluid students and those who identify as women but are biologically men presented more complex situations, which were navigated on an individual basis). Many other restrictions existed outside of the campus, including a prohibition on drinking, a social norm disapproving of public displays of affection, a requirement to "dress modestly" (which for women generally meant shoulders and legs should be covered), and a general mandate to respect the local laws and customs.

The new university's ample resources made up for any inconvenience from these restrictions. *New York Magazine* reported an interview with two students about life at NYU Abu Dhabi: "Only the Americans complain about their lack of liberty, and when pressed, they concede that the compensations on offer by the university are pretty sweet. 'There's this sailboarding thing,' says Bailey, smiling wide on Skype. 'Horseback riding. Deep-sea diving. That's another reason that I came here. It's like, . . . Oh, wow, there's so many resources.'"[22] At the same time, some students reacted against what they saw as an ill-defined notion of global citizenship within their new community. They tried to engage in the robust ecumenical dialogue that Sexton had envisioned, but they didn't always want to engage in deep discussion with one another about topics that could prove stressful and contentious. As a result, in recent years the university has developed a new Inclusion and Equity Accountability Framework, an Office of Inclusion and Equity, and has pledged to "work together to address and dismantle systemic racism, and strive to become an inclusive and equitable community anchored in mutual respect and solidarity."[23] This type of approach suggests that NYU Abu Dhabi is beginning to rely more on American-style diversity, equity, and inclusion approaches to its global campus. It remains to be seen if this approach will forge new ground in the way that Sexton originally imagined.

Despite some of these tensions, student responses to the first years of instruction were quite positive and helped fuel interest in the new university from other prospective students around the world. As one student wrote about the experience in 2014, "my peers were and remain some of the most remarkable people I have ever met: writers, founders of academic journals, world-class musicians, and frighteningly talented chefs. They were brilliant and at times startlingly compassionate."[24]

Building the Faculty and Curriculum

Among the first faculty at NYU Abu Dhabi's 2010 opening were fifteen from New York, some of whom offered courses in a three-week January term course, and others who came for a full semester or academic year. The rest of the approximately forty faculty for that first year would have their permanent base in Abu Dhabi, helping the new university more than reach its goal of a faculty-to-student ratio of eight to one, with a three to one ratio in the first year.[25]

By 2012, approximately one hundred faculty were "local," with tenure-track appointments at NYU Abu Dhabi; this core group was joined by approximately two hundred faculty visiting NYU and the other NYU global campuses. Visiting NYU faculty were able to use the global campus arrangement to teach one of every eight semesters abroad. The home campus in New York played a central role in hiring new faculty and overseeing the curriculum but included the local faculty in all decisions and in committees at both NYU and NYU Abu Dhabi. While the NYU campus provided a start to the emerging new culture of NYU Abu Dhabi, the new curriculum provided the opportunity to bring into reality some of the vision of the founders. Diane Yu, one of the founding team, described the unique elements of the academic approach as including "interdisciplinary, multidisciplinary, and comparative offerings," "global components" in the curriculum and study abroad, and "no classic departments but rather larger, integrated clusters."

In the first years after launch, the curriculum included a set of eight core courses, including an "Islamic world" requirement, and a set of "J-term" classes offering intensive instruction in a single topic over two to five weeks, in either January or June, with many of the courses offered abroad. The core courses were organized into four areas: Pathways of World Literature; Structures of Thought and Society; Art, Technology, and Invention; and Ideas and Methods of Science. Students selected two courses in each area. They could choose from twenty-two possible majors, and they could also take two or more semesters abroad within the NYU "Global Network," one semester for intensive language development, and one to help conduct research for the capstone project. The NYU Global Network today includes three degree-granting campuses in New York City, Shanghai, and Abu Dhabi, as well as global academic centers in eleven of the most dynamic cities in Africa, Asia, Europe, and South America.

Bloom described how the NYU Abu Dhabi curriculum combined with the NYU Global Network was poised to deliver on the aspiration to educate global citizens:

> This is to not just educate you about Islamic culture, about the politics and sociology and history of the Middle East importantly, but it was about learning to be a global citizen, in a broad sense. And what does it mean to move your sense of belonging from a nation, or a locality to belong to the world, for seeing yourself as someone who is invested in not just the relationship between, let's say, France and the United States, or China and the United States, but someone who has really invested in developing a world of certain kinds of responsibilities and a peaceful world.

Bloom's words described a vision that would prove more complicated to implement on the ground.

Controversies on the Home Front and Academic Freedom

The NYU Abu Dhabi program had been in operation for just two years when NYU faculty began raising objections to Sexton's leadership and voicing concerns about academic freedom within a country run by an autocrat. The UAE as a country has banned political parties and vests all executive, legislative, and judicial authority with the seven hereditary rulers, or emirs, who each head one of the seven emirates. Freedom House, a US-based foundation, gave the UAE a rating of "not free" and ranked it as seventeenth from the bottom out of one hundred countries for its overall level of freedom, with comparably low scores for political rights and civil liberties.

On the home campus, many faculty feared that NYU's principles would be hard to maintain within this context, and protested Sexton's decisions at home and abroad. A 2013 article in the *New Yorker*, "The Imperial Presidency," describes how Sexton "had failed to provide an academic rationale for the scope and the pace of the university's growth."[26] This criticism arose in part from Sexton's decision to hire an additional 125 tenure-track professors for the New York campus between 2004 and 2010; he also doubled the number of full-time adjunct instructors (ineligible for tenure) at the same campus. Such investments couldn't be sustained, critics argued. Additional controversy over the costs of construction in New York raised concerns about possible tuition increases and the need for more student enrollments, trends some faculty felt could "eventually degrade our student body." Sexton counters by noting that in that same period NYU created full-time "contract" positions for faculty that included many of these non-tenure-track faculty, which included benefits, sabbatical rights, and representation in university governance.

The Abu Dhabi project only aggravated these home-front concerns, which triggered fierce resistance to Sexton's vision for a global campus. Some faculty suspected that the new global expansion was conducted "at least partly, as a solution to a real-estate problem." Faculty complained that they were unable to make a rational judgment about the new campus in Abu Dhabi, as negotiation and other materials were not shared widely. Some faculty felt that Sexton had thus "failed to honor a basic principle of the university, which is built on the idea of free and open debate."[27] Sexton notes that the negotiations for the new university took place privately with Sheikh Mohamed, at the sheikh's request. The disputes about his alleged excessive use of executive power in NYU's global expansion eventually resulted in a vote of no confidence in Sexton, which passed by 298 to 224 in March 2013.

The concerns at NYU about academic freedom couldn't be separated from cultural issues surrounding the Emirati legal code in the UAE. As pointed out in a 2012 *Chronicle of Higher Education* article, "under Emirati law, remarks that are deemed insulting to the seven emirates' ruling families and government officials, or to Islam—or that are seen as causing social unrest—can lead to prosecution. Demonstrations are illegal. Swearing in public and engaging in homosexual relations are also crimes." The article further stated that the foreign branch campuses were seen as "a bubble" and, despite assurances of academic freedom, "researchers and other academics who work in the Emirates say they use caution in broaching topics such as AIDS and prostitution; the status of migrant laborers; Israel and the Holocaust; and domestic politics and corruption. Any critical discussion of the Emirates' ruling families is an obvious no-go zone."[28] But in a 2012 interview, Bloom insisted that "there was a guarantee that we can enjoy academic freedom, and it has been implemented in every way." He sought to reassure critics: "There is no interference, no sense of concern, fear, or anxiety."[29]

In 2009, NYU issued a statement of shared values with the Abu Dhabi government, which promised contractors involved in campus construction would obey UAE labor laws. The statement included assurance that workers would receive at least one day off per week, and employers would forgo the typical practice of confiscating workers' passports and forcing overtime work. NYU negotiated with officials in Abu Dhabi to address concerns from students and faculty about UAE labor laws and treatment of migrant workers. The resulting agreement would be put to the test as soon as construction began in 2010 on NYU Abu Dhabi's lavish new Saadiyat Island campus.

The difficulties soon become hard to ignore and generated a number of high-profile articles, which reported alleged exploitative labor practices within the NYU Abu Dhabi construction site. In the first year of construction, it appeared that many workers, mostly from India, Pakistan, and Bangladesh, had received harsh treatment. Workers at the Saadiyat Island campus, interviewed by the *New York Times*, revealed they had to pay recruitment fees in order to work and were forced to put in eleven or twelve hours per day, in stark contrast to the agreements NYU had made several years before.[30] Other reports described how workers were forced to work in the summer heat and were earning wages below even the minimum of $0.80/hour.[31] By 2014, a well-publicized labor strike in Abu Dhabi came to an end when police swarmed into the crowded worker compound, beat several workers, and placed dozens in jail before deporting them.

This revelation resulted in an apology from Sexton, in which he called the treatment "if true as reported, troubling and unacceptable."[32] Sexton's caveat was based on his awareness that despite having negotiated extensively with contractors for some of the best working conditions in the UAE on behalf of the more than six thousand workers building the new campus, not all the contractors could be monitored completely for compliance. NYU commissioned former federal prosecutor Daniel Nardello and his consulting company to systematically investigate how well the contractors had met NYU's labor requirements.[33]

Almost simultaneously, NYU Abu Dhabi was reaching a watershed moment: the first commencement ceremony was to be held at the new Saadiyat Island campus. The ceremony, on May 25, 2014, featured former US president Bill Clinton as the main speaker. In a triumphant atmosphere, the principal leaders from NYU, NYU Abu Dhabi, and the UAE government celebrated the graduation of NYU Abu Dhabi's first cohort. Clinton told the graduates: "We are going to share the future. But the remaining job is to define the terms of our interdependence so that it is full of peace and prosperity and promise. Today there is both promise and peril. You represent the promise."[34] Clinton also referred to the controversies surrounding working conditions at the new campus. He noted that the concerns raised about the workers provided "an opportunity to address in concrete, real flesh-and-blood form, one of the representative issues of equality and identity in the twenty-first century."[35]

Sexton's address shifted the focus toward the student successes and did not directly address the labor controversy, which was dominating press accounts of NYU Abu Dhabi at the time. "Four years ago we set out to develop a new approach to higher education," he said, "merging Abu Dhabi's goal of becoming one of the world's great idea capitals with the ambitions of NYU's global network university. The young men and women who graduated today are proof that we have succeeded."[36] The success of the NYU Abu Dhabi experiment for students did indeed seem validated, as graduates from the first class obtained jobs in high numbers as well as prestigious fellowships, including three recipients of the Rhodes Scholarship, one Schwarzman Scholar, and one NSF scholar. But lingering questions remained about the broader enterprise, and a new phase of evolution was needed to bring the new institution to maturity.

In April 2015, Nardello's company released its report on labor conditions. The report concluded that NYU "intended to improve the conditions for workers" and "made a real effort to implement the Labor Guidelines," which benefitted the majority of workers "to varying degrees." However, the report also found that a loophole in the guidelines "disenfranchised thousands of workers" from the protections that NYU had negotiated, amounting to about 30–35 percent of the worked hours. This loophole exempted workers who had worked fewer than thirty days or who were working on contracts valued at less than $1 million.[37] NYU has worked to close this loophole, and produces regular labor compliance updates, which describe in detail any lapses within ongoing operations at NYU Abu Dhabi.[38] While the process has not satisfied all the critics, it has provided evidence of continued improvement in working conditions, which, while not meeting US standards, are far above the prevailing standards in UAE before NYU Abu Dhabi arrived.

Evolution and Revision

As the new campus was being constructed, a parallel effort was undertaken to remodel NYU Abu Dhabi's curriculum. The rationale for the core curriculum was to "grapple with profound and enduring questions about the human and social condition while developing essential intellectual skills" through eight core courses, two in each of in four areas. This breadth was an attractive idea while founding the institution, but finding space for these eight courses proved onerous for students interested in moving quickly toward their area of academic focus and also became difficult to staff. A simultaneous reconsideration of the NYU core, known as the "Morse Academic Plan," provided an opportunity for both institutions to retool their curriculums.[39] By 2014, students were also noting that the "cross-cultural perspectives" that were also promised within the core were not always being provided. Many courses remained focused on topics from the United States and often were older courses redesigned to work as core courses. Students complained that the curriculum often treated "texts not written in Europe or the United States as little tokens." The problems with the core were acknowledged by Deputy Vice-Chancellor Hillary Ballon, who stated that the "conversion of courses that had been designed as disciplinary courses into cores was a pragmatic response to a first year problem" and agreed that their goal was to "not just produce a general education program that had a strong Western bias."[40]

By 2015, faculty and students had agreed on the need to reduce the number of courses by merging two of the four required areas, and yet students wanted to also help define the new core curriculum. The solution to involving students in the design process was developed by English professor Bryan Waterman, who created a "Hack the Curriculum" event to discuss the possible alternatives. Waterman himself seemed perfect for the task, as in his previous life as a student he himself had rebelled against what he felt was an outmoded curriculum. His feelings were so strong that he dropped out of Brigham Young University in protest, after complaining about how the institution lacked the academic freedom to discuss controversial topics like abortion rights, colonialism, and LGBTQ+ rights. This protest prevented him from completing his undergraduate degree but did provide material for his first book, *The Lord's University*, which described the controversies within Brigham Young. His academic career moved forward with a PhD in American Studies from Boston University, which led to his position at NYU the following year.

Waterman, who had been a professor of literature at NYU since 2001, "fell in love" with NYU Abu Dhabi when he joined the desert excursion offered for prospective students in 2011, where he enjoyed "racing to the top of sand dunes" and was excited by the "rainbow of cultures" within the students.[41] Waterman convened his "Hack the Curriculum" event in September of 2015, with small teams of three to five students developing proposals while downing portions of falafel and shawarma long into the night. The two winning proposals from the event were sent to the Core Curriculum Committee, which met throughout the year and developed a draft proposal for consideration by faculty. Waterman described the goal as "a core that both offers breadth and flexibility and still provides the feeling of a common intellectual experience at the heart of undergraduate education."[42]

The following fall semester, the NYU Abu Dhabi faculty voted for a new structure of the common curriculum, reducing it to just six courses. The new curriculum design aimed to bring "plenary moments" to the core program, which could be a guest lecture, film screening, art exhibit, or other performance, and would serve to bring the community together to consider common themes at key moments. The new design consisted of two core colloquiums focusing on global challenges, and then one course selected from each of four areas: art, design, and technology; cultural exploration and analysis; data and discovery; and structures of thought and society.[43] The compromise enabled the four area courses to provide a wide mix of disciplinary perspectives, but also included the interdisciplinary colloquium courses that addressed "profound and enduring questions" with an emphasis on "significant global challenges."[44]

NYU Abu Dhabi also has been pioneering interdisciplinary course sequences in science and engineering. Westermann says the NYU Abu Dhabi sequences in Foundations of Science and Foundations of Engineering are unique, with math, physics, biology, and chemistry—"the primary colors of science"—all taught in "interactive modules." The STEM curriculum focuses on problem-oriented and design-oriented thinking, with students in engineering challenged to take on substantial design experiences in their first year and also taking a required course called Engineering for Social Good. In their subsequent years they expand on those emphases in more advanced work and capstone projects.

Another unique element in the curriculum involves the Arab Crossroads Studies major, which arises organically from the location in Abu Dhabi. Westermann says that importing a Middle Eastern studies approach entirely unchanged from NYU would be "the last thing you want to do," so instead the faculty in the program have worked to be "a little bit humble" and "listen to what people have to say and contribute there." The program explores Abu Dhabi's context in regional history, politics, environment, and the energy sector. It also, Westermann says, "looks east to India across trade routes and west to Africa in a way that isn't so common in Middle Eastern studies programs in the United States."

By 2017, however, just as all these curricular efforts were hitting their stride, the forces pushing globalism forward seemed to be in retreat. Nationalism and political retrenchment had replaced earlier optimism about a new global outlook in many nations. Many students also began to focus more on their future job prospects than on the global ideals that had launched the university. In a 2017 interview, Bloom urged universities to sustain a "global perspective" that could build "a world of common understanding." He delivered a forceful pushback against education for job placement. "If we just educate for careers, I think you're going to get a continuation of the kind of division and divisiveness that we experience so much today." He explicitly noted that "the model that we provide will help to shape a view of global universities. . . . [T]hey are not only about providing excellent education but [also about] providing a new way of looking at education." He saw this new outlook essential for "developing agents of common humanity and agents of a more united world."[45]

Once again, however, the vision struggled in the face of realities on the ground. Setbacks and controversies continued as stories circulated on the new campus about denied visas, academic freedom infringements, and continued issues with labor. NYU journalism professor Mohamad Bazzi went public about a denied visa for teaching at NYU Abu Dhabi, which he claimed was due to religious discrimination; and additional allegations suggested that such events were more widespread than previously thought. New NYU president Andrew Hamilton apologized to the campus community, stating that "we were deficient in our communications" and pledging to "immediately improve how we deal with future cases."[46] Additional faculty alleged that they had been denied visas and experienced restrictions on their internet. Within UAE, civil rights activist Ahmed Mansoor, who was not related to the university, was imprisoned by the government, an event that prompted a faculty petition to the NYU administration urging action.[47]

Perhaps the most dramatic controversy involved the imprisonment of Durham University postgraduate student Matthew Hedges in late 2018. The UAE government accused Hedges of trying to steal "sensitive national security secrets" and gather information on the war in Yemen using "two different identities to gather information about his targets." Hedges was arrested in May 2018, and although he signed a confession in Arabic stating he was an MI6 operative, he denied that he was spying and claimed that he had just been researching for his PhD studies. After being sentenced to life imprisonment, he was suddenly pardoned in November 2018 and released to the British embassy.[48] This combination of events prompted a faculty forum in

Abu Dhabi on December 18, a gathering that NYU professor Andrew Ross, who himself alleged his research in UAE had been impeded by political concerns, described as a "tipping point."[49]

Hamilton, who had succeeded Sexton in 2016, responded to these concerns about visa denials and academic freedom but also stated his support for the program by highlighting its successes. In the same statement that delivered his apology, he argued that:

> NYU Abu Dhabi has proven itself an academic success—though less than a decade old, it has attracted distinguished faculty from leading institutions, and produced Rhodes Scholars and graduates who have gone on to top graduate schools, professional schools, and employers. It has also provided an education to students from around the world, many of whom would not otherwise have had the opportunity for a top rate liberal arts experience. NYU Abu Dhabi is one of the most diverse academic communities in the world, with students and faculty from more than 115 countries. The character of classroom teaching and discussion there would be entirely familiar to faculty here. Its research success puts it in the vanguard of research institutions in the region. This is enviable, and we should not lose sight of it.[50]

NYU president Hamilton's statement attempted to shift the tide of public opinion by focusing on NYU Abu Dhabi's ability to deliver placement at top employers and graduate programs and its place among the vanguard of research institutions, but lacked the expansive vision of "secular ecumenism" promoted by his predecessor. Sexton himself has written on these controversies since leaving office and makes the distinction that academic freedom protects inquiry and expression "inside the university" and "does not create in the academic class a set of uber-citizens who get superior rights of expression outside the walls of the university." Sexton also denies any discrimination in visa allocations by UAE but notes that "there was no way that the university could guarantee unbridled movement across a sovereign border."[51]

Entering Young Adulthood

With new leadership at the home campus since 2016 and a new vice-chancellor in Abu Dhabi, NYU Abu Dhabi is writing the next chapter in its history. Returning to NYU Abu Dhabi as vice-chancellor in 2019, Westermann represents both new leadership and a full circle return to the early days of NYU Abu Dhabi, when she served from 2007 to 2010 as the university's first provost. In a recent interview, she reflected on how she was appointed back in the very beginning—before NYU Abu Dhabi existed—and she cherished the institution from its birth. When she returned to NYU Abu Dhabi in the chief executive role, she says, "The baby had become this handsome young adult, and it seemed a great opportunity to help it become a fully well rounded grown up."

Westermann has grand ambitions for NYU Abu Dhabi. The aim is for the thriving university to become a full anchor institution the UAE and the MENA region, and she looks forward to expanding its global impact. She wants to grow the student body from 1,500 students to an initial steady state of around 2,000, and expand the graduate offerings, which on her arrival included ninety PhDs in STEM fields offered jointly with NYU in New York. In the graduate sphere, Westermann sees great opportunities to offer unique master's and PhD programs that lean into NYU Abu Dhabi's interest in promoting innovative work between the disciplines and to leverage the enormous diversity of the talent attracted to the university and the country. In areas of professional education like business and management, too, NYU can offer NYU Abu Dhabi great start-up wherewithal and faculty strength. The university is already on the way to achieving these goals, with a new master's in economics, a new MFA in fine arts, and additional graduate programs in arts and sciences and engineering as well as professional degrees being planned. A new vice-provost for graduate programs, Carol Genetti, recently joined NYU Abu Dhabi from the University of California at Santa Barbara. Says Westermann: "I think over the next five to eight years, we could see several hundred students coming into those programs." She has also hired a new provost, Arlie Petters, a mathematician who was previously the dean of faculty affairs at Duke University.

With its new leadership, NYU Abu Dhabi does appear to be approaching a new era of expansion and growth. A recent press release noted that the university had hired forty-five new faculty in 2020 alone. Like their students, these faculty are international, hailing from twelve countries.[52] At the ripe old age of twelve years at the time of this writing, NYU Abu Dhabi has survived the most difficult parts of its formation period and is settling into an adolescence—or even young adulthood—as a new university. As it continues to grow and consolidate its role as a leading research and liberal arts university in the MENA region it will have to negotiate the ongoing challenges of delivering a liberal arts education in a nation that does not value freedom of speech over all other considerations.

As Sexton reflects on NYU Abu Dhabi, he acknowledges its struggles but is proud of how the university in many ways has realized his lofty global vision, even with some obstacles and setbacks: "It would be wrong to claim complete success either in NYU New York, NYU Abu Dhabi, or NYU Shanghai. Institutions, like people, are metaphoric victims of original sin, and we're not going to achieve perfection in this world. I will say, in terms of the internal dynamic of what I'm calling secular ecumenism, the easiest place to see that was NYU Abu Dhabi." Since its founding just twelve years ago, NYU Abu Dhabi has grown to become one of the most productive research engines in the MENA region. The new campus has achieved so much impact in research, it has boosted the ranking of NYU itself. NYU Abu Dhabi also serves a key role in fostering talent from around the world and feeding it back into careers in the UAE government and into other sectors in UAE and beyond. Within the first five graduating classes, it is possible to document the relocation of the global population of NYU Abu Dhabi's students into new countries and regions. These shifts include the movement of over 40 percent of the North American students to other parts of the world after graduation, and a shift among students originating in Sub-Saharan Africa and South Asia to a wide variety of countries, with 60 percent of these students moving to other parts of the world. Perhaps most interesting is the net migration of graduates toward the MENA region, with 36 percent of NYU Abu Dhabi graduates staying within the MENA region, despite only 16 percent of incoming students originating there. This net shift of graduates toward the MENA region could be evidence of progress toward Sexton's vision of building Abu Dhabi as a "global idea capital" for the world.[53]

Fully realizing that vision will require more work, however, partly because of the geopolitical uncertainties in the Middle East region and the limited freedom within the UAE. Navigating between the very different cultures and legal environments of the United States and the UAE has been a constant challenge for the institution and was a source of the working-condition and visa controversies. This disconnect continually challenges both students and faculty as they balance the freedoms and increasingly American-style approaches toward multiculturalism with the social norms and laws of the UAE outside the walls of campus. NYU Abu Dhabi especially has unresolved issues in how to navigate differing norms regarding homosexuality and gender relations, which are very different in New York than in Abu Dhabi. The reverberations of global and US culture have most recently taken form in continuing debates about how best to promote social justice. The murder of George Floyd in 2020 profoundly impacted the NYU

Abu Dhabi campus, and triggered campus discussions of racism, diversity, inclusion, and equity. Students protested against cultural appropriation and demanded more diversity within their faculty, while suggesting that the curriculum was Eurocentric and needed to be "decolonized."[54] The administration responded with a new "Accountability Framework" and also is instituting community-wide training in equity and inclusion, reviewing hiring, and working toward "Globally Dismantling Racism in Relation to Disciplines and Social Practices."[55]

Despite ongoing challenges, NYU Abu Dhabi has built a unique multicultural community that includes students from 115 countries and faculty from around the world. This makes it a uniquely global campus with the potential to engage deeply in intercultural issues and to pioneer new types of interdisciplinary scholarship and teaching. This potential is being realized with signature programs such as the Arab Crossroads program, high-profile interdisciplinary research conferences,[56] and new interdisciplinary institutes such as the al Mawrid Arab Center for the Study of Art, the Center for Behavioural Institutional Design, and the NYU Abu Dhabi Water Research Center.[57] While NYU Abu Dhabi is not yet fully the "secular ecumenical university" envisioned by former NYU president John Sexton, it is moving forward in prestige and building a considerable research presence, which should assure continued growth and influence in coming years.

4

In Asia for the World

YALE-NUS COLLEGE

In 2011, two years before the Yale-NUS campus opened, Charles Bailyn; the newly appointed inaugural Yale-NUS Dean, Lily Kong; the lead administrator of the project from the National University of Singapore (NUS); and Jeremiah Quinlan, the Yale-NUS admissions dean, put on a series of "road shows" in Singapore to pitch the concept of the new Yale-NUS College to skeptical parents and their high-school students. Intended to promote the benefits of a liberal arts education, the meetings took place in public halls and schools across Singapore. Bailyn and Quinlan, both on loan from Yale, stayed in Singapore for months at a time to meet with officials at NUS and to spread the word about the new liberal arts program, to be known as Yale-NUS College, to the wider Singaporean public. As Bailyn described it:

> The three of us went on a road tour of elite high schools in Singapore advertising this new educational venture, which as yet didn't exist. There was no curriculum, there was no campus, there was no faculty. And these are very smart students and so they would ask us all these questions and we would make stuff up. And Jeremiah and I are pretty quick on our feet, so is Lily, and we just with great authority asserted how things were going to be that no one had thought about it until that very moment. And it was actually astonishing how true it turned out to be.

The launching of Yale-NUS College arose from growing interest in the liberal arts across Asia and within Singapore in particular. Yale-NUS is more than a branch campus of Yale University and differs markedly from other new liberal arts projects in Asia. Among its distinctions, Yale-NUS is "a true partnership between two great world universities; second, it includes a financial model placing the operating costs on NUS; and third, it confers a separate degree that comes from Yale-NUS College, and not Yale or NUS."[1] These differences have made Yale-NUS College almost—but not quite—like a stand-alone American liberal arts college. The Yale-NUS degree is based on the Yale NUS curriculum, managed by the Yale-NUS faculty but with accreditation from the NUS. Lacking full status as a stand-alone institution, and in the absence of Yale's full backing for the degree, Yale-NUS has faced unique challenges and questions around autonomy. The arrangement allowed the venture to reach great heights of success, but also may have created the seeds of its ultimate closure as a stand-alone institution.

Singapore as an Education Hub

While many American accounts of Yale-NUS College focus on the role that Yale University played in the start-up, those histories are incomplete. Yale-NUS College arose from decades of effort by the Singaporean government and NUS to strategically increase the quality of higher education in Singapore. In 2015, the young city-state celebrated its fiftieth anniversary as a nation, and in this relatively short time had built a vibrant and diversified economy—one that by 2016 provided the third-highest per capita income in the world,[2] with leading industries in the financial sector, high-tech manufacturing and design, biomedical research, and petrochemicals, along with a large sector in shipping and resource management. Crucially, much of this growth came from the rise of knowledge industries, which account for over 70 percent of Singapore's GDP.[3]

Singapore's growth and its education strategy have been inseparable. As early as 1965, shortly after its founding as a nation, Singapore established universal primary education. The official language of instruction is English, but bilingual education is mandatory, with Chinese, Tamil, and Bahasa Melayu all taught in addition to English. Singapore also includes tracks at the secondary level for polytechnic, technical, arts, and pre-university education. The nation is ranked at the top levels globally for the high salaries its teachers receive and for the extensive training and learning opportunities that teachers are offered each year. In his book comparing top global education systems, Marc Tucker also credits Singapore's central planning for the ascent of its schools in global rankings. "Singapore has perhaps a uniquely integrated system of planning," explains Tucker. "The Economic Development Board plays a central role and coordinates with the Ministry of Manpower. The Ministry of Manpower works with specific industry groups to identify critical manpower needs and project demands for future skills within a work skills framework. These are then fed back both into pre-employment training and continuing education and training."[4] The quality of the Singaporean secondary school system enabled the country to consistently attain top rankings in the Program for International Student Assessment achievement tests, with the country finishing second globally in this exam in 2018.[5]

Before Yale-NUS was launched, Singapore was working to improve its educational sector at all levels—primary, secondary, and tertiary. In 2005, Singaporean minister of education Tharman Shanmugaratnam announced "a new phase in education," which included a focus "on quality and choice in learning" and "a shift from learning content to developing a habit of inquiry," and was bringing changes that were "percolating through our schools and tertiary institutions."[6] Across Singapore, educators were looking to offer higher quality and a greater range of choices for students at all levels. As the nation's oldest and most prestigious university, NUS formed a key component of Singapore's strategy for globally recognized higher education. It now resides in the top ranks of world universities, with centers that lead the world in cancer science, quantum technologies, mechano-biology, and environmental and life-sciences engineering. The opportunity to partner with Yale University to build a premier liberal arts college was a natural outcome of NUS's growing clout and prestige. The potential collaboration also fed into Singapore's strategy of attracting top global talent to help initiate new sectors of its economy and knowledge industries. With a strategy in place, Yale and NUS began assembling a leadership team to build the new Yale-NUS College. Given the challenges involved, the right leaders would prove essential.

Yale Appoints a Dean

Charles Bailyn, the A. Bartlett Giamatti Professor of Astronomy and Physics at Yale, began discussing the role of inaugural dean of Yale-NUS College in 2010, before the college existed. With a BS from Yale and a PhD from Harvard, he held impeccable academic credentials. His doctoral dissertation on X-ray-emitting binary stars had won the Trumpler Prize for best North American Astrophysics PhD, and he had received the 2009 Bruno Rossi Prize for his research on the masses of black holes, distinctions that gave him a very high level of academic credibility among both the Yale and NUS faculty. His administrative credentials were also impressive: Bailyn had served on the Yale College Education Committee, the Yale College Teaching and Learning Committee, and at the Yale Center for Media Initiatives. A popular and charismatic teacher as well, he had been one of the first professors at Yale to record his sought-after astronomy course in the Open Yale online education site, thus giving him early experience with online teaching.

In his initial conversation about the new college with Yale president Richard Levin, Bailyn recalls Levin beginning with a question: "How would you like the opportunity to reinvent the liberal arts college curriculum from the ground up with no pre-existing conditions?" He recounts what happened next:

> He knew, of course, that I had a profound interest in this. And so I expressed interest. And it was only then after I had already halfway signed on that the word Singapore was even spoken. And I had never been to Singapore. I'd been to Asia once. I had no particular interest in Asia, or at least I thought I didn't. And then a month or two later, I found myself on a plane with the initial group of seven faculty and administrators from Yale who went to visit NUS to investigate this possibility.

Bailyn soon focused on the unique nature of Singapore and its blending of cultures. As he puts it:

> I became fascinated by the place . . . but that wasn't where I started. Where I started was curriculum. And one of the things about Singapore in particular . . . is, what do you do with the humanities? What do you include? . . . There's no organizing principle as there is with Western culture.

It was not long before cultural differences complicated the road-show messaging about the new liberal arts program. First, within Singapore and much of Asia, "colleges" typically educate for the final two years of high school, unlike in the United States, where a "college" refers to a higher-education institution, like the many liberal arts colleges across the country. Bailyn and his colleagues resolved this initial confusion by reminding audiences of parents and students that Yale-NUS would be a bachelor's-degree-granting institution backed by the full prestige of both parent institutions. The use of the word "college" was intended to convey the "collegial" nature of the smaller university and its parallels with counterpart institutions in the United States.

Bailyn and Quinlan encountered a second confusion about the liberal arts on the same road shows. Singaporean parents and prospective students thought that "liberal arts" meant an education in poetry, painting, and abstract philosophy, not to include any of the sciences. Says Bailyn: "One of the things that helped in dealing with the parents was the fact that I'm a scientist and I had gone to Yale as an undergraduate, and over half my undergraduate courses had been non-science courses just by the way an American liberal arts education is set up." Audiences voiced particular curiosity about how one could become competitive as a scientist while taking so many unrelated courses. Bailyn tried to explain the rationale to them. "I had taken all this history and literature and stuff in college," he says, "and then when I got to graduate school, I was a little bit behind. But I knew things that the other students didn't—like how to write." This key difference made him even more effective in science than many of his peers. His stature as a top Yale scientist also lent credibility to his explanation—and prestige to the new Yale-NUS College, helping assure Singaporean audiences that the new institution was top-notch, backed by nothing less than Yale University.

Global Ambitions for NUS and Yale

The arrival of the new Yale-NUS College at NUS marked the culmination of decades of growth and numerous international experiments at NUS before the agreement with Yale was signed in 2011. NUS is the Singaporean flagship university, founded in 1905 and named an autonomous educational institution in 2005. NUS president Shih Choon Fong introduced new procedures for hiring, promoting, and granting tenure to faculty in 2006, replacing the earlier civil service model for faculty hiring and promotion. With growing budgets for expanding research and hiring top global faculty, NUS began moving into the ranks of the world's best universities. That growth has continued to the present day: in 2021, the *Times Higher Education* rankings placed NUS as twenty-fifth in the world, and the Quacquarelli Symonds(QS) rankings placed it at eleventh.[7]

Innovative interdisciplinary programs and new international partnerships helped drive NUS's growth and its rise in the global rankings and made it the perfect place for the Yale-NUS experiment. As far back as 1996, NUS leaders had initiated the Special Project in Science (SPS), which provided top science students with advanced interdisciplinary training in science—placing special emphasis on emerging research problems. Within the SPS is the "discovery science module," in which students conduct an independent research project and are supervised by faculty across multiple departments. NUS leaders had also developed their own version of a core curriculum by 1998, inspired by comparable programs at US institutions such as Harvard. NUS invited dozens of US academics to visit throughout the 1990s and 2000s to share some of their ideas, and the resulting curriculum included both cross-disciplinary and multidisciplinary knowledge elements. By 2001, NUS had developed partnerships with several dozen universities across the world and had hosted over 350 international students and sent 289 NUS students abroad.

Prior to Yale-NUS College, NUS had also developed its own residential liberal arts undergraduate program: the University Scholars Program (USP), initiated in 2002. The USP offered unique interdisciplinary courses in the first two years and then integrated these students into NUS for more traditional disciplinary study for years three and four. The USP was intended "to nurture a pool of brilliant students by developing their potential for leadership and intellectual excellence," according to an early report on the program. It aimed to bring together "the best and brightest students from different faculties into a learning environment that catalyzes their intellectual passion and stretches them to their utmost."[8] Service-learning and experiential courses included a 2003 course in Mo Mot Village, Vietnam, where students engaged in "building a kindergarten while simultaneously documenting Hmong culture and village life."[9] The USP also developed joint courses with global universities, such as a course with Yale University, "Religions in the Contemporary World," that joined students from Yale with peers at NUS and included conversations with Tony Blair and Yale faculty. By 2011, the USP had received its own dormitory within the new University Town, which was also the site of the new Yale-NUS College.

NUS had ample experience in founding new institutions with international partners before the agreement with Yale. The Yong Siew Toh Conservatory of Music started from a 2003 partnership with the Johns Hopkins University Peabody Conservatory and by 2008 was a stand-alone conservatory on the NUS campus. The new Duke-NUS Medical School was established in 2005 as a laboratory of new kinds of medical education.[10] Duke-NUS opened its doors in 2008 to its first incoming class of twenty-six students from seven countries, and offers a joint MD degree from both NUS and Duke University. The program provides a unique postgraduate form of medical education that includes research and leadership training and employs an innovative team-based learning pedagogy known as Team-LEAD, which stands for "Learn, Engage, Apply, and Develop."[11] NUS was ready for the creative challenges that an international partnership with Yale would bring.

Establishing a global presence seemed the natural next step for Yale as it approached its three hundredth anniversary and implemented its "Fourth Century Initiative." Levin had a vision for Yale to become "a truly international institution." In a 1996 speech, he described the university's global commitment as one that emphasized excellence in undergraduate education:

> First, among the nation's finest research universities, Yale is distinctively committed to excellence in undergraduate education. Second, in our graduate and professional schools as well as in Yale College, we are committed to the education of leaders. . . . Beyond these commitments, we must recognize that the leaders of the twenty-first century, in virtually every calling and profession, will operate in a global environment.[12]

Like NUS, Yale had greatly expanded its global partnerships and programs beginning in the early 2000s. It had already established international summer internships in twenty-eight countries and helped launch the International Alliance of Research Universities, a consortium of leading world universities that today includes Yale, Oxford, Cambridge, NUS, ETH Zurich, Peking University, the University of California (UC), Berkeley (UC Berkeley), the University of Copenhagen, the University of Tokyo, and the Australian National University.[13] International programs expanded rapidly from 2005 to 2008 and included training opportunities for senior government officials from China and India, extensive research collaborations with China (such as biology research at a Peking-Yale joint center, and nanotechnology at Yale-Beida center), and a proposed Yale Institute of the Arts in Abu Dhabi. The Yale International Framework of 2009 also listed a jointly taught summer course at NUS with Yale and NUS faculty and students, and projects on tropical forestry in Singapore, but the liberal arts college in Singapore was not yet part of Yale's extensive international strategy.[14]

NUS also had global ambitions as it entered its second century. In 2008, NUS president Shih Choon Fong presented the initial idea for a liberal arts college in Singapore to the Claremont Colleges, proposing to call the new venture Claremont-NUS College. Shih argued that the new college would "prepare our students for the global economy, equipping them with a competitive edge in our culturally complex world."[15] Some of the Claremont faculty were excited about the initiative's potential to promote interdisciplinary work and a more global outlook at their institution. Many other Claremont faculty voiced concerns about how academic freedom could be assured within Singapore and the project's financial and logistical scope. Despite three visits to Singapore from the presidents of the Claremont institutions, and detailed plans for making the new Singaporean liberal arts college a full member of the Claremont Colleges, the Singaporeans abruptly changed directions and began discussions with Yale University, abandoning the Claremont Colleges. David Oxtoby, the president of Pomona College, suggested that the abrupt change of direction may have been associated with the Claremont Colleges' insistence that the new liberal arts college be independent of both its founding Claremont Colleges and of NUS.

By 2010, however, productive discussions had begun between new NUS president Tan Chorh Chuan and Yale's Levin. They began negotiating a partnership, immediately recognizing the compatibility of a new global college in Singapore with their respective visions. Their institutions had already collaborated through the prestigious International Association of Research Universities, which enabled leading world universities to work together on jointly developed courses and research projects. Yale remained deeply interested in expanding its international programs, training global leaders, and providing a liberal arts education for undergraduates. NUS sought to create new forms of residential liberal arts for its undergraduates and was rapidly growing both in international stature and in partnerships with US institutions. Together, they could achieve their shared institutional missions.

In 2010, Levin cowrote a prospectus for the new Singapore college with Yale's provost, Peter Salovey, outlining its governance and financing. They presented the idea to the Yale faculty for review and discussion in September 2010. Levin and Salovey cited the unmet global demand for higher education and Yale's status as one of the world's leading universities as two factors for founding Yale-NUS College. As reported in the Yale alumni magazine:

> Levin and Salovey mention other motives in their letter, including a growing imperative for universities to invest abroad. "We do believe it is inevitable that the world's leading universities by the middle of this century will have international campuses," they write. U.S. and European universities have hundreds of partnerships and joint ventures in Asia and the Middle East, and the demand for higher education in both regions is growing tremendously.[16]

In a 2013 interview, President Tan commented that the Yale-NUS College would help create "differentiated pathways" for higher education and would support Singapore's strategic positioning in "ten to fifteen years' time"— and perhaps well beyond that. His list of top priorities included developing online education, the "nexus between education and employment," as well as a refocus on education and teaching. The Yale-NUS College would catalyze these areas, he hoped, "not to replicate the liberal arts model, but to enhance the value proposition" of higher education.

Controversies in New Haven

Discussions at Yale about the Yale-NUS College provide a case study in press relations and academic governance. An editorial in the *Yale Daily News* just days after the release of Salovey's prospectus presaged many of the most controversial aspects of the agreement:

> Yale has never before operated, even in partnership, a full-fledged overseas campus with its name on it. Even though half the seats on the board of directors of the new college will be Yale appointees, and even though Yale will have say in the admissions criteria for students, faculty searches, tenure appointments and institutional assessments, it will be difficult to ensure the quality of the day-to-day education on a campus nearly 10,000 miles away. It also will be very difficult to ensure that academic freedoms are maintained in a country where public demonstrations and chewing gum are banned.[17]

Town hall meetings among tenure track or "ladder" faculty debated how the new college in Singapore would be governed and staffed, and whether the Yale faculty supported the idea. Haun Saussy, chair of the Yale Council on East Asian Studies and cochair of the Yale oversight committee, expressed a more sympathetic view of why Yale would embark on the project, appealing to the university's long history of educational experimentation, as reflected in its motto: "Lux et veritas." To Saussy, the *lux* and *veritas* of a new Yale-NUS College would "incorporate lessons and values from our long experience here and contextualize them in ways that can be partly foreseen and remain partly to be discovered. It would be an experiment in intercultural learning."[18]

Over two thousand professors received invitations to the first meeting, but only twenty-five attended. The *Yale Daily News* indicated that all seventeen professors they interviewed supported the venture. Linda Lorimer, vice-president and secretary of the university, reported that the administration "received 290 e-mails from alumni and 25 from faculty about the plan, with 72 percent of alumni and 64 percent of faculty expressing full support and 11 percent and 8 percent opposed, respectively."[19]

Concerns about Yale-NUS College revolved around political rights in Singapore, which has been called an "illiberal democracy," despite being known as a long-standing magnet for global talent. Expatriate workers make up nearly 20 percent of Singapore's population, including both a high-wage and high-skill group of workers in technical industries and a large unskilled workforce in trade, construction, and service industries. The rise of Singapore was led by Lee Kuan Yew, prime minister from 1959 to 1990, and by his eldest son, Lee Hsien Loong, who has served as prime minister since 2004. Lee Kuan Yew also founded the People's Action Party, which has ruled Singapore since its founding with a reputation for firm enforcement of the nation's strict legal code. The latter includes several provisions that infringe on people's rights to gather for protest and withholds legal rights for gay and lesbian Singaporeans. While hardly the authoritarian state described by many critics, Singapore's restrictive political system and legal code did create what to many appeared as an existential threat to an academic institution based on liberal values and academic freedom.

While Yale's faculty had mixed views about the new initiative, several outspoken faculty voices, covered extensively by major media, shaped public perception of the new Yale-NUS College. One particularly prolific opponent to the plan, a lecturer in political science named Jim Sleeper, regularly conducted interviews with major papers and submitted numerous editorials against the Yale-NUS College, largely basing his opposition on academic freedom concerns. Sleeper summarized his objections in a 2015 article, "Innocents Abroad? Liberal Educators in Illiberal Societies." He took a cynical view of ventures by MIT, Yale, and NYU in Singapore, China, and Russia, and he cited an open letter from the American Association of University Professors to the Yale community: "'In a host environment where free speech is constrained, if not proscribed, . . . authentic liberal education, to the extent it can exist in such situations, will suffer.'" He particularly took Singapore to task for its lack of press freedoms (ranked 153 of 180 nations in 2015) and its tendency toward "Kafkaesque legalism to restrain artistic expression and political activity."[20]

Editorials and news stories covered the incarceration of British author Alan Shadrake for writing about Singapore's judicial system in an unflattering way, the lack of rights for gays and lesbians in Singapore, laws in Singapore against "unlawful" assembly (which prohibit demonstrations with as few as five people without prior approval from the government), and Yale's motivations for opening the new college. Despite vocal opposition from a small minority on campus, Yale administrators moved forward with the plan. Levin felt that the opportunity to engage Singapore in the new college could help liberalize its society, as the alumni magazine reported:

As to the larger question of whether Yale should get involved with Singapore at all, Levin's answer is unsurprising, as he has maintained a similar stance on China for many years. He argues that the best course of action is to "engage and hope that through conversation and interaction there's going to be some advance in mutual understanding and perhaps some liberalization of the society."[21]

Yale created an advisory committee for the college that included equal representation from Yale and NUS and thereby aimed to uphold academic freedom. This assurance included a guarantee that faculty and students at the new college "will be free to conduct scholarship and research and publish the results, and to teach in the classroom and express themselves on campus, bearing in mind the need to act in accordance with accepted scholarly and professional standards and the regulations of the college." Yale also received assurances from Singapore that the Yale-NUS nondiscrimination policy would be "fully consistent" with Yale's own. Anthony Kronman, former dean of Yale Law School and Yale faculty advisory committee member, put it succinctly when he said, "We have been given the strongest possible guarantees by the government of Singapore and by NUS that on the campus of the liberal arts college, the principle of freedom of expression will be honored just as on the campus of Yale in New Haven."[22]

In March 2011, a budget was established for the new project that met the approval of the Yale administration. Yale had insisted on sufficient resources for facilities and faculty salaries, as well as lifting the usual Singaporean requirement that international students receiving heavily subsidized education in Singapore fulfill a "service obligation" by working for a period in the country afterwards for companies based in Singapore. Financial aid would be offered to international students in the new college, providing a subsidy that made the costs of Yale-NUS significantly less than those of comparable private liberal arts colleges in the United States (Singaporean tuition for 2014 was S$15,000, and international students paid S$30,000, which corresponds to about US$12,000 and US$24,000 respectively).

The site for the college, a 10.5-acre lot adjacent to the NUS campus in an area known as University Town, would be developed by Pelli-Clark-Pelli and Forum Architects to house the college's one thousand students in three separate residential colleges surrounded by new instructional space, laboratories, studios for music and art, and classrooms. The University Town location was adjacent to several other emerging new residential undergraduate programs at NUS as well, including the USP. The new College of Alice and

Peter Tan occupied another residential tower in 2013, prioritizing citizenship and community engagement with overseas and community service projects. A third new residential college, Tembusu, was dedicated to science, technology, and society, and a fourth, still named RC4, was developed to focus on systems thinking.

Despite steady progress in planning for the new Yale-NUS College, in April 2012 over two hundred Yale faculty met to vote for a resolution that expressed their concerns about freedom in Singapore. The resolution began with a statement about "the history of lack of respect for civil and political rights in the state of Singapore" and demanded that Yale "respect, protect and further principles of non-discrimination for all, including sexual minorities and migrant workers, and . . . uphold civil liberty and political freedom on campus and in the broader society."[23] The resolution passed despite Levin's opposition: the president felt that "the tone of the resolution, especially the first sentence, carried a sense of moral superiority" that he felt was "unbecoming."[24] Levin proceeded to launch the new Yale-NUS College, mindful of the need to balance concerns from the Yale faculty while fulfilling the larger goals of the project for Yale and NUS.

The First Yale-NUS President

By May 2012, after all the agreements had been signed and the controversy in New Haven started to settle, the new Yale-NUS College appointed its inaugural president. Pericles Lewis was already working on the new venture as the chair of the Yale-NUS humanities search committee, and his administrative credentials included serving as director of graduate students and director of undergraduate students in comparative literature and the literature major at Yale. His undergraduate degree came from McGill University, and his PhD was from Stanford. His deep roots in the humanities formed a great complement to Bailyn's science background. Lewis had written extensively on modernism, with three books out from Cambridge University Press; and he had won the Heyman Prize for outstanding scholarly work for a junior member of the Yale humanities faculty in 2002. These impressive achievements were coupled with his experience in new technologies: Lewis maintained an online center for modernism, known as the Modernism Lab, which describes itself as a "virtual space for collaborative research on modernism."[25]

Lewis brought a cool unflappability and presidential sensibility to his new job—as well as a sense of humor and an appreciation for irony, key traits for any faculty member contemplating an administrative role. If modernism in literature is described as the tendency to "break away from traditional verse forms" and "seek new methods of representation appropriate to life in an urban, industrial, mass-oriented age,"[26] as Lewis had written, then Yale-NUS College can be seen as modernist as well: the new institution sought to break away from traditional colleges and seek new methods in its curriculum and teaching.

Despite lacking previous executive administrative experience, Lewis jumped into the challenge, joining lively debates on Yale's campus about the new college and its curriculum. He suggests that his lack of experience was best for the experiment he was being asked to lead. "Frankly," he says, "an experienced president didn't really want to take on something . . . we were told not to call a risky experiment, but it was a little bit risky, and definitely an experiment. So, they were looking for somebody to lead it, and I wound up being that person." He credits his background as a Canadian, his familiarity with colonial and postcolonial countries, and his extensive travel experience in Asia with helping him get up to speed on NUS and Singapore.

As president, Lewis learned quickly about the unique challenges of university administration in an Asian context. He immediately saw the need to choreograph meetings and run them differently than the raucous debates that often took place at Yale: "Singaporeans, in general, don't like to have conflict in meetings. So, you tend to go to the meeting and the decision is actually reached by the time you get to the meeting, or it's reached after the meeting, but the meeting is just to affirm the decision that everybody agrees on. Americans tend to be a little more conflict-oriented in meetings." Lewis initiated the development of Yale-NUS's mission statement by thinking carefully with the entire community about the values of the new college. A former English professor, he was sensitive to the need for the perfect choice of words. The mission statement needed to concisely reflect the culture and values embodied by the new institution. The resulting Yale-NUS College mission statement took the unique form of a haiku:

A community of learning,
Founded by two great universities,
In Asia, for the world.

Some of the inspiration for this haiku came from a conversation with Tan Chorh Chuan, the president of NUS. President Tan told Lewis, "Pericles, when you're writing these mission statement kinds of things, they should have the compactness of a haiku where every word means something." Lewis notes that the statement lacked the exact number of syllables required for a haiku, but it did have an interesting parallel with the lyrics of a traditional Yale song that includes the line "for God, for country and for Yale." At heart, the mission statement is an aspiration for globalization rooted in service. Says Lewis: "If you say, for the world, the point is, we're trying to create a cosmopolitan ideal . . . a sense that you belong to a broader community than just your own national community."

Building a Common Curriculum for the World

Beautiful and concise as this mission statement was, it also reflected challenges faced by the curriculum-development team. Bailyn describes the problem with humor:

> Fine. So you've narrowed it slightly. Now you're talking about Asia. Maybe Asia and the West or something. That was always denounced by the faculty as the Rudyard Kipling formulation. East is East and West is West, and that this is an imperialist way of approaching it. . . . Asia is almost as broad as the entire world. Right? There's China. There's India. There's the Middle East. There's Southeast Asia, fourteen different varieties of it. What do you even mean by Asia?

Yale-NUS planners ultimately developed a curriculum independent of a local dominant culture. Singapore itself arose from a mixing of influences that included China, India, Malaysia, and the UK. As Bailyn describes it: "one of the interesting things about being in Singapore is you had to actually answer that question because you weren't in China. You weren't in India. You weren't in Japan. You weren't in the Emirates. One of the features of Singapore is there's no dominant culture." Interdisciplinary learning and breadth of study, new concepts within most of Asian higher education, became central design principles and selling points for the new Yale-NUS College. Students would take ten required courses in humanities, sciences, political theory, modern social thought, mathematics, and science, and then they would apply this core curricular learning to a more specialized course of study, much like a major within a US liberal arts college. Instead of having distribution requirements that many students fulfill by taking unrelated, distinct courses, Yale-NUS decided to implement a common curriculum, having students take the same ten courses at the same time.

The blueprint for the new Yale-NUS common curriculum is eloquently described in the 2013 Yale-NUS College Curriculum Report—perhaps a uniquely complete document of the vision and context for a start-up university curriculum. The report places Yale-NUS within the history of global higher education and emphasizes the centrality of the common curriculum in shaping the institutional culture for faculty as well as for students. The report describes how "faculty must create a whole set of courses together, teach them together, and find ways of reviewing and revising them together," which would produce better collaboration and governance for the faculty. In the eyes of the Yale-NUS team, a traditional distribution requirement in a curriculum "opens the door to faculty considering themselves primarily as free agents or entrepreneurs, rather than as members of a collegiate community of learning." Such disconnected courses, according to the Yale-NUS team, "may have contributed to the gradual decay of effective faculty governance that observers of American collegiate education have noticed and often lamented."[27]

Perhaps the most exciting aspect of the project for its founders and the inaugural faculty was the chance to reinvent liberal arts education both in the structure of the curriculum and in the context of Asia. Yale-NUS also planned to move beyond traditional lectures and seminars by "devoting attention to team-based learning and various forms of experiential education," breaking new ground not only in the content for the curriculum but also in terms of the pedagogy. As Bailyn and the founding faculty dived into designing the new curriculum, they experienced both excitement and some healthy anxiety about the challenges. They wanted "to include everything in a global perspective," Bailyn says—an aspiration that turned out "to be impossible because there's way too much."

This new curriculum was unique, in part, because students would take their courses in synchrony. "From a dean's point of view," Bailyn says, "there's no practical way to construct a committee to create a common curriculum when you haven't had one before." Most core curriculums offer a general education requirement where students choose from a list of courses. But the prospect of designing an entirely new *common* curriculum offering a unique global curriculum in humanities, social sciences, and natural sciences proved attractive to incoming faculty. Bailyn worked with committees at Yale on the effort, while NUS hired dozens of "inaugural faculty" who convened as a team one year before the launch of the new college in fall 2013. Bailyn describes what followed:

We had the great good fortune of having this incubation year . . . where faculty could hang around and argue about this for a whole year before they actually had to teach that course. And so it was like a year-long liberal arts conference except that you knew that next August, you would have to teach this. And that was a cattle prod of considerable power because you had to actually decide stuff. You couldn't just agree to disagree. And some of the arguments were completely trivial but very fierce.

In addition to curricular design, Bailyn was tasked with hiring a total of one hundred new faculty for the new college, with twenty-five in the first year alone. Bailyn and the team were faced with a nearly unprecedented situation, even in the scale of the advertising needed for the new positions. Bailyn called up the *Chronicle of Higher Education* and told the staff member that he needed to place job ads for twenty-five tenure-track faculty members across the arts and sciences. "There was this pause," he says. "Then the person on the other end . . . was like, 'Okay.'" That first year, he recalls, Yale-NUS had a significant fraction of all the tenure track jobs in philosophy worldwide. "We needed six junior philosophers all at once," he says. "And boy, they were good."

Bailyn and the hiring committees also engaged in cluster hiring of twenty to thirty faculty each year throughout the first few years, where top candidates were selected to attend a series of workshops together. During these workshops, candidates received information about the new college, worked in small groups to discuss the new common curriculum, and met Yale executives such as Levin and Lorimer, hearing directly from them about the new college. This process began in August of 2011 and included more than eight separate workshops with groups of thirty to forty prospective faculty attending from across the United States and beyond in the first year alone, with nine more workshops in the subsequent three years. The workshops served as group interviews where prospective faculty could be observed working with others, helping design courses, and discussing teaching, giving hiring officials a good sense of their potential for the challenging work of designing a new core curriculum in Singapore.

As developed during this incubation year, the new curriculum included nine interdisciplinary sequences in the humanities, social sciences, and natural sciences, with titles like "Comparative Social Institutions," "Philosophy and Political Thought," "Scientific Inquiry," "Integrated Science," "Quantitative Reasoning," "Foundations of Science," "Current Issues," "Historical Immersion," and "Literature and Humanities." More than survey classes in a single subject, these courses would provide a synthesis of Eastern and Western literature, philosophy, political theory, and culture, as well as immersing students in scientific inquiry and key modes of thought common to all science disciplines.

During these same months of curricular planning, Yale-NUS College had its temporary home on several floors of a gold-colored, glass-windowed bank building in downtown New Haven. From these offices, Bailyn and the team of inaugural faculty debated the works of Aristotle, Plato, Lao Tzu, Confucius, and the political philosophy of the Enlightenment. They fanned out into New Haven for further discussions at night at Mory's eating club and other New Haven venues. They were visited by scholars from across the United States and the world, and they also took trips to visit some of the best liberal arts and sciences programs in the United States—the Claremont Colleges, Vassar College, and Olin College of Engineering. During these visits, the inaugural faculty paid close attention to course design and also sat in on lectures and laboratories.

Ambitions ran high for the new curriculum. It wasn't just going to transform Singaporean education—it was also, ideally, going to have an impact on the Yale campus back in New Haven. Bailyn describes a feedback loop in which initiatives started in Singapore could be adopted at Yale. "The way the feedback loop would work is we will invent some new things, try them out," he says. "Just the process of thinking them through will give people ideas." Yale faculty could teach for a semester or a year at Yale-NUS and then return, bringing back courses and teaching methods to New Haven. Anthony Kronman, Sterling Professor of Law at Yale, described this part of the project in glowing terms: "It's an opportunity to think about all of this without the baggage and prejudices that hamper curricular reform and liberal education in the United States. We can draw on a relatively blank sheet the outlines of a program that would be Western, Asian, completely free and fresh."[28] One key challenge of the new common curriculum was how to offer interdisciplinary science courses to all the students, including those who would become science majors. Founding president Pericles Lewis hoped that the common curriculum would "bridge the gap between the sciences and the social sciences, to bring STEM into the fold to make it STEAM" (the acronym for the combination of STEM and art).

While many aspects of the Singapore college were new and innovative, the core approach to teaching at Yale-NUS is rooted in simplicity. In the words of the 2013 Curriculum Report, Yale-NUS College was designed with "a focus on articulate communication," "open, informed and reflective discourse," and "conversation" between individuals as the primary element of learning, just as in ancient times.[29] As the report put it, "among the goals of a college curriculum is to help students make sense of that experience together, through a set of conversations about some of the most fundamental questions and problems of human existence."[30]

The Approach to Steady State

The combination of this common curriculum, the breadth of study, the institutional prestige, and interdisciplinary and global focus proved very attractive to potential students. Yale-NUS recruited a spectacularly talented group in the initial and subsequent student cohorts, drawing young people from over sixty countries, with about half hailing from Singapore. With the first applicant class, Yale-NUS was able to achieve a selectivity even higher than Yale University's, accepting only 4 percent of the students who applied. By 2020, with four graduating cohorts already on the job market, Yale-NUS College enjoyed a 6 percent selectivity rating and was one of the most sought-after liberal arts programs in the world. Admission to Yale-NUS remained slightly more competitive than admission to Yale University, which offered acceptances to 6.54 percent of its applicants for the class of 2024. By some accounts, Yale-NUS College was accepting only 1–2 percent of its applicants, making it one of the most selective institutions in the world, and yet it is important to note that this figure includes a large number of applicants who had applied to Yale and opted to share their applications with Yale-NUS College.

The intimacy of the campus, with its "community of learning" from around the world, affords students unique opportunities in cross-cultural learning. As Joanne Roberts, the current president of Yale-NUS College describes it:

> Our classes are small with up to 18 students on average. I was teaching a course in economics, and I realize that almost all the students in the classroom are from different places. So, they have as much to learn from each other as they have to learn from you. I think that's part of what makes teaching here so rewarding.

Like the inaugural faculty, the initial class of students played a key role in developing the college, its curriculum, and its cocurriculum. Roberts described the emerging culture of Yale-NUS College in a 2021 interview:

> I think that we created a very nice culture of co-creation with our students. This means that our initial cohorts of students, even though things

weren't necessarily entirely nailed down, in terms of our co-curricular programming and our residential support, those students really helped us create the institution and they feel that ownership and that is something that's very, very beautiful.

The cocreation process with students includes a critical discussion about the common curriculum, perhaps the signature component of Yale-NUS education. Students have criticized it as overly Western and insufficiently attentive to the culture and traditions of more locally rooted writers, thinkers, and communities. Faris Joraimi, an undergraduate and director of academics for the Yale-NUS student government, criticized the common curriculum for its lack of any writing from Singapore's own traditions. Joraimi noted that Yale-NUS curriculum designers cautioned against the dangers of "producing a rootless elite who regard themselves as part of a rarified world of educated professionals but who lack deep ties to particular places and real communities."[31] In particular, Joraimi felt that the college's notions of Asia were "reductive" and overly simplistic: "To an outsider's eye, tracing the development of Chinese thought for three consecutive semesters may seem a triumph for diversifying the academy. But to the non-Chinese Singaporeans, the heavily Sinophone curriculum feels no different from their experience growing up with a public education system and an official discourse that privilege Confucian values and places the burden of assimilation on them." "A university education in Singapore—even if it is for the world," Joraimi concluded, should involve "some considerate regard for the knowledge that Singapore and its cultural hinterland have generated."[32]

Not only have students actively cocreated the curriculum, but their achievements after graduation have also validated the Yale-NUS educational model. Employers have noted that Yale-NUS graduates come with "strong writing and problem-solving skills as well as the ability to take the initiative."[33] In the first five graduating classes, alumni included two Fulbright Scholars, two Yenching Scholars, two Schwarzman Scholars, a Rhodes Scholar, and an Ertegun Scholar. Numerous start-up companies have been launched by Yale-NUS graduates, demonstrating the power of the liberal arts to catalyze entrepreneurship.[34] As Roberts describes it: "Our first few cohorts of students have achievements such as winning Rhodes scholarships, getting into PhD programs in top schools in the U.S. which have great conversion rates, from internships to placements and leading firms. I think that having that proof point early on has been really important in terms of promoting our value to Singaporean parents." Yale-NUS faculty have also had impressive achievements. Among its 130 full-time faculty, 15 have an h-index over 20, a sign of extremely high research productivity. By comparison, top US liberal arts colleges Williams, Amherst, Swarthmore, and Pomona College have 19, 16, 16, and 14 faculty with an h-index above 20, respectively. The comparison is even more remarkable considering that Yale-NUS has had less than a decade to establish its faculty scholarship. By 2021, Yale-NUS College was reaching a kind of institutional adolescence, which Roberts described in an interview:

> I think we're in that teenage moment, and occasionally you feel a bit of that tension. I want to be innovating all the time but at the same time, we need to find a balance between teaching and research. Trying to find that right balance for people while bearing in mind the weight of the service, which was such a huge part of those first few years, is part of this consolidation moment as well.

Yale-NUS in its "teenage" years faced some of the same challenges that all liberal arts colleges face—from finding an optimal balance for faculty between research, teaching, and service to fine-tuning faculty governance and the curriculum. Roberts pointed out that getting these details right is part of the "consolidation moment," as will be finding the right balance of voices in deciding certain tradeoffs:

> [I] think this consolidation phase is partly about figuring out, where are the places where we really want faculty voices, and where are the places where we want some steady hands? We don't want everything to have to be decided every time. So, we want some consistent rules. We want to institutionalize things, systematize what goes where, how decisions are made.

One recent controversy tested the limits of academic freedom at Yale-NUS and generated a number of articles in the global press. The issue concerned a week-long short course, Dialogue and Dissent in Singapore, planned by Singaporean playwright Alifan Sa'at in 2019, that was abruptly cancelled the summer before it was to be taught. Yale-NUS president Tai Yong stated that the cancellation was necessary to prevent international students from losing their visas for engaging in political activity, but his explanation did not satisfy everyone.

Yale's president Peter Salovey issued a statement on the controversy. "Yale has insisted on the values of academic freedom and open inquiry, which have been central to the college and have inspired outstanding work by faculty, students and staff."[35] Salovey requested an investigation to be led by former Yale-NUS president Lewis, who was then Yale's vice-president for global strategy. A report based on interviews with administrators, faculty, and the instructor of the course concluded "that the decision to cancel the module was made internally and without government interference in the academic independence of the College."[36]

The incident nevertheless generated international attention, including a *Washington Post* editorial, which stated: "Although only 16 students were enrolled, the decision has revived a debate on whether American liberal arts colleges and other Western universities are compromising their values of academic freedom and the free exchange of ideas when they expand into places with restrictive political climates such as Singapore, the Persian Gulf states and China."[37]

The Fate and Impact of Yale-NUS

Although the controversy eventually abated, Yale-NUS would soon face a much greater and ultimately existential challenge. The campus was stunned by the surprise announcement on August 27, 2021, that NUS was taking charge of Yale-NUS, dissolving it as a separate institution and merging it with the legacy USP from NUS, and renaming it "New College." Faculty, staff, and students received notice of this sudden consolidation in a hastily convened "town hall" announced just one day before the merger was official. The decision was made by NUS president Tan Eng Chye and shocked both the Yale-NUS College leaders and the leadership at Yale. Notably, Yale-NUS president Tan Tai Yong was not part of the decision. He told the student newspaper that he was "gobsmacked and flabbergasted" by the news.[38] NUS explained that the merger of Yale-NUS and USP to create New College would save funds and expand access to interdisciplinary and liberal arts education within Singapore. NUS president Tan told reporters that New College would provide "broader access and inclusiveness for students across NUS to be exposed to and benefit from a broad-based, interdisciplinary education." In a later statement, he also pointed out that "the evolution of USP and Yale-NUS into the New College . . . brings together the best features of both institutions and expands access to multiple pathways, disciplines and specialisations."[39]

Since the announcement of the Yale-NUS "merger," many have speculated on potential deeper motivations for the premature demise of the Yale-NUS College. The possibilities of additional agendas and motivations—

beyond the official reason of needing consolidation for financial efficiency and greater enrollment—have been discussed in social media and newspaper accounts. Some of these other factors might include concerns about the political dangers from liberalism and dissent on the Yale-NUS campus, resentment within NUS about the lavish resources given to Yale-NUS, or other political concerns within NUS about limited benefits to itself or even unwanted competition from Yale-NUS for the best students and for research awards. These factors may well have been in play, as well as profound mismatches in culture and priorities between Yale and NUS, which may have made the partnership unsustainable regardless of the NUS decision. These mismatches included limited interest and concern on the part of Yale for Singapore's larger goals in the project, and a rather drastic disconnect in the academic cultures of NUS and Yale, with differing approaches in some key areas such as faculty governance and the role of the individual "citizen" within an academic community. The academic cultural differences included the philosophy of assessment of students (NUS strictly graded students using a "curve"), methods of disagreement and debate within a campus, different ways of conceptualizing academic freedom and professor autonomy in classrooms, and some different cultural assumptions about the nature of the liberal arts and the larger purposes of higher education. Perhaps some of the seeds of the Yale-NUS merger can also be found in the early statements of leaders focused more on building Yale-NUS "in Asia for the World" than on the specific needs of Singapore.

Regardless of the precise motivations, and even if the NUS New College retains substantial parts of the Yale-NUS curriculum or pedagogy, the merger threatens the unique academic culture created within Yale-NUS. The merger will also upend much of the heroic effort given by faculty, staff, and students for over a decade in building the Yale-NUS College curriculum, cocurriculum, and community. But the merger doesn't diminish the success of Yale-NUS College as an academic institution, as it had reached the top levels of research and teaching quality in just a few years after its founding.

Despite its premature demise, Yale-NUS College developed an extremely innovative common curriculum, which has been widely recognized for breaking new ground in terms of integrating East and West and developing new interdisciplinary approaches in undergraduate education. Yale-NUS College has also demonstrated high intellectual integrity in how faculty can reinforce and improve teaching practice through team teaching and provide faculty development through their Center for Teaching and Learning. Like NYU Abu Dhabi, Yale-NUS created high expectations for research on its campus and hired numerous junior faculty who published extensively in the best journals and produced excellent monographs published by the best university presses. Through its strong connections with both Yale and NUS, Yale-NUS was able to push beyond many of the boundaries limiting research on typical liberal arts campuses. In some fields, like urban planning and social sciences, Yale-NUS also developed a niche within Southeast Asia and leveraged its location in Singapore to become a world leader in scholarship. Yale-NUS managed to attract truly excellent students and had a higher selectivity than Yale itself. Yale-NUS placed its graduates in the top ranks of Singapore's civil service and with important firms.

From its founding, however, Yale-NUS was limited in its ability to sustain a full laboratory science program, since its campus lacked research laboratories and it had to use space on the neighboring NUS campus. The impacts on Singapore, on NUS, and at Yale from Yale-NUS College were only just beginning to be seen but perhaps were not yet at the levels envisioned at its founding. Singapore's motivation for Yale-NUS to train creative workers to spur economic growth in Singapore collided with increasing nationalism within the country, perhaps providing a chilling effect on the new campus. Several batches of Yale-NUS graduates had just begun to provide benefits to the Singaporean economy, and yet perhaps the Singaporean government's goals were threatened by the number of them who left Singapore after their education to work elsewhere.

By merging Yale-NUS with the University Scholars Program at NUS, the goals of Singapore and NUS to create larger cohorts of Singaporean students with liberal arts training may still be possible, and yet without the same unique academic programs and unique culture that the founders of Yale-NUS worked so hard to create. Yale's ambitions in founding Yale-NUS were a central part of its third century global strategy to advance Yale as a "truly global university," and this plan will have to be continued in other ways, as Yale finds more sustainable methods for increasing its global impact. Some of the impacts of Yale-NUS on Yale include over 150 Yale faculty having spent some time on the Singapore campus, ranging from days to over a semester, and in some cases Yale faculty have returned to New Haven with modules or courses they designed in Singapore. However, as of 2022, no major curricular changes at Yale or other larger impacts on the home campus had been realized. As such, it remains to be seen if the huge investment of funds and personnel in creating the Yale-NUS campus and curriculum will live up to the lofty rhetoric of the college's founding.

5

A Culture of Continuous Innovation

OLIN COLLEGE OF ENGINEERING

It was July, 1, 2020, and Gilda Barabino was beginning her first day as president of Olin College of Engineering. Barabino was the second president the institution had known since its founding twenty-three years earlier, and the day represented the first ever hand-over of power for the institution. Like a nation undergoing its first transfer of authority, Olin College had reached an important threshold of institutional adulthood, transitioning the presidency from Richard Miller to a new generation of leadership represented by Barabino.

Barabino's journey to Olin entailed a circuitous route that included many states and service in the US military before she began her academic career. She was born in Alaska (her father was based there in the military) and spent some of her childhood and young adult life in New Orleans, where she attended public high school and went on to the historically Black Xavier University, where she received a BS in chemistry. She decided to shift into chemical engineering, and in 1986 became the first African American woman admitted to the graduate program in chemical engineering at Rice University in Houston, Texas. When she earned her PhD a few years later, she became only the fifth African American woman in the country to earn a doctorate in the field. Barabino continued onward with faculty and administrative appointments at Northeastern University, Georgia Institute of Technology, Emory University, and the City College of New York.

The contrast between the two Olin presidents was remarkable in many ways. Miller was born into the fourth generation of a farming family in rural California and was raised in the farmhouse of its eighty-acre ranch. He began his academic career at UC Davis, graduated with a BS in mechanical engineering, and went on to get an MSc at MIT and a PhD from the California Institute of Technology. He continued in academia and spent seventeen years on the engineering faculty at the University of Southern California (USC) and UC Santa Barbara. Miller then served as dean of the College of Engineering at the University of Iowa beginning in 1992, until being contacted by the president of the F. W. Olin Foundation in 1999, who asked Miller what he would like to change about engineering education. Miller visited the foundation to discuss his ideas, and when he returned home, he wrote up an extended letter about what he thought Olin should do and then put the letter in a drawer. After he received an offer to serve as Olin's inaugural president and first employee, that letter wound up becoming the blueprint for the new Olin College.[1]

Miller began his process as founding Olin president by seeking senior faculty who were frustrated with the state of engineering education to form an advisory board and then hiring younger faculty who had the passion to make the new college a reality. Within a year, Miller and his team had hired his first dozen employees, including four vice-presidents and key founding faculty. He called on his advisory board to "rethink what it means to be an engineer" and "what it means to be educated in the twenty-first century." He also asked the group, "What do you remember from your undergraduate education?" He describes the response that the board members gave him:

> And so we went around the table. . . . Silence! I mean, I remember I had physics and I'm talking to a physicist. So you would think it was Halliday and Resnick, but don't ask me to do a quantum mechanics problem today because I haven't touched it in 20 years. Everybody had trouble even remembering the topics that we had taken as undergraduates, except for one. The senior capstone project. Everybody remembered that project.

This insight—namely, that the most powerful undergraduate educational experiences involve self-directed capstone work, not typical classwork—resulted in the decision to place project-based learning and design throughout all four years of the new Olin College curriculum, culminating with a yearlong senior design problem. Design problems were already required in the engineering curriculum, thanks to the requirements of the Accreditation Board for Engineering and Technology, but generally came only after a long series of courses, and often as only the last semester of a student's education. Miller and Olin, by contrast, infused project-based and experiential learning from the first semester onward, as they were convinced it was far more effective for student learning. Says Miller: "We got fascinated by the idea that projects have this amazing ability to penetrate your understanding and to stick with you for generations later. This experiential learning thing is not better by a fraction of a percent, it's orders of magnitude better in terms of sticking in your head."

Creating the Ideal University

In the late 1980s, the National Science Foundation and the engineering community began calling for reform in engineering education. The aim was to equip students with a wider variety of skills during their studies—from business and entrepreneurship to creativity and human-centered design—to provide education that included more of the social, political, and economic contexts of engineering.[2] Key thought pieces generated during this period of reform include a 1994 report from the American Society for Engineering Education, "Engineering Education for a Changing World," which recommended engineering education that was more "relevant, attractive, and connected," and urged "individual missions for engineering colleges," since "the world now demands new models."[3] The report called for a revised engineering curriculum, one that placed more emphasis on team skills with active learning environments, and a systems perspective that would incorporate the "societal, economic and environmental impacts of engineering decisions."[4] The report urged this redesign to promote international economic competitiveness and greater diversity within engineering, to take "full advantage of the nation's talents," and to train engineers "to serve as technology and policy decision makers."[5] In 1996, the National Science Foundation restructured its priorities, emphasizing greater integration of research and teaching and issuing a press release that described the ideal university environment: "Picture an ideal university: It has a pervasive culture promoting collaborative research between professors and students; there are internet links between research labs, libraries, and students; and there is an emphasis on discovery-based learning techniques throughout science and engineering curricula. This should be the norm. Often, however, it is not."[6]

In response to these calls for transforming science and engineering education, the Olin Foundation, led by President Lawrence W. Milas, decided that it
could best maximize its impact by creating an entirely new institution, one that
could respond to the call for dramatic reform of engineering education nation-
ally and globally. Olin College was named after Franklin W. Olin (1860–1951),
an engineer, entrepreneur, and professional baseball player who had studied
civil engineering at Cornell. In 1938, he dedicated a significant portion of his
personal wealth to a private philanthropic foundation, and over the following
decades his organization would award grants totaling $300 million to con-
struct and equip seventy-eight buildings on fifty-eight independent college
campuses. The foundation board located the new Olin College in Needham,
Massachusetts, fourteen miles west of Boston. To enable the new college to
accomplish its ambitious goals, the foundation made a gift of $460 million,
allowing Olin to be built from scratch in what was then the largest gift ever
for higher education.[7] With a ready-made financial foundation in place, Olin
College received its charter in 1997 from the Commonwealth of Massachusetts
as an independent nonprofit institution. Its first faculty members had joined
the college by September 2000, and the college opened in the fall of 2002.[8]
The new college would be the Olin Foundation's largest and final gift: all of
the foundation's remaining assets were transferred to the college in 2005.

Once founded, Olin College began to attract significant attention. Its
curriculum was unique for its interdisciplinary approach and project-based
learning spanning all four years. Henri Petroski, a professor of civil engineering at Duke University, described in a 2006 report how Olin was able to redefine engineering: "It's a common misconception that engineering is applied
science, in other words, that you know all the math and the science and you
almost just look up a formula somewhere and crank out your engineering
design," he said. "It doesn't really work that way. Olin seems to recognize
that this is getting the cart before the horse, so they are apparently trying to
do it the other way. I'll be very interested to follow them."[9]

The idea of having students embark on difficult design projects first and
then learn relevant content while building these projects in real time seems
daunting if not dangerous at first, a venture with a strong chance of failure. But
this risk-taking approach is intentional at Olin and underlies its institutional
culture, which was codesigned by a group of the first students and faculty
in 2001, along with the curriculum. Miller and his founding team included
David Kerns, a former Bell Labs electrical engineer who became Olin's first
provost, and Sherra Kerns, former chair of Vanderbilt's electrical engineering
department who became Olin's founding vice-president for innovation and

research. The team began its work in earnest with a small group of faculty and students in what has now become legendary—the Partner Year.

The Partner Year

Picture this: a group of faculty and students huddled together in their farmhouse and temporary structures, tasked with designing the curricular nuts and bolts of the institution they've come together to form. They begin working. The first thirty students (selected from over six hundred applicants) gather with fifteen to twenty founding faculty to test out some of the class concepts and teaching approaches. The ensuing discussions and planning will become known in Olin lore as "The Partner Year." As Miller recalls, there was a lot of interest and skepticism in the project in those early days: "We were located fifteen miles west of MIT. And what did they expect? We're going to walk up to the front door of MIT, 'Excuse me. A few of us in a farmhouse out here fifteen miles [away] got the right answer. MIT's got it wrong.'" The intense interest meant that "it felt a lot like trying to invent cold fusion on live TV with everybody watching." With scrutiny creating an audience whose members might be eager to "watch them fail," the Olin team tried many original approaches. Says Miller:

> We broke every rule. Olin doesn't have tenure. Olin doesn't have departments. Everything at Olin has an expiration date. We asked the students to help us. In fact, the whole thing about bringing the kids in was transformational. The Olin partner year, we had fifteen boys and fifteen girls who lived in a parking lot in trailers for a year while the campus was being built. How the heck did we get them to come? They didn't even get course credit for this. They had to start over again the next year.

After a year of testing out ideas, the faculty and students were ready for Olin's official opening in the fall of 2002. "The Olin Experiment," a case study in *IEEE Spectrum*, gives examples of the new college's teaching approach, including "a bio-inspired introduction to design" that included such challenges as building a mechanical hopper (which might be patterned after beetles, fleas, or other insects) and a glass wall climber. The case study describes this second challenge:

> The second project, more challenging, is the glass wall climber, which the students make out of plastic pieces, electric motors, pneumatic actuators, and suction cups. To fabricate the parts they need, they use Olin's two

machine shops, which have a plastic thermoformer, a laser cutter, and other tools that they are certified as freshmen to operate. And to evaluate the climbers' traits—a gecko's gait, for example—the students hold an entertaining demonstration. "Lots of stuff in engineering are done without a whole bunch of science. These students are quite capable of a lot of stuff now, and we don't need to deny that."[10]

When Olin opened its doors, the Partner-Year students joined the first incoming class of seventy-five students to begin Olin's first official year as a college together. A surprise problem quickly emerged. The ambitious curriculum kept students up building things until one or two in the morning, and within a few weeks many were exhausted. Some frustrated students began to crack under the pressure. Faculty had underestimated the time and effort that students needed to complete the team design tasks. Student frustration grew so intense that protests broke out a month after classes began. Students contended that they were staying up late to complete assignments for several days on end, and consequently could not stay awake in their classes. Some even considered leaving Olin. The administration responded by declaring a moratorium on classes and reevaluating the workload and curriculum. Thus began a key moment in Olin College history, which became legendary as the "bouncy castle moment."

This seminal incident is recounted by founding faculty member and current Olin provost Mark Somerville, the chief architect of the college's foundational year.[11] Somerville recalls the attitude of the faculty, many of whom had been thinking, "We had spent a ton of time designing all this amazing stuff, right? It was going to be the best thing ever." And yet after just two weeks, "students were breaking down crying and falling asleep in class and just completely burned out because . . . they were trying too hard." Both faculty and students had asked too much of themselves and each other, and "they were expecting more of themselves than was reasonable. . . . Our eyes were all bigger than our stomachs and their stomachs." The answer was the "bouncy castle," now a beloved object of Olin culture:

> So we set up a bouncy castle down on the fields and basically took the day off with students and had the egg toss that turned into the throw eggs at professors thing, and then called everyone together and said, "We screwed up. We tried to push too hard. You tried to push too hard. No homework for the weekend. On Monday, we're going to come back together and figure out together how we can make this work and how we're going to change things."

Somerville also recognized that this incident was an "important cultural moment" that continues to resonate within Olin College whenever the community faces an unexpected challenge that requires a reset: "People still today at Olin, talk 'Oh, we need to have a bouncy castle.' . . . [T]his term bouncy castle means something collectively. And there'd been a number of points in our history when we had what we call 'bouncy castle moments.'" The construction of Olin's permanent campus also included a few surprises. Miller recalls how, in the early days, Olin was at risk of being, as he puts it, "blindsided" by setbacks. Despite the foundation's extraordinary gift of $460 million (which removed the financial uncertainty typical of start-ups), Olin faced its share of unplanned construction emergencies. Miller likens founding a college to being a country doctor—you have to be prepared to handle everything that comes your way. (He recommends that those who do this kind of work cultivate a "long fuse.")

The initial facilities consisted of farmhouses and trailers, but as they began construction of the full campus, builders discovered a twenty-two-inch gas main for the city of Boston ran right through the center of the property: substantial engineering redesign would be needed to accommodate this pipeline. They also discovered a historic aqueduct that had to be preserved and learned that much of their campus was on "registered land" or wetlands, requiring multitudes of applications and permits. These setbacks delayed their opening by a year but gave the team more time for developing the curriculum and hiring new faculty.

Despite these delays, Olin College would rise to a level of prestige and press attention well beyond its humble beginnings in a farmhouse setting. Miller describes how Olin was founded with advice from Joe Platt, president of Harvey Mudd College, who provided two "big ideas" to the founding team. Harvey Mudd College itself was an innovative start-up several decades earlier and has provided top-quality liberal-arts-infused engineering education within the Claremont Colleges since 1955. The first principle: make sure your students are excellent. "Ten excellent students are better than forty average students"—even if this meant lower enrollments in the first years. The second principle: be mindful of the institutional tendency toward conservativism, and continually strive to keep the curriculum, the instruction, and the institutional culture fresh. New generations of faculty and of students all want to share that sense of being at a new institution, and the leadership at Olin wanted to meet this expectation. As Miller recounts, Platt's full quote was that "there's no more powerful force for conservatism than having something to conserve. Right now you have nothing to conserve—but in 10 years, you will have trouble prying the white knuckles of faculty off the steering wheel to make any changes." Miller points out that this is what led to Olin's founding principle of "everything at Olin should have an expiration date."

To attract the best and brightest—Platt's first big idea—Olin offered full scholarships to all incoming students who might otherwise choose to go to MIT or Stanford. Overseeing this process was Olin's first provost, Mike Moody, former Harvey Mudd College mathematics chair. Moody also helped recruit and hire some of the first faculty and today has a named professorship in honor of his contributions.[12] The relationship between Olin and Harvey Mudd is worth noting here, since Olin leaders modeled portions of the new college after the slightly older science and engineering institution. Both Olin and Harvey Mudd are based on intense collaboration with students and hands-on and project-based courses; and like Olin, Harvey Mudd's core curriculum has requirements in the humanities, social sciences, and the arts.

The winning combination of outstanding students and an exciting new curriculum and institutional culture placed the college in a strong position to attract top-quality faculty. Today, Olin receives about 150 resumés for each open position, even though these faculty jobs come without tenure. New generations of faculty and new generations of students continue to contribute to building Olin College long after its launching, and the leadership strives to make this expectation of continuous innovation a central part of the institutional culture.

The Emergence of Olin College Culture

To build on Platt's second big idea—continuous innovation—Olin College faculty, students, and administrators together built processes to promote renewal and refinement of the institution. According to Somerville, there is "enormous opportunity from a cultural perspective in starting a new organization," even though culture is not usually the overriding concern of faculty in a start-up university. Conversations within start-up institutions typically center on the curriculum and other business but begin to embody a new culture through participants' interactions—usually without the founders recognizing this. Somerville advises start-ups to be more conscious of this emergent culture and to be more intentional in fostering this process and helping it take shape. As he puts it: "You consistently see this emergence of a culture theme in these organizations that's important and that if you go into it with your eyes open . . . there's probably a lot of opportunity to be intentional around culture." Perhaps unique to Olin is the role students played in building the institution—and the mind-set of cocreation that helps inspire Olin's instructional environment. As Somerville puts it: "On some level, students are not consumers in a startup organization, they are co-creators. And that's almost by necessity when you're doing a startup. A startup that tries to avoid that, you can't actually avoid that as a reality. . . . I think there's an enormous benefit in that framing students as co-creators." By making students cocreators, Olin founders learned a key lesson: there is value in "reframing the student from a consumer mindset to co-creator mindset." This repositioning offers a "huge educational opportunity" and increases learning, according to Somerville.

To this end, Olin faculty identified specific curricular goals they wanted to implement during the Partner Year and beyond. They envisioned a curriculum that motivates students, that includes design throughout, and that culminates with a senior capstone that is representative of professional practice. They also sought a learning environment that would be intentionally social, so that students could gain experience *working as an individual, as a member of a team, and as leader of a team*—valuable stepping stones toward becoming professional engineers after graduation. The curriculum also emphasizes communication, helping students communicate logically and persuasively in verbal, written, numerical, and visual formats. And it includes "space for a true international/intercultural immersion experience" that allows students to gain perspective "beyond the confines of their own backgrounds." The hope is that Olin's curriculum will prepare graduates to "predict, create, and manage technologies of the future, not simply respond to the technologies of today."[13]

Many elements of this curriculum blend and cross the boundaries between engineering and liberal arts. For example, Olin's Grand Challenges Scholars Program "uses a combination of formal courses and informal experiences to help students grow into their identities, participate in a community of practice, and find a role for themselves in fulfilling Olin's mission of doing good in the world."[14] The program was invented in 2009 by Olin, Duke, and USC. It was recently recognized with the Gordon Prize of the National Academy of Engineering (NAE) and had been adopted by ninety-seven universities by 2022. The liberal arts are reflected in Olin's commitment to interdisciplinary courses, as well as in its emphasis on educating the whole person. Olin encourages personal growth by giving students the space to pursue extracurricular interests and nontechnical skills, a common philosophy at many liberal arts colleges.

Olin's culture goes beyond curricular innovation to include fresh approaches to faculty development. To begin with, the college does not award tenure to its faculty. Vincent Manno, dean of faculty during Olin's second decade, explained in a 2013 interview that the reappointment and promotion process involves a constant answering of two questions: "Where are you going as an individual?" and "Where is the institution going?" If the answers suggest that both the faculty member and the institution are "going to the same place," then he or she is reappointed. In the early days, the reappointment process posed difficulties, since many of the first faculty did not have a complete understanding of the expectations being placed upon them. Manno described how Olin's leaders took great care to ensure that faculty expectations were managed carefully during hiring and that good mentoring occurred. These shared expectations include having an impact externally and internally. Such an impact can include traditional forms of scholarship (publications in academic journals, patents, etc.) or educational research, and/or curricular innovations that draw national attention. It all sounds straightforward, but in practice the lack of tenure and shifting expectations caused problems from 2006 to 2010, a period Mark Somerville calls "Olin's darker years." By 2010, Olin's first class of students had graduated, and the college was no longer a brand-new start-up. A new style of leadership and communication seemed necessary. "Okay, now we've got the plane in the air," says Somerville, recalling those moments. "Now we need to figure out how do we operate at steady state."

As part of this aspirational steady state, the institution began to place more emphasis on research. But for faculty members who had been burning the midnight oil to build the institution, the new focus appeared to be a kind of bait and switch. Some faculty wondered if the administration was asking them to "go back in your lab and publish those papers that you haven't published." Others concluded that Olin had "just changed the goalposts," according to Somerville.

With confusion growing about whether Olin was taking a turn toward conventional faculty scholarship, Olin leaders had to respond. Somerville described how, after 2010, Olin administrators decided to shift reappointment and promotion criteria and modify the faculty hiring process in a way that aligned with the institutional mission and placed greater emphasis on curricular innovation. This effort represented what Somerville calls a "more intentional cultural shift," necessary to preserve the unique Olin student experience: "We need to recognize that if we want the student experience to be a certain way, we also need to think about the faculty experience in a certain way. We needed to think about the institutional structures in a certain way and those things all have to mesh together in ways that make sense." This shift in emphasis, which affected both faculty hiring and faculty review, brought with it an awareness that Olin's ultimate impact, or its "coin of the realm," as Somerville says, would be on global engineering education, not research in a traditional sense: "Olin does have people that are engaging with lots of schools around the world around how to change engineering education. Olin does have graduates who are going on and doing really exciting and successful things. But the coin of the realm for Olin is not publications." Today, Olin's faculty members operate with the understanding that the curriculum they teach is constantly evolving. The college has a yearly process for curricular assessment and improvement, with a retreat each year for staff, students, all faculty, and even external constituencies to "review student work and student competency development."[15] The presentation of Olin culture as dedicated first and foremost to educational innovation serves as an antidote to the perceived overemphasis on research activity by faculty, a focus that Miller believes does not serve students well. In other institutions, he says, it's "all about prestige and it's all about winning the Nobel prize. And it's all about published articles and grants." What happens to students in that atmosphere? Not much. It's a culture "that's got to change," he says.

Another of Olin's distinctive cultural traits involves collaboration among students, faculty, and staff. The college makes a genuine effort to bring these three groups together and help them form vibrant and generative teams. One example is the Olin Public Interest Technology Clinic, described on its website as a "student-led effort to cultivate pathways and opportunities for Olin's students, faculty, and staff to be creators, engineers, designers, artists, and activists." In addition to running a summer fellowship program, the clinic uses a variety of innovative methods to recognize needs and design solutions as well as foster student creativity for the benefit of communities in need.[16]

This emphasis on creativity drives much of the Olin educational method. For Miller, "the bottom line is creativity as a way of thinking," which "requires courage and it requires a sense of belief in your ability to do something before you can get serious in trying it." Creativity is not something you can learn from a book. "Reading a book about creativity is about as useful as reading a book about swimming," says Miller. "You have to get in the water and move your arms around. And it's the only way you're learning." The traditional engineering curriculum, with its hierarchical nature and emphasis on applied science, is like classical music, he argues: it teaches students to "reproduce the notes that Beethoven wrote two hundred years ago, and you do this exactly the same tempo and everything that he did." Useful to a point—but not conducive to discovery and innovation. Olin's curriculum, in contrast, operates more like jazz, and as Miller says, "jazz has to start from inside and is more of an extemporaneous conversation than a recital."

Olin's Second President

A new era for Olin College began with the appointment of its second president, Gilda Barabino, in 2020. Barabino's prior work included serving as dean of the Grove School of Engineering and the Daniel and Frances Berg Professor at the City College of New York. In these roles, she doubled the retention rate in engineering; developed new master's programs in data science and engineering, cybersecurity, and translational medicine; increased research; and enhanced the representation and success of women, minority faculty, and underserved student communities.[17] In 2020, she was elected to the National Academy of Medicine for "shaping and transforming the face of biomedical engineering through the integration of scientific discovery, engineering applications, and the preparation of a diverse biomedical workforce" as well as for "seminal discoveries in sickle cell research." In 2018 she received the Presidential Award for Excellence in Science, Mathematics, and Engineering Mentoring, and she was elected to the NAE in 2019. The NAE recognized her for "leadership in bioengineering research and inclusive models of bioengineering education and faculty mentoring."[18] Barabino is also a well-known researcher in the fields of cellular and tissue engineering and sickle cell disease.[19]

Though Miller and Barabino came from very different paths, they share a common passion for undergraduate education, experiential learning, and for redefining engineering with a sharp focus on project-based learning. Barabino has promised to bring Olin College of Engineering into a new phase in its development. At twenty years old, Olin College is a mature start-up that has become a world-recognized leader in engineering education. By one 2018 MIT ranking, Olin and MIT were both named as "the top leaders in engineering education globally."[20] More than its rankings or size (Olin has fewer than four hundred students), Olin's curriculum and its example have influenced many other institutions. For example, Fulbright University Vietnam modeled its codesign year after Olin's pattern. Olin also has collaborated with leaders from USC and the NAE to expand the use of project-based approaches in engineering education. In recognition of their work founding Olin College, in 2013 the NAE awarded Olin College's three founding leaders, Richard Miller, David Kerns, and Sherra Kerns, the Bernard M. Gordon Prize, which recognizes innovation in engineering and technological education.[21]

In addition to her experience and expertise, Barabino had the opportunity to bring a fresh look to Olin as an outsider to the tightly knit community. She notes that the process is "daunting because there's that history . . . a track record that's already there." Her goal is to keep what's working while also trying out new ideas—or as she puts it, to "capture the essence, the core that drives everything" while keeping "fresh and agile and doing something new" at the same time. In a 2020 interview, she described herself as a "tempered radical," a pioneer in her own life who learned how to overcome isolation and find support. A tempered radical, she says, strives to affect change, but also works within the system and creates that change from within. Barabino elaborated on this concept in an interview with the Olin student paper just weeks into her new presidency:

> If you think about "tempered" in the sense of a metal becoming tougher from alternately being heated up and cooled down—if you're a tempered radical, maybe in a certain setting you increase the heat, you push harder, you put on more pressure. . . . It's the tempering that allows you, hopefully, to be more effective, because different situations call for different kinds of reactions.[22]

On her first day as president, Barabino arrived on a campus filled with welcome messages from students. Chalk drawings in bright colors brightened the brick paving in the central oval welcoming Barabino to the "Olin Family." Whimsical drawings included dragons, colorful hearts, and a modified Olin logo showing it to be the "College of Engineering and Fun." Barabino responded with a chalk message of her own: "I love my Olin Family."[23] Soon after, a car parade featured students, staff, and faculty, who drove past Barabino honking, waving, and displaying signs of support. A tour of campus was followed by a socially distanced lunch, since her first year as president was also the year the COVID-19 pandemic started.

Barabino immediately felt an affinity to her new community. "My connection to Olin was immediate and it was deep," she said. "At a time when the global challenges we face are increasing in complexity and enormity, we must rethink how we educate engineers to meet new challenges."[24]

Expanding Creativity and Diversity at Olin

How to encourage creativity across a diverse student body? Olin here benefits from its small size, with under four hundred students. Being small allows for nimbleness within the curriculum and within the community, helping faculty and students brainstorm continuous innovation. Barabino says that Olin's small size gives it the ability to "change on a dime" to modify the curriculum and pedagogical approaches, in partnership with a faculty used to working "across disciplines, across boundaries." The end result? Students become "more engaged in the learning process," she says. In a related manner, Somerville describes the importance of having a shared framework for institutional culture to help faculty understand the emergence of Olin's distinctive academic ethos. He invokes Edgar Schein's three levels of organizational culture as one framework that works well at Olin:

> I think that shared framework is really useful from an explanatory power perspective and also from a design perspective. So, having that shared language around what we even mean by when we talk about what's the culture, the idea that you would talk about artifacts, and espoused values, and underlying assumptions, having that be part of the vocabulary of the people in the organization is probably helpful.

Along the way, Olin began to mature, and its organizational culture began filling out key components: core values, rituals, and artifacts. Instead of a conscious development of culture, in other words, Somerville argues that culture *emerged* over time; and soon the college had "a bunch of espoused values and underlying assumptions and rituals." Looking back, he wishes they had done even more in this direction. If they had been more conscious of how the institution was being shaped by their activities, he says, they could have made "better, and more intentional design decisions about building culture and maintaining culture." A lack of this cultural awareness can lead start-ups into a "valley of death," he says:

> If you talk about startups in general, most startups start off with a great sense of energy and . . . there's that initial phase of, "This is going to be great. This is going to be awesome. We're going to change the world." Then there's the valley of the shadow of death. And lots of startups don't make it through the valley of the shadow of death. . . . But I think a lot of that valley of the shadow of death has a lot of cultural stuff that actually is often too to blame for that.

As a part of this emergent organizational culture, Olin challenges students with design projects that are so difficult that there is always a chance of failure. Miller recalls the initial design challenge for Olin students that began three weeks after their arrival:

> And we told them, "We want you to design build and demonstrate a pulse oximeter, and we want you to do that in five weeks, and here's the patent literature on a pulse oximeter that has a little schematic diagram with transistors and things. And by the way, I know you don't know what a transistor is, but you'll figure it out. Oh, and there's a bunch of tools over there in the corner, and there's some old guys here that will answer any questions that we know how to answer, but we never built one of these things either, so just see what you can do.

"We fully expected it to fail," Miller says. But five weeks later, the students had built a pulse oximeter, and it was working. Its performance even matched the device used by hospitals. The experience encouraged Miller and the Olin faculty to have students jump into the design before going through all the theory—or as Miller puts it, "You don't need two years of calculus and physics before you can pick up a wrench." This embrace of risk brings progress. "Have you heard of the Wright brothers?" he says. "The whole aircraft industry was pioneered by these two bicycle mechanics who jumped off the hill a million times with these wings on their back."

For Miller, engineering is not, at heart, an applied science or a body of knowledge. It is a process: "The process is about iteratively asking questions and figuring there must be a better way and you improve it. Everything that you touch that was engineered today is built on that process, and guess what? We're not teaching it in mainstream universities. The only thing we have taught in engineering schools was the senior project at the end." Design at Olin thus begins with a "realization process," one that requires engineers-in-training to imagine and understand the needs of the people using the object, an exercise that shapes how it is built and marketed. Olin calls this approach "user-oriented collaborative design." Another word for it might be "creativity."

Liberal Arts and Interdisciplinary Engineering

In addition to its unique culture and philosophy, Olin has structural differences that set it apart from a typical engineering program. The college does not have academic departments but instead organizes faculty into a single interdisciplinary group.[25] Olin education moves through three phases: the foundation (emphasizes mastering and applying technical fundamentals), specialization (students choose their fields), and realization (students apply their education to real-world problems).[26] Within this phased approach, students can choose from a wide range of engineering degrees, which include electrical and computer engineering, mechanical engineering, and engineering with concentrations in bioengineering, computing, design, and robotics.[27] Olin requires every student to explore starting and running a business before he or she can graduate, and all Olin students participate in a yearlong industry-sponsored senior design project, or a yearlong project for a nonprofit organization.

One of Olin's signature innovations is its forging of strong connections across liberal arts, business, and engineering. Partnerships with nearby Babson College and Wellesley College have provided an essential extension of the Olin campus into these areas, while broadening the range of courses available to Olin students. These partnerships also give Olin students the chance to meet and work with peers who are not headed into engineering careers—a welcome diversity. Connections like these reduce the "opportunity cost" of attending an engineering school and make Olin more like Stanford, with a greater range of class options and of potential classmates. The synergies with Wellesley, Babson, and Olin enable them, together, to form a "virtual university." Says Miller:

> If you were to imagine us as a virtual university, that we're the engineering school, Wellesley is the College of Arts and Sciences and Babson is the business school, and we're close enough. . . . I brought with me a map of the University of Michigan, and I said, "So here's the engineering quad up there. That's farther than it is between Olin and Babson and you have to ride a bus to get there."

Through this "virtual university," Olin students can take liberal arts classes alongside students majoring in humanities and social sciences, an opportunity that Miller considers a great strength. "I'm a graduate of MIT and Caltech, and I can tell you it's a different experience if you take poetry with a bunch of engineers in the room," he says. "As opposed to taking poetry at Wellesley, where there were people who were planning to be poets, it raises the bar." As Barabino and Miller have both stressed, in the long run, the real innovation of Olin College is not technology, curriculum, or even pedagogy. Instead, as Miller puts it:

> It's about people, and you don't learn about people from differential equations. . . . The Navier-Stokes equations don't tell you how people

work with each other, and they don't listen. Most engineering deans just think, "well, we need an engineering school and a business school. Oh yeah, this liberal arts stuff is like for philosophers or something." And we say no, it's how people's motivations determine everything. As IDEO has shown, all innovation occurs at the intersection of Feasibility (what engineering schools teach), Viability (what business schools teach), and Desirability (what arts and humanities teach). Only if you understand all three can you create value. And that's what this is about.

For her part, Barabino is excited about the beauty of integrating liberal arts, entrepreneurship, and engineering, which recognizes that engineering is a practice that is both "social and technical." In her words, "engineering starts and ends with people." This element, the "constant infusion" of the human side, constitutes the key difference at Olin—and a major draw for potential students.

Preserving Innovation after the Start-Up

Miller discourages other start-ups from copying Olin's curriculum, class-rooms, or books, but says emulation has been the approach of many would-be Olin Colleges overseas. Institutions trying this strategy are missing the point, he says. "It's about experimenting. . . . And it's indigenous to your culture and to your location. And you can only find that out if you do these experiments." Some of the unexpected setbacks of Olin's start-up wound up being keys to its success. Miller jokes that another start-up might try what Olin did, delaying the opening for a year filled with risky experiments. He summarizes Olin's early approach as trying things that might fail—and then purposely watching them fail. By allowing students to have opportunities for failure, you open them up to achieve more in the long run. "[These] kids are way more resilient and capable than you think they are, when you trust them and you give them something important to do," he says.

As Olin reaches its adolescence and approaches adulthood, Miller now as ex-president remains concerned about how the college manages change as it evolves over time. Even now, students and faculty want to feel as if they are part of the pioneering early days. To this end, Olin continues to invent new traditions such as "Build Day," proposed by students to enable them to feel that they, too, are "building" Olin. The college stops all classes, and students gather to share ideas on how to improve campus. They also showcase inventions, reconfigure labs, engage in discussions with faculty about the curriculum, and offer performances of different types.

Faculty have also enabled reinvention at Olin through continuous innovation that starts with prototyping new ideas within courses. This effort is made easier by the common practice of team teaching, says Somerville:

> We do a lot of team teaching at Olin. And so, generally when this happens, it's actually multiple people that are involved in the reinvention process. . . . It's not a neat scientific experiment. It's much more of an ongoing prototyping mindset. The approach that we use is one that says, "If you want to prototype something, you can build it, you can prototype it," and after a couple of years, that's the point when you actually need to . . . bring it forward and say, "We built this prototype and we think it's working and we think we ought to put it in place."

Somerville cautions that leaders should be aware of how much time it takes to develop a curriculum and give faculty at least two to three years for revisions and refinement, since faculty will then "get better at what they're doing and learn from each other." In recent years, Olin has also placed new emphasis on the social and human factors in how teams of students and faculty work together; and with this increased attention, project-based learning brings an opportunity for reflection about how the team environment is working. Olin is able to "navigate by being very flexible about the ways that people innovate," says Somerville, and encourages its faculty to "innovate by substitution, as opposed to innovation by addition."

As she entered her third year of the Olin presidency, Barabino focused on helping students and faculty reflect on their shared work and suggest improvements. This process of communal reflection helps instill ethics in the team, which can enable thoughtful engineers to exercise "design refusal," where engineers speak up and say, "I'm not comfortable with how this technology is going to be used." Olin seeks to develop this kind of ethics in engineers, along with a greater awareness of how engineering is fundamentally geared toward service to others. In the long run, that commitment to serving humanity might be the most important element Olin students take away from their college years.

The new era of Olin involves a consideration of how to engineer a more diverse and inclusive campus at all levels. In fall 2019, Olin's student body consisted of 386 students, balanced between men and women, who were invited to join the college community after a rigorous on-campus interview process that evaluated their ability to work on teams, among other things, and after being admitted they received 50 percent tuition scholarships. A total of 7 percent of Olin's students were international students, 8 percent were first-generation college students, and 13 percent qualified for Federal Pell Grants.[28] As of 2022, 46 percent of Olin's domestic students identified as "students of color" and 22 percent of its forty-two faculty members are reported as members of minority groups.[29] However, both statistics include Asians within the "minority" or "students of color" categories, even though this group is typically not underrepresented in engineering. The Olin Board of Trustees is also less diverse than its students. Of the seventeen board members in 2022, only five were female and only one was African American.[30] Barabino has appointed an executive leadership team whose members are 75 percent female; but there is more work to be done. Barabino is working on "broadening the circle" of voices, she says, and is including members of the board, alumni, and community in Olin discussions as part of this process.

Olin is increasing its emphasis on collaborations with its traditional partner schools—Babson and Wellesley—as well as with institutions with more diverse student populations, such as Paul Quinn College, Xavier University (Barabino's alma mater), and other HBCUs. New partnerships are also being developed in Israel and other countries. With these collaborations, and the insights of a new and mobilized president, Olin will continue to reach more diverse groups of students on an increasingly global stage.

Olin's partnerships also go beyond higher-education institutions. The college is also pursuing connections with the Boston Museum of Science, Greentown Labs, the Chan-Zuckerburg Biohub, and Citizens of the World, a nonprofit community organization in Cambridge, Massachusetts, to create new immersive experiences for students. And even more innovation might lie ahead: Barabino says that the college is considering a new academic calendar, one that might depart from the traditional setup of semesters, academic years, and summers off. "Why can't we mix these blocks up?" she says. "Why can't we look at our curriculum and say, maybe you get the degree in three years?"

Barabino is making sure that Olin extends its community to welcome more diversity. She wants Olin students, faculty, and staff to regularly ask, "Are we hearing all voices? Seriously, are we? Does everybody feel that same level of comfort and sense of belonging?" In answering these questions, she hopes to address enduring inequalities that include the educational arena but also press beyond it. In the end, she envisions Olin graduates using their careers in STEM to bring service, equity, and justice to their communities.

Olin's start-up is ongoing. As Somerville notes, at this stage the Olin experiment is "less a product and more an ongoing process." What makes a start-up work "is actually the messiness of it," he says. In his view, start-ups "are like gardens"—easy to seed; harder to grow, cultivate, and weed. The messiness of the experiment shouldn't be seen as a detriment. In some ways, the Olin story suggests that the messiness "bug," as Somerville puts it, can become a guiding feature to innovation in the future.

Olin College of Engineering, in less than twenty years, has managed to rise to the top of rankings of engineering schools, tied with MIT for top engineering school in the world. This remarkable level of recognition has enabled the school to achieve a worldwide impact in engineering education, with hundreds of leaders of engineering schools around the world visiting and establishing connections to help emulate some of the unique ingredients of success that Olin has designed in its founding. With the focus squarely on design thinking and student-centered education, Olin has invented a new way to educate engineers that integrates design projects across all four years, culminating in a yearlong design project. It has also pioneered the integration of liberal arts and business into its curriculum and has strong partnerships with complementary schools nearby that strengthen the Olin education with greater breadth and diversity of curriculum.

Despite this impressive achievement, Olin is a small college, which directly reaches fewer than four hundred students in Massachusetts—a tiny undergraduate program reaching an overwhelmingly US-based student population. With its new president, Gilda Barabino, Olin aspires to bring in more diverse voices and reach underrepresented populations to help broaden and diversify future leaders of engineering. As a top-ranked engineering school, one might imagine even larger horizons for Olin—perhaps a greater research presence, an expansion of its size, development of some graduate programs, or a more international impact. Olin has instead begun through its new partnerships and collaborations to focus more intentionally on its role as a paragon of engineering education, which may have substantive impacts outside of its walls. This role is consistent with Olin's initial charge to revolutionize engineering education, and expanding its scale of impact would be in keeping with its founding rhetoric. To borrow an analogy from engineering itself, the initial design of Olin can be likened to the design of a cargo ship, which is intended to deliver its goods. Perhaps after successfully completing the building and determining how to operate the ship, the larger mission and intention for the goods can now be fully considered. As Olin enters its third decade, the world will be watching this next exciting phase of its journey.

6

The Intangibles of Excellence

FULBRIGHT UNIVERSITY VIETNAM

On March 23, 2016, President Barack Obama stepped up to the microphone at the National Convention Center in Hanoi, Vietnam. He spoke about economic and security cooperation, including promoting the Trans-Pacific Partnership and lifting the embargo of US arms sales to Vietnam. Alongside these weighty issues, Obama announced that Fulbright University Vietnam (FUV) was set to open its doors in the fall—the country's first nonprofit, independent university. "Even as we keep welcoming more Vietnamese students to America," he said, "we also believe that young people deserve a world-class education right here in Vietnam."[1]

To launch this unique partnership, the United States would provide almost $50 million, and Vietnam would donate rent-free land in Ho Chi Minh City. In his speech, Obama highlighted the hallmarks of the university-to-be-born. At Fulbright University Vietnam, he said, "there will be full academic freedom and scholarships for those in need. Students, scholars, researchers will focus on public policy and management and business; on engineering and computer science; and liberal arts—everything from the poetry of Nguyen Du, to the philosophy of Phan Chu Trinh, to the mathematics of Ngo Bao Chau."[2] The new venture emerged from cross-cutting interests held by Vietnam and the United States. The Vietnamese government had a strong interest in normalizing relations with its former foe in order to reap economic benefits and build in-country expertise capable of advancing *doi moi*, the national strategy of moving toward a market-based economy.[3] In the United States, a powerful desire to heal the wounds of the Vietnam War was driven by a group of veterans of that conflict who now occupied high office: Secretary of State John Kerry and Senator John McCain, as well as former Nebraska governor and senator Bob Kerrey.

"The Vietnamese suffered as did most of the countries who were under colonial control," says Kerrey. "They suffered as a consequence of the French [not] allow[ing] independent colleges to develop. And then the Communists come in and they're a little hostile to independent thinking. And so, you bring that historical streamflow together and what Vietnam was missing was a truly independent college that was their own."

In 2007, Kerrey, then president of the New School, a New York university, hosted a forum during which Vietnam's president Nguyen Minh Triet and his education minister Nguyen Thien Nhan discussed the idea of founding an American-style university in Vietnam. Although both sides had some reservations, the two governments created an advisory group cochaired by Thomas (Tommy) Vallely, another Vietnam War veteran who was especially close with Kerrey, and Tran Thi Ha, then director general of the Ministry for Education and Training's higher-education department.[4]

Vallely, a radio operator with the marines and the recipient of a Silver Star for gallantry, had plunged into Vietnamese life and culture and was passionate about bringing together American veterans with their former Vietnamese opponents. In 1989 he launched Harvard's Vietnam Program as part of the Ash Center for Democratic Governance and Innovation at the Kennedy School of Public Policy and established the Fulbright Economics Teaching Program in Ho Chi Minh City in 1994, a partnership between the University of Economics in Vietnam and the Kennedy School. "Tommy placed the idea of building an American-style university in Vietnam on the two countries' agenda for cooperation," Fulbright's Xuan Linh and Viet Lam later wrote.[5]

Central to the university's emergence was Vallely's personal relationship with Dam Bich Thuy, chief executive officer of ANZ Bank. Dam was the first leader of an international bank's operations in Vietnam. A Fulbright scholar with an MBA from the Wharton School, she would become Fulbright University's founding president in 2016. Back in 2007, she and Vallely sat together in her Hanoi office and discussed the prospects for creating an American-style university in Vietnam.[6] Dam's daughter had gone through high school and college in the United States, so Dam understood the American educational model and how it differed from the more routinized approach in Vietnam. At the time, she told Vallely that she thought the new university was a wonderful idea. Privately, however, she remembers thinking: "Yeah, nice idea. Nice dream. Never happen." She would soon prove herself wrong.

The Intangibles of Excellence

In 2010, Laura Chirot, a New School researcher based at the Fulbright School in Ho Chi Minh City, and Ben Wilkinson, who worked with Vallely in the Vietnam Program at the Ash Center at Harvard, put together a strategic analysis for turning Dam's idealistic dream into a reality. The resulting white paper, "The Intangibles of Excellence," made recommendations for the creation of an "apex university" in Vietnam, an educational institution capable of reaching "high levels of quality in teaching and research, as measured by internationally-recognized standards."[7]

Such a university, they argued, was central to the development of a knowledge-driven economy that would make Vietnam economically competitive. Yet while the government of Vietnam, a socialist republic with a one-party system led by the Communist Party of Vietnam, had paid attention to the practical inputs necessary to support such an institution—finance, land, buildings, and technology—missing were the intangible elements of institutional autonomy and governance: "Without a fundamental reordering of the relationship between academic institutions and the state," Chirot and Wilkinson wrote, "no level of financial resolve will be enough. At the institutional level, a commitment to a core set of values—chief among them academic freedom and an affirmation of merit as the sole determiner of membership—must be encoded in a university's DNA."[8]

Their paper drew on the work of Professor Hoàng Tụy, a major Vietnamese mathematician and the chairperson of an independent think tank in Vietnam, the Institute for Development Studies (IDS). "The crisis in education is above all else a crisis of quality," a 2009 IDS report contended, "meaning that education has not only *fallen behind*, but is *heading in the wrong direction*, isolated and out of sync with contemporary global trends. This is a consequence of many years of *systemic management failures that have degraded education*."[9]

Both the Ash Center and the IDS white papers pulled few punches in describing the problems Vietnam faced: inefficient and bureaucratic structures, scientists trained under a Soviet model that left them out of touch with international standards, pay inequities, and a fundamental lack of understanding of what it meant to have or create a research university. The result, the authors argued, was an impatient desire for "quantity over quality and fame over real achievement" in Vietnamese higher education.[10]

The solution? As early as 2004, Tuy and other prominent intellectuals had recommended that Vietnam should "build a single new modern, multi-disciplinary university that can be a 'pilot' for university reform."[11] The 2010 Ash paper echoed this recommendation. The culture and politics at existing Vietnamese universities had become so cumbersome and problematic, the authors maintained, that reform within the system was impossible. A "green field" approach was the only viable option.

To guide this new approach, the Ash paper identified central features of an apex university for Vietnam. A first feature was research excellence, especially in fields that could serve as incubators for economic change and growth. "Faculty at an apex university occupy important positions in national intellectual and political life," the authors wrote. "Through independent, critical research and analysis, faculty members contribute to informed policy debates, providing an important counterweight to research produced by institutes attached to state agencies."[12]

A second key feature of an apex university, and the place where Vietnam should focus its initial efforts, involved high-quality *undergraduate* education. Vietnam's greatest shortage, the authors argued, lay in its pool of highly skilled workers. Providing excellent teaching in the undergraduate arena was a singular responsibility of a new university. It would reduce the worker shortage while simultaneously creating a pathway for a smaller number of the top students to pursue advanced training abroad.

The Ash study caused shock waves throughout Vietnam's educational system. Nguyen Xuan Thanh, a founding member of Fulbright University, recalled that the proposal prompted "both excitement and fear in Hanoi."[13] It amounted to an opening salvo, a direct challenge to educational business as usual—the network of public universities, for-profit training programs, and government-to-government ventures that made up Vietnam's current system. "Tommy was very firm that the U.S. government and the team would not be interested in creating something which had no chance to be great," says Dam. "Because if we just want to create another university like many others that already existed in Vietnam, we had better things to do."

The Ash paper wasn't the only innovation on the educational horizon during this period. The Fulbright Economics Teaching Program (FETP) also played a role in helping the new project move forward. Established back in 1994, the FETP had built significant credibility in Vietnam by the time Vallely and Dam introduced their proposal. It had enrolled more than

1,200 policymakers and trained more than 40 percent of Vietnam's National Assembly members as well as 18 Politburo members, including the prime minister and now president Nguyen Xuan Phuc, thus contributing to a more open culture of policy deliberation. While some worried that Vietnamese contributors to FETP publications might face consequences for their outspokenness, the analyses generated by these efforts were generally praised as beneficial. "Our credibility [with the government] arises from criticism," FETP's Vu Thanh Tu Anh said in 2020. "Although criticism itself does not create value, it is truly valuable when done in a constructive manner for the common good. Sincere and science-based criticism gives you power in debate."[14]

During these same years, the Vietnamese government expanded the remit for more open discussions, launching the Vietnam Executive Leadership Program at the Kennedy School in 2008. The program offers weeklong discussions among government and private-sector leaders and faculty experts at Harvard. "We know that our input is not always well received," said Vallely, "but at least we have played our role in the policy debate. And the great thing about Vietnam is that they like us doing it."[15] As these discussions and debates expanded and built trust within Vietnam, US diplomats were also engaged in strategic meetings with their Vietnamese counterparts on ways to counter China's growing influence in the region. *Politico*'s Isabelle Taft commented that Vu "notes that the Vietnamese government granted FUV approval in principle only in June 2014, just as thousands of Vietnamese were protesting China's deployment of an oil rig in a contested area of the South China Sea."[16] It was against this backdrop that the Ash paper recommendations for establishing a new kind of university in Vietnam were received. Ultimately, the Communist Party and Vietnamese government endorsed the Ash paper's strategies. "Why don't you give what you proposed a try?" is how Vallely remembers the government's response.[17]

Vallely and Dam brought complementary personal strengths to the ensuing approval process. "Tommy is a loud guy who bursts into the scene and thunders in with a vison," says Ryan Derby-Talbot, FUV's first chief academic officer. "It's that strong energy that was enough to shake people into trying something new." Taft describes Vallely as "tall, given to the hearty arm-grabbing of a Boston pol and with a booming voice that reveals his Massachusetts upbringing ('ideas' are 'idears')."[18] But in Vietnam, it was important to "have a finesse person to smooth that out and make things work and that was really Dam," says Derby-Talbot. "Negotiation with the ministry and the political realities was something she did really well." Vallely said simply: "She's way less combative than I am."[19]

Controversy and Control

Fulbright's first days were not idyllic. Critics didn't hesitate to weigh in on the new institution. For some international observers, Fulbright was a colonial enterprise that sought to imprint American values on Vietnamese youth. The name itself, Fulbright, honors an American senator from Arkansas who opposed US involvement in the Vietnam War and created the Fulbright Program to send US students abroad. (Fulbright's founders say that it was the Vietnamese stakeholders who advocated for the Fulbright name as a way to highlight the quality of the institution.)[20]

Financial considerations, too, generated heated criticism. Who controlled the money? The Trust for University Innovation in Vietnam, an American nonprofit organization chaired by Vallely and registered in Massachusetts, provided the US funds, which came from South Vietnam's wartime debt to the United States. Some Vietnamese expressed concerns that the decision-making rested too much on the American side. Ton Nu Thi Ninh, Vietnam's former ambassador to the European Union, wrote that Fulbright must not be "an institution in Vietnam conceived and decided upon by Americans disregarding our self-respect and dignity."[21] International scholars also raised questions about Fulbright's role in pushing both an American model of higher education and market-based economic approaches for Vietnam. What motivations were really at play here?[22]

Questions about colonialism and control came to a head in criticisms of Bob Kerrey's role as chair of Fulbright's board of trustees. As reported by a 2001 investigation, Kerrey had commanded a Navy SEALs unit that massacred twenty civilians in Thanh Phong in 1969. Viet Thanh Nguyen, a Vietnamese American author who won the Pulitzer Prize in 2016 for his novel *The Sympathizer*, criticized Fulbright for focusing too much on Kerrey's role—the story of an American soldier making amends and reconciling with the past. Instead, Nguyen argued, much greater attention should be paid to the historical suffering of the Vietnamese people. He proposed that the Fulbright campus include a memorial to the civilians who died at Thanh Phong, both to honor them and to prompt questions about how and why they were slain.[23]

Yet critics within Vietnam were gentler on Kerrey than Nguyen, a US resident, had been. "Like many other American veterans who fought in Vietnam, Bob Kerrey made up for his mistakes by helping to end the embargo, normalize relations with Vietnam, expand the bilateral relationship, and, most especially, by strongly supporting the development of Vietnamese human capital," Nguyen Minh Thuyet, a former member of Vietnam's National Assembly, said in a 2016 address.[24]

More fundamental criticisms zeroed in on the willingness of the Vietnamese government to avoid interfering in university governance. Vu told *Politico* that the autonomy FUV sought "was a hard sell in a country where universities are strictly controlled by the government."[25] Moreover, while government and Party leaders might agree in principle to a new venture, education officials lacked any experience in dealing with a university that wielded significant autonomy and academic freedom. The application itself signaled trouble as it weighed 10 kilograms and required a hand-truck to deliver ten copies to the Ministry of Education and Training. The ministry made clear that FUV's founders might aspire to building a new university but that content of instruction had to remain the same. Given this strongly worded statement, tensions over autonomy and academic freedom seemed inevitable.

"It Felt like a Tech Launch"

The Ash paper did not specify what kind of undergraduate education Fulbright should adopt. It supported the idea of a general education curriculum but left to others whether the overall model should adopt a US-style liberal arts approach or a specialized training strategy more common to Europe, India, and other parts of the world. The university-to-be was a high-profile project, but no one quite knew what it was. In the run-up to President Obama's 2016 announcement, Dam, Ben Wilkinson, and other members of the founding team had begun visiting American universities to inform their thinking about what kind of university to build. "I still vividly remember our trip from Boston to New Hampshire," says Dam. "It was a long journey, and the roads were blanketed with thick snow. Ben drove the whole way, carrying Ngan and me in a family car. We discussed all the way and then drafted Fulbright's foundational mission and precepts. This mission document was later hung at our first office. When Fulbright had its official campus, this mission remained unchanged."[26] A decisive moment came when the team met with Rick Miller, the president of Olin College of Engineering in Massachusetts. Olin's willingness to innovate in engineering education inspired them to think less about importing an American curriculum and more about inventing their own. Mark Somerville, a leading architect of the Olin curriculum, joined the discussions and soon signed on as a senior advisor for Fulbright. Somerville told the Fulbright team that their first task was to get to know their target students. Dinh Vu Trang Ngan, a founding member of the academic team, agreed, setting out to visit high schools, crisscrossing Vietnam by bus. She found students eager for a new kind of education, for a university where faculty would support them in pursuing their boldest dreams.[27]

By the summer of 2017, Ryan Derby-Talbot, a mathematics professor who had been working at a start-up university, joined the Fulbright team. Derby-Talbot came from Quest University Canada, a school that had been launched in Squamish, Canada, in 2007, with the goal of harnessing students' natural curiosity rather than requiring a pre-set curriculum and majors. While Quest enjoyed many initial successes, Derby-Talbot wasn't one to turn down a good challenge. When the Fulbright opportunity arose, he took the plunge. "Wouldn't it be great to do a 2.0 version?" he remembers thinking. He would go on to become FUV's first chief academic officer.

Soon after joining, Derby-Talbot found himself transplanted from the scenic Garibaldi highlands of British Columbia, with its glaciers and fjords, to the iconic Bitexco Tower, a giant skyscraper in a posh district of Ho Chi Minh City. There, he found a small group of twenty staff working in a start-up environment: a small open space with no walls and a beehive of activity. With bankers and financiers occupying the rest of the building, the Fulbright team members were constantly tripping over one another, bustling in and out of their two meeting rooms and hosting events to explain what they were planning. "It felt like a tech launch," says Derby-Talbot, "where it's Apple's new product and everyone's excited and wants to hear about it. There's this sense in Vietnam of a willingness to try things, of being early adopters."

Top on the agenda for the fledgling institution was how to recruit students and hire faculty. On the student side, they wanted applicants who were willing to take a risk in joining an institution that did not yet exist. Their admissions process included a group interview in which students had to work in teams to design a new product. In one exercise, teams competed to design a paper airplane that would fly farther than their rivals' planes.[28]

Some applicants found this experience exhilarating. When Ly Minh Tu received a full scholarship to Wellesley College and admission to FUV, she had to decide whether to deviate from the only destination she had imagined for herself—college in America. She chose Fulbright and participated in the codesign year. When incredulous friends and family asked why, her answer was twofold. Pragmatically, she was drawn to the prospect of creating networking opportunities at home, rather than struggling to do so from abroad. Idealistically, she was motivated by the opportunity to be a pioneer in the service of her nation. "Among the letters of admission, Fulbright's stood out the most," she says. "I remember reading the first lines in that letter, saying 'How can we build the best university for the students, for this century, for Vietnam?' With just one question, Fulbright made me completely reevaluate my decision-making process."[29]

Fulbright also introduced a new concept to Vietnam: financial aid. To offset the higher tuition the university would charge, it would follow the US model of offering need-based financial support. This had never been done before in Vietnam, and no process existed for assessing family need and wealth. Early on, the Fulbright team would review Facebook and other websites, asking "Where does your family go on vacation? Describe the kind of cars your family drives," to assess a family's need for financial aid. Despite its newness, the financial aid process allowed FUV to enroll students like Khang A Tua, who came from the H'Mong ethnic minority group and a poor, rural family. The group interview process was daunting for Khang but ultimately gave him confidence—he came away convinced that he could succeed at FUV:

> When the professors and the admissions staff asked me questions in English, I couldn't make sense of what they were asking, let alone answer them. I decided to answer them in Vietnamese, and the other candidates helped me translate my answers into English. I was so moved. I was their competitor; they could have chosen not to help me to increase their chance of getting in. But they didn't do that. I knew then that I wanted to learn alongside these friends.[30]

FUV provided Tua with financial aid and with language and learning support as part of its pre-first-year bridge program.[31]

Fulbright created a group interview process for faculty hiring, also. Candidates had to demonstrate their abilities and interest in joining a highly interactive institution. Group interviews brought together engineers, poets, artists, and historians, with each candidate required to give an "impact talk," which meant a more broadly engaging presentation rather than a research seminar. "We asked questions like 'What would you invent newly?'" says Derby-Talbot. "'What are courses you've never taught that you would love to teach? Why do you want to be in an interdisciplinary environment? What does it mean to build a plane while you're flying it?'" Interviewing for a Fulbright job needed to feel a lot like Fulbright itself—dynamic, collaborative, and always leaving room for the unexpected.

The university attracted adventurous scholars seeking new ventures and vistas. In a letter to students titled "In You I Trust," Nguyen Nam, a founding faculty member who today oversees the Vietnam studies major, reflected on his experience: "It brings me joy by encouraging the discovery of what the rising generation of Vietnamese can do and achieve. Together, we mutually learned from one another with laughter, tears and silent moments of meditation. It also gives me hope for a brighter future for our country in a globalized world. This is why I joined Fulbright."[32] Fulbright did not offer tenure to its faculty. Labor laws in Vietnam required that all contracts be renewed every two years; but even apart from this law, the university's founders did not want to commit to a lifetime contract for a faculty member when they needed flexibility to figure out what kind of programs and what kind of faculty were most essential. Fulbright's first cohort was made up of faculty like Nguyen, drawn to the prospect of a nation-building project, as well as those either fresh out of their PhD programs or seeking a change after growing disaffected with their current institutions. "That mix of people came together with a huge pool of trust that gives this job to them: let them do whatever they think they can," says Dinh, "and then see what happens."

Codesign Year

Under the guidance of Somerville and then Derby-Talbot, Fulbright decided to follow the model developed at Olin College and host a codesign year prior to the actual launch of the university. In the fall of 2018, an enthusiastic group of fifteen faculty and fifty-six students huddled together in the industrial park to begin a process that would create Fulbright University and its undergraduate curriculum.[33] The group worked for long hours. Their efforts included prototyping new courses and designing majors, writing a course catalog from scratch, and designing student government and dorms. They were tasked with generating three ideas for every project—what Dinh remembers as "a new idea, a bold idea, and a crazy idea."

Dinh earned a BA from Bates College in the United States and a PhD from the University of Cambridge, worked at the Kennedy School of Government at Harvard, and taught in the Fulbright graduate program in economics in Vietnam. In 2016, she would become Fulbright's first director of the undergraduate program; today, she serves as dean of undergraduate studies. But at the time, she recalls fondly being told that the new idea should be something that hadn't been done before but was plausible. The bold idea should differ from standard practice and reside a little bit outside of everyone's comfort zone. "And the crazy idea," she says, "should be impossible, nuts, absolutely nonsense." The goal was to push back on the tendency of faculty to replicate what they knew and to encourage students to bring fresh ideas. The initial result was widespread confusion. Faculty trickled into the codesign work over the course of a few months. Somerville arrived and took everyone through a design sprint in which they learned how to do fast prototyping of courses and curriculum. Faculty were instructed to take a single week and quickly develop 1.0 versions of courses that would then be modified in subsequent versions.

Students then joined faculty in monthlong colearning modules. Two to three faculty would be paired with twelve to fifteen students; the faculty offered sample teaching lessons and students read research papers on the value of active learning. Working together accustomed faculty and students to nontraditional roles. It also provided a common language for community members to talk about the choices the faculty were making in designing the courses.

Neuroscientist Kinho Chan and applied linguist Pam Stacey began their monthlong module on rhetoric by explaining that persuasive writing in the West means clearly stating your point at the outset. This claim prompted students to explain that was the opposite of how things work in Vietnam, where writing is intentionally opaque and the reader has to look for subtle indications of meaning. This contrast led to a conversation about how persuasion works in different cultures. The result? The new course became much more of a dialogue between East and West and more firmly rooted in the Vietnamese context than its originally planned version: this was the codesign vision in action.[34]

At end of the month, faculty and students presented their work to each other as well as to board members, government officials, and the general public. "Those were some of the best events," recalls Derby-Talbot. "It gave everyone a chance to see the process unfolding. It also gave the faculty and staff a big shot in the arm because they saw the students' continued engagement and accomplishments." An unexpected ancillary benefit: the codesign process helped create a group of students who were true believers in Fulbright. They then spread the word about the new university's philosophy and mission to others. Their enthusiasm and buy-in became the best possible advertising to reach skeptical parents and potential students throughout the nation.

Many in Vietnam had assumed that Vietnamese students would find it difficult to transition to a seminar-style education where they were expected to play an active role in learning. Most students had come from high schools where they were required to sit with their hands on the desk and address the teachers with great deference. "Vietnamese students have a rebellious heart," says Dinh, "but look very obedient. But inside they were like a storm. Now here they are from inside and outside. Yeah, troublemakers. And we loved it. We learned about the endless boundaries of our students."

Teaching the American War in Ho Chi Minh City

A key flashpoint in the codesign year and the initial years that followed was how Fulbright would handle the government requirement to teach mandatory courses in subjects like the history of the Vietnamese Communist Party, Ho Chi Minh thought, and Marxism. Typically, a foreign university operating in Vietnam would seek an exemption from mandatory course requirements, and many observers expected Fulbright to follow suit.[35] But FUV's founders knew that receiving special dispensations denied to other universities would blunt their new institution's impact in Vietnam. Accordingly, Fulbright promised the government that its faculty would teach the required ideology courses in a way that students found engaging, in contrast to the tired "tick the box" approach adopted at most institutions. They would teach Marx in the context of German thinkers and Ho Chi Minh thought in the context of Vietnamese history, for example.

To further build trust with ministry officials and with the larger public, Fulbright leaders also made a key tactical move: the university would openly share what and how its faculty were teaching. So, they put the course descriptions online and allowed anyone from the government to sit in on the class and to talk with the students. Fulbright did not specifically advertise every reading or assignment, but neither did it seek to hide them.

Delicate subjects included teaching about what in Vietnam is called the "American War." Vietnamese students learn a specific view of that war in high school. At Fulbright, their assignments included excerpts from Ken Burns's documentary *The Vietnam War*. "For the first time," Dinh says, "the students were listening and hearing about the other side of the war. And it is not the history printed on the walls or in the books." The core aim of the course was to introduce students to the idea that history has layers and can be interpreted from different perspectives. "I remember now vividly that day, students getting out of that class fully in tears," says Dinh. They were shocked, she recalls, as history suddenly shape-shifted. They now understood that history "is a story to be told and depending on who's telling the story, it's a different story." This experience was particularly meaningful for Dinh, whose father had fought in the war against the United States but had blessed her attending college in America in the late 1990s.[36]

Critics of FUV did not see this story in such a positive light. Mark Ashwill, a former recipient of a Fulbright grant who now runs an educational consulting firm in Vietnam, regards this approach as far too America-centric. "While the suffering of the Americans is tragic, it pales in comparison to that of the Vietnamese," he writes. "Save the lion's share of your tears for them and the sacrifices they made to defeat the latest in a formidable array of foreigner invaders. . . . What a perversion of history to focus on U.S. suffering in a war it should never have fought."[37]

Fulbright's faculty took seriously the task of navigating an unwritten set of sensitivities. They understood that the autonomy they had been granted came at the cost of being willing to allow others to watch them closely. In their minds, they had a duty to wield their freedom carefully, in a way that "makes students interested but also makes the government OK," recalls Dam. In class, faculty and students also learned to navigate between open discussion, including criticism of the government, and topics that went too far. The graduate program's record of analyzing and assessing specific government policies made it clear that such criticisms were tolerated and even welcomed. Faculty learned that it was acceptable, even desirable, to bring different perspectives to bear in analyzing a problem, so long as the analysis was framed in academic terms. There were, however, some red lines faculty were instructed not to cross, including direct criticisms of the single-party system and proposals for alternatives to it.

The same red line applied to activity outside the classroom. Fulbright's leaders, worried about potential student protests against the government, rehearsed scenarios for how to handle conflicts over free expression on campus. But such clashes over academic freedom were never put to the test. "The percentage of students who really have a desire to talk about politics is very low to begin with," says Phan Vu Xuan Hung, a founding member of the faculty. This reluctance to talk openly about sensitive subjects emerged, at least in part, from the students' internalized understandings of what is and is not permissible to discuss in Vietnam. It was also shaped by a more prosaic factor: students—and their parents—remained laser focused on completing degrees that would lead to employment.

Many of FUV's families work in business and are eager for their children to study practical subjects, readily translatable fields that will equip them to take over the family enterprise or succeed elsewhere in the commercial world. These families seek out FUV because they understand that a pragmatic education—in economics, social studies, and psychology, for example—is the university's bread and butter: here Fulbright benefits from the brand and reputation created by the FETP in years previous. Their interest also reflects the recruitment efforts at Fulbright that have highlighted the liberal arts and engaged teaching. Coupled with the absence of laboratory space, these factors mean that FUV has been a less attractive option for students interested in math, engineering, and science, and the pure arts and humanities in general have been of less interest to students. The most popular majors at FUV are in the social sciences and in computer science. Today, still in its early years, the university's emphasis has settled squarely on social science analysis and its practical applications to solve public policy problems facing Vietnam.

From Blank Slate to First Draft

If onlookers were to mistake the codesign year as something out of a Silicon Valley start-up, they could be forgiven: Fulbright leaders intentionally sought a fast-paced, corporate feel for their planning year. They wanted to avoid anything that smacked of the slow-moving bureaucracies typical in established universities. "We were trying to use the language of design thinking startups, entrepreneurship, boot camps, the spirit of failing fast, and prototyping because it helped generate a shared buy-in to the idea that Fulbright was fundamentally innovative," says Derby-Talbot. "It's harder when you talk about liberal arts innovation—'here's an innovative course that combines agriculture, engineering, and literature'—for those outside of academia, that doesn't sound as sexy as a sprint using agile management to produce a draft curriculum."

Creating a curriculum from a blank slate initially excited many of the newly recruited faculty. Yet not everyone felt comfortable with the start-up feel of the planning year. The language and processes of design thinking were new to many. For some Vietnamese faculty in particular, the process did not give sufficient respect for hierarchy and the elevated role of a senior professor over junior colleagues and students. For other faculty, design thinking was too focused on getting things done fast. They wanted time to step back and think things through.

"Design thinking by itself was not enough to provide the kind of measured thought about assumptions in education that can lead to a really valuable institutional program," says Derby-Talbot. "Training programs that come out of Silicon Valley treat education as though what you need to do is just have a better way of delivering information." To accommodate these concerns, Fulbright leaders augmented the typical design sprint process by building in time for more extended discussions and analysis.

The blank-slate approach soon took off, generating excitement and interest. Early curricular drafts coalesced around the idea of self-designed majors in which students would weave together different forms of knowledge and apply them in practical projects. But as the initial weeks and months turned into half a year, counterpressure began building to see results. Parents, students, government agencies, Party officials, board members, and other supporters all wanted something specific to react to and promote. Some came to see that the Olin College–inspired design process might not fit the goals for Fulbright. "Olin's goal was to change the way engineering was taught, so it helped them to experiment," says Dam. Olin wanted:

> to get design into the DNA of their students and to continue changing. [But] in the U.S. there are 1,000 universities, if you are tired of co-design you can go to another university. You don't have to go to Olin. In Vietnam, the expectation of the society from Fulbright is huge, much higher. They expect something concrete, relatable, understandable, [and] much earlier than the co-design process would allow.

Halfway through the codesign year, the board of trustees sent a memo to Fulbright faculty seeking more specifics on the curriculum and the majors under development. Individual board members also brought to the table particular ideas that they wanted to see incorporated. As time went on, it became clear that some stakeholders had become less enamored of the codesign process. They wanted to see solid outcomes, a viable curriculum that included specific features, such as a major in computer science.

In the end, Fulbright planners settled on a combination of ideas that emerged from the codesign process and from the specifics that stakeholders had superimposed on top of it. In years one and two, the curriculum offers a core of skills-based courses, together with three linked courses that connect the disciplines. The core courses provide a foundation in critical thinking, communication, and methods of analysis, as well as civic engagement, ethical reasoning, and collaboration.

Distinctive to the Fulbright curriculum is the dual concentration on local challenges facing Vietnam and students' capacity to combine or synthesize existing knowledge in innovative ways. In addition to three required courses in the humanities, quantitative reasoning, and scientific inquiry, the core curriculum also includes a course on modern Vietnamese culture and society and a course on design and systems thinking. Fulbright also expects students to learn to connect knowledge and skills across courses and think beyond individual disciplines. It accomplishes this by requiring that students take a least one "stream" of three linked courses drawn from the traditional areas of arts and humanities; social sciences; and math, engineering, and science.

Fulbright's most distinctive contributions to education have come in its emphasis on Vietnamese art and culture and in its incorporation of Vietnamese case studies through the curriculum. In addition, the Vietnamese studies major makes it very different from similar majors or programs offered at institutions outside the country. This major enables a student to combine a comparative approach to the study of Vietnam with a specific disciplinary focus. "Vietnamese studies are very limited in many American universities," says Dam. "We try to make it more overarching. From day one, we have focused on this as our signature program."

After a year of codesign, Fulbright's first entering class of 120 students began classes in September 2019. By then, the board had appointed Ian Bickford as provost after the departure of Derby-Talbot. Bickford came from Bard College, whose president, Leon Botstein, is on the Fulbright board. Bickford had been part of efforts to build Bard-affiliated programs in Myanmar, and he arrived in Ho Chi Minh City with a mandate from the board to establish a recognizable lineup of majors. Under his direction, Fulbright settled on a set of nine majors: engineering, computer science, integrated science, economics, psychology, literature, history, art and media studies, and Vietnamese studies. Each major requires a capstone project, and all students must also complete an experiential learning requirement.

The Meaning of Innovation

The uncertainties in the codesign year reflected the difficulty of producing something viable quickly. Design thinking promises to unleash creativity and develop "fast prototypes." But its practitioners at Fulbright also sought to build a culture of innovation that would adapt and grow over time. They recognized that they would not get things right in their first iterations.

Instead, they sought to seed an agile culture of community members who were comfortable with constant change. This dynamic state, however, was enormously difficult for stakeholders, who did not know what was going to emerge and whether it would be any good.

The codesign year also elicited different understandings of the purpose and nature of the university. For some, Fulbright's innovation lay in cross-cultural status: it was an American-style school in Vietnam. As a new high-quality university for Vietnam, it should emulate the most prestigious universities in the United States—it didn't need any more innovation than that. References to Fulbright becoming the "Harvard of Vietnam" marked these particular aspirations for the university. Such ideals "put a certain impression in people's minds," Derby-Talbot recalls. "Trying to do something innovatively means that you are actually doing something different from what Harvard might do. That was a constant source of tension by itself."

Dinh offers a related perspective. "I think the ministry is actually easy [to convince], [and] the public," she says, "because once we have good stories and the students will share them, it's great. [But] the university board, they don't see what happens every day. They will have 'Geez, these guys are creating this crazy concept of teaching. Is it going to work?' The benchmark they know is MIT, Chicago, Harvard, and this is not like those."

For other participants, what made Fulbright stand out were its experiments in teaching and learning. Creating a new kind of educational institution was the most important takeaway, the most creative element, of the Fulbright venture. The Olin College approach, which stressed that education is always a work in progress and in constant need of revision, drew individuals with this mind-set to the institution. The codesign year, says Dinh, "was a roller coaster, chaotic and messy, but a great time nonetheless. We learned about ourselves, the products, and the teachers." For her, it felt like being at Apple before the first iPhone was developed. They didn't know what they were building, and it took a deep process for the result to emerge. This was especially so for faculty from overseas, who needed a crash course from their students to learn what would resonate in Vietnam.

Adapting an American-style liberal arts education for Vietnam while simultaneously experimenting with teaching and learning that pushed the boundaries inevitably created tensions—both among the faculty themselves and between the faculty and the board. "Many Vietnamese faculty members were there first for their country and the establishment of something of benefit to Vietnam as a whole," says Derby-Talbot. In contrast, many non-Vietnamese faculty members were more there to build something new and exciting for students in general. Sometimes this would lead to conflicts about risk. For example, a faculty member might propose a completely crazy idea, something really different. And a Vietnamese faculty member might counter, saying "no, we need something that's going to work here. It doesn't need to be radical." They were trying to scale back the risk a little bit because it felt like it was putting too much at stake for Vietnam.

The need for a coherent and consistent set of messages drove the Fulbright team to seek some way to resolve or reconcile these disparate perspectives. At first, the messages about the university were different and even competing. Then, attempting to combine all points of view into one resulted in bland, watered-down communications that tried to be all things to all people. "Our collective editing drained the spark from the messages," wrote Derby-Talbot and Andrew Maguire, then in charge of special projects at Fulbright, "leaving them flat and generic. Our blank slate, once the canvas for a grand portrait, had devolved into a patchwork of mixed pictures that we were trying to blend together."[38]

Eventually, they settled on a clear message: Fulbright improved education both by adapting American traditions to Vietnam and by developing new approaches. For Derby-Talbot and Maguire, this resolution taught a surprising and essential lesson. "Rather than thinking of an institution's blank slate as an empty canvas," the two wrote,

> one should imagine it instead as a piece of tracing paper. The tracing paper lays atop the traditions and established ways of the institutions that have come before. The critical question then becomes what to trace, and what to leave open for drawing newly. Without this alignment, the blank slate can lose coherence, and end up looking less like a master painting and more like a finger painting.[39]

For Bob Kerrey, this was as it should be:

> All we knew was that Vietnam needed an independent college. The debate about what's going to be taught is a sign that it's working. You don't ever want to get it so fixed that change is impossible. Once you say with certainty, "I know what the curriculum ought to be," it generates distrust. Because the curriculum itself needs to change. It needs to change regularly. It shouldn't be in five years what it is today.

Impact and Trajectory

Fulbright's impact has reverberated in several ways in Vietnam. Most fundamentally, it has introduced the concept of a liberal arts education as an option for Vietnamese students to remain at home and obtain the kind of education that used to require them to leave the country and pay much higher tuition. "You don't [have to] enter university knowing for sure that you are going to be a doctor or an accountant, or a pharmacist," says Dam. "You have [time] to explore your potential." This approach appears to be gaining some traction. Applications for admission to the class of 2024 increased 240 percent over the previous class, and the university enrolled 170 students, 50 more than they had initially planned.

Dam also points to Fulbright's impact in the financial aid arena. In Asia, she notes, there is significant emphasis on being rewarded for meeting standards of merit. "But then again, merit also drives inequality in education. So, we introduced need-based financial aid and are helping other universities think about how they are going to provide access to students from lower economic backgrounds." By bringing the concept of financial aid to Vietnam, Fulbright officials changed a cultural conversation. Close to 30 percent of applicants for the Class of 2024 are students whose parents did not attend college. At the same time, Fulbright's value proposition is growing as more Vietnamese families who have the means to pay tuition are seeking admission for their children.

Beyond its campus impact, Fulbright seeks to be a pathfinder for other universities in Vietnam. It sees itself as breaking barriers in higher education that will enable others to experiment with their own innovations. In this regard, the most important legacy Fulbright may leave in Vietnam came about early in the process of seeking a charter: a change in the law governing higher education. When it launched, Fulbright did not fit existing categories for a university in Vietnam, which covered either public institutions that charged little tuition or private for-profit institutions often of dubious value.[40] Initially, the government sought to carve out a special category within which only Fulbright would operate with greater freedom. But while this exceptionalism would facilitate the university's development, it also limited the impact Fulbright could have down the road. "When you are special," says Dam, "permission could be withdrawn at any point. [And] if you continue being special a lot of people will not try to follow you because they are not special." Fulbright leaders successfully pushed to revise higher-education law itself in Vietnam, so that whatever independence they possessed could be claimed by other universities as well. As a result, today Fulbright is a Vietnamese university, not an overseas campus or a joint-venture university. "Because we are given academic freedom and autonomy," says Dam, "by law, every Vietnamese university should be able to enjoy the same thing."

Fulbright's impact is also ongoing. The university has ambitions to scale up in Vietnam and to enhance its regional and global reputation. On May 16, 2021, the university celebrated its fifth anniversary, a date marking the line between a start-up phase and what they see as a scale-up phase. From the beginning, Dam says, the goal was not simply to create a small liberal arts college with 1,000 or 1,500 students. Instead, they aimed to eventually grow to an undergraduate population of 3,500 to 4,000 students and to add targeted graduate programs that would bring the total student population to 5,500 to 6,000 students. This would position Fulbright as smaller than a traditional public university in Vietnam but larger than a purely undergraduate college.

Fulbright took an important step in this direction in 2019, when the Fulbright School of Public Policy Management, an outgrowth of the FETP, received accreditation for two of its programs from the US agency known as the Network of Schools of Public Policy, Affairs, and Administration. This is the first graduate program in the Southeast Asian region to receive this accreditation and places it among a small group of schools in the network located outside the United States. Fulbright is also expanding its partnership programs to include a new cybersecurity program in collaboration with the University of Texas.[41]

In February 2022, Fulbright announced a commitment of $40 million from eight inaugural members of its founders' circle to support the initial stage of building a flagship campus in Saigon High-Tech Park. This is a significant gift both in terms of its amount and as a signal of the impact the university is starting to have in Vietnam. Private philanthropy is highly limited in the country, as it is across Asia, especially in support of universities. "Our founders believe in the transformational power of education," Dam says, "and it is their faith in Fulbright's relevance to the future of Vietnam that motivated this historic act of giving." (In a bid to unleash more donations, she is seeking to focus attention in Vietnam on the value of a US-like system that would allow tax deductions for charitable giving.)[42]

Fulbright has also benefitted from direct support from the Vietnamese and US governments. In an international private-public venture, the Vietnamese government recently donated a fifteen-hectare parcel of land for the university to construct an environmentally advanced education complex.

The US International Development Finance Corporation also provided $37 million in a twenty-year direct loan to support the first phase of construction for these new facilities.[43]

Fulbright has also begun to build up its regional reputation by creating an outreach arm to other Southeast Asian countries, and—not content to remain merely a regional institution—it is bolstering its international reputation by seeking accreditation in the United States by the New England Commission of Higher Education. "People ask, 'Are you going to focus on serving Vietnam or are you going to be more ambitious and make it more international?'" Dam said on the school's fifth anniversary. "In the long term, we want to be competitive internationally, drawing top students from around the world even as we remain committed to our mission of service to Vietnamese society."[44]

In its first five years, Fulbright wrestled with what it means to be a deeply Vietnamese institution that offers an American style of liberal arts education. The initial lack of clarity on how the Vietnamese and American features of the institution came together gave rise to an opaque institutional identity that occasionally hampered decision-making. Turnover in academic leadership also made it difficult to establish a clear curricular vision. Provost Bickford departed after one year, and new provost Jay Siegel was unable to relocate to FUV owing to the COVID-19 pandemic: he parted ways with the university after just three months. Yet its dual identities also enabled Fulbright to find its shape over time as, like a diamond, it could be turned first in one direction and then another to display a specific facet when needed. Today, as the university pursues greater regional and global aspirations, it continues wrestling with questions about its core character—and with new challenges, such as whether to operate solely in English or to teach in both English and Vietnamese.

With its historical connection with Harvard's Kennedy School of Government, Fulbright might well choose to position itself as an emerging Harvard of Vietnam. But the small size of the institution and its limited research capacity makes realizing this ambition difficult in the long run. The isomorphic forces of emulating Harvard can also sit awkwardly next to the imaginative, student-centered liberal arts emphasis and the inventive curriculum that emerged from the codesign year. In its start-up phase, the university gravitated toward younger faculty who loved teaching and mentoring students in close relationships. Making the transition from a small, experimental undergraduate college to a more high-powered research institution, should Fulbright choose to fully pursue that aim, will require shifts in the kind of faculty that the university invites on board. It will also mean confronting the same kinds of challenges that medium-sized universities in the Unites States regularly face—tensions between maintaining small class size in an intimate and nurturing undergraduate environment and recruiting more research-oriented faculty who require lighter teaching loads and are more accustomed to the time-saving lecture format.

Still, at just five years in, it is now possible to reflect on how far Fulbright has come since its founding. As president, Dam says that she expected it would take much longer to convince Vietnamese parents and students that a liberal-arts-style education would be a good bet for their future. "We thought it would be hard to recruit students to take risks in an adventure like this," she says. "Actually, I found that my skepticism was overdone. Society in Vietnam was very open for change."

7

Archimedes's Lever

ASHOKA UNIVERSITY

Pramath Raj Sinha is the son and grandson of writers from the ancient city of Patna, which sits on the Ganges River in northeastern India. To support his family, his father launched a textbook publishing business, and Sinha would accompany him on marketing trips: "We called it canvassing," he told the journalist Sonya Choudhury in 2017. "We would fill the car with calendars and diaries and call on schoolteachers with these gifts. I thought it was a lot of fun; only later I realized it was serious marketing."[1]

Sinha was admitted to the Indian Institute of Technology (IIT) Kanpur to study a subject he knew nothing about: metallurgical engineering. Like many Indian students forced to specialize too early, he hated it. "I was stuck," he says. "I had no flexibility." Later, in a PhD program in mechanical engineering and applied mechanics at the University of Pennsylvania, he reveled in an academic culture that encouraged him to explore additional and more varied interests. But that experience didn't last. "Once I took up a formal academic job, it was very restricting for somebody like me, who likes to do multiple different things," he says. "And I found that I was learning more and more about less and less, and that's not how I wanted to live my life."

Sinha walked away from academic life and joined the consulting firm McKinsey and Company. As a partner at the firm in the 1990s, he helped launch the Indian School of Business (ISB) in Hyderabad, taking the institution from an untested proposition to a top-twenty global ranking. He took a leave of absence in 2001 to become the school's founding dean; and by the mid-2000s, ISB's success had emboldened several other groups of entrepreneurs to imagine building an entire university from scratch. "All of us always saw the need," Sinha says, "but we didn't have the courage or the time."

By 2008, Sinha would become the linchpin connecting two groups of Indian first-generation entrepreneurs who wanted to build a university that would compete with the most prestigious institutions in the world. A small group of IIT alumni sought advice from Sinha about starting a Nobel laureate–producing engineering college. The group was well suited for chasing such an ambitious dream. Vineet Gupta, who founded one of India's largest test prep companies, led the IIT group. At the same time, Ashish Dhawan, a private equity founder, and Sanjeev Bikhchandani, an internet entrepreneur, approached Sinha with the vision of establishing a top-notch liberal arts college in India. Dhawan had graduated from Yale College in the early 1990s, and Bikhchandani from St. Stephen's College (a long-standing liberal arts college within the University of Delhi) in the mid-1980s. Over lunch one day, the two began to dream. "I cherished the period of my life at Yale," recalled Dhawan, "and always felt it made me a different person relative to my peers in high school. So, the two of us were very passionate about building Ashoka."

Overcoming the Colonial Legacy

Dhawan and Sinha's passion should be seen against the backdrop of the Indian higher-education system, which is the third-largest in the world, following China and the United States. Yet to date no Indian university has ranked among the top two hundred in the *Times Higher Education* World University Rankings.[2] The founders of Ashoka University saw Indian universities as lagging in purpose and content. The legacy of the British model of precollegiate education meant that students were funneled into narrow areas of specialty from which they could not escape. Starting in the 1950s and 1960s, the system began embracing technical education in the belief that a poor country needs to grow its own engineers, doctors, and lawyers. Professional degrees in these fields became prestigious, and demand created supply as parents told their children (especially their sons) that they had to earn such credentials.[3]

India now has over fifty-two thousand higher-education institutions and enrolls over thirty-five million students, quadruple the enrollment from 2001. Physical campuses have swelled beyond their capacities, and only recently has the government moved to expand options for online education.

At the same time, India has seen growth in high-quality research and smaller and more elite institutions. Since 2000, India has implemented a dramatic expansion of its vaunted IIT system, which has grown to include seventeen new IIT campuses, an increase from just six campuses before 2000 to twenty-three, across every region of India, in 2021. Yet Indian higher education still reaches only a fraction of the estimated fifty million young people who need it among the country's total population of 1.4 billion. Only around 25 percent of students graduating from high school pursue higher education, and the government wants to double that figure by 2035.[4]

Existing Indian higher-education institutions lack the capacity to admit all qualified students. Even students scoring 95 percent on their twelfth-grade exams fail to gain admission to sought-after universities such as the University of Delhi, and find themselves scrambling for alternatives.[5] Often dissatisfied with the inadequate options available in their home country, every year half a million Indian students travel abroad for their studies.[6] In response to the overall growing educational demand in India, entrepreneurs have founded a number of private Indian universities since the 1990s, schools that now compose 80 percent of the higher-education system.[7] These new institutions were lightly regulated, however, and few incentives exist for their faculty to produce high-quality teaching or research. "We saw all of these other universities mushrooming," Sinha says, "but they were very poor quality and much more commercially oriented, and we realized there was something missing."

Determined to do something about the problem, Sinha convened two groups of entrepreneurs who would become the founding team of Ashoka: "I just said, 'you guys are very similar age groups, similar vintage, similar motivations, why don't we come together?'" Initially, they planned for a multifaceted approach to the social sciences as well as gearing up for an engineering and a business school. But when the 2008 financial crisis hit, talk shifted to a more focused but still radical proposal amid an economic downturn: building a liberal arts and sciences university to help students gain a more holistic foundation. Sinha, Dhawan, and others did not want to just create another professional school. They were passionate about the liberal arts ideal and keenly aware that to succeed they would have to narrow their scope.

"By then my own thinking had evolved to the point that I thought setting up a technology-only institution no longer made sense," says Sinha. "Instead, we needed to be multidisciplinary." The curriculum had to venture beyond a smattering of subjects across different disciplines, and it had to offer students the flexibility to make choices about their areas of study that were not predetermined by their high-school performance or an entrance test. "That was the big insight," says Sinha. "In India people were crying out, 'Hey, I don't know if I want to study psychology or economics, can I just come and check it out and then maybe decide? And maybe I can do both? Can I do a little of both?'" He saw a market need that aligned with the founders' mission.

Dhawan went even further, highlighting the broader social imperative for a different kind of education. "What we need in India is not just economic change," he told the *Financial Times*, reflecting on those early conversations. "What we need is societal transformation." After completing his MBA at Harvard and a stint at Goldman Sachs, he had returned to India in the late 1990s to establish one of the country's leading private equity funds. In 2012, he left investment management to launch a grant-making and public-policy think tank focused on systemic change in India's primary and secondary schools. He saw a similar urgency to drive change in higher education. "You need people who are willing to question the status quo," he said in 2018, "who are independent thinkers and who know how to write well and express themselves well in spoken form. India doesn't have enough of that."[8]

The entrepreneurs pooled their resources and convinced powerful friends and colleagues to join their group of founders. Eventually, some of the wealthiest business leaders in India joined the founding team through their financial contributions. For planning purposes, the founders' group narrowed to a core of four: Sinha, Dhawan, Bikhchandani, and Gupta. They met monthly in Dhawan's office at the Oberoi Hotel in New Delhi. By 2010, this group had identified twenty-five acres of land to purchase in Sonipat, Haryana, thirty miles from Delhi. Dhawan and Bikhchandani agreed to provide the capital to purchase the land, and a wider group of supporters made a founders' grant to support student scholarships.

Creating the Rhodes Scholarship of India

The founding group wanted to set sail with their new university quickly. Their experience in finance and technology had conditioned them to see the value of a fast launch. But their experience with the Indian government had taught them that regulatory and construction-approval delays could keep them at dock for years. So they came up with a plan to start a postgraduate liberal arts program before they received formal approval to build a university. Named the Young India Fellowship (YIF), the program was designed "to rekindle the desire to learn and explore" and provide a "multi-disciplinary learning environment created by some of the best and most inspirational teachers from India and the world."[9]

The founders were betting that they could demonstrate the overall value of their liberal arts approach by offering selected students a year of this type of education *after* they had completed more specialized degrees elsewhere. The program was designed to draw on both Indian and visiting international faculty, and the group launched a search across India for the most talented recent graduates to become the first fellows. Then, they waited. Would anyone express interest in something that had never been offered before in India? "We were genuinely concerned that nobody was going to show up," recalls Dhawan. One thousand applications later, they selected fifty-seven students who "were frustrated with having been funneled down this narrow path and really had missed out on what they genuinely wanted to study," he says. "They were passionate about something else." These were exactly the students the founders had been hoping to find.

The program made its initial home at the Sri Aurobindo Center campus in South New Delhi. To attract high-quality faculty, organizers offered eight different six-week terms that provided intensive experiences for students and teachers. Visiting faculty gave courses on topics ranging from "The History of Science and Technology" to "Visual Communication and Storytelling." Students took twenty-six total courses over the year. They also participated in an eight-month-long experiential learning module (ELM), where they worked in teams to address a real-world problem for schools, environmental organizations, government ministries, health-care companies, and workforce training programs. Student contributions ranged from content creation and operational support to data analytics and business development. Fellows can also create their own ELM project, and over the years several have evolved into successful start-ups, such as Barefoot Edu, which builds educational leadership and improves school systems, or into programs at Ashoka such as the Centre for Studies in Gender and Sexuality.[10] Along the way, students were mentored by the YIF staff and attended guest lectures from a wide range of intellectuals, entrepreneurs, and world leaders. In one year, the YIF featured ninety-three guest lectures, including visits from Madeline Albright, former US secretary of state, and other high-profile speakers.

The YIF experience left no doubt in the founders' minds that Indian students were ready for a liberal arts approach to education. These students brimmed with curiosity and questions. The first graduates of the program did well in their initial work or graduate study placements, and by year three the program was receiving three thousand applications for one hundred spots.[11] The brand name took off, and the difficulty of admission led the media to call the YIF "India's Own Rhodes Scholarship."[12]

The YIF thus filled the gap between the founders' aspirations to launch quickly and the reality that regulatory approvals and construction would take years. This interim period proved to be crucial in other ways as well. Each YIF student was sponsored by a single donor, a structure that helped recruit supporters and build a culture of philanthropy. As donors witnessed the quality of the students and the increasing selectivity of the program, they became attached to the group's mission, making it easier for the founders to ask them to write bigger checks as they began to build the university. The graduates of the first class and subsequent classes themselves became compelling spokespersons for the future Ashoka University—and a dynamic network for recruiting future students.

This interim period further enabled the founders to test the waters in a low-cost way and to build a recognizable brand for a product then unknown in the Indian market. It helped them begin assembling an international roster of visiting faculty and to discern who among these guest professors was especially committed to the liberal arts and sciences and the Ashoka project. "From a recruitment standpoint," Dhawan says, "it helped us to shop the vision and gave us confidence that we should stick to the liberal arts and sciences and not fan out to any other area." The YIF also gave these founders, a group dedicated to speed, time to focus on quality, helping them avoid fatal mistakes early on: "You're not just scrambling to pull together things; you can be a little bit more deliberate when you're unsure about the demand or your value proposition," Dhawan adds.

Built by the Elite, for the Elite?

Once the founding team members had successfully demonstrated the appeal of a liberal arts education, they forged ahead with their broader vision. Ashoka University was named after Emperor Ashoka (ca. 304–232 BC), known for his renunciation of war and promotion of peace and Buddhism throughout India. The campus opened in 2014 after the founders had gained regulatory approval, acquired the land, and built the initial academic buildings and student residences.

The story of Ashoka's campus is intertwined with several other elite higher-education institutions, all neighbors in the newly developed Rajiv Gandhi Education City near the village of Sonipat, formerly a quiet rural village an hour and a half outside of Delhi, in Haryana State. As part of a plan to develop Haryana, the state government acquired over two thousand acres of agricultural land in 2006 and then offered this land to new start-up universities in India. The Haryana Private Universities Act of 2006 enabled relatively rapid development and approval for these new universities in exchange for reserving 25 percent of seats for students from Haryana, along with some fee concessions for local students. By 2017, Education City had transformed the tranquil farmland into a hive of educational ventures, with parcels for an expected thirteen private and public institutions. One of these was Ashoka University.

Students who found their way to this new campus were able to take different kinds of courses before deciding on a major, allowing them to explore their intellectual passions. Students weary of the Indian public university system rejoiced in what one described as the "fresh, young and very modern" education Ashoka was offering.[13] The new university attracted students like Aritra Sutradhar from Kolkata, who wanted to study music, astronomy, and computer science. "It was tough in [high] school with no flexibility," he told Malini Goyal from the *Economic Times*. "I want to get into the music industry, but I do not want to limit my options right now."[14] The university began with a first cohort of about 120 students in 2014, and by 2021 had enrolled over 1,860 undergraduates.[15]

Students also enjoyed a level of freedom not often experienced at Indian universities. A full-time, residential education, the undergraduate program at Ashoka has no curfew prohibiting movement on or off campus for male or female students, and there are no rigid class-attendance requirements—both of which are the norm at most Indian universities. "Ashoka treats students the way they should be, as adults," Sandeep Sen said in 2014, a Young India Fellow. He contrasts this approach with his own undergraduate experience in Bangalore, where "college life was fun, the experience of education was not."[16]

Ashoka's founders struggled to create a sustainable financial model without the kind of endowment enjoyed by the top US institutions that Ashoka considered as peers in terms of educational quality. They set a fee structure well below US costs but still very high by Indian standards, and then they offered financial aid. "At the Williams and Amhersts, the cost per student is about $80,000, half of which comes from net student fees and half from the endowment," says Dhawan, "so the real challenge we are faced with is how do you bring that $80,000 down to $8,000 or $10,000?" As a start-up, Ashoka lacked the endowment that most elite US schools relied upon to cover half or more of the total cost per student.

At the same time that Ashoka has had to meet financial challenges, a persistent criticism within India is that it is a university "of the elite, for the elite, by the elite," as one former Young India Fellow put it.[17] The writer charged that the university is really just a way for wealthy Indians to offer a high-quality education for their children at a lower cost than sending them abroad—an "elite solution for elite problems." Writing of his experience at Ashoka in 2018–19, this former student continued:

> The university's target customer was someone who was excellent at English, came from a reasonably rich family, upper-caste, uncompromising, and had aspirations of infinite freedom only the elite could dream of. . . . Students from the lower castes cannot even imagine to apply as the fee charged despite scholarships is exponentially exorbitant. The campus is sanitized of caste issues as there is little to no representation of students from lower castes.[18]

At more than $11,000 for annual tuition, Ashoka's cost remains out of reach for most Indian families. The university's students often come from the upper middle-class and are more likely to have studied at the better high schools. Many of them are comparing offers to attend Ashoka or to go abroad for college. Yet the university does provide financial aid to almost 50 percent of the undergraduate class, including full financial support (covering tuition, residence, meals, and stipend) to about 20 percent of the class. The average need-based scholarship awarded is over $4,000. The class of 2021–22 is Ashoka's largest and most diverse, with 690 students. It includes 6 percent of students who are the first in their family to attend university, and 35 percent of the students come from outside the major metropolitan areas. A total of 57 percent of undergraduates are women, 42 percent are men, and 1 percent describe themselves as other. International students compose 6 percent and come from twenty-five countries.[19] Sinha acknowledges that Ashoka is elite by dint of being a small, highly selective institution. But, he says, "we don't want to be elitist. We are proactively searching for deserving students from unrepresented communities. There is no other private university in the country that's making the same effort to reach out."

Ashoka's financial model invokes several strategies, including offering lower faculty salaries, which are comparable to faculty pay in the United States after accounting for the reduced cost of living in India; insisting on a two-plus-two teaching load, which also keeps out faculty who are looking to be at a research university with lower teaching requirements; and offering a limited number of majors. "We can't afford to have eight faculty and three students," says Dhawan. "You want a certain minimum critical mass to offer courses and to be able to provide a rich experience for the undergraduates, but you don't want to offer infinite choice." Ashoka also runs much leaner administratively than comparable US institutions. "Even though you want the liberal arts model from the US," says Dhawan, "the real innovation is staying away from the cost disease that has plagued education there and rethinking the model so that it's viable in the Indian context."

The Kama Sutra and the Mahabharata

The promotion of Ashoka University as the Ivy League university of India signaled quality to Indian parents. Yet Ashoka's founders and early faculty leaders entertained even more ambitious dreams. They wanted to build a university that would be distinguished by its intellectual and cultural heft. Before its 2012 launch, Ashoka's founders put together an all-star academic council to guide its intellectual development. Headed by the distinguished Indian sociologist Andre Beteille, who had been teaching in the YIF, this group included Kaushik Basu, who at the time was the chief economist at the World Bank; Ramachandra Guha, an authority on the history of modern India; Christophe Jaffrelot, a French political scientist who specializes in South Asia; Devesh Kapur, a professor of political science at the University of Pennsylvania at the time; and Pratap Bhanu Mehta, a well-known academic and public intellectual who was then the president of a Delhi-based think tank, the Centre for Policy Research. Beteille would become the university's first chancellor in 2014, and he was joined by the historian Rudrangshu Mukherjee, who was also teaching in the YIF program and became the first vice-chancellor responsible for academic affairs. In 2017, Mukherjee succeeded Beteille as chancellor, and Mehta joined full-time as vice-chancellor.

This group and the early faculty members faced several significant constraints as they sought to create a liberal arts university in India. Externally, just at the moment that most members of the first class had matriculated, a new government came to power and scrapped all four-year degree programs in order to reduce costs and extend the capacity of India's struggling education system. To approximate the liberal arts ideal, Ashoka had to pivot to a hybrid three-year plus one degree, which limited curricular options. After completing the three-year bachelor's degree, students could take a one-year postgraduate diploma in advanced studies and research, which enables them to apply for graduate programs in countries that require four-year degrees.

The extra year also allowed students to complete capstone research projects under faculty mentorship, a feature of the best US liberal arts colleges.

Other constraints on innovation were internal to the university. Initial curriculum development efforts bogged down in disagreements over teaching core content versus teaching different modes of thinking. Over time, these two perspectives began to take on different contours. "We discovered the nature and structure of knowledge now lends itself to different kinds of debates about what the goal of the curriculum should be," says Mehta. "The transformation of the disciplines itself, where disciplines and subdisciplines are decided more by method than by the object of study," had significant effects. "My quantitative political science friends have more in common with the economists than they do with other colleagues. In the sciences this revolution is quite extraordinary now." Ashoka faculty had to ask themselves: "Are we simply taking some old models and reproducing it, or are we in some sense pushing the frontiers of what one can do in the organization of teaching and pedagogy that takes on board profound changes in the structure of knowledge?"

This increasingly expansive line of thinking led to proposals for experimental new approaches. One was called the Ashoka Quest, where students would integrate forms of experiential and practice-based learning that were particularly attuned to the Indian context. In this model, a student would spend an entire semester studying relevant fields while immersed in a rural or urban Indian context. The goal was twofold: for students to learn by doing, and for them "to build a social conscience and a social commitment," says Sinha. He continues:

> Indian students tend to be very protected in the current generation because parents know how much competition there is for them to get admitted to university. And so they protect them from the real world. This was an opportunity to get them exposed and everybody bought into this vision of the quest. For one semester, everybody will go on this quest to discover themselves and discover their passion.

This idealism, however, proved impossible to sustain in the face of the government's decision to mandate three years for undergraduate degrees—not to mention the financial resources it would have taken to support the program. It never got off the ground.

Instead, the faculty at Ashoka directed their energies toward creating a distinctive set of foundational courses that would help students transition from the traditional Indian school system to a liberal arts education. A robust general education program immediately distinguished Ashoka from other Indian universities, which tend to pay lip service to requirements for breadth in favor of quickly funneling students into majors. By contrast, Ashoka requires nine foundational courses: critical thinking; great books; literature and the world; Indian civilizations; environmental studies; mind and behaviour; economy, politics, and society; mathematical thinking; and principles of science Students must also take two cocurricular courses in the arts or languages.

In the early days, some of these courses appeared quite similar in content to other great books courses in the West, albeit with one or two Indian texts added to the list. Over time, though, a more seamless integration between texts from different cultures took place. Mehta recalls that "we had to build it up slowly rather than right from the start." The Indian civilization course traces the emergence of modern India and evolutions in its culture, religion, and politics. Students read Mahatma Gandhi's *Hind Swaraj* (*Indian Home Rule*), a seminal piece of work on social ills and self-rule. They also read the *Kama Sutra*, which the world considers to be a book about sex but also is a deep work of anthropology and philosophy. (Some more conservative parents were disturbed to discover that this text was being taught.)

The course also introduced students to traditional texts like the *Mahabharata*, one of the two major Sanskrit epics of ancient India. Teaching these texts, especially in high schools and public universities, has been a controversial issue in India. Ashoka's founders believed that it was important for students to understand and debate the meaning and influence of these texts on Indian history and politics and to place them alongside the classics of the Western tradition. "For us this was very exciting, we were not just doing Greek texts and the great writers of English in Europe, but really bringing it back home as well," says Sinha. Indeed, one consequence of the rise of nationalism in India has been to attach new interest and cachet for students for their own civilizational identity. "Our students want to be able to argue in a language that can use the *Mahabharata* and other culture-defining texts," says Mehta. "There is a kind of civilizational zeitgeist that is getting back to those texts, we hope in a much more intelligent way."

Beyond the foundation courses, students can choose from eleven disciplinary majors, nine interdisciplinary majors, and seven minors. The introduction of interdisciplinary majors was completely new in the Indian landscape. At Ashoka, these range from computer science and entrepreneurial leadership to politics and society. Some of the most interesting majors emerged from the interplay between students' intellectual interests and parental concerns for employability. After students were exposed in their first year to courses in Indian civilization and Indian history, a significant number of them asked to switch from majors like economics to history. But when parents balked at allowing their children to do so, the university developed a major in economics and history. The problem then became convincing the regulators. "'You're not allowed to do this,'" Sinha recalls being told. "'Students have to do one degree and then they have to do a second degree. And only then can you give them two majors.' So we had to really fight the system to get them to understand that there's a way to construct these and times have changed."

A third constraint common to other start-ups centered on the place of the natural sciences in a liberal arts institution. Ashoka started with a focus on the social sciences and humanities. While they wanted to add the natural sciences, the founders initially discovered that the capital costs associated with that effort were overwhelming. As it turned out, however, Ashoka's largest gift (as of 2020) was for a school of biosciences. At the time, the deeper challenge revolved less around funding than around the nature of modern scientific and quasi-scientific knowledge. The requirements to be competitive in increasingly specialized disciplines have become daunting. This is true of economics as well as physics and chemistry. "Economics can require students to study eight math courses just to do economics today," Mehta says.

As a result, the challenge for Ashoka became less about integrating Indian and Western perspectives in the curriculum and more about balancing the requirements of excellence and rigor in those majors while also giving students as much choice as possible in a liberal arts environment. Too many prerequisites and specialized courses and the undergraduate experience would become more like graduate training; too few such courses and students might not be competitive for admission to top graduate programs. While the numbers are small, initial reports indicate that the university has found the right balance between disciplinary training and a broader liberal arts education: six of the first twelve physics majors received full scholarships to graduate study abroad. So, too, the university has managed to assemble the top-ranked economics faculty in the country, a distinction that will serve undergraduates well as they apply to graduate school.[20]

From Consumer to Producer

As Ashoka responded to these challenges, its leaders simultaneously had to shape and define a new faculty culture. Ashoka's founders believed that who they hired and who they tenured would send a critical market signal. High-quality research and stringent tenure standards thus constituted a crucial part of their overall strategy. For its launch year, the university drew heavily on academics who had taught in the YIF to populate its first seventeen faculty hires: most were Indian nationals, but several were international faculty who would play important roles in building the institution. In its early years, Ashoka also telegraphed its global ambitions by recruiting visiting faculty from top-ranked institutions in the United States and the United Kingdom. Ashoka was especially attractive to nonresident Indians, an official category that includes people of Indian birth or ancestry who live outside of the country, who could now return home while still teaching at a Western-style institution. By 2018, two-thirds of the faculty had obtained PhDs from leading universities in the West, and a third of the faculty came from abroad.[21]

By necessity, many of these early hires were junior faculty: few senior scholars were willing to join an institution with a still-unknown future. Even by 2017, the economics department had thirteen junior faculty and just one senior faculty member. Since then, senior hires have become easier to make as the institution's reputation has grown and as the ideological and bureaucratic difficulties of working within India's public universities have increased, effectively luring away candidates who might have gone elsewhere a few years earlier. "If I'd asked giants in their field to join Ashoka ten or even five years ago, they would have said 'no,'" says Mehta. Faculty were drawn to Ashoka for its grand ambitions, its low teacher-student ratio, the quality of its students, and the greater freedom to design and teach their own courses than is typically available in India.

Sinha's experience in the early 2000s building the Indian School of Business (ISB) in Hyderabad influenced Ashoka's approach to building its permanent faculty. The ISB is now ranked in the top twenty business schools in the world, and one strategy Sinha employed there was to leverage relationships with Wharton, Kellogg, and other top-tier US business schools to create a large visiting faculty presence. In building the faculty and shaping the culture at Ashoka, however, Sinha, Dhawan, and the academic leadership opted instead to build up the university's own full-time faculty. In disciplines such as computer science, where it was hard to recruit faculty initially, Ashoka's leaders were willing to wait until the quality and brand recognition of the new university had reached the point of attracting the kind of candidates they sought for permanent appointments.

The bimodal age distribution of faculty recruits also gave them another reason not to scale the institution too fast. Ashoka found its greatest success in hiring faculty either coming directly out of PhD or postdoc programs or in the fifty-plus age category whose children had left home. The expectation was that it would take up to twenty years to build a world-class faculty, and that it would be a mistake to rush that process. "There's a risk you won't get the best faculty because your reputation will not be as strong and you'll hire the wrong people at the get-go," says Dhawan. "I'm always a believer you have to bide your time and grow into it, as opposed to imagining you can just turn on the switch and become a great institution from day one."

Faculty of Indian origin were their most likely targets. In this pool, some fields proved easier to hire than others, with greater recruitment success showing up in the humanities than in the natural sciences. So while the university waited to staff certain fields, it gained early traction in hiring for fields such as South Asian history and politics. Scholars in these fields appreciated the opportunity to directly shape Indian intellectual and political culture at an institution that was free from the stifling bureaucracy and intense politicization of traditional Indian universities. Political pressure pervades every aspect of university life at many traditional Indian institutions, from faculty hiring to student admissions and curriculum. These pressures, coupled with the sharp increase in student enrollments and protracted underfunding, had caused many of India's brightest stars to decamp for Western universities.

Ashoka promised a way to reverse that brain drain. This market reality coincided with one of the new university's deepest intellectual aspirations: to gather in leaders from the Indian diaspora, who, in conjunction with colleagues who had been teaching at Indian universities as well as non-Indian scholars, would establish India as a site for world-class scholarship and a well of creativity and discovery. "Over the last eighty or hundred years," Mehta told the *Financial Times* in 2018, "India has for the most part been a consumer of knowledge—the big ideas get produced in western societies and we just apply them." But things could be different now. Ashoka could "move India from being just a consumer of knowledge to a major producer of knowledge."[22]

Between Academic and Entrepreneurial Cultures

Hiring the right faculty, constructing a curriculum, recruiting students, and building a campus required a delicate balance between the traditional ethos of academia and the more entrepreneurial culture of the private sector. By 2018, they had raised over $140 million from a hundred donors, each of whom gave at least $300,000, and by 2022, two hundred donors have given over $200 million, the largest shared philanthropic effort in India. Recognizing all these donors as part of a broader group of founders enabled the university to bootstrap the operation and build a collective whose members felt personally invested in the success of the institution. Being a founder gave special acknowledgement to these early investors. Ashoka required donations of $1.5 million to become a trustee, a status that allowed donors opportunities to offer their counsel, though not to have a say in governance.[23] The actual governance of the institution is carried by a ten-person body that includes the chancellor and vice-chancellor, a representative from the state of Haryana, and seven others. This group, in turn, delegates authority to a board of management that has four trustees and a wider group from the academic and administrative leadership of the university. There is also an academic council that consists solely of scholars, which is responsible for curricular and other academic matters.

This tiered structure of involvement and oversight helped Ashoka resolve a central problem facing private institutions in India: how to raise sufficient funds to run the university while preventing a single individual or family from exerting excessive influence over decision-making. Ashoka would operate under a system of collective governance rather than becoming subject to the desires of a primary donor. "We have said no to many people who have been willing to give us large amounts of money but wanted proportionate representation on the board or significant naming rights," Sinha said in 2018. "This is the crux of institution-building that people don't understand."[24]

The entrepreneurs who founded Ashoka also brought special attention to the cultural and human dimensions of launching a start-up. Typically, faculty join an existing university that they see as a platform to facilitate their own work. At a start-up, the founders knew from their own experience, it was crucial that everyone see the success of the institution as part of their work. Ashoka's founders brought lessons from outside of academia into the conversation, such as how the Mayo Clinic, a renowned academic medical center in the United States, had built a strong partnership between doctors and support staff.

The founders also saw that new universities offer a rare opportunity to build academic structures that do not simply replicate what has gone before. "The cement hasn't started to dry yet," says Dhawan. "You don't have hardened walls between disciplines." For Ashoka, this opportunity translated into designing a physical infrastructure that intentionally placed faculty from different disciplines and departments in proximity to one another. Ashoka's founders imported another lesson from their corporate backgrounds: setting metrics for five-year strategic growth that integrate financial resources, student enrollment, faculty hiring, and physical plant.

As much as Ashoka's founders sought to inject a more entrepreneurial culture into the DNA of the university, they also had to guard against giving too much influence to the university's extended network of financial supporters. Business leaders love speed and scale, says Dhawan. In their world, the practice is to build quickly, starting with relatively inexpensive, poor-quality products, and then move up the value chain to produce products that improve over time. "In business, that's possible," Dhawan says. "But in higher education, if you start wrong, you're doomed forever. Once your reputation is established, it's very hard to break out of that. It's almost like a self-fulfilling vicious cycle with recruiting faculty and students. And business leaders don't automatically get that. It's not just another sector, and so the way you set it up has to be different." Business leaders also struggle to understand the shared governance model, Ashoka's founders learned. They had to educate donors that interfering with faculty recruitment or curricular development ends up undermining how universities work and how they attract and retain high-quality faculty and students. Donors also wanted the institution to concentrate in areas like artificial intelligence, machine learning, and big data. "There's a real need to convince people that we can't start from a narrow technology perspective," says Dhawan. "Understanding the humanities and what makes us human is even more critical today. But the desire often is to align the university with technology trends." At Ashoka, there was also constant pressure to make the curriculum more vocational by including subjects like accounting and law. The founders did not want Ashoka to be completely disconnected from real-world employment, but they were constantly reminded of the temptation to make everything more vocational from the beginning. To their minds, there are some skills that can be learned later on, and adding them to the mix for undergraduates would undermine Ashoka's distinctive value proposition.

It seems fair to say that Ashoka's founders brought a special combination of creativity and humility to these efforts. They injected an entrepreneurial spirit while recognizing limitations on their reach and that of other donors. Still, the balance between institution building and academic autonomy is a difficult one to maintain. This is especially so in the context of a third factor looming in the background of Ashoka's development: the turmoil roiling the waters of Indian politics. From the beginning, Ashoka faced criticism that it was an elitist bastion for left-leaning intellectuals; and a series of controversies have made it difficult for the university to protect free expression without being perceived as taking sides on political and cultural issues.[25]

Academic Autonomy and Institution Building

In 2016, six Young India Fellows sent a mass email to the entire Ashoka community, calling on recipients to sign a letter of solidarity condemning the Indian government's use of deadly force in the disputed territory of Kashmir. Debate raged over email as some students rejected the use of terms like "occupation" and questioned the letter's proposal that a plebiscite should determine the fate of the region. The university passed a resolution distancing Ashoka as a formal sponsor of the letter, and administrative leaders issued a new policy requiring approval before Ashoka-wide emails could be sent.

Far from quelling the conflict, two staff members in academic affairs and a mathematics instructor who had signed the letter resigned, and media reports began questioning Ashoka's commitment to freedom of speech. At the same time, Hindu activists condemned the university for allowing the letter to be issued in the first place. In a message to students, Vice-Chancellor Mukherjee sought to distinguish between students' freedom to express their views and the university's duty to stay out of the fray in India's heated political atmosphere: "Ashoka is trying to teach all you to question, to doubt and even to challenge, [but also to be] conscious that this freedom operates in a particular cultural and political context."[26]

In 2018, another controversy engulfed the university. Activists criticized Ashoka for teaching an allegedly anti-Hindu and anti-Brahmin graphic novel, *A Gardener in the Wasteland,* as part of its Great Books course. They charged that the book constitutes hate speech and exemplifies how Ashoka encouraged its students to "grow up deracinated & clueless about [their] own history and with self hatred."[27] Others called for the novel's author as well as the professor who assigned the book and the university administration to be charged with sedition for spreading hatred. Varnika Gangavalli, a first-year student, told an online newspaper, "The Great Books course was about historical oppression. . . . [B]ut I can't say that we were being indoctrinated."[28] For its part, the university issued a statement affirming the faculty's freedom to use a diverse range of materials:

> It is the hallmark of a mature education that students confront a diversity of arguments, including some uncomfortable ones. The university aims to ensure that students are equipped to think critically about issues and form their own views. Ashoka University is committed to freedom of academic thought, without bias of any kind.[29]

Incidents like this one periodically resurface on social media, and the university has to continually manage the public fallout.

When Mukherjee succeeded Beteille as chancellor, Ashoka's founders recruited Mehta to succeed Mukherjee as the university's academic leader. Mehta was well established as both a scholar and a commentator on issues of public import, and he would continue to write and speak publicly as vice-chancellor. In 2005, he had served as a convenor of India's National Knowledge Commission, a body set up by then prime minister Manhohan Singh to guide the government on educational reform. On the commission, Mehta worked with others to imagine a "green-field" strategy for higher education, including a blueprint for a private, not-for-profit university. The Indian economy was booming at the time, and they tried to interest philanthropists in funding the venture. But it became clear that no wealthy donors would do so and also give autonomy to the institution. Mehta eventually resigned from the commission in protest over the government's mandating specific numerical quotas for affirmative action in education that he regarded as political tokenism rather than serious strategies to advance social justice.[30] The Ashoka founders made the pitch to Mehta that their venture was the opportunity he had been imagining as part of the commission: building a great university outside of the public sector. The sale was an easy one: "I didn't have to think for more than 5 minutes" before accepting the role, Mehta says.

But the timing of his appointment was politically inauspicious. The Bharatiya Janata Party (BJP) under Narendra Modi had come to power during the year of Ashoka's founding. Prime Minister Modi had formed his first government in 2014 and wasted no time implementing the principles of *Hindutva* ("Hindu-ness"). The party is highly critical of the secular policies pursued by the previously dominant Indian National Congress; it advocates for an Indian society that is defined by Hindu values and sees Muslims as second-class citizens. After an electoral loss in 2018, the BJP returned to power in 2019 in a landslide victory and began pressing its Hindu-centered politics with greater vigor. It was in this context that Mehta's increasingly vocal criticisms of the government brought intense scrutiny to Ashoka.

In order to separate his dual roles as public intellectual and university leader, Mehta elected to step down as vice-chancellor while staying on as a professor: "I didn't want to risk Ashoka's future because of my personal history and profile, and we wouldn't be sacrificing any principle if I voluntarily stepped down." In setting up the university, he later explained,

> we were conscious of the fact that one of the reasons we wanted a liberal arts institution was to provide a space where people could step away from the ideological identification of universities. JNU [Jawaharlal Nehru University] was considered this bastion on the left and there was an effort to create right-wing universities. Frankly, it'd be a tragedy if that's the game Ashoka got into.[31]

Sinha and Dhawan shared this same aspiration for Ashoka to cultivate independent thinkers without letting the university itself become associated with a particular political movement or party. They were acutely aware of the importance of protecting free expression—and also of the fact that the state of Haryana, in which Ashoka resides, wields ultimate control over the institution. Sinha contrasts this delicate situation for Ashoka with a university like Princeton, "where you've been around for three hundred years, and you are in the United States, and nobody can touch you." In the Indian setting, he argues, it is crucial to uphold your beliefs in a way that does not jeopardize the institution that nurtures and protects them.

By 2021, tensions between free inquiry and an increasingly nationalistic government could no longer be contained. Mehta resigned from his faculty post at Ashoka amid reports that the government had placed indirect pressure on the university to sever ties with him. Arvind Subramanian, an economics professor at Ashoka who had once worked as chief economic adviser to Prime Minister Modi, also resigned from his position, characterizing Mehta's treatment as a fundamental affront to academic expression and freedom. Faculty and students protested Mehta's resignation, and an international roster of academics issued a statement of solidarity.[32]

The university disputed any claims that the government had pressured Ashoka to fire Mehta, even as it acknowledged lapses in institutional processes and reaffirmed its commitment to academic autonomy and freedom. A statement jointly issued by Mehta, Subramanian, and the Ashoka leadership read: "Pratap and Arvind would like to emphasize that Ashoka University is one of the most important projects in Indian higher education. And they remain lifelong friends and well-wishers of the institution and are committed to its success wherever they are."[33] In a letter to students, Mehta acknowledged the weighty difficulties involved: "We live in complicated times. India is bursting with creativity. But the dark shadows of authoritarianism are also hovering over us, putting us all in often uncomfortable and sometimes dishonourable positions. We will have to find principled and intelligent ways of overcoming this condition." For his part, Sinha believes that "as founders, all you can do is keep yourself focused on what it takes to protect the institution against the forces that could destroy it. It's about accepting the practical reality of what it takes to build the institution, and making sure that it survives and thrives." In the aftermath of these unsettling events, Ashoka put in place measures to reduce direct contact between the governing board and the faculty and to support free inquiry and expression by appointing a former Supreme Court judge as the university's first ombudsman.[34]

Archimedes's Lever

Ashoka University has successfully created a high-quality liberal arts college that in many ways is unique within India. Students who compare Ashoka to other Indian universities see it as a place where undergraduates are more genuinely excited by learning and where faculty are more committed to teaching and mentorship. Quacquarelli Symonds, the global ranking organization, placed Ashoka among the top five private universities in India in 2022 (top thirty among all universities) and as the top-rated university based on its percentage of international faculty. Research Papers in Economics in 2022 ranked Ashoka's economics faculty as the top department in India and thirty-first in Asia. Its faculty also includes leading intellectuals in the humanities and the social sciences. Students, too, have found considerable postgraduate success, from winning international fellowships like the Rhodes Scholarship and Millennium Fellowship to securing placements at global firms such as Accenture, McKinsey, and Deutsche Bank, as well as at India-based private and nonprofit organizations such as Zee Network, Zomato, Samhita, and Teach for India.[35]

Ashoka's influence can also be seen in its demonstration effect—the ways in which its new organizational form and pedagogical culture have become a reference point for broader transformations in Indian higher education. These transformations are apparent in the spread of similar kinds of ventures across India. Between 2015 and 2020, 230 new privately funded universities opened, a 66 percent increase in five years. Among the prominent new entrants are KREA University in the state of Andhra Pradesh and Rishihood University in Haryana's Sonipat, near Ashoka. Ashoka has also pioneered a collective governance model and a strategy for fundraising without ceding too much authority to donors, efforts other institutions have sought to emulate. Rishihood University, for instance, characterizes itself as a "collective philanthropic initiative."[36]

More broadly, Ashoka's imprint can be seen in the National Education Policy issued by the government in 2020 and in subsequent government promulgations. The policy document validated the liberal arts approach within Indian education and urged broader implementation across India. It reflects the kinds of changes that Ashoka has pioneered, especially a more interdisciplinary and holistic approach to education. The Indian government has relented in its three-year requirement for higher education, partly in response to programs like Ashoka that needed four years for students to explore a wide range of subjects and conduct original research. A proposed framework released in March 2022 by the University Grants Commission, a government body, includes requirements for all universities to offer general education, interdisciplinary coursework, and a capstone research project.[37] Ashoka, Dhawan says, has become a "sort of Archimedes' lever" for moving India away from the narrow and overly specialized British model of higher education that has dominated the country for 150 years. "All this is a far cry from what Bikhchandani [one of the original four founders] envisioned back in 2007 when he first met Dhawan to discuss their shared concerns about the state of Indian higher education," the journalist Amy Kazmin wrote in 2018:

> Over coffee, the two rapidly agreed they should work together on a university project and Dhawan offered to match Bikhchandani's donations, rupee for rupee. "He said, 'yeah, good idea, I'm on. . . . [H]ow much do you think you'll put in?'" Bikhchandani recalls. "We were under the impression the whole university would take $5m to do. So I said, I'll put in 20 per cent; you'll put in 20 per cent and get three more people. It was something I could deal with and not get intimidated. If I had known it was going to cost this much, I never would have done it."[38]

Ashoka is now seeking to further maximize its own influence by growing in size while maintaining the distinctive aspects of a residential liberal arts campus. "With just one or two thousand students, you're a little college and I don't think you can have the knock-on effects of influencing the rest of higher education," says Dhawan. "A minimum critical mass, he says, is "at least 5,000 students, but possibly closer to 8,000 to 10,000 students," including graduate students. Plans for scaling Ashoka University have already gotten underway, as the foundation stone for a twenty seven acre extension of its campus was laid in September 2021. This new campus will add 3,500 students to the university, increasing its enrollment to over 6,000 students by 2027. The overall investment will more than double the size of the campus, enabling the university to continue giving greater attention to the sciences and to graduate education.[39]

As much as Ashoka's success to date has depended on its quick attainment of a high prestige factor, the university also appears to be meeting its deeper aspirations: to become a major producer of knowledge, not just a consumer, and to prepare a new generation of students to solve societal problems in the Indian context. Ashoka has developed a unique specialization in Indian culture and civilization that has attracted scholars from around the world and been a seedbed for ideas at a moment when India's cultural identity and citizenship is hotly debated. Faculty have been influential commentators on social, legal, and cultural issues, including controversial topics such as religion and citizenship. For students, Ashoka's intellectual impact in this area is helping them think about what it means to be both rooted in the Indian context and globally connected. "We don't want to be a copycat of any institution," says Dhawan.

> We are in India and as a university we need to understand India's societal problems. And we need to understand the context, the history, the civilization and culture. And yet, we're part of the larger global ecosystem. So, having a fine balance between the two, there's a chance to be more global and yet be rooted in the Indian context.

Yet despite these rousing successes, the pursuit of prestige can create a high degree of institutional isomorphism that limits further innovation. This is especially the case as Ashoka builds more graduate programs, within which the pressures to conform to existing international standards exceed those for undergraduates. It is also important to note that high tuition costs make it difficult for the university to reach across and touch all sectors of Indian society, even with its significant commitment to providing financial aid. Here, the Ashoka model resembles those comparable institutions in the United States in which students from the upper socioeconomic ranks predominate.

How will Ashoka navigate its commitment to academic freedom and open inquiry in a stifling political environment? While free inquiry at Ashoka is much prized by students and faculty, society at large is slower to evolve, and entrenched beliefs are difficult to challenge. This final and perhaps most formidable tension will need to be managed carefully for Ashoka to retain its mantle of excellence in the liberal arts.

8

Building an African Renaissance

ASHESI UNIVERSITY

In March 2002, Patrick Awuah and Nina Marini were beginning a new venture far beyond what their training at the Berkeley MBA program and Microsoft had prepared them to manage. Both Marini and Awuah had conducted extensive planning on the business side for running a new university, and they were now living with thirty students in a rented house in Awuah's native Ghana. It was the first year of operations for his new university, to be named Ashesi, or "beginning" in the Akan language.

As they surveyed the scene during that fledgling year, they realized that starting a university was much harder than they had anticipated. One of their first obstacles was gaining accreditation from Ghana's National Accreditation Board (NAB), which repeatedly delayed the planned launch of the university. Several months earlier, the fall 2001 opening was postponed by a full academic year, and Awuah and Marini convened an urgent—and literal—"back-of-the-napkin conversation" in an airport to review how much cash they would need and how to limit their losses during the delay. Despite the extreme financial pressures, they decided to launch Ashesi University in March 2002 with thirty students in homes converted to dormitories.

While they waited for the NAB, Awuah and Marini set up books in a makeshift library placed in one bedroom within the rented house and negotiated with scholars eager to start as Ashesi's first faculty members but unsure of exactly what the new university was going to be. The lack of a clear start date made recruiting challenging. "It's hard to recruit people when it's a new institution, completely untested, run by people who weren't academics," Marini says. "We were asking people to take a pretty big leap of faith."

The residential campus made up a key part of the vision for Ashesi. Awuah and Marini both had firsthand experience of how residential liberal arts can transform students, with life-changing experiences in and out of the classroom—Awuah at Swarthmore and Marini at Haverford. Those years had left each of them eager to build a similar kind of living/learning community for Ashesi. But the costs were daunting, and some of their donors from Microsoft had recently seen losses in investment funds, placing additional financial pressures on the team. The plan to use rental houses would help bridge the gap, they hoped, while they raised funds for a permanent campus. Marini recalls the strong reaction from visitors in the early days, who would say, "What? You're in houses, what? That's not a university." This initial impression shifted once the Ashesi University receptionist was greeting guests and giving them a tour. "They would leave with a completely different impression," says Marini. "People would get excited. . . . [E]ven the receptionist started being more than a receptionist because she was so excited about what we were doing. We would just turn people on."

In that first semester, Ashesi had just eight faculty, many on part-time contracts that partly conflicted with the semester calendar. Course scheduling was challenging. Awuah and Marini had to stagger the class schedule so that students could fit the limited faculty into their lineup, sometimes having to take two or three intense courses at a time. As Marini recalls, "We were so in startup mode, we embraced that startup mentality, lean and mean, and we'll just make anything happen. . . . Those early years it was absolutely critical and it served us really well."

The Return to Africa

Awuah's return to Africa had seemed unlikely when he left on a scholarship to study in the United States decades earlier. He had received a full ride to Swarthmore, where he would work toward double degrees in engineering and economics. After graduating, he landed a job as a program manager at Microsoft. Awuah describes this period as one that allowed him to escape Ghana's chaotic military dictatorship, where conditions were so dire that "finding food was a daily challenge for most families, including mine." Life at Swarthmore was a haven by comparison. The college offered "a new way of questioning, developing, and testing ideas," he says, transforming his way of thinking. At Microsoft, he worked on dial-up internet technologies and earned a reputation as a gifted closer, bringing challenging projects to completion. During his time there, he says, "I turned my back on Africa."

Awuah stayed with Microsoft for eight years. He met his future wife Rebecca there. He returned from a brief visit home after his first year at Microsoft even more convinced that he had made the right choice to leave Ghana when he did. "I was extremely disillusioned," he says of his experience during that trip. "Nothing worked. I came back to the U.S. and told my colleagues at Microsoft that I would never return to Africa to live."

His detachment didn't last. When a series of crises hit the African continent, including the Rwandan genocide and the war in Sudan, Awuah began to feel compelled to do something to help. When his first child was born, this sense of duty only deepened. He needed to give back to Africa. "When I looked for the first time into my son's eyes," he says, "I realized I had been extremely arrogant to think that I had within me the power to disown a continent. Africa will matter to my children, to the way they see themselves; the way the world sees them." Even as he began rediscovering his Ghanaian and African roots, however, he struggled to discern his own role. "Like so many others who wish to create progress in Africa, I found that my first question was 'Where should I begin?'" he said in 2012.[1]

Awuah began by applying his liberal arts training—his ability to ask the right questions and his problem-solving skills—to study the continent as a whole. "I investigated local challenges—neighborhoods without water, high unemployment, swelling slums, dysfunctional hospitals. And for each problem, I asked myself, 'Why?'" he says. He soon realized that in addition to the struggles of emerging from centuries of colonial plundering, many of Africa's problems fit a pattern, one where "people in positions of responsibility . . . were neither fixing problems nor creating solutions." The answer? He envisioned a new kind of educational offering that could create Africa's future leaders. This new model would combine "elements of a traditional liberal arts college with world-class majors in business and technology," he says, and it would also fight corruption in Africa: each student would be required to take a four-year leadership seminar series dedicated to ethical formation and the greater good.

The Business Plan for the New University

With these convictions driving him forward, Awuah stepped away from his life at Microsoft to earn an MBA at Berkeley, a degree that would help him design a business plan for the new university. He began planning in 1998 with Marini. Their first step entailed conducting a feasibility study in Ghana. After they visited the country to gather research data to inform the business planning, Awuah set up an advisory group that engaged faculty from UC Berkeley, Swarthmore, and the University of Washington to help with curricular design. At the same time, Awuah and Marini worked with some of Berkeley's architecture students to come up with initial plans for the new campus. On Marini's telling, Awuah was "convinced of the power of a liberal arts education" because a liberal arts graduate knew how to problem solve: they became "a see-er of solutions as opposed to a see-er of just problems everywhere." This "big stark difference" was something Awuah had noticed in the evolution of his own thinking, compared with those who stayed in Ghana for their higher education.

Their initial approach considered Ashesi primarily as a business problem. They studied whether Ghana offered a sustainable marketplace for a liberal-arts-based college, and they worked to determine the best degree programs and price points for different majors. They also investigated whether a residential campus would be of interest to Ghanaian students and asked if graduates would be entering a viable marketplace: was anyone hiring what these future graduates might be offering? Since Ghana has high unemployment even among graduates of the best-rated universities in the country, this latter question was especially important. Marini and Awuah wanted their students to find jobs after graduation. They sensed a strong demand in Ghana for "a new type of higher education," one that would be "more analogous to parents sending their kids abroad to the U.S. or Europe typically, for a different price point." While such an elite education would not be in reach of most Ghanaians, having it available within the continent of Africa would open the possibility of more sustained impact, as Ashesi's graduates could remain within Africa to help solve problems and provide much-needed leadership.

Marini would ask groups of middle-school and high-school students to imagine this new university. She describes the excitement she would see on their faces when they considered the idea. She would hear from the students, "Can I go? When can I apply?"

It was really refreshing and inspiring. And it made it clear that this was a project that, even if it didn't work, we'd be trying to do something really important and very impactful. And that was just very enticing for me personally, and I think it underpinned the project with a sense of purpose that was really important in the trying years

The Ghanaian education system, as in much of Africa, was an outgrowth of the colonial period. The British introduced Christian missionary schools while they ruled Ghana, and European-style education expanded after Ghana achieved independence in 1957. Free and compulsory education in the country was not introduced until 1961, with English as the formal language. Compulsory education in Ghana through grade nine reaches 81 percent of Ghanaian children, a higher percentage than many sub-Saharan African countries, and one that produced a literacy rate of 71 percent among adults in 2010. Secondary education became tuition-free in 2017 but still reaches only a minority of students, primarily in urban areas. Only 29 percent of students attend secondary school in Ghana, and only 42 percent complete the last grade of middle school, according to 2018 data.[2] The Ghanaian education system lacks trained teachers, especially in rural areas where literacy rates are much lower, particularly among women and girls.[3] Despite consuming over 18 percent of all government funds (amounting to 4 percent of Ghana's GDP), the education system in Ghana desperately needs additional resources, as well as many more trained teachers and leaders. Awuah and Marini wondered if those new teachers could come from the ranks of Ashesi University's graduates.

Higher education in Ghana followed a comparable timeline and was launched under British rule in 1948 with the University of Ghana and in 1952 with the Kwame Nkrumah University of Science and Technology (KNUST). In succeeding decades, Ghana's higher-education landscape has rapidly expanded. The number of universities had risen from just three in 1990 to seventy in 2014, and the number of students studying at university in Ghana increased dramatically from 16,161 in 1980 to 440,000 in 2017. Despite this huge increase in capacity and student enrollments, the best students still typically choose to study abroad, a population that included 52,000 students in 2018, a 50 percent increase over 2012.[4] The public University of Ghana (with 38,000 students), KNUST (with 42,000 students), and the University of Cape Coast (with 75,000 students) stand among the most prominent institutions in the country, but none of these Ghanaian institutions were ranked among the top thousand world universities in the 2022

Times Higher Education World University Rankings.[5] Faced with sobering statistics, Awuah and Marini recognized that a new high-quality university within Ghana was urgently needed.

Building Social Capital for Ashesi

Awuah and Marini returned from Ghana and promptly began fundraising. They launched the Ashesi Foundation, seeking philanthropic support from former coworkers at Microsoft and from former Berkeley classmates. The timing for seeking major gifts seemed perfect: the tech sectors of Seattle and the Bay Area were in what Marini describes as the first "high-tech startup bubble," a hopeful moment in time where "there was just this sense that anything was feasible, a startup is not a big deal, you can make it happen," she says. Marini and Awuah pitched their idea to potential donors, focusing on the need to prepare students in Africa for high-paying and rewarding careers. Their pitch was less about the liberal arts and more about "hard skills" such as business, computer science, medicine, and engineering, Marini says. The goal was to create degree programs that landed graduates good jobs—meaningful and well paid—right away.

Marini's skills complemented Awuah's powers of persuasion. A native of Tokyo, Marini was a former financial analysist who had graduated from Haverford College with a degree in history. Her experience also included extensive public relations, complementing Awuah's training in economics, engineering, and business.[6] Awuah and Marini set up an office in Seattle to serve as headquarters for both the Ashesi Foundation and the new university. They hired Matthew Taggart to help with grant writing and fundraising. The office resided directly above a pub, the Red Door Ale House, which featured plentiful noise from live music and a strong smell of smoke. Awuah describes the colorful scene of those early days:

> Our office was right above the bar, and the Fremont neighborhood was a neat place to be. There was a lot of activity, human movement, and there were restaurants and cafes around us. It had this sort of this quirky energy in that neighborhood that we really loved. The second floor of the building had other startups. There were some software startups and an architecture company in that space. We had this little architectural design—a cardboard model of the campus—that we set up in our office, and it made for a great conversation starter when people would come visit our office. We loved this space except there was this one little detail

we had missed, which was that there was a lot of smoke, cigarette smoke coming up from the bar. We solved that problem by installing a HEPA air purifier.

This Seattle headquarters became the Ashesi equivalent of the Hewlett Packard garage—the legendary place where the magic first happened. Just as in the case of corporate start-ups like Hewlett Packard and Apple, such humble beginnings later have historic impacts, as the founders wrestle with the fundamental concepts of their new institution and set the tone for the new institutional culture. Awuah reminisces about those exhilarating early days:

> I do think about those days. It was really cool! We had this routine. There was a place we always went out to lunch, and they had the best cookies, so we always got these big chocolate chip cookies for lunch. It was the three of us, Nina, Matt and me, with this model saying we were going to build a university in Africa. It was this sort of curious project in that building.

Their project quickly attracted interest from others in the building. Visitors were struck by how unusual their group was. Awuah says they would notice that

> it's just three of you just going to go build a university in Ghana. None of us was a professor. We've been customers of universities when we were students, but we hadn't actually been involved with the business of a university either in an administrative capacity or on teaching or research, so it was a somewhat unlikely group to be planning this project.

Awuah, Marini, and Taggart, the first three members of Ashesi University, were not academics, but they knew where to find some. They recruited a research expert from Microsoft and twenty-four professors from top universities to help them plan. Awuah thinks of this strategy as bringing talent onto the team and building credibility. "Even though I wasn't myself a professor, I had some very capable minds working with me," he says. He brought his own business savvy and a resolve to "run this thing on sound financial principles," and he believed strongly that it was a sustainable venture. In numerous talks and interviews, he made a strong case for Ashesi, describing a university devoted to training leaders who, in turn, would help ignite an "African Renaissance." This movement would be propelled by a new generation of ethical and entrepreneurial changemakers.[7] He envisioned a world that "will be a different place for all people of African descent in . . . thirty, fifty years from now." Since at the time only 5 percent of college-aged students attended college in Ghana, even a small institution like Ashesi could have a powerful impact on the country. Those 5 percent could be placed in positions that would shape policies within Ghana's courts, hospitals, schools, and across the nation. And if they admitted students from across Africa, not from Ghana alone, they could see a similar multiplier effect across the continent, Awuah argued.[8] "When I think about an African Renaissance," Awuah clarifies:

> I really am thinking about an Africa that has emerged to be an equal partner in the world polity—so economically doing well, culturally doing well, an equal player on the world stage. I'm also thinking about an Africa that is more interconnected within itself, and an Africa where the young people on the continent feel a sense of pride and confidence.

His vision for Africa includes a future where "net migration is zero," and where Africa offers opportunities that "people from other parts of the world want to come to." In this scenario, African people possess "the same human rights, fundamental rights as you'd expect anywhere in the world."

Awuah and Marini made an effective team. Together, the duo's extensive network of connections in the tech world enabled their fundraising effort to pick up speed quickly. Many supporters gave money even though they were not fully convinced of the feasibility of the pair's plan. "Some of those same people told me that they thought this was a really crazy idea," Awuah says, "and that we'll support it because it's Patrick." One of his former professors at Berkeley warned, "It's going to cost you five times what you think it's going to cost." Awuah guessed the venture was going to cost around $2 million. The professor replied, "It's going to cost you $10 million." The professor proved to be correct.

Finding the Market for Liberal Arts in Africa

To gather more information about the market for the university, Marini and Awuah conducted surveys across Ghana from all potential stakeholders. Their targets included parents, representatives of industry, and officials from across Ghana. The team found clever ways to encourage participation by parents, who sometimes seemed wary of surveys. "We had the brilliant idea of hitting up the churches," says Marini. Pastors would pitch the survey to parishioners on Marini and Awuah's behalf, resulting in much higher completion rates. The research that Awuah and Marini conducted within Ghana gave them a data-driven basis for refining their plan. They wound up with 3,300 surveys; they conducted hundreds of focus groups and formal interviews, and they evaluated data from Ghana's Ministry of Education and the Ghana Statistical Service. They presented their collective findings in a feasibility study, which documented both the demand and the support for their proposed university from sectors across Ghana.[9]

Since the liberal arts were not commonly practiced or studied in Africa, the team avoided mentioning the phrase. They wanted to avoid misunderstandings: "What is this liberal arts thing? What are you really going to teach?" Marini received this question whenever the term came up in conversation. Confusion over the meaning of liberal arts also posed an obstacle to accreditation, as some accreditors thought that the liberal arts were "a waste of time if someone's going to be an engineer." But since nearly all Ghanaian focus groups agreed with the idea of "more options, quality education, stay in Ghana," the pair made this language a priority. Before Ashesi, students who wanted to pursue their education in Ghana had limited options, with most enrolling in education or business programs within the large public universities. Local universities also offered fewer opportunities for women, with men making up more than two-thirds of university students in Ghana. In addition, very few of the Ghanaian students train in advanced fields of science and engineering, and such expertise is much needed for the future development of the country.[10] Marini recalled the energy of Ghanaian focus groups, who had "a hunger and so much support for . . . better options, but more access too." The top universities in Ghana—such as the University of Ghana Legon and Kwame Kumasi University—were still able attract some of the best and the brightest students within the national system. But as Marini put it, students at these institutions "were trained to regurgitate, to memorize and regurgitate. And so they weren't prepared for the working world."

Validation for the Ashesi concept came from job recruiters within Ghana, who were struggling to find talented workers for industry. Marini describes them as saying, "Okay, I'm going to hire the more expensive talent and spend a year, a year and a half training them before I put them in front of a customer or have them work on any meaningful project." This seeming lack of preparedness for the industrial workforce meant that recruiters often considered any local talent to be untrained—and would often hire from abroad to save on training hours. It was shocking, Marini says, "just how much of a gap there was between the types of graduates that were being created versus what was needed." She and Awuah hoped Ashesi's proposed curriculum could help bridge this gap. The new university promised to use liberal arts approaches to develop so-called "soft skills," including communication, collaboration, and working with complexity. Ghanaian university graduates typically "didn't know how to deal with ambiguity," Awuah says. "Or they didn't know how to communicate powerfully and effectively, or they couldn't engage with people outside their fields very well."

Awuah and Marini came away from these months of planning even more convinced that Ashesi University was the right response at the right moment in Ghana's history. After meeting with leaders in industry, the military, and civil society, they felt the mission of the new university had been validated: Ashesi would prepare ethical leaders for Africa, equipped with professional skills and liberal arts approaches that encourage the kind of questioning Awuah discovered at Swarthmore. Yes, the leaders Awuah and Marini met with had discussed finance, engineering, medicine, and the professions, but they had also spoken about the need for ethics, the humanities, and the social sciences. Says Awuah: "In the minds of the leaders that we spoke with here, there is not a separation. There's not a disconnect. They need all of this."

From these discussions the team designed a curriculum based on professional majors but with a core curriculum in humanities, social sciences, math, and other liberal arts subjects—to be taught in a way that avoided rote memorization and repetition and encouraged thinking for oneself. This new Ashesi University curriculum would not be an African version of Swarthmore, but instead would remove the separation between professional skills and traditional liberal arts subjects.

Earning accreditation was a daunting and unexpected challenge for the unconventional new university. Ghana had created an accreditation board just one year after its return to democracy in 1993. By 1996 only a few private universities had been formed, largely traditional religious schools. Awuah had created the Ashesi Foundation in 1999 and worked simultaneously to build financial support and gain accreditation. He summarized the accreditation problem in a 2012 publication: "The board, following the prevailing African model, thought students should take classes only in their field of study, such as engineering or business, rather than 'waste' students' time with leadership seminars."[11]

Despite the team's Herculean efforts, disaster seemed unavoidable if the accrediting bodies could not recognize the value of liberal arts, or if, sensing some value in the approach, they nonetheless worked against it to prevent competition with existing Ghanaian universities. Marini described this tension as "an inherent conflict of interest . . . where they're evaluating potential new universities that would eventually be competitors." Members of the accreditation board included professors and administrators from established Ghanaian public universities, who resisted approving the new university.

The board created maddening and ever-growing obstacles to accreditation. "They wanted to see our physical facility," says Marini. "They wanted to see who was going to be on our faculty. . . . They wanted to see a library full of a certain number of books. They wanted a student-to-toilet ratio of a certain amount that you would never find in any of those public univer sities."[12] Lacking accreditation, Ashesi was not even allowed to advertise, and while its faculty and facilities were all ready for it to launch, it had to wait out the academic year of 2000–2001 until its accreditation had been formally approved.

Finally, in September 2001, the NAB gave Ashesi University permission to operate under the mentorship of the University of Cape Coast, and in March 2002, Ashesi University began instruction. The team worked quickly to offer their new curriculum, developed with their advisors from Swarthmore, Berkeley, and the University of Washington, and they launched with a strong financial base of support from the Ashesi Foundation.[13] Their assets began with a motivated and dedicated set of faculty and staff who worked from a few rented buildings to provide education to just thirty students. From these humble beginnings, an internationally recognized institution would emerge, one that would enroll over one thousand students by 2017, and which received a presidential charter from the president of Ghana in 2018, making Ashesi a fully independent university that can confer its own degrees.[14] Awuah's vision was finally becoming a reality.

Launching Ashesi's Campus and Curriculum

Though the initial years of the university were not easy, the energy and vision of the team and their start-up mentality forged in their early days above the tavern in Seattle kept them moving. Their business model was in development since 1998 and included several key components to reduce costs. These measures included removing majors, such as premedical studies, that would require expensive equipment and focusing on majors that would offer employment for graduates. Awuah offered $300,000 of his own money to get the project started, and his first business plan estimated they would need $8.5 million more to get the campus running. In the first year of operation, Ashesi's makeshift campus centered on a three-bedroom house that housed the admissions office, library (in one of the bedrooms), a computer lab, a classroom, a health center (in the garage) and a cafeteria, which was just enough space for the thirty students enrolled in the first year. The first year of operations included an annual tuition cost of $4,000, and the university had just a few faculty during the first three years, but had increased capacity to a hundred students per year by the end of three years. Donations were able to cover the start-up costs for the first three years, and the business model projected that increasing enrollments and tuition revenues would cover an increasing share of the expenses each year, with additional donations making it possible to eventually build a campus for the university.[15]

Despite a strong donor base in the United States, Ashesi did not break even financially until 2009, even facing a period between 2003 and 2004 when closure was a real possibility. A key landmark in Ashesi's growth and stability was the development of its new one-hundred-acre campus, inaugurated in August 2011. Located about an hour's drive away from the capital city of Accra, the campus today includes well-appointed classrooms as well as design labs, research labs, machine shops, workshops, and also a sports center, health center, and waste-treatment center.[16] One new building, known as the Hive, includes two cafeteria areas, student leadership offices, and also meeting rooms for student groups and even a campus radio station. Ashesi's health center played a key role during the HIV/AIDS pandemic by providing voluntary counselling and testing services in collaboration with Family Health International.[17] The new campus uses sustainable architecture, is partially powered using photovoltaics, and has systems to store and reuse rainwater. Similar to many American liberal arts universities, Ashesi also offers well-appointed residential housing to its over 1,200 students, with about 50 percent of the university's students living on campus.[18]

As Ashesi developed its footing and stride, its visibility across Ghana and Africa grew—and employers began noticing its students and its first graduates—building its reputation for quality. In 2005, the first "pioneer class" graduated, and 100 percent of them found job placements, with 90 percent staying in Africa.[19] This record was maintained in subsequent years, with 98 percent of the 2010 graduates receiving offers in four months, and over 90 percent receiving placements in the classes of 2012 and 2013 as well.[20] By 2021, Ashesi graduates had also received prestigious scholarships, like the Schwarzman Scholarship, and graduate school placements in top universities around the world. Currently, 18 percent of Ashesi students come from outside of Ghana, representing over twenty African countries, and the university plans on increasing this fraction to 30 percent, to expand its impact across the continent.[21] These positive outcomes have buoyed Ghanaians' impressions of both the humanities and the liberal arts. Awuah describes this transition to a more accepting mind-set of the university's educational mission: "Then as businesses hired people from Ashesi, they recognized that our students worked differently, and they asked us, what are you doing differently from other universities? . . . [W]e described that we were teaching the humanities differently, . . . the way it ought to be taught. In a way, we're sort of helping educate the market here about the power of a multidisciplinary education." Ashesi's positive reputation began attracting exchange students from the United States, many of whom were struck by the difference in courses from what they had previously experienced. Since 2015 Ashesi has operated an exchange program with the US-based College of Wooster. The program includes a faculty exchange component, and students from Ohio also regularly study in Ghana. One US exchange student described her Ashesi finance course as among the most useful she had taken in her college career, according to Awuah; she later landed a job at Goldman Sachs. Awuah believes that liberal arts programs around the world can learn from the innovations at Ashesi, which "embrace the full definition of the liberal arts around multidisciplinary learning" and tackle problems from multiple perspectives, including corporate and professional angles.

Students from abroad bring energy and new ideas to the equation, but in the two decades since its founding, Ashesi has specifically adapted its curriculum to better meet the needs of students within Africa. Students arrived with varying degrees of preparation in mathematics, prompting Awuah and the team to modify their first math course, calculus, to include topics in pre-calculus and algebra to help students shore up their skills. Another innovation involved developing a "focus course" based on interdisciplinary themes rooted in real-world issues within Ghana. One example is a course on cocoa as a focal point connecting students to the agricultural, economic, political, trade, and environmental issues surrounding the cocoa bean crop. Another example is a course on the automobile, which explores the economic, scientific, and environmental issues surrounding the vehicle and its supporting industries.

Ashesi's curriculum offers just six bachelor of science degree options through its four departments: Humanities and Social Sciences, Business Administration, Computer Science, and Engineering. Undergraduate BS degrees include business administration, management information systems, computer science, electrical and electronic engineering, computer engineering, and mechanical engineering. Regardless of major, all undergraduate students pursue a multidisciplinary core curriculum that, according to promotional materials, "develops critical thinking, creative problem solving, ethical reasoning, and effective communication skills." All students take courses offered across all four academic departments to broaden their perspectives.[22] Students engage this breadth of courses (also including mathematics, business, and computer science courses) to develop critical thinking skills, or, as the website declares, "to explore the connections between fields of knowledge, separate relevant information from the irrelevant, question assumptions, reflect on others' views, and navigate the world's most complex issues."[23]

The Ashesi required curriculum includes the courses "Giving Voice to Values," "Foundations of Design and Entrepreneurship," and "Text & Meaning," along with other communication and writing courses, an African studies elective, the signature Ashesi four-course leadership sequence, and more specialized courses in one of the six major fields. Cutting across Ashesi's four academic departments are eight learning goals: ethics and civic engagement, critical thinking, communication, leadership and teamwork, innovation and action, curiosity and skill, technological competence, and professionalism.[24] Ashesi also offers numerous experiential learning options, which "shape students with the drive to take risks, recognize the limitations of theory, critically analyze the complexity of every issue, and the humility to learn from and empathize with diverse and under-served communities." Student clubs, study-abroad opportunities, service learning, and entrepreneurial projects provide this hands-on learning that extends beyond the classroom. This unapologetic emphasis on leadership and grounded experience forms a distinctive component of Ashesi's liberal arts vision.[25]

Training Ethical Entrepreneurial Leaders for Africa

Ashesi's leadership-development curriculum didn't emerge in a vacuum. The leadership courses arose, in part, from an incident early in the institution's history involving elections for student-body leaders. Candidates for student government in Ghanaian universities were often males with highly charismatic personalities, but not always possessing genuine leadership abilities. After Ashesi's first student government election, Awuah set up a meeting with students to review their election process and their conceptions about leadership. He recalls this moment as "the first leadership seminar at Ashesi," one that enabled the university to become "more intentional and structured" in its leadership pedagogy. The final result was a set of four leadership seminars, which students all take as part of the core curriculum today.

Where is African history and culture in this curricular plan? All Ashesi students must take a set of courses in African studies to develop their understanding of Africa's past, present, and possible future, and to help them become leaders in Ghana and across the continent. As the university has evolved, more consideration has been paid to local knowledge and wisdom as well, including the stories of everyday people and elders within African communities. Accordingly, the curriculum now includes not only authors from Europe and around the world but also voices from Africa. The Ashesi curriculum is thus not simply one that has "de-colonized" but also one that supports "African futurism." Says Awuah: "We're imagining what we want Africa to look like, and we are structuring the curriculum to help us get there. Rather than looking at it with a kind of a negative lens, we're looking at it with a positive forward-looking lens, which makes the conversation a lot easier and gets everybody's buy-in." Awuah sees African futurism as requiring a combination of optimism, ambition, and humility. He urges a more confident African approach to education, one that engages in dialogue with an increasingly globalized world. "Anybody who says we should only have African content is exhibiting a lack of confidence in Africa, in my view," he says. The curriculum doesn't shy away from African content, however. "Ghanaian Popular Culture" and "African Philosophical Thought" both orient students to Africa's current realities. Joseph Oduro Frimpong, who has taught both courses, says they help students "take everyday experiences as sources of knowledge," so that they come away at the end of the semester understanding local sources of knowledge "as places of equal value to attain an intellectual breadth."

In his teaching, Frimpong highlights local African knowledge—such as the proverbs he learned from his own mother—as sources of wisdom and a cultural treasure. These insights, he says, extend beyond what he learned at Southern Illinois University, where he "was taught all the concepts in anthropology that did not mention the local experience." He contrasts his educational experience in the United States with the experience of his mother, who lacked a formal education, owned a pub, and spoke in proverbs that transformed her son's life over time. Frimpong asks his students to interview their own mothers and family members, and local people such as taxi drivers. In one assignment, he asked students to document taxi inscriptions, a particularly fascinating facet of Ghanaian popular culture: "On the back of these vehicles, a lot of them have some kind of inscription or some kind of statement. Sometimes they are talking about their enemies. Sometimes they're talking about . . . inspiring stuff." Frimpong asked his students to interview taxi drivers about the meaning of these inscriptions, which might include maxims, sometimes with grammatical errors: "No food for lazy man." "If you don't do hard work, then you don't eat." "Hope never lost." He tells his students, "Don't focus on the grammar, or else you lose the bigger picture," urging them to concentrate on the stories that motivated these drivers to write their various inscriptions.

What's the payoff? Frimpong wants his students to realize that these drivers are highly competent, highly thoughtful individuals in their own right, or "highly critical people that process information and then arrive at a sort of conclusion." That process and its eventual outcome, he says, is a form of local wisdom, warranting respect and critical attention.

Now that Ashesi University has passed its twentieth birthday, the institution has reached a certain level of maturity. It has received overwhelmingly positive coverage by the media for its new model of liberal arts education. In 2019, Ashesi was the only private university in Ghana included in the *Times Higher Education* University Impact Ratings, and it also ranked among the world's top 301+ universities. The ranking data report cites Ashesi's strengths as including the categories of "Quality Education, Gender Equality, Reduced Inequalities, and Partnership," and commends the university for advancing the UN Sustainable Development Goals.[26] The business mentality that Marini and Awuah have brought to the new university appears to have paid off, at least according to Marini: "The business mentality served us well, especially in the early years, because we knew we didn't know everything we needed to know. And so we really embraced input and advice and involvement from others. . . . [W]e didn't have any pedagogical ideology that was like, 'It has to be this way.'" As with any innovative start-up, Awuah would remind the team that "there's always more to do." He has challenged his colleagues to fight off the tendency toward complacency. Marini, too, feels that this constant drive and propensity to push forward is embedded in the culture of the staff and faculty.

As Ashesi transitions from a start-up to a more seasoned university, it will need to navigate past its initial founding vision and founding leadership toward the next generation. "Founder syndrome" describes a common problem that start-ups face: the inability to make that transition toward new leadership after an intense period of launch and early implementation. "It takes a very visionary person to be able to do something like this," says Marini. That dominant leader can at times make it difficult or seemingly unnecessary for others to step into the leadership pipeline—and Ashesi has not been immune to this challenge. Building the capacity for succession and for distributed leadership thus depends heavily on institutional culture, which in the case of Ashesi has had over two decades to develop—with an explicit emphasis on training leaders for Africa's future, and hopefully for Ashesi's future as well.

The Ashesi University Culture

Today, Ashesi University, perhaps more than many universities, is more than a curriculum, a campus, or a group of faculty and students. Awuah and his team have worked to build a community and a culture that blends the diverse cultures of business and academia—and of the United States and Ghana. Awuah characterizes this culture as imbued with "a very deep sense of ethics and integrity and trust." Initially shepherded by faculty and administrators, this culture now belongs to the students as well, who have taken ownership of it—a good development, says Awuah. "If the students don't own it, then we failed," he adds. Planning conversations, town-hall meetings, retreats, and other community events have helped strengthen this communal approach to culture. Of central importance is the university's student-implemented honor system, a code of conduct unique among Ghanaian institutions and the first within Africa.[27] University statements praise the honor code as "a significant step in Ashesi's mission to educate a new generation of ethical leaders in Africa." Student led and student enforced, the code is depicted as key to a durable culture of trust on campus.[28]

A related element of the Ashesi University culture is gender equity. In a departure from other universities in Ghana, Ashesi has placed a priority on recruiting female students since its inception. After only 25 percent of the applications for the first class were women, Awuah tasked the admissions team to "make sure that we got the number of women applicants to rise over time" and required annual targets. Currently, Ashesi enrolls 46 percent female students, and its number of female faculty has grown from 25 percent to approximately 40 percent today. Awuah is proud to point to this gender equity and notes that 55–60 percent of his board members are women. In addition, women compose 50 percent of his executive team.[29]

The representation of women at all levels in the organization, even in male-dominated fields like engineering, has translated into more empowerment and a culture of true gender equity. Says Marini: "I think it really sets the tone. It sets a tone for the culture. And I think it got established pretty early on. Our first dean of academics was a woman with an incredible background. And so she was our most senior leader, the most experienced leader on campus with a very inspiring presence." Students also embody the spirit of gender equity, and Awuah rejoiced when in 2006 the student council elected the first female president of a student council in any university in Ghana. Female students are "just right there with their male counterparts in terms of stepping up as leaders and feeling like they have a voice," he says.

One example of Ashesi's commitment to women leaders can be found in the appointment of the university's current provost, Angela Owusa Ansah. Ansah's education mirrors the global mindset of the Asheshi University education. She was educated in Ghana for her BA in psychology and then received advanced degrees in Spain, the United States, and the United Kingdom, fulfilling a residency at Oxford University. She brings a new approach in her leadership, and will no doubt greatly extend the teaching and research capabilities of the Ashesi faculty, as she has extensive experience working with faculty at Elon University and is a strong advocate for applying the scholarship of teaching and learning to improve student learning.

Ashesi is able to leverage its unique cultural richness to help students celebrate the many cultures of Africa. Special events in the campus dining halls alternate between East African and South African food, and Ashesi has developed a new matriculation ceremony as well, where students all wear their traditional attire. Another Ashesi event known as the *kalangu* aims to bring students together and expand their sense of equity. *Kalangu* is a Swahili and East African word that means "talking drums." But the word also conveys a deeper cultural meaning that celebrates communication, community, and belonging.

Ashesi's faculty embody an important component of this broader culture of diversity, and come from many different African countries, often with different educational systems. As Marcia Clark, former provost of Ashesi, wrote in a recent piece, "over the years, the faculty of Ashesi found the university or the university found the faculty." By 2016, Ashesi had twenty-six full-time faculty, which included twenty from Ghana, and ten part-time faculty, all of whom were Ghanaian. Many of the faculty had studied in the United States as undergraduates, and about half of them did their graduate work there.[30] Ashesi works to bring the community of students and faculty together as a learning community that can have the capacity for substantive impact on Africa. Examples include making progress on the World Health Organization's Sustainable Development Goals, which are intrinsically interdisciplinary. By 2021, Ashesi was able to document specific projects advancing over a dozen of the SDGs, which includes workshops by Ashesi faculty for Ghanaian youth to help spur economic growth in rural Ghana, helping to improve fertilizers and developing new organic fruit production to boost agriculture in the region, developing new biomedical devices to monitor cancer and help improve testing of malaria vaccines, offering STEM teaching workshops for Ghanaian teachers, and many other projects.[31]

The Future of Africa and Ashesi University

Looking forward, both Ashesi University and Africa face daunting challenges and vast opportunities, especially in the face of the COVID-19 pandemic. Awuah notes that the lack of vaccines in Africa is indicative of the larger problems facing the continent. "If Africa or many African countries had developed the vaccines and were producing their own vaccines, we wouldn't even be having this conversation," he says. "The conversation would be, where are the vaccines most needed? Where are they most being produced?" Rather than just providing vaccines for Africa, Awuah believes a better way would be to engage African countries with internal capabilities for developing new vaccines:

> If you're going to invest in health in Africa, would you invest in a research institute in the global north to come up with vaccines and other things for tropical diseases and send them to tropical countries? Or would you go and strengthen institutions and develop the people and the leadership in those countries to develop their own vaccines and treatments for tropical diseases? I would say the second, the latter, is more truly global than the former.

As Ashesi plans for its future, it is navigating what Marini refers to as a "tension between staying in motion yet staying in one place." The curriculum remains focused on ethics and good leadership amid the overarching challenge of finding solutions for the continent. The university's forward motion includes its major partnerships with top universities around the world like ETH Zurich (the Swiss Federal Institute of Technology), and Arizona State University, who want to be part of a new global community centered on Africa. Awuah explains his vision for truly mutual partnerships with universities from both the Global North and Africa, describing a "community of practice where we're sharing equally with each other, where we've softened the borders between our institutions."

From these partnerships, which are known collectively as the Education Collaborative, Ashesi leaders hope to build a collaborative research community, fostering linkages among liberal arts education, the employment sector, and the advancement of larger social goals. According to Awuah, this community will help establish a ranking or measuring system for key metrics, including job placement, gender parity and gender balance, campus safety, and research outputs. The measurements could also assess how Ashesi and other universities advance sustainable development goals, helping universities hold themselves accountable.

Ashesi's successes to date might suggest that the university should grow larger and scale up its offerings. But Marini believes the success of Ashesi arises from its modest scale, which enables it to produce a small number of highly influential graduates while serving as a model for higher education in Africa. "It would've been easy for us to get pulled into a scale mentality," she says. "But Patrick was pretty clear like, 'Our scale comes through the long-term impact of all of our graduates over time.'" Despite Ashesi's burgeoning reputation and strong demand for its graduates, Marini and Awuah plan to maintain Ashesi's small and personalized size to foster student leadership and a shared sense of community.

Ashesi maintains a goal that at least 20 percent of its graduates develop new start-up companies to provide employment for Ghanaians. This goal is helped by a host of entrepreneurship programs, which include D:Lab, Ashesi's design lab; community entrepreneurship courses; the Ashesi Startup-Launchpad; and the Ashesi Venture Incubator, which helps Ashesi alumni incubate new companies. Ashesi graduates are proving Marini's statement that "a Ghanaian can go do a high-tech startup." Examples of start-ups from Ashesi graduates include Nubian VR, which develops virtual reality content for Ghanaian schools, and a company called Cyst, which uses AI to help make mobile payments. Ashesi students have also won international competitions based on student ideas for new products, including a futuristic hair braiding device, a prototype baby incubator and crib, and a cost-effective cocoa-pod-breaking machine design.[32]

Ashesi is building alliances with other small colleges such as those in the Global Liberal Arts Alliance, which includes twenty-eight universities centered on the US-based Great Lakes Colleges Association, to collectively redefine best practices within undergraduate education. One example was the 2016 faculty development workshop at Ashesi University, which brought together faculty and administrators from the College of Wooster with their counterparts from Ashesi to discuss how to build undergraduate research programs and effective mentorship for undergraduates. From such collaborations, like-minded institutions can work together to foster innovation, entrepreneurship, and quality education. Marini hopes the example that Ashesi is setting will encourage new people to enter the higher-education market and create new institutions. Perhaps there could be "multiple Ashesis in different countries," she says

Ashesi University, now reaching its "adulthood" as a start-up university, might be considered in some ways to be a rather conventional type of institution if it were in the United States or Europe. But Ashesi is revolutionary in what it offers for students in Ghana. The Ashesi team had to overcome innumerable obstacles as they built and launched their university, facing resistance from within Ghana. Active resistance came from existing Ghanaian higher-education institutions and accreditation procedures, and the lack of familiarity in Ghana with liberal arts made the task even more daunting. Despite long odds, the team at Ashesi simultaneously listened to a broad array of stakeholders, which included parents, the government, employers, and community leaders. Through such careful research, Ashesi was able to improve its messaging and its mission, while also educating these diverse stakeholders in Ghana about the power of a liberal arts education. In just a few years, the Ashesi team was able to create, launch, and develop to maturity a vibrant, functioning, well-managed liberal arts campus that innovates in many different ways. Ashesi's emphasis on developing a new generation of entrepreneurial and ethical leaders for Africa inspired its leaders to develop entirely new levels of student leadership and empowerment, student autonomy, student ownership of the honor code, and many other aspects of university operation.

The goal of Ashesi to help develop a new African Renaissance and allow African countries to fully enter the global stage and take their place alongside other wealthier nations as equals has not yet been realized. But Ashesi is only twenty years old, and it has so far offered a continuous stream of graduates who are beginning to make impacts within Ghana and across Africa. Ashesi in many ways embodies a Swarthmore type of education adjusted for the needs and culture of Ghana with great promise for impact in the coming decades across the entire continent of Africa. However, Ashesi also has not yet managed the transition away from its initial founding president and visionary, Patrick Awuah. Managing this transition and connecting more broadly with other higher-education institutions within Africa and beyond will mark the next stage of Ashesi's development and will help Ashesi and many countries of Africa reach a new stage of maturity and leadership.

9

A Global Solution, African Born

AFRICAN LEADERSHIP UNIVERSITY

When Fred Swaniker was four years old, a military coup forced his family to flee from his native Ghana for Gambia. Four years later, when a new coup erupted in Gambia, his family had to walk through the night to find a safe house. He then spent the next decade growing up in Botswana and attending high school in Zimbabwe. His father died when he was sixteen and living in a mining town in Botswana, where his mother had been asked to start a school. There were already two expensive private schools in the town, staffed by European teachers and serving mostly expats and those who worked for the mine. The new school was meant to be an affordable one for people from the town.

When Swaniker finished high school, his mother said to him, "Okay, this is going to be your gap year experience," and made him the headmaster. "So for a year I ran this school, I taught the classes, I managed the teachers, and I'd go home in the afternoon, she would give me coaching about what to do the next day," he says. That was his first experience in educational entrepreneurship as a powerful force for transformation.

His mother also taught him other lessons. She used only African teachers and focused on instilling values as well as facts and figures. She was willing to think about what needed to be done differently in an African context, rather than copying models that came from the West. "My mother went off the beaten path," Swaniker says. "And so, I saw what can happen if you dare to be different, and to actually just listen and say, 'What actually are the needs of the society, and how do I design for those needs?' versus just coming with a preconceived notion of what's going to work."

After just three years in operation, his mother's school beat the other two schools in the national exams. Two years later, it outdid every single school in the country—and went on to do so for the next twenty years. "I learned a lot from that experience of how to build education institutions of excellence with limited resources and in creative ways," says Swaniker. "My mother invested in what really matters in education, which is great faculty, great students, and a great curriculum. And if you have those three things, you can put them under a tree, and you'll have a great school."

Growing up in multiple countries on the African continent infused a Pan-African perspective in Swaniker. Everywhere he went, he experienced the beauty of the region and witnessed the people's resilience and spirit. He saw countries with solid infrastructure and great education, like Botswana. On television, he saw Nelson Mandela's refusal to leave jail until apartheid came to an end. He also carried in his memory the failures of governance in Ghana, Gambia, and elsewhere on the continent. Zimbabwe had seemed like a model for economic development until it, too, fell apart, under the corrupt rule of Robert Mugabe. He started thinking about what it was really going to take to unlock Africa's potential, asking what these different countries shared in common.

As he reflected on the root cause of these problems, Swaniker always came back to one thing: leadership. "When institutions are weak," he says, "leadership makes or breaks the success of a country." He began thinking about educational institutions as crucibles for the development of future leaders, not as ends in themselves. And if you begin with that premise, you have to ask yourself, as Swaniker says: "What would you do differently to maximize the probability that leaders come out of this institution?"

After his gap year, Swaniker left Botswana to attend Macalester College in Minnesota, where he felt a strong sense of community. He soaked up the idea of school as a place that nurtures individuals and helps them form relationships and explore who they are. At the same time, he was disturbed to find that students who studied computer science, economics, and business were seen as selling out and students who studied whatever they wanted without regard to finding a job thought of themselves as superior. Education, he concluded, needed to move beyond this divide between learning for learning's sake and learning to get a job. It ought to develop practical skills and tap into a young person's motivation to pursue their deepest passion. He was also shocked by the expense and inefficiency of a system in which a four-year degree included less than two years of actual instruction, and where the physical plant sat inactive for five months every year: "I got two years of education from going to Macalester for a four-year degree," he says.

Following a stint working for the consulting firm McKinsey and Company in South Africa, Swaniker enrolled in the Graduate School of Business at Stanford. The classes were fine, but what really inspired him was the spirit of innovation and entrepreneurship:

> There's Yahoo and there's Google and Cisco and all these companies, and every person on campus was thinking about the next startup. One thing I noticed is that there's nothing different about the air or the water in Silicon Valley. It tastes just the same as in Africa. The only difference is that they take a sixteen-year-old kid with an idea seriously, and then next thing that becomes Apple, it becomes Google, it becomes Yahoo.

Over the next two decades, Swaniker converted his dreams of educational entrepreneurship into reality. He and his partners raised almost $800 million and launched an independent high school in South Africa, established two university campuses in Mauritius and Rwanda and regional hubs across the continent, and started a short-course career-accelerator program and a global employee recruitment and outsourcing entity. If that makes your head spin, here's a simpler description: Swaniker and his colleagues built a transcontinental web of interlocking companies and nonprofits with a university at the core. In 2019, *Fast Company* named African Leadership University (ALU) one of the most innovative organizations in the world, and CNN declared it to be the "Harvard of Africa".[1]

From Academy to University

Swaniker and several partners began by launching the African Leadership Academy (ALA) in South Africa. The new institution offered seats to students from across the continent to complete their final two years of high school. In 2008, its first year of full-time operation, the ALA received one thousand seven hundred applications and enrolled ninety-six students. The school quickly exceeded Swaniker's boldest expectations as the acceptance rate demonstrated strong demand. Soon, however, the limits of the project became apparent: the new high school could serve only a tiny fraction of the more than twenty thousand students who were by then applying. What's more, 80 percent of ALA graduates would leave Africa upon graduation to study in the United States and Europe, thus contributing to a brain drain from Africa. That wasn't why Swaniker had started his school. He wanted all those gifted young people to begin stepping into leadership roles right at home.[2]

The African employment landscape has been changing rapidly, with its young, dynamic, and entrepreneurial population seeking opportunities in education and business. Africa's working-age population has the highest rate of entrepreneurship in the world (22 percent), stretching from 9 percent in Algeria to around 40 percent in Nigeria and Zambia. In many countries, annual economic growth rates are ticking upwards and poverty rates are declining. In 2013, Macky Sall, president of Senegal, told an audience at Harvard that Africa is "the continent of the future," owing to its abundant natural resources, burgeoning workforce, and enterprising spirit. Africa is rich in mineral reserves and has roughly 8 to 12 percent of the world's oil and natural gas reserves, respectively.

Swaniker calls Africa either a ticking time bomb or an immeasurable talent pool, depending upon how quickly and efficiently the human capital of the continent is developed. By 2035, Africa is projected to have the largest workforce in the world, yet in sub-Saharan Africa nearly 60 percent of those aged fifteen to seventeen are not enrolled in school. At the same time, only two African universities have reached the top 250 of worldwide college rankings, and both are located in South Africa. The real and perceived uneven quality of African degrees drives African students to foreign destinations in huge numbers.[3]

Swaniker vowed to counter this trend by building world-class universities in Africa—institutions so strong and reputable that the best talent did not have to leave the continent. But how? What would it take to build a campus, hire a faculty, and fund the entire enterprise? "As we started doing it, there were so many things that led me to realize that we need to do this in a very unconventional way, if we're going to be able to pull it off," he says.

A key insight came from the ALA students. In a required course on entrepreneurial leadership, they absorbed how to take the initiative and to continually push themselves to learn and grow. Meanwhile, in a computer science course down the hall, students took charge of their course to teach one another advanced concepts. Sidee Dlamini, a founding member of ALU, recalls the number of times Swaniker shared this generative moment with the team. Students taking an online Udacity course called "How to Build a Search Engine" began meeting three times a week to pause the asynchronous lecture and work though knotty problems together. A student from Morocco later told Swaniker that this computer science course was her favorite: "Fred's like, 'What? Isn't that the class that doesn't have the teacher?'" says Dlamini, who grew up in Swaziland and would go on to earn a master's in development economics from UC Berkeley in 2015. "And she was like, 'Yeah, but we've been teaching each other. And I know how to code and I program now. Because we had to do it ourselves and use Google, we figured a lot out.'" That was a light-bulb moment for Swaniker. A peer-to-peer learning philosophy was the path to a financially viable and scalable program.

Once that big idea took hold, there was no looking back. In a 2014 TED Talk, Swaniker described his vision to establish twenty-five university campuses across the continent that would educate three million new leaders in Africa by 2035. The proposed African Leadership University attracted millions of dollars of start-up capital from Silicon Valley investors such as the Omidyar Network and individual donors. Swaniker's initial plan to establish the university in South Africa quickly went awry. A university for the entire continent would require students and staff from outside the country and obtaining South African entry visas was almost impossible. This limitation meant he would have to look elsewhere to build his first university. "We were not building another university for South Africa," says Dlamini. "We're building a Pan-African university. So, it's important for us to be in a location that was welcoming to people from across Africa."

Swaniker and his team turned their sights to Mauritius. In contrast to South Africa, Mauritius made it easy to do business across the continent, allowing students from Africa and staff and faculty from all over the world to enter the country without visas. The new campus was also able to partner with Glasgow Caledonian University to offer UK-accredited degrees. In the fall of 2015, ALU welcomed its first cohort of students from twenty-three countries; another 120 joined in January. In these early days, students lived in hotels and took a bus to a business park for classes and meetings. They could see a large crane in the middle of a nearby sugarcane field where the residential campus would be built. Once the campus was ready for use, students found classrooms named in honor of leading Africans, including UN secretary-general Boutros Boutros-Ghali, Ethiopian runner Haile Gebrselassie, and South African writer Bessie Head. Axum, Kongo, and Songhai dormitories represent notable African civilizations.[4]

ALU moved to launch its second campus soon after, in Rwanda. The Rwandan government offered strong support and provided ten hectares of land in Kigali's Innovation City (KIC), which serves as a hub bringing together technology companies, incubators, and universities. KIC is at the heart of President Paul Kagame's "Smart Rwanda" strategy to make the country a player in the knowledge-based economy by investing in broadband infrastructure and educational initiatives that emphasize digital skills.[5] ALU is joined by a second university, Carnegie Mellon University Africa, and construction has begun on the University of Rwanda Centre for Biomedical Engineering and E-health. "We expect a spike in demand for more digital solutions, both in government and the private sector," says Tesi Rusagara, managing director at KIC. "The ecosystem being built in Rwanda . . . will be critical in driving the creation, adoption and scaling up of tech-enabled solutions . . . across Africa."[6]

In 2016, ALU began its operations in Rwanda by opening its new School of Business, which offered a twenty-month Africa-centered MBA program for executives and rising professionals. Soon afterwards, in the fall of 2017, ALU Rwanda enrolled its first 270 undergraduate students. The Rwandan campus also hosts ALU's School of Wildlife Conservation, which offers undergraduate and graduate programs. By 2019, the Rwanda campus had grown to over 800 undergraduate students and 105 in the business school. A nonresidential university complex was built in 2020, a 70,000-square-foot building of pale tan brick that spills down the rolling Rwandan terrain. The complex was designed to reflect the university's disdain for large lecture halls in favor of smaller classrooms and work spaces that facilitate peer and self-paced learning.[7]

By 2021, ALU had attracted a diverse cohort of students from over forty countries in Africa. One thousand seven hundred students were enrolled at ALU, three-quarters of them in Rwanda and one-quarter in Mauritius. Women account for over 55 percent of enrolled students. And whereas the ALA costs $30,000 per high-school student in South Africa, the total cost of attendance for ALU in Mauritius hovers around $16,000 annually—and even less at the Kigali campus, which charges $12,000. Still, most students are on scholarships and there is still a large unmet need for affordable education across a region that is bursting with talent and has an intense desire for change.

Turning a University on Its Head

For Swaniker, Dlamini, and other early members of the ALU team, traditional university education methods had become irrelevant, inefficient, and insufficiently attentive to teaching practical skills and igniting passion. Universities had become stuck on content transmission in an era where information was easily accessible almost anywhere, they argued. The monopoly on knowledge that universities once held was based on information scarcity: in past generations, obtaining key facts or data required going to the university, to the library, or to the professor. Today, in contrast, a child in rural Africa can access more information on their mobile phone than was available to someone who was doing a PhD at Oxford thirty years ago. Yet universities were still behaving as if they constituted the sole sources of knowledge available.

Swaniker likes to ask his audiences, "How many of us remember specific things we learned in college or graduate school?" Rather than content, he says that what most students remember are the relationships they forged and the specific skills they got a chance to practice. The ALU designers set out to translate this relationship- and skills-based vision into a curriculum. The curriculum designers surveyed 150 companies in different parts of the world to identify the skills they found were missing when students arrive at work from college. The designers mapped seven overarching skills, which they grouped into four categories—how to think, how to be, how to do, and how to learn—and broke down further into 135 specific learning outcomes. During their first year at ALU, students take core classes to develop what the university calls twenty-first-century meta-skills:

- **Leading others:** empathy, diversity, relationship building, feedback, collaboration
- **Leading self:** self-awareness, proactivity, lifelong values, self-improvement, self-regulation
- **Entrepreneurial thinking:** system thinking, identifying opportunities, human-centered thinking, creativity and innovation, continuous iteration
- **Critical thinking:** authentic inquiry, evidence/research analysis, arguments and judgments, synthesis
- **Quantitative reasoning:** data contextualization, uncertainty and modeling of the real world, empirical research, data-based decision-making, quantitative problem-solving
- **Communication for impact:** audience, writing process, voice, organizing for effective communication, storytelling, presentation
- **Managing complex tasks:** scoping, structuring, planning, coordination, execution

This core encompasses traditional skills often seen at other universities, such as critical thinking and quantitative reasoning. It also focuses on applied skills, including entrepreneurship, complex-task management, and telling compelling stories for different audiences. Each one of these concepts is broken down into specific subcomponents, such as understanding how a complex system works and how to prototype, iterate, and validate practical interventions in the system. The ALU curriculum also places a distinctive emphasis on the personal traits students need to manage themselves and lead others. In and out of the classroom, students learn about discipline, relationship building, and collaboration. Character-building habits and self-awareness are constantly discussed and nurtured at ALU. The required common core aims to build individual students' self-confidence, their sense of efficacy, and their belief that through discipline and passion they can shape their own future. Faculty and staff continually urge students to "do hard things," a message reinforced in the university's social media as #dohardthings.[8]

The student experience is based on a four-part learning cycle: discovering what you don't know and what you need to learn, individually learning at your own pace and in your own way, peer learning from those who have learned it and can explain it to you, and facilitated group learning where you can apply and extend your learning to other contexts. For the first part of the learning cycle, the core course helps students realize gaps in their learning, which they can address through the rest of their time at ALU. Students can take courses online and work on assignments at their own pace. Peer learning is a core component of ALU's pedagogy, and students learn some of the challenges of working together with others through various collaborative projects. Faculty also facilitate discussion sessions with students. Small class sizes enable close interactions with faculty members. As students are pursuing their interests, they meet on a regular basis with the faculty, where they receive mentoring and are held accountable to the plans that they develop.

Alongside other foundational courses, a course in entrepreneurial leadership introduces students to what has come to be called "human-centered design thinking," which developed in the 1960s in the United States at the intersection of work in the design, management, and engineering fields. In the course, students use the BUILD (believe, understand, invent, listen, deliver) model to assess and address a particular African problem; their final task is to construct a business model for starting a company to address the challenge. Another of the core courses of the foundation year at ALU enables students to work on a specific project with a social enterprise or business partner that ALU has identified. The course "is aimed at helping students manage complex tasks in an organized manner, hone their project management skills and affords them the opportunity to develop their inter-personal skills by working in teams." In class, students learn the content they need to tackle their project and faculty advise them on how to produce a final product. Students then work in teams and complete specific tasks such as convening stakeholders or developing solutions. The project thus combines critical thinking and research along with organizational skills and a real-time experience.[9]

In comparison to the staid programs for new students at traditional uni-versities, students at ALU are energized by their first-year leadership core. Wassa Cisse, a student from the Ivory Coast, describes how being at ALU fired her imagination and belief in herself. She met presidents, prime min-isters, "and those you always see in the TV, but you could never be close to. But I was close to them and I had a picture with them. I could shake their hand. And then we are like, yes, now we are probably equal or this is where we will be." Francophone West Africa, she says, doesn't pay enough atten-tion to wildlife conservation, which is her focus of study, "so I see myself as leading by example. I believe that we need young people, young women, bright people motivated and ready to do the job. And that's me in five words." Another student, Mimi Mutoni from Rwanda, says simply: "one of the things that I admire most about some of our current students is that they don't wait for opportunities to come their way, they take it upon themselves."[10]

From the second year on, students curate more specialized and self-directed in-person and online courses, engage in peer learning, take on indi-vidual and group projects, and complete an internship. One required course in the second year focuses on African history, politics, society, and culture. It draws on the humanities, social sciences, and the arts in order to provide a context for students to think and act in the African context. Taken together, the required courses and individual, group, and experiential learning are all part of what ALU calls "a mission, not a major." Faculty and staff encourage students to join their personal quest for achievement based on self-mastery to a purpose bigger than themselves—a mission that comes from tackling a complex and critical problem. Students are introduced to seven grand chal-lenges, which are global in nature and have specific resonance in the African context: urbanization, education, infrastructure, health care, climate change, governance, and job creation. Commensurate with ALU's can-do philosophy, students are also exposed to a set of grand opportunities in areas ranging from natural resources to culture and design. Frank Muhire, a student from Rwanda, describes his mission as getting companies to achieve "greener, smarter, and fairer results. Having a mission is very crucial because sometimes you get distracted and sometimes you tend to think that you don't have a direction," he says. "A mission has helped me to see the small, tiny things that I do every single day, how they feed into the bigger picture."[11]

ALU has fundamentally reconceived the nature and purpose of the traditional departmental major. Brian Rosenberg, former president of Macalester College and an advisor to ALU, describes the traditional structure as a holdover that "is done this way because it has been done this way. In reality, there is no compelling reason for a student to 'major' in English unless the student plans to pursue a graduate degree in English—these days, neither a common nor a wise choice."[12] ALU's reimagining of a major as a mission is instead rooted in the belief that knowledge is more cross-functional and that learning does not come primarily from classroom experience. ALU's approach turns the traditional model on its head and is rooted in a 70:20:10 rule of learning: 70 percent of learning comes from doing; 20 percent from relationships with mentors, coaches, and peers; and 10 percent from the classroom.[13] "We learn best by doing," Swaniker says simply. "Yet today most education focuses on that 10 percent—the classroom experience. We wanted to give them the full 100 percent."

Far more than a traditional university, ALU places a premium on student responsibility, independence, and initiative. "Here you will find no silent temple to books and knowledge," reports the journalist Aryn Baker: "In fact, the university's Pure Learning Library has no books at all. Instead, there's a cacophonous din of competing ideas, as students convene in animated groups around communal tables, shouting out solutions while feverishly diagramming them on the whiteboards that panel the walls." Jeremah Nnandi, a second-year computer-science student from Nigeria, told Baker: "We aren't really encouraged to be quiet here. We believe that the best way to learn is from our colleagues. Regurgitating the stuff you memorized from books just to pass an exam isn't really going to solve Africa's problems, is it?"[14]

And the results? ALU students struggle to adjust to a primarily self-directed education and peer-learning pedagogy. Many come from traditional high schools in which rote memorization and testing are the primary means of education. "We always go through a period where they all want to kill us for this model," says Dlamini. "They hate it. They're protesting against it. And then at some point, they get it." Even after students adjust, it remains to be seen whether the intense focus on learning by doing provides sufficient content and coherence. Can students truly curate the depth of knowledge they need and connect individual courses into a larger arc? This question is especially the case when students are learning from prerecorded massive open online courses (MOOCs), the limits of which have become apparent in recent years.

ALU's educational model also requires a radically different role for faculty, who become more facilitators than experts. This role demands a shift in identity as well as pedagogy: faculty have to recognize that they are not the most important part of the process. Faculty who have specific areas of academic expertise are, in Swaniker's experience, too often focused on transmitting what they know and insufficiently attentive to lighting a fire in students to learn on their own. In practice, this orientation means that many faculty at ALU are practitioners with industry experience, rather than traditional PhDs, of whom there are relatively few available in Africa and who add significantly to the university's cost structure. Utilizing so many such practitioners is a significant departure from traditional hiring practice and a key to scaling the university by keeping costs low; it is both a necessity and an intentional design feature. Yet are academically trained faculty more central than ALU initially recognized for providing high-quality instruction and for helping students to construct a coherent learning journey? Perhaps so. As the model evolved, faculty hiring shifted toward a more even mix between practitioners and those with academic backgrounds. The practitioners tend to teach more in the first-year program, while instructors with master's degrees and PhDs teach upper-division courses in the program, so that specific areas of content and analytical skills complement more practical knowledge.

Making It Safe to Innovate

Like a force of gravity, university stakeholders exerted pressures on the novel institution to conform to an easily recognized model. If new ventures like ALU want to succeed in their mission, they need rocket engines to counteract those forces. These engines have to help students, parents, faculty, accreditors, donors, and others remember that their institution is different by design. To this end, ALU leaders created a shield—an external perception of normality—that protected their ability to innovate. "Sometimes you have to play the game that exists in order to play the game you want," says Swaniker. "What we've done is essentially use a Trojan horse approach, where we had to be a bit more conventional in the beginning."

What did this shield look like? First, ALU offered a traditional-looking campus despite the nontraditional learning model. Students can picture themselves sitting on the grass outside the classrooms and moving into dorms with friends. This effect is powerful, even for institutions like ALU where students do not spend all their time on campus. Second, because "missions, not majors" is hardly a reassuring program to accreditors or parents, ALU started out by offering conventional-sounding degrees in business, social science, and computing. Over time, regulators in Rwanda worked with ALU to approve a BA in something slightly less conventional—global challenges—and in Mauritius ALU obtained approval for a BS in entrepreneurial leadership. In both countries ALU offered the leadership major as the primary degree, with a carve-out for a separate degree in one field, software engineering, where it recognizes a need for greater specialization. Over time, employers and parents appear to have become sufficiently comfortable with the notion of a bachelor of science degree in leadership that prepares students for work in many different sectors. The strategy has been to translate core offerings that fit the institution's goals into language that others can understand and embrace.

Finally, ALU leaders recognized that they needed to demonstrate student success using conventional metrics. An impressive 85 percent of graduates find jobs within six months, according to the university, compared with what it says is five years for college graduates in Kenya. And 95 percent of job placements are in Africa, including at leading global firms like KPMG (Kenya), Bain (Nigeria), Dalberg (Ethiopia), Pernod Ricard (South Africa), Cellulant (Kenya), and PWC (Ghana). Around 5% of students find employment outside of Africa, especially in the United Kingdom (Facebook, Goldman Sachs, Bank of America Merrill Lynch), as well as France, Estonia, and Lebanon. A hundred new ventures have been launched by 135 graduates; drawing from data for thirty-eight of those start-ups, ALU says that its alumni have created over ten thousand jobs and that, on average, an ALU entrepreneur creates eleven jobs.[15]

To date, twenty-five students have enrolled in graduate studies in the United States, the United Kingdom, Europe, China, and South Africa. These students are attending MBA and master's programs at schools such as Stanford, Harvard, the London Business School and Sciences Po; and they are enrolling in PhD programs at the University of Edinburgh, the University of Cape Town, and the University of Massachusetts, Amherst. Students have also received fellowships for postgraduate study, such as Melissa Kariuki from Kenya and Arinze Obiezue from Nigeria, both of whom won a highly competitive scholarship to attend Schwarzman College at Tsinghua University in China. In between graduating from ALU and taking up her scholarship, Kariuki had been working as a product manager at Google;

Obiezue worked as a content designer at Meta (previously Facebook).[16] Swaniker is proud of the reputation the university is building. "One of the main things people are buying when they go to college is the stamp," he says. "I went to X, Y, Z. So we also need to make sure that we build a brand and students can feel good about themselves. These are some of the things that we do to counter the force of gravity. But I can tell you, it's not easy. It keeps trying to pull us back."

To resist that gravitational pull, ALU consciously sees itself more as an entrepreneurial start-up than a traditional university. Its leaders do not sound like most higher-education leaders; instead, they speak about building a product, product management, and customer and user experience. "We really treat our institutions like they are tech companies, innovative tech companies," says Dlamini. "We say we work for higher education, but it's never felt like it. I truly felt like I work in Silicon Valley." Practices that reflect this Silicon Valley culture include ALU's use of Slack, Asana, and other technology tools more often associated with start-up companies than with universities.

The university's hiring process borrows heavily from Google's talent acquisition strategies, with hiring officers focused on finding employees who are aligned with ALU's values and beliefs. This commitment to mission-based hiring began in the first days of institutional planning, when Swaniker handpicked every member of his team. He found Dlamini in New York, another member in Palo Alto, and a third in Ghana. He was willing to turn away applicants who might look good on paper and came from the right universities but seemed more interested in a conventional approach. Too much experience within higher education encouraged too traditional a mind-set, he found. Instead, he looked for people from outside the sector who would question everything.

At ALU, the largely youthful employees are given permission to brainstorm, to test, to fail, and to keep trying. "I had so much permission to do anything and everything," says Dlamani. "And it was okay. I worked through the weekend because it was fun. Eighty-hour weeks were not grueling. We just dare to be audacious. Every target we set is ridiculous. It's always ridiculous, but it just brings out the challenge." At the same time, Swaniker studied the way that top-performing companies like the Four Seasons Hotel infused a shared culture and common practices across its multiple holdings. Like the Four Seasons, as ALA gave birth to ALU in Mauritius, and then in turn to ALU in Rwanda, employees from the older institution were sent to populate the newer one to ensure consistent replication.

Discontent and the Emergence of the
African Leadership Experience

Despite the attention given to organizational culture at ALU, conflicts emerged in its early years. The founding team had formed a tight unit, but to succeed the institution had to scale up fast, and doing so meant that these founding members had to let others contribute to the building process. Ceding responsibilities and decisions wasn't easy for everyone, and there were some tense moments. At one point, the article "'Give Away Your Legos' and Other Commandments for Scaling Startups" became required reading across the organization.[17]

Conflict also escalated when the university had to attract fee-paying students, after a first year in which students all received scholarships. For some ALU staff, the very idea of requiring fees went against a fundamental principle of the new university—to provide an education at low or no cost to African students. This conflict reflected the flip side of recruiting leaders and instructors who are committed to a certain set of beliefs. Policy changes become sources of tension, not just over how to make a change but about whether certain changes violated core tenets of the organization.

This dynamic became most apparent in a debate over what it meant to be an African institution. ALU's leadership thought that it doesn't matter where an idea comes from if it works. "African means simply African born," says Dlamini. "A global solution that is African born." By contrast, some administrators and faculty thought it was paramount that ALU be built by Africans for Africans. In their minds, it was crucial not to mimic or adopt any policies or practices that smacked of a Western way of thinking or acting. They criticized the core curriculum and the focus on lifelong learning skills as being too American.

ALU also faced existential questions over its very survival. Educating a few thousand students every year on expensive campuses would not achieve the goal of training three million leaders by 2035. Despite scaling up the Rwandan enrollment to five times the size of the original Mauritius campus, a move that drove tuition down to $12,000 annually, ALU's tuition price is still far out of reach on a continent where the median annual university cost is $2,600 and the majority of people earn $3 a day. (The university experimented with an income-share system where students would pay back a percentage of what they earned after graduation. While repayment rates were high, ALU soon found itself on a poor public-relations path to becoming the largest income-share-agreement provider in the world at a time when such agreements were being vocally criticized as little more than indentured servitude.) To meet its goals, ALU could not afford to be expensive. Traditional campus models often depended so heavily on donors to provide financial aid that they couldn't be looked to as viable examples. Neither campus could persist with its current enrollment, let alone grow, as the actual tuition and fees paid by students accounted for just 11 percent of the operating budget.

Facing these questions meant the entire ALU community had to rethink its model: If the goal was to create leaders, a traditional set of small-scale universities would not suffice. The original vision was not sustainable. This conclusion led to significant turmoil and staff turnover. Three academics who made up the social sciences department all resigned; eventually, ALU dismissed nearly half of its staff. Internal critics of the shift saw it as a betrayal of the institution's commitment to the highest quality of education, unrelated to a student's ability to pay. A former staff member criticized the move as being "too manifestly corporate" and having "lost the essence" of ALU. She characterized that essence as "dialogue, debate, and knowledge creation and exploration, with Africa—and not only corporate Africa—always at the core. Those possibilities have really diminished in the new context."[18]

In the wake of this upheaval, a new strategy gradually emerged that prioritized flexibility and modularity. One immediate move was the creation of the new African Leadership Experience (ALX), a career accelerator program that dispensed with physical campuses and formal accreditation and relied even more heavily on peer-to-peer learning than on traditional faculty-led instruction. ALX set up shop in Nairobi in 2018 and targeted eighteen- to twenty-eight-year-olds who had graduated from traditional universities and/ or had some work experience but sought additional training. ALX distills the core leadership-development programs offered at ALA and ALU into a low-cost, modular program. In 2019, program leaders raised $30 million in a private equity investment led by a Danish retail billionaire to expand beyond Nairobi and build a series of lifelong learning centers, starting with Johannesburg, Lagos, Cape Town, and Casablanca.[19] (This investment comes with a personal dimension: Swaniker's name is Danish and he is descended from the last Danish governor of Ghana.)[20] ALX's program offerings range from four weeks to twelve months and include job readiness, financial and data analysis, entrepreneurship, cloud development and cloud engineering, and software engineering. Remarkably, since 2021, ALX has expanded its presence from three countries to more than forty, and it has gone from training fifty software engineers to training fifty thousand.[21]

In an unusual move that reflected the continuing turmoil at ALU and ALX, Swaniker posted an article on LinkedIn entitled: "Five Reasons Why You Should NOT Work at ALX."[22] These reasons capture the key elements of a model that began as a humble in-person high school academy and was now seeking to compete on a global stage as both a university and a career accelerator:

1. **"You don't want to scale."** Citing business examples from Emirates Airlines and Apple to Google and Four Seasons Hotels, the article declares: "We believe that organizations that scale well actually enhance their quality as they scale. Quality gets better, not worse, with size."
2. **"You want to build something conventional,"** meaning a model focused on faculty and disciplinary majors rather than peer-learning and mission-driven majors.
3. **"You think 'revenue' is a dirty word."** To drive impact, and to not rely on governments or donors, ALX has to invent a new business model.
4. **"You want a 'safe bet.'"** "We are a community that would rather fail trying to achieve something extraordinary than succeed at something ordinary. There is no easy way to say this: There is a chance that what we are doing could fail."
5. **"You don't want to build something global."** "While we are proud of our African roots, we see ourselves as a global innovation born in Africa."

If any of these features of ALX trouble the applicant—if the "mindset freaks you out"—then ALX is probably not the right place for you, Swaniker writes. "We've had many phases of misalignment," says Dlamini. "We still have, it's like every year and half, we come back to it: 'Guys, this is the vision. This is how we're going to do it. If you're misaligned, let's have a conversation because we need to move with people who are aligned.'"

Excellence at Scale—ALU 2.0 and The Room

The global pandemic played a key role in the evolution of ALU as it embraced aspects of the ALX model. The pandemic forced ALU to take a closer look at its cost structure and to recognize that most of the university's expenses were not directly related to learning. These costs came in the form of housing, food, and travel to campus several times a year. ALU leaders decided to pivot from this fully residential program model. In its newest iteration,

ALU is reimagining itself in a distributed residency model, where students come to Mauritius or Rwanda only for several months at the beginning of their first year. After that, they return to their homes, where ALU is building regional hubs. These hubs do not have permanent faculty but are essentially coworking spaces with internet access, electricity, and, they hope, a sense of community and student life.[23]

This structure leans even more strenuously into the peer-learning model of education and will test its resiliency. Students who begin with a traditional, campus-based experience and then transition to far more independent learning in regional hubs will need to be even more self-directed than earlier ALU graduates. They will be learning in and out of the classroom from a wider array of instructors and sources than ever before. Where will the commitment to doing hard things come from, absent a vibrant community of peers and teachers who share a common campus?

It may be, however, that the regional model will better situate students to believe in themselves and the importance of their mission. In the original model, students would spend three to four years in Mauritius or Rwanda, where they would study global challenges such as urbanization. But after studying in Mauritius, where traffic and sanitation problems are few and far between, students would return unprepared for the scale and complexity of these issues in a city like Lagos. By way of contrast, in the new, distributed ALU model, a student will be embedded in Lagos or other sites for three years and immersed in the community, completing internships with problem-solving organizations and starting to prototype solutions. In year one, students will launch their experience by spending one term on campus, one term in a Pan-African or an international hub, and one term in an internship. In year two, they will personalize their learning journey by spending two terms in a hub and one term in an internship; in year three, they will do the same. And as part of year three, students complete a capstone project that integrates their three years of learning and doing.[24]

Building from this new model, ALU projects enrollment to grow significantly—from two thousand to twenty thousand students in five years—and the price to drop dramatically to $2,000–3,000 annually. This would be an astonishing accomplishment. With the benefit of scale, the university will move from collecting roughly $3 million in student fees to approximately $40 million annually, a growth trajectory that, along with significant fundraising and control over expenditure, could make the institution both more sustainable and more accessible. This shift also entails a fundamental transformation in the type of student that ALU seeks to recruit. The campus-based model was organized around African students who already constituted something of a global elite in their academic preparation and ability to pay some portion of tuition and fees. The new model seeks to recruit from a much larger market of students, what ALU calls the "rising middle class," the members of which will require an even more significantly reduced price than ALU Rwanda.[25]

If it works, it could be game changing for everyone involved. The hope is that this model will leverage visiting faculty from the world's great universities and from leading companies, experts in their fields willing to spend a month in residence at a hub and offer workshops. These visitors will not be formally compensated but will work as a way to travel and contribute to Africa's development. They will not be the only teachers, of course: the model also has its own paid faculty, as well as additional courses delivered by faculty on Coursera, edX, Udemy, and other platforms. Swaniker wants students to find "those two great courses from Stanford, those two great ones from MIT, those two great ones from Harvard and Oxford, and curate them in one place—online, as related to your mission that you're pursuing." In doing so, he expects that costs will go down and the student experience will be enriched.

Swaniker argues that the United States has figured out how to offer high-quality education better than anyone—but only for the very few and at a cost that is unsustainable. The United States has also figured out how to do education at scale, but often with low quality. As much as ALU and ALX have been fundamentally shaped by Swaniker's education at Macalester and Stanford, he explicitly refuses to copy a model he sees as flawed, even doomed. "If you have a high-quality product," he says, "you should assess your quality and your effectiveness by how many people you touch with that high quality product, because you're here to transform society. And so, we are choosing to be different, in saying, 'We actually believe that you can now do high quality and scale.'"

This strategy embodies his view that ALU is building a leadership model in Africa that will then spread all over the world, including to the United States. Thus, as much as ALU has adopted and adapted many core principles and practices from the West, its ambition goes beyond changing education and leadership training in Africa. Swaniker likens what ALU is doing in education to what happened when mobile phones first emerged on the scene. The core technology didn't come from Africa, but many subsequent innovations happened faster in Africa, where inertia and the status quo had less of a hold and where there was a stark necessity to drive down costs.[26] Says Swaniker: "In Africa, we have a clean slate, and we're using that clean slate to innovate and build a new model of higher education. But it's not just a model for Africa, it is a model that's globally relevant and we are going to take it to scale globally."

In December 2021, ALU announced the next step in meeting its global ambitions: setting up regional hubs in the United States, one in New York City and one in Silicon Valley near Stanford. The hubs will bring students from across Africa and across the United States to learn together in the ALU style. The Silicon Valley hub is a collaboration with the venerable Carnegie Foundation for the Advancement of Teaching, and it aims to bring together students from underrepresented communities in the United States with their African counterparts to create a pipeline into jobs in technology and financial services. "The African Leadership University has established a new standard for postsecondary education," says Carnegie president Timothy Knowles. "The program is rigorous, affordable, experiential, career aligned, and scalable. Most important, it develops ethical, entrepreneurial leaders, dedicated to addressing the world's most complex and important challenges."[27]

In December 2021, Swaniker added yet another element to the ALA, ALU, and ALX ecosystem: a global talent-matching solution called "The Room." The new offering aims to connect students and workers to in-demand technical careers in Africa, Latin America, North America, and Europe. The plan is to start in Africa but ultimately build a global community of ten to twenty million members in fields ranging from software engineering and cloud computing to product management and cybersecurity. For job seekers, The Room will offer mentorships, network building, and learning opportunities. For companies, The Room will identify, cultivate, and offer access to talent in pockets of the world that have typically been untapped. Programming will feature virtual services coupled with in-person talks, conferences, pitch festivals, ideas summits, lifelong learning workshops, problem-solving sessions, performances, and communal meals.[28]

Audacity and Risk-Taking

The sheer audacity of what Swaniker and his colleagues have achieved is remarkable. The ALA in South Africa is a beacon for high-school students across the continent. ALU in Mauritius and Rwanda has produced strong student results at a fraction of the cost of a traditional university. These new institutions have placed student agency at the core of their educational model in a way far beyond most other institutions that claim to be "student-centric." Equally impressive, both ALA and ALU have undergone a series of leadership transitions, with new leaders emerging from within and from outside the organizations.[29]

This loosely confederated ecosystem of schools and companies has raised almost $800 million in support. This figure would be astonishing in the United States and it is simply astronomical in Africa. The traditional ALU campuses in Mauritius and Rwanda have received almost $100 million, and current projections call for ALU to invest another $100 million to achieve sustainability over the next five years. ALU's largest partner is the Mastercard Foundation, along with hundreds of philanthropists and foundations who are committed to taking the long view of social change. Recent grants seek to supercharge the network over an eight-year period. To achieve sustainability over those eight years, the business model has had to evolve—sometimes dramatically. ALX initially sought to drive upfront student costs down by offering a subscription model in which students pay a flat-rate fee to a talent agency that provides mentoring and coaching. This approach proved to be a nightmare to administer, even as it created a debt-collector relationship with students, and so it was scrapped. The financial approach at ALX and The Room has developed into a business-to-business model in which companies pay subscription and placement fees; The Room is also looking to tap into the outsourcing market.[30]

Yet the speed and evolution of the educational and financial models raise some fundamental questions. The most critical is whether quality can be offered at scale in education as it can be for hotels. Has the new ALU pushed its academic-content-lite model too far, leaving students to cobble together an education from MOOCs and other forms of online learning that are too disconnected? In recent years, students across the globe have experienced the limitations of learning from prerecorded courses, which can promote passivity rather than engagement and may not be connected coherently. As much as ALU's first-year program on campus offers a fresh take and energizes students, the risk remains that the key skills absorbed in that year remain disconnected from sufficient mastery of necessary content. Can students receive a meaningful education in a university whose library doesn't have books? So, too, it remains to be demonstrated that ALU's expanded roles for mentors, coaches, and visiting faculty can be fully realized in ways that provide consistent instruction and deep learning. Are academically trained faculty more central than ALU currently allows? All of these questions take on additional force when applied to the regional-hub strategy, which will need to find substitutes for the intense community environment of a traditional college campus, which offers critical support for students as they find their way.

As other university leaders do, Swaniker points toward the success of ALU's initial graduating classes as proof that what he's doing is working. Even more, he asks: What's the alternative in the African context, where just to catch up to India's level of enrollment in higher education would take building over a hundred universities every year for fifteen years? Swaniker and his colleagues are betting on establishing deep relationships between instructors and students and among peers, pushing students to direct their own learning, and—most profoundly—instilling in students a fundamental belief in themselves and their ability to move mountains. Taken together, they see these features as both absolutely necessary for students in Africa and as a rebuke to the highly choreographed education in which students at most universities simply have to show up for rehearsal. Seen this way, ALU is not a low-quality online university but a distributed university that intentionally includes only 10 percent of in-class time because the primary forms of learning are with peers and mentors and in the field doing research or shadowing professionals.

Still, Swaniker and the other ALU leaders have themselves identified quality control as a central concern. Its strategy to mitigate this risk is to partner with Amazon Web Services to build a system for tracking student outcomes and identifying interventions to ensure that students graduate and succeed in finding meaningful work. As the ecosystem scales, other challenges will grow alongside it: more students will need access to reliable electricity, internet, and coworking space. Adequate human support structures are especially needed, as students will now spend most of their time outside of a traditional campus and community. The regional hubs will succeed or fail to the degree that they can approximate the intensity that students feel when going through the same experience on a shared campus.[31]

Looming over the entire enterprise is the question of financial sustainability. Cost estimates for the entire African Leadership set of initiatives project that more than $3 billion will be needed over the next decade. A lot rides on the bet that a network of nonprofit schools and for-profit companies can secure sufficient philanthropy, scale access and drive costs down, and tap into a huge recruitment and outsourcing services market. Yet the African Leadership's principals have a clear-eyed vision of the challenges and the possibilities that lie ahead. No one has figured out how to create thirty million jobs in a decade in Africa. How the network achieves results will almost certainly change over time and will require equal measures of audacity and steadfastness.

10

Critical Wisdom for the Sake of the World

MINERVA UNIVERSITY

Ben Nelson paced the hallways of Harvard Business School. After nine months of trying, in 2011 he had landed a thirty-minute meeting with Larry Summers, former president of Harvard University. The meeting was to take place between 6:30 and 7:00 p.m., and Nelson didn't know at which of four different entrances to the building he was supposed to meet Summers. Finally, at 6:48, Summers burst through from one of the hallway doors and asked, "Why are we meeting?"

Nelson launched into his pitch. He proposed a new kind of university, one that would change higher education by revolutionizing the entire teaching enterprise. Minerva's curriculum would focus on cognitive skills that transcended traditional academic fields. It would emphasize the ability to transfer concepts from one field to another and apply them in new and unfamiliar settings. Minerva's pedagogy—or how faculty teach these concepts—would draw on research that showed how students learn much more from applying their new knowledge in the classroom rather than simply receiving information through lectures.

Minerva's location would be simultaneously everywhere and nowhere. The university would deliver its courses through a state-of-the-art online technology that promised to reduce costs by 60 percent. This technology platform would allow students to take up residence in global cities over the course of four years. (At the program's launch, Berlin, Buenos Aires, Hyderabad, London, San Francisco, Seoul, and Taipei were selected.) The reduced costs would further allow Minerva to expand its educational reach by admitting its entire student body without regard to socioeconomic status or national origin: this new university would be global both in its teaching locations and in its students' diverse countries of origin.[1]

Nelson's proposal struck a chord with Summers, who seized on the idea that this vision could solve a significant problem with higher education: how to bring an Ivy-League-quality education to students who deserve such an opportunity but, because they are not American, rarely receive such a chance. He told Nelson that he would chair an advisory board to support the new institution.

Summers's offer provided the validation that Nelson needed. At that point, he had no funding, no faculty or staff, no accreditation, and no technology—"not a single line of code." Most crucially, Nelson lacked what he saw as the most fundamental ingredient to bring his vision to life: prestige. "Minerva was a figment of my imagination," he says. And every time he talked to potential supporters, they told him his ideas would never work. He set out to prove the naysayers wrong.

Brand and Specs

Nelson has the energy of a charismatic reformer devoted to a messianic cause. He weaves a narrative that is one part educational philosophy, one part data, and one part sheer audacity—and his vision elicits both deep devotion from audiences hungry for change and deep doubt from some faculty and journalists.[2] Tom Vander Ark, the first executive director of the Bill & Melinda Gates Foundation, described his first meeting with Nelson in 2014: "It's those moments—when, with animation and passion, an edupreneur describes an ambitious plan to change the world . . . that I smile and think to myself, 'that will never happen.' But with Ben . . . I immediately knew that the vision was entirely possible and that he actually had a shot at pulling it off." By contrast, Chris Peterson in the MIT Admissions Office speculated in 2012 that "Ben Nelson, Wharton grad and former M&A consultant, has realized that . . . [he] can load his comparatively under leveraged international students with loans that will return an appreciable rate to his investors."[3]

Before founding Minerva, Nelson had no previous work experience in higher education. After stints in various corporate settings, he served as chief financial officer and then president of Snapfish, an online photo-hosting and printing service acquired by HP in 2005. His meeting in the Harvard Business School hallway with Summers was set in motion by a piece of advice he'd received from Silicon Valley iconoclast Peter Thiel. "You have a nice plan," Thiel said. "You want to build the best brand in higher education, which fundamentally means that you're going to have the best students. But in order to attract the best students, you have to have the best brand. You haven't explained to me how you're going to crack that chicken and egg problem."

This question led Nelson to seek the brand prestige of Harvard's president. He understood that in contrast to the world of commerce, the currency of higher education is status, not money. New entrants in this market can't simply succeed by improving efficiency because no one actually knows what is being purchased: college is a veritable black box of research, education, coming-of-age experiences, athletics, and, ultimately, reputation. As former George Washington University president Stephen Trachtenberg memorably put it, "College is like vodka"—a flavorless beverage that people will spend more on if it comes with a brand name because that name signals something about the buyer, not about the product.[4]

For Nelson, current brands in higher education were old and tired, and if you looked under the hood the specs were terrible. Stanford, Harvard, and all their followers had become ossified around preserving their exclusivity:

> Stanford and Harvard have become diploma mills. They're not certifying education, since it's virtually impossible to get a C, much less flunk out. What they're certifying is a pre-existing condition, which is: Are you rich? Despite all their yammering about inclusivity, what they're really celebrating is providing a tiny bit more access to an exclusive club because exclusivity based on wealth is what they have ossified around. And that kind of ossification is a major inhibitor to innovation.

Nelson wanted to upend this entire model. He planned to focus on outcomes—engaged learners who apply their knowledge in the real world in ways that everyone can see matter. He set out to ignore the exclusivity the market currently wanted and base his model on what he thought the market *should* want.

In thinking about how to go about this project, Nelson found himself drawing lessons not from another university but from Tesla, a Silicon Valley company. Tesla backed up its audacious claim to build the world's greatest car by focusing on efficiency, acceleration, power, and distinctive touches like a huge navigation and control screen. Similarly, Nelson wanted to tie the Minerva brand to the specs, to a curriculum and teaching strategies that produce superior results. These specs, he hypothesized, would redefine what counted as prestigious. At the same time, he would aggressively highlight the failures of traditional universities to actually improve learning. This strategy paid off in enormous media coverage, including an *Atlantic Monthly* cover story that positioned the launch of Minerva University as "The Future of College." In a neat bit of ju-jitsu, observers asked whether this upstart, yet-to-be-built university could displace the Ivy League, not whether it could compete with a private liberal arts college or a public university.[5]

The specific strategy was twofold: selectivity and data to measure what students learn. One, Minerva would utilize a few external signals of quality and prestige—its student selectivity that wasn't dependent on wealth (today, fewer than 2 percent of applicants are admitted) and its ability to attract brand-name academic leaders (Larry Summers, as well as Minerva's founding dean and the architect of its curriculum Stephen Kosslyn, who had been the dean of social sciences at Harvard). Nelson also recruited high-profile political and educational leaders like Bob Kerrey, the former senator, governor, and president of the New School, who was also deeply involved in launching Fulbright University Vietnam, who became Minerva University's board chair. Two, Minerva would then relentlessly focus on the promise of more and better data about what students actually learn. Social proof plus academic proof would establish the Minerva brand as a high-quality, prestigious institution that was inventing the future of higher education.

Financing and Accreditation

Nelson had a theory of change and the support of the president of the best brand in American education, Harvard. But in 2012 he still lacked financial backers. "My history with venture firms was that they'd say: 'You're crazy,' and laugh me out of the room," he remembers. It took a while before he could capture his vision in a concise and compelling pitch. There were so many moving parts to his plan, and higher education was famously resistant to change.

Eventually, he found the right group in Benchmark Capital, a storied venture firm whose investments include Silicon Valley darlings like eBay, Uber, and Twitter. Each of its six partners listened to Nelson's pitch independently; one partner, Kevin Harvey, leaned especially hard into the idea, and the firm committed to fund Nelson's entire $25 million ask. "I have never had a chance to back a venture with a mission so strongly epitomizing our own of enabling great entrepreneurs to change the world for the better," said Harvey. "That's why our partnership agreed to committing the largest seed investment in our history."[6] In two successive rounds in 2017 and 2019, investors would commit funds that increased the total support by another $128.5 million. Key supporters included the TAL Education Group, a K-12 after-school tutoring service in China, and Bytedance, the Chinese technology company behind TikTok. Both investors said that they saw in Minerva's teaching and technology a recipe for making a high-quality education available to a vastly expanded number of students globally.[7] (In 2022, Bytedance donated its stock in the company to the university in support of its nonprofit educational mission; its founder remains on the university's board.)

The idea to leverage private investment was straightforward, if unorthodox: to overcome the barrier to entry posed by a lack of state support or a private endowment, venture capital funding could be used to launch the university. The new university would be established as a nonprofit, tax-exempt educational institution and be governed by an independent board in which investors would be in the minority. Minerva University's board members include a prestigious mix of scholars, including Randy Schekman, who shared the 2013 Nobel Prize for Medicine; Bertil Andersson, president emeritus of Nanyang Technological University; and Wendell Pritchett, the former provost at the University of Pennsylvania and chancellor of Rutgers University-Camden—as well as ed tech thinkers and doers, including Michael Horn, Stacy Childress, and Diane Tavenner.

Initial start-up support would come through a for-profit entity, called Minerva Project, which would own the intellectual property developed for Minerva University and could, if the university succeeded, pursue ways to monetize it. "You needed a for-profit organization that understood how to develop valuable intellectual property, technology, business methodologies, a brand, a go to market capability," says Nelson, and you "needed a nonprofit that would be the showcase." The relationship between Minerva Project and Minerva University is a novel one, and questions often arise about it. The university and the company have separate and noninterlocking boards. The project owns the intellectual property developed in building the university, and new materials the university develops are jointly owned if the project does not pay for their creation. The university's academic leadership controls its curriculum and the university's board approves new programs.[8]

Leveraging others' prestige as social proof—check. Focusing relentlessly on quality that can be demonstrated—check (at least in principle). Financing to launch immediately—check. Still, in higher education, even a combination of prestige, quality, and funding is not sufficient to launch a new venture. One last hurdle facing Minerva was how to win accreditation by the regional governing body, the Western Association of Schools and Colleges (WASC). Without accreditation, a new university cannot attract well-qualified students and faculty. If most venture funders had laughed at his plan, WASC's leaders told Nelson that he was trying to do the impossible. No one could launch an accredited institution on day one: the existing process required an institution to graduate its first class before being reviewed for accreditation. They suggested that he hire a consultant to develop a plan.

As it happened, Teri Cannon, who had just stepped down as the executive vice president at WASC, had read about Benchmark's investment; Nelson's vision of a selective, global, and highly effective teaching institution "just spoke to me," she says. A lawyer by training, Cannon knew that WASC was actively looking for ways to maintain quality oversight while enabling new entrants into the education market. She arranged for a meeting with the presidents of the Claremont Colleges, a distinctive arrangement of seven colleges who share a campus neighborhood in Claremont, California. Two schools expressed interest in learning more: Pomona College, a highly ranked and respected liberal arts school, and the Keck Graduate Institute (KGI), which focused on graduate programs in life and health sciences, engineering, pharmacy, and genetics.

Cannon, Kerrey, and the Minerva leadership team met with the president and other leaders at Pomona, who had a lot of doubts about the proposed venture. Why should they lend their institutional prestige and hard-won status as one of the top-flight teaching institutions to an upstart Silicon Valley guy with an undergraduate business degree? "I remember this vividly," says Bob Kerrey. "They had four pages of single-spaced questions that made clear they didn't want to partner with us." The experience underscored what Kerrey knew from his time as a university president, but Nelson had yet to experience so directly: knowing you want to change the curriculum and changing the curriculum at an existing college or university are two different things. "It's very, very difficult," says Kerrey, "and I'm sympathetic. Change is hard and can involve a lot of political trauma."

The meeting with the KGI went much better. KGI was younger than the liberal arts colleges in the Claremont consortium and had an entrepreneurial bent. It had no existing undergraduate faculty who might voice reluctance to participate in such a novel venture. In discussions with its president, Shelly Schuster, an agreement was forged in which KGI would use its existing accreditation to incubate Minerva. KGI would provide oversight, and tuition dollars would flow through KGI on the way to Minerva. Remarkably, KGI did not ask Minerva to pay anything for this arrangement. "It was a real partnership with a meeting of the minds and shared values," says Cannon, "and the idea of active learning and innovation really appealed to KGI."

Minerva now had a willing partner and went back to WASC to seek its blessing. Kerrey sensed that the decision could go either way. "It seemed from the questions that about half of the commission were afraid we were going to fail and about half of them were afraid we were going to succeed," he says. Kerrey understood the Commission's hesitation. This meeting took place at a time when most of the new players in higher education were for-profit online entities growing at an incredible pace and leaving in their wake high dropout and poor completion rates. Minerva was swimming upstream, and WASC needed a reason to approve such a new and risky venture. A politician skilled at reading the room, Kerrey called on WASC not to lean so heavily into its role as gatekeeper that it kept out new players trying to accomplish some good. "To their credit, WASC was looking for a way to be innovative and they trusted us," he says. "They took a chance and approved the new arrangement."

Critical Wisdom and Curricular Structure

Despite Minerva's focus on technology and learning outcomes, its core vision revolves around a more traditional notion of higher education and its purpose. Nelson took his cue from two of his former professors, the historian Lee Benson and the political scientist Ira Harkavy, who had taught a seminar on the history of higher education at the University of Pennsylvania. Benson and Harkavy were early leaders of applied, community-based research for undergraduates. They traced this interest back to the founding principles of American universities, including the writings of Benjamin Franklin and Thomas Jefferson, and, later, John Dewey and others. Franklin and Jefferson had understood education as preparing citizens to govern in a republican form of government. That capability meant being able to draw on different fields of knowledge to make wise decisions. What Franklin and Jefferson called "practical" or "useful" knowledge, Minerva calls "practical knowl-edge" and distinguishes it both from a narrowly vocational form of train-ing and from the pursuit of knowledge purely for its own sake. Nelson staked his claim on precisely this notion. Minerva's Latin motto, *Sapienta critica*, means "critical wisdom," to which Nelson adds "for the sake of the world." The premise is that systematic thinking enables learners to look at novel problems they've never encountered before and know what to do in response—and this preparedness is the true definition of wisdom.[9]

As much as Nelson revered Franklin and Jefferson, he and Kosslyn both believed that modern education must also be rooted in the sophisticated understanding of how students learn that has emerged over the last thirty years in cognitive, developmental, and educational psychology, a field known as the science of learning. Ironically, for all faculty invest in mastering their individual disciplines, few employ key principles about how students retain and apply what they are being taught. "It would be difficult to design an educational model more at odds with the findings of current research about human cognition than the one being used today at most colleges and universities," writes Diane Halpern, a professor at Claremont McKenna College, and Milton Hakel, a professor at Bowling Green State University.[10]

These twin sources—a traditional focus on preparation for citizenship in a republic and a modern emphasis on the science of learning—informed Minerva's commitment to a highly structured curriculum in which general education, majors, and electives are tightly linked. At Minerva, the curriculum (rather than the individual course) forms the fundamental unit by which an education should be structured. All courses are tied together by a set of key habits of mind (cognitive skills that come to be triggered automatically) and foundational concepts (fundamental knowledge that is broadly applicable), which are collectively known as Habits and Concepts, or HCs. Each HC receives a specific hashtag designation, which enables students and faculty to track their progress over time. Examples include #biasidentification (identify and explain how biases result from psychological mechanisms), #breakitdown (organize problems into tractable components and design solutions), #complexcausality (identify ways that multiple causes interact to produce complex effects), and #audience (tailor oral and written work by considering the situation and perspective of the people receiving it). The aim of this cross-contextual scaffolding is to continually reinforce students' understanding of these core HCs and their ability to apply them across disciplines and contexts.[11]

Students are introduced to these HCs as part of eight cornerstone courses, which make up their first year of education. They encounter and apply a concept to a case study and later demonstrate their ability to use this concept in a research paper. Students are initially asked to demonstrate "near transfer," or their ability to use the same concept in a similar context, perhaps through a presentation pitching a business idea to potential investors. As students become more adept at using the given concept, they must apply it in seemingly unrelated areas, or what Minerva calls "far transfer." For example, for #constraints, they might be asked to construct mathematical equations that satisfy a set of quantitative constraints, negotiate a deal that satisfies multiple stakeholders, design a natural-resource-management policy that incorporates growth rates and population dynamics, or develop an urban transportation plan that accounts for foot, bicycle, and vehicular traffic. "We think of the HC as constituting not so much a set of things that everyone ought to know," writes Joshua Fost, who oversaw the development of the general education curriculum, "but rather, a set of tools that everyone ought to use—something akin to a basic cognitive operating system. Our aim is [to] anchor these tools so robustly in the minds of our students that they reach for them and apply them in all relevant contexts, quickly and naturally."[12]

A student's ability to transfer or apply learning from one context to another is an area of considerable debate among scholars as to whether it's possible, under what conditions, and whether it can be accurately assessed. Fost and his colleagues created a grading policy that seeks to explicitly incorporate evidence of learning transfer, while acknowledging that the concept is itself slippery and requires ongoing research.[13] Rather than the more traditional high-stakes, summative exams favored by most universities, Minerva students receive low-stakes, formative feedback for every day in class and on every assignment. The HCs "time travel" across a student's experience at Minerva. In years two through four, students are graded both on the specific topics of their advanced courses and on their ability to apply the HCs in increasingly sophisticated ways. Not until students complete their education are actual letter grades for their first-year cornerstone courses finalized. This approach is further reinforced by a distinctive set of culminating events for seniors called "Manifest," in which students teach their own class. Students are assessed on how they apply what they have learned as far back as their first year rather than only on their specific area of advanced work.

As Minerva students advance, they become more self-directed in their studies, including codesign of their fourth-year coursework and an independent project that incorporates both intensive research and creative problem-solving. In between the cornerstones and the capstones, students in their second year select a major: arts and humanities, business, computational sciences, natural sciences, or social sciences. Majors at Minerva are not organized by discipline or topic. Instead, each major includes three or four foundational courses followed by more distinct areas of concentration. For instance, a student might concentrate on data science and statistics within a major on computational science. Electives are drawn from other existing majors and concentrations.[14]

Building a Fully Active Pedagogy

This highly coordinated curricular model at Minerva University didn't appear overnight. The first stage in its evolution came in 2014 when Kosslyn and Nelson were joined by five divisional deans and several younger faculty. The core team worked out of an office suite on Market Street across from San Francisco's Civic Center. At the same time, the fledgling university recruited a founding class of twenty-eight students from fourteen countries to test out the beta version of the first-year cornerstone courses and to provide feedback on the overall Minerva experience.

These students, who lived in an old building in the upscale Nob Hill neighborhood, paid no tuition and had only minimal personal expenses, then took a gap year; and twenty-two of them rejoined the university in 2016. At that point, together with a second set of just over one hundred students admitted in 2015, they jointly formed the inaugural class as sophomores. The twenty-eight founding-year students remember that first year as both demanding and energizing. "When my friends at other universities were going to parties, I remember very intense academic workshop sessions on Friday evenings," Yoel Ferdman says. "And whenever we gathered in the common room, we'd find ourselves debating pedagogical practice. We felt we had a very active role in co-creating the university."

Yet the Minerva curriculum proved both overwhelming and disjointed for some students. Every class and every week they would encounter a completely different body of knowledge that they had to master just to be able to participate. The designers had so disconnected concepts from content and context that students became unable to keep up. In the first two weeks alone, students barely slept, owing to the formidable number of assignments they had to complete. "It was just theory. It wasn't based on humans," Nelson says, looking back on those early days. Not surprisingly, the cornerstones underwent a radical overhaul: the number of HCs was reduced and they were clarified, syllabi were completely rewritten, and a set of "Big Questions" was introduced to ground the application of the HCs and to build through lines in the curriculum: Can war be avoided? How can we feed the world? Should machines think like humans?[15]

All of the first-year courses were taught by the small complement of founding deans, as there were not yet any regular faculty. In the fall of 2014,

Vicki Chandler joined Minerva as the dean of natural sciences (she later became the provost.) A geneticist and National Academy of Sciences member, Chandler had taught at the University of Oregon as well as at the University of Arizona. She looked at the full curriculum approved by WASC and saw a long list of courses for each major that required significant review, culling, and coordination. From this list, Chandler and the other deans developed a nine-course matrix of required courses for each major, which would check three boxes: it would highlight key concepts and tools, ensure that every course offered had the rigor of a required course, and keep costs low by only teaching courses as electives that were already embedded in the overarching curriculum. A student majoring in arts and humanities, for instance, could choose to focus in one of three tracks, taking three courses each in the areas of historical forces; philosophy, ethics, and law; or arts and literature. Those same courses would be electives to students majoring in a different track, such as social sciences, or in another college. For any major a student must complete a minimum of eight to nine courses from their major and a minimum of five courses from one or more other colleges.

Advanced tutorials modeled on the Oxford system emerged as a solution to the problem of ensuring that students developed sufficient depth. Students identify topics that build on their majors and take deep dives into advanced material as part of small groups facilitated by a faculty member. Recent examples range from bioinformatics, quantum computing, and climate change to feminist theory and practice, the ethics of big tech, and the philosophy and psychology of education. In the natural sciences, tutorials are driven primarily by research papers in an area of interest to the students. Minerva does not offer traditional labs in the natural sciences. Students have virtual labs as part of their coursework and work with publicly accessible primary data to generate hypotheses and design experiments to test them. This approach of no laboratory courses is a radical departure from the practices at most colleges and universities, and the expectations of funders like the National Science Foundation. If successful, it would suggest that millions of students and thousands of universities have mistakenly invested billions of dollars and half of their contact hours. "My feeling about the lab courses is that it wasn't a big loss," says Chandler:

> In a lot of institutions, you need lab courses because they teach science in large lecture halls. The students are sitting there passively getting all of these facts thrown at them. It's really only in a lab that you're working with a smaller number of students and maybe doing inquiry-based

or project-based things. Whereas all our classes are designed to be inquiry-based and project-based and our students learn to think like a scientist.

Minerva students who want to pursue scientific careers gain real-world lab experience during the academic year through partnerships with local universities like the University of California at San Francisco or Hanyang University in South Korea—or in the summer as part of a research experience, typically at R1 (very high research activity) universities. Students from the first graduating class have gone on to PhD programs in top-ranked departments such as physics at UC Berkeley, systems biology at Harvard, computational neuroscience at Princeton, and computer science at the University of Chicago. "They found that they were not disadvantaged when they went to graduate school because of their coursework and research experiences," says Chandler.

Across all classes, Minerva employs "Fully Active Learning," a pedagogical approach that has its roots in cognitive and behavioral research. The core concept? Active participation in courses carefully structured to enhance retention and engage key ideas can lead to significant increases in student learning. Nelson argues that students in traditional universities quickly forget what they've taken in passively and that they are rarely pushed to apply a core principle in one field to another. By contrast, he claims that over four years Minerva students improve their ability to apply what they've learned across fields and in different contexts.

Minerva employs a fully flipped-classroom approach, in which classes are ninety-minute intensive sprints through debates and collaborative projects based on readings and assignments completed before students come to class. In the cornerstone courses, faculty work from a common lesson plan and draw from a shared repertoire of teaching practices. (Advanced courses reflect the same practices but are crafted by the individual faculty in ways that draw out and apply the core concepts taught in the cornerstones.) Examples of key practices include using explicit prompts that prime students for focused learning or push them to integrate the class discussion, as well as intermixing different types of problems to keep attention fresh. Other examples focus on using information repeatedly over time rather than cramming it in, and applying the same concept in unexpected situations. All of these practices are well known to scholars; what Minerva has done is to codify them into a system that faculty can deploy effectively across the entire curriculum.[16]

This format receives additional support from Minerva's advanced virtual learning environment, called "Forum." For readers doubtful about the quality of learning that can take place online using technologies like Zoom, it is important to note that Minerva's Forum platform was built from the ground up to facilitate active learning. The platform facilitates both small group discussions and multiple levels of interaction among faculty and students in which students must constantly formulate their own ideas and communicate them using a variety of means. Rather than simply transferring traditional methods for classroom instruction into online formats, it allows for students to engage in verbal, written, and visual ways, including whiteboards, collaborative workbooks, emojis, hand-raises, and chats. Classes typically begin with a reflection prompt, incorporate a series of small breakout group activities in which students collaborate on problem-solving, and end with a synthesis activity.[17]

Going further, Forum integrates course development and management tools such as syllabus and lesson-plan construction and grading, which creates a data-rich environment for students and faculty to track individual progress. All classes are recorded, and instructors evaluate and provide feedback on students' in-class contributions. Critics worry that this kind of data gathering creates a harried environment of constant monitoring. "Staff can see when a student logs on, how long they spend on an activity, how much they contribute to a discussion," Allison Littlejohn, professor of learning technology at University College London, told the *Guardian*. "There are real problems with this method: it puts a lot of pressure on students, and there are issues with privacy and surveillance. Everything a student does is monitored."[18]

Minerva faculty challenge this view; students who are uncomfortable with this system don't apply or accept admission, and professors see the data as enabling them to identify students who may be struggling to participate and to design ways to include them. The data also undergirds a system in which master teachers support new instructors in learning the ropes and provide a "sense check" of what's going on in the classroom. Even veteran instructors work with master teachers to regularly discuss and test out advanced topics in learning science, such as what kinds of questions lead to the most productive kinds of active learning. Sharing metrics across different courses or faculty also helps instructors to identify their own blind spots and provides fodder for collective faculty problem-solving: Was an instructor dominating the classroom or were students struggling with English-language proficiency on difficult or technical subject matter? At the same time, faculty recognize that data require context to interpret and that "there isn't a one-size-fits-all for an ideal class session," as Katie McAllister, who leads the social science division, writes. Instead, she continues:

> Meaningful engagement requires a deep belonging that relies on trust, student agency, and a positive classroom dynamic with opportunities for meaningful participation. Metrics offer a starting point for more objective and data-informed conversations about cultivating active and engaged students. Understanding when and how our students are engaged enables instructors to foster a greater sense of community, increase belonging, and build rich learning environments.[19]

McAllister joined Minerva in 2016 after completing her PhD in neuroscience and working in consulting for four years in London. At the time, she was skeptical about online education. As an undergraduate at the University of British Columbia, she loved her innovative in-person seminar classes in the Science One and Cognitive Systems programs. Might Minerva's proponents fall into the trap, she wondered, of the "tech 'move-fast-and-break-things' mentality and ignore the good things that actually happen in traditional institutions"? McAllister comes from a family of educators, and she also knew that large lectures and many of the traditional practices at universities are incredibly ineffective. She joined Minerva knowing that it had set itself to root out these practices. At first, faculty could feel stifled by the high level of oversight of their teaching. Over time, a culture among Minerva faculty has emerged that melds the art of teaching with the science of learning. Faculty call it "scripted improvisation," says McAllister, in which the goal of improved learning on the part of students is achieved by faculty "riffing on the script to make a different kind of music with whatever section of students you have in front of you."[20]

Cities and Students

As much as Minerva's founders focused intensively on curricular design and pedagogy, they found that their best recruitment tool had little to do with what went on in the classroom and more to do with what took place when class was not in session. Students gravitated to Minerva because it offered experiential living in a global rotation of cities. Formal instruction at Minerva, as a university, is largely virtual, but each year it rents living space for students, locating them in seven cities through which they rotate and in which they carry out experiential learning in person. After the first year in San Francisco, students take up residence for a semester each in Seoul, Hyderabad, Berlin, Buenos Aires, London, and Taipei, before returning for a culminating month in San Francisco.

This rotation, where students spend four months each in different cities, is intentionally different from the traditional semester or study-abroad experience. Rather than seeking to immerse students deeply in each culture, Minerva wants students to apply the underlying concepts they are learning—say, about #conformity or #powerdynamics—in different contexts and then move on. The goal is to generate as many opportunities as possible to enhance students' pattern-recognition capabilities—to stress their minds so that they focus relentlessly on the application of core frameworks rather than on the context itself.

Minerva has staff in each location who work collaboratively with a team of global directors to create a model for what will be done in each city. Staff come from twenty-eight different countries, and less than half of them are US citizens.[21] Students undertake location-based assignments that engage them in the life of the city: they work with government agencies, community organizations, and local businesses. In lieu of university-provided facilities, they use the same libraries, parks, and gyms as do local residents. Rotating students across continents seven different times is costly and complicated. Yet this approach surprisingly serves both Minerva's educational philosophy and its commitment to keeping costs low. "We don't pay for anything that isn't going to contribute directly to students' learning, growth, and development," says Cannon. "So, we don't own buildings, we don't have climbing walls. We don't have gyms. Students who want to join a gym do so in the city where they're living; we teach them how to fish."

Some students have criticized Minerva's approach, which requires them to figure out how to navigate different cultural contexts on their own, as insufficient. Izzy Rousmaniere from the class of 2020 observed that "without guidance as to how to build one's capacity to interact with culturally different classmates and contexts, students fall into patterns of self-segregation in both the community and the city, and often respond to difference with insensitivity or disrespect rather than adaptation."[22] Faculty and staff have agreed with this assessment, and a greater attentiveness to cultural immersion and the ability to be self-aware and act appropriately has emerged. "What I was seeing was that some students really got a lot out of that global experience and other students did not," says Cannon. "If they weren't really bold and built to jump into a city, they were not getting as much as they should have. So, we first created an intercultural competency course that was credit-bearing and then expanded it to cover all areas of learning outside of the classroom."

Initially, experiential and classroom learning were treated more like 747s flying in formation—aligned but separate, an unexpected replication of practices in traditional universities. Faculty would be surprised to learn what students were doing outside class as they explored new cities, and student-life leaders weren't fully read into the core concepts students were learning in class. The Minerva commitment to a fully intentional, holistic education wasn't being realized. Today, faculty and their student-life and experiential-education colleagues more explicitly link in-class and out-of-class learning, and they jointly offer a required half-credit course every semester called "Integrated Learning." The course covers five areas—self-management and wellness, interpersonal engagement, intercultural competency, professional development, and civic responsibility—each of which connects experiential, personal, and academic learning via the same underlying learning taxonomy used in class. This approach reinforces the concept of "far transfer," in which students apply the same concepts in different contexts. While the five areas covered are commonly heard on college campuses, what's distinctive here is how the academic HCs (Habits and Concepts) are so tightly woven in. For example, self-management and wellness is undergirded by six HCs, including #selfawareness and #emotionaliq; interpersonal engagement and intercultural competency cover seven and ten HCs respectively, some which are shared, such as #biasidentification; and professional development and civic responsibility reference ten and eight HCs respectively, and get at key concepts like #purpose and #compexcausality.

While truly integrated learning had to evolve over time, and remains a work in progress, Minerva devoted significant attention from early on to creating a distinctive set of rituals to bind the community across social, experiential, and academic experiences. Friendsgiving is a multicultural feast near the Thanksgiving holiday that is by and for students, and Quinquatria is an annual festival that falls five days after the Ides of March and is the traditional Roman holiday celebrating the goddess Minerva that paid homage to pedagogues in Roman times—for this the university hosts a feast and a student talent show. Civitas connects students with civic partners for applied project work, which culminates in Symposium, an end-of-term "demo day" of the results. Manifest is a monthlong culmination at the end of senior year, which includes defenses of a multisemester capstone project and Consequent, a reimagining of the typical commencement speech, in which students lead a two-hour online seminar with professional and international luminaries.[23]

Minerva's curriculum, pedagogy, and global rotation of cities demand unusual maturity on the part of its students. Its unique approach requires an admissions process as distinctive as these core programmatic elements. Minerva is especially attentive to the ways in which standard admissions systems in the United States are too often skewed by income status. Accordingly, the university does not charge application fees or evaluate students with any visibility of their gender, race or ethnicity, region, or income. No preference is given to athletes or students from feeder schools. Candidates complete and submit their applications entirely online, including interviews.

Rather than rely on standardized tests like the SAT or ACT, Minerva has developed its own set of admissions challenges, including a prerecorded interview and a live essay. Applicants do not know what the questions will be or what the university is looking for in its assessment. "I remember there was a question [that] asked me to list as many uses of a bowl that aren't the traditional use of a bowl," says Yoel Ferdman, a student in the founding class. "I really felt like the admissions process was assessing my brain, both the cognitive and the creative parts." High-school grades are taken into account in the context of a student's specific region and high school, rather than as a comparison across schools globally.

The university's student body is remarkable both for its global origins and for the high proportion of lower-income students. Today, more than 85 percent of an entering cohort of Minerva students come from outside the United States, and the population of more than six hundred students represents over eighty countries. In descending order, the ten countries from which Minerva draws the largest number of students are the United States, China, Ukraine, Vietnam, Brazil, Pakistan, Kenya, Nigeria, Egypt, and India. Nearly 60 percent of students come from families with annual household income below $50,000, and about 44 percent come from families whose annual income is less than $25,000.[24]

Most international students studying in the United States pay full tuition and are ineligible for financial aid. By contrast, Minerva is one of very few US-based institutions that is need-blind and provides substantial financial aid regardless of country of origin. In 2021–22, more than three-quarters of the students received financial aid (grant, work-study, and loan) and the average financial aid award was over $28,000; the average outright grant was almost $18,000. The cost of attendance per year for that academic year was $34,000–38,000, depending on which year a student is in, which is less than half the cost of elite private schools in the United States. Just 23 percent of students pay the full cost; in other elite US-based schools more than 50 percent of applicants are able to do so. In short, Minerva is highly selective—admissions rates hover in the 1–2 percent range—but highly inclusive when it comes to wealth and family status.[25]

Students who attend Minerva are oriented toward applied, entrepreneurial, and professional roles, and the education is particularly well suited for work in these arenas. McAllister, who previously worked for the Boston Consulting Group, says that core principles and activities at Minerva "are exactly what we were doing at BCG, but we didn't have them so clearly codified as in the HCs: identify the right problem, break it down, do a gap analysis, and look for complex interactions and emergent properties." Of the graduates from the classes of 2019 and 2020, 75 percent are employed in private companies and nonprofit organizations. While some students have found their way into traditional career tracks at firms like Morgan Stanley, more appear to have sought work at technology and entrepreneurial companies such as Google, Tesla, Softbank, or smaller start-ups.[26]

More than 13 percent of graduates have started their own enterprises. Among the first two graduating classes, three teams of students applied to, and were accepted by, the highly competitive Silicon Valley incubator Y-Combinator. Two recent graduates from Egypt won the Microsoft Imagine Cup Award in Education for inventing a program that enables a student from anywhere to control robotic tools in a remote lab. Another alumnus, who came from Spain, was selected for the *Forbes* 30 under 30 award for cofounding the Transcend Network, which hosts fellowship programs for early-stage founders of companies in educational technology. Students have also found employment across the nonprofit sector at organizations such as Innovations for Poverty Action, Color of Change, and the Washington Institute for Near East Policy. More than 15 percent of Minerva graduates have gone directly into graduate programs at Harvard, Cambridge, the University of Chicago, UC Berkeley, and other highly competitive institutions.[27]

For Minerva's founders, the most distinctive feature of these results is their origin: they come from a small student body heavily weighted toward low- and middle-income students. The founders see Minerva's student successes as vindication of the belief that talent is equally distributed around the world and across income brackets. Harvard and Stanford might boast of equally successful outputs, but they are drawing on a larger class size and a student body hailing from the top of the income ladder. Minerva's students have had to overcome barriers that many of these Ivy League students might not be able to imagine.

Faculty Culture

Minerva faculty, like Minerva students, operate in a distinctive culture that is recognizable as an elite university but also dramatically different. To begin with, Minerva offers faculty long-term contracts rather than a traditional tenure system. A faculty member is initially appointed for one year and then, if renewed, receives three-year rolling contracts. Roughly two-thirds of Minerva faculty are full-time. Part-time faculty often hold an appointment at another institution or prefer more flexibility in their teaching commitments.[28] Among the perks that Minerva offers to its faculty members is the flexibility to live anywhere. As Bob Kerrey, the former New School president and Minerva board chair, puts it, "parking is a big deal in higher education," and faculty at Minerva never have to worry about making it to the classroom from a faraway lot.

Both full- and part-time faculty receive the same payment per course, and those who teach more than a threshold number of courses also receive medical benefits. Part-time faculty are encouraged to participate fully in faculty meetings. "If they have a criticism, they have a complaint, or they have an observation and a great idea, they're taken as seriously as someone who is full time," says Chandler. Notably, all Minerva faculty share the same voting rights. "We do not have the concept of somebody being adjunct or part-time and, therefore, in a lesser or different category or different pay scale than someone who's full time. We don't separate."

Faculty come from fifteen countries, and 40 percent of them are female.[29] The absence of tenure generates anxiety about job security for some faculty, although few appear to have been let go once they have successfully completed their first three-year contract. One real challenge faculty face is having to teach based on the time zone in which students are located, which can lead to very early morning or late night sessions. The university tries to minimize these challenges, but overly taxing schedules combined with the intensive preparation required to teach according to Minerva's standards has led some faculty to leave the university. Grading is particularly arduous, as faculty provide extensive feedback to students on a weekly basis as well as meeting with them regularly outside class.

Minerva supports and celebrates faculty research, but it does not seek to emulate the teacher-scholar model held up as the *beau ideal* by liberal arts colleges.[30] "We're not an R1 institution," says Chandler. "We're not even a liberal arts institution that supports research and requires our faculty to do research with their undergraduates." Research and teaching aren't mutually exclusive, she says, but contrary to what most schools claim, the two activities also are not codependent. "Especially at the undergraduate level, you don't need to be the world's expert in X to be a teacher of it. You just have to stay on top of your field, especially if you're teaching upper division classes, and our faculty do that."

Critics from traditional colleges and universities, especially in STEM fields, have questioned whether research and teaching can be separated so easily. They point to high-profile educational studies validating the need for research experience for undergraduates and research aligned teaching.[31] And yet, while the benefits of research experience for students and inquiry-driven learning in STEM are well established, several studies have shown little or no correlation between the quality of teaching by professors and their research productivity.[32] In fact, Nobel laureate Carl Wieman has noted that the key factor in effective STEM teaching is to teach students "expert thinking," which requires disciplinary expertise combined with additional expertise in the complexities of effective STEM teaching and assessment of student learning.[33] For its part, Minerva explicitly cultivates and rewards instructors for focusing their full attention on the art and science of teaching rather than asking faculty to meet two overlapping but often contending masters, research and teaching. "The most important thing about a man or woman who teaches at Minerva," says Kerrey, "is they have to love to teach and have to be good at it. That is absolutely essential. And the good news is, there's lots of people living on this planet that love to teach and who are good at it, and that's who we recruit."

Despite being dispersed geographically, Minerva has developed an intentional culture of collaboration among faculty. No faculty member "owns" a class, and instructors who teach in the same course meet weekly. Far more than in traditional universities, faculty regularly review and revise syllabuses and lesson plans in an annual process overseen by the provost and supported by the heads of the different colleges. A formal approval process for major changes includes review by the Faculty Curriculum Committee, the provost, and the Minerva board.[34] University-wide working groups on curriculum and pedagogy are coordinated by the provost and driven by the faculty. One working group reviews student learning data and recommends ways to provide better formative feedback that will promote student learning. Another group concentrates on how students demonstrate their ability to apply ideas from one field to another or in new and unexpected contexts. A third group examines how well HCs are scaffolded across the entire curriculum, noting areas of strength and areas that need strengthening.[35] "Our culture really values iteration and improvement, so there is a system that supports it, and there's teamwork that supports it," says Cannon. "On every team, there are people who are design thinkers, and when we see a problem, we deconstruct it and then we do a design sprint around it."

Faculty also create their own interest groups—for example, one group formed around how to better integrate environmental sustainability across the curriculum and in experiential activities outside class, which led to the creation of an interdisciplinary minor. "Our faculty talk about teaching," Chandler emphasizes. "They talk about what worked this week, what didn't, what do we want to change in our lesson plans? How are we going to get a better reading for this or that topic?" Faculty hold regular online drop-in sessions for students, coordinate live grading parties, and gather once a year for an in-person retreat in San Francisco. When a faculty member recently got married in Minnesota, twelve faculty flew in for the event. "I thought the hardest part of my job was going to be hiring faculty and keeping them happy," says Chandler, "and it turned out to not be true."

Faculty evaluations are as innovative as the student evaluations. Faculty are assessed both on their individual teaching and on their contributions to the shared courses, overall curriculum, and life of the university. For inhabitants of traditional universities who are used to limited or no oversight of their teaching, the level of attention Minerva and its faculty pay to teaching can seem unnerving at first, and some have wondered if the system there is punitive. Certainly, a faculty member who thrives at Minerva must be willing to regularly give and receive feedback on teaching techniques and curricular planning. An instructor who wanted to be mostly left to his or own devices would not be a good fit. But faculty who stay at Minerva experience the collegial atmosphere as energizing rather than Orwellian.

The faculty's well-defined role as guides offers a further example of Minerva's coordinated approach to a student's learning journey over a four-year arc. It also represents perhaps Minerva's most pugnacious challenge to the established model of elite higher education. Most colleges and universities make their biggest investment in colocating their faculty and students on a single or primary campus. The underlying assumption is that daily interactions in a common or shared space forge a sense of community and drive intellectual synergies that would otherwise go missing. Yet, says Nelson, what more often happens is that students get four different instructors each semester, instructors who rarely talk to one another and often have little idea of what core concepts their colleagues have taught students. "It's lunacy," he says. "It's like trying to teach somebody to play a sport and assigning different coaches who each have a different idea of what they think you should learn. It's so patently obvious that you cannot educate someone to do anything with that formula."

Surprisingly, given that Minerva faculty and students don't share a campus, their connections run deep. Given the heavy demands placed on faculty at Minerva, McAllister says that, along with pedagogical innovation and a highly collegial environment, a primary factor in faculty retention is the relationships they forge with students, relationships that they have been very purposeful about nurturing. "Because we know there is going to be the distance, it makes us more cognizant about when and how we reach out; we prioritize it in a different way than if we were in the same place." Classes are limited to fifteen to twenty students, and the classroom experience is intensive, so faculty quickly find out who is interested in feminist theory or neuroscience and how the faculty member can guide students to further pursue these interests. McAllister regularly has students who take her cornerstone course, move on to advanced courses, conduct research with her over the summer, and they then copresent and copublish the results. "I've taken quite a few students to conferences and every time I feel like our contribution to the broader space of higher education is so much more valuable when we can help bring student voices into these conversations," she says.

Sustaining the Vision

In June 2021, the WASC formally awarded accreditation to Minerva University independent of its relationship with the KGI. This successful accreditation marks the last stage in an eight-year process from the university's launch and signals the formal end of the start-up's initial phase. While praising Minerva's Forum technology as a "remarkable medium" to "support active learning, outcomes-based curriculum, and assessment," the review team characterized Minerva as an educational rather than technology-driven organization. It commended Minerva for focusing on scientific evidence of effective pedagogies, for building an institutional culture of continuous learning and innovation, and for its strong emphasis on teaching excellence. "While higher education is rife with ideas for reform," the team wrote, not only is Minerva "a well-conceived model that incorporates the results of learning science, but also a full and successful implementation of that concept was achieved in what is record time for this sector."[36]

The WASC report also flagged concerns about student access to sufficient library resources and about the impact of not offering physical laboratory space in the natural sciences. More broadly, the report team urged Minerva to carefully assess the relationship between curricular breadth and depth: "There is an inherent albeit healthy tension between the time dedicated to holistic, overarching skills and abilities aimed at in the cornerstones curriculum and the subject matter proficiency that may be needed by Minerva graduates."[37]

The team paid close attention to whether the university has sufficient operational autonomy from Minerva Project: "The for-profit Minerva Project has put millions of dollars at risk to develop a platform (Forum) that can be distributed to other clients and thus prospectively monetized. The non-profit provides the example of what the learning platform can do and is essential to the for-profit's business strategy. Thus, the concern: with such pressures is Minerva independent?" The accreditation report answered this question in the affirmative, stating that it was persuaded for several reasons. First is a service agreement signed in 2021 that gave the project no say in whether the university continued to use the company's learning platform after ten years. "As a public critic of other models of higher education," the report asserted, "Minerva Project could not survive as a commercial entity if it engaged in coercion of Minerva." Second, the team reported that there is "a clear delineation of roles and responsibilities that provide Minerva with control of all academic course content, curriculum and teaching decisions." Last, it found that the university's board acted to protect its autonomy, including the board's oversight of an agreement with the company that safeguards the university's independence even if the company is sold or key founders are no longer involved.[38]

The accreditation team's other major area of concern focused on Minerva's ability to continue providing high-quality education at a significantly lower price point than its peers. A related concern asked if students fully understand their total costs of attendance after financial aid, especially in relation to their ability to participate in unpaid experiential offerings. The WASC team's attention to financial sustainability points to shifts in Minerva's underlying business model and theory of change in higher education. The initial plan was to scale the university to seven to ten thousand students after graduating an initial cohort and demonstrating the university's academic quality, selectivity, and global reach. In an expanded plan, Minerva would both benefit from a more advantageous cost structure and be able to directly challenge America's elite universities. "We would start to inflict pain," says Nelson. "We go and steal 20 percent of the incoming Harvard class, 20 percent of the Stanford class, and we don't let them ignore us.

We force them to change." Elite universities would have to adopt Minerva's approach in order to maintain their status.

The problem Nelson encountered was simple. The business model to scale the university could not work. "What I incorrectly assumed was that because we're so much cheaper, we'd have half of our students be full-pay, and maybe another quarter will take out a small loan and we'll raise some scholarship money for the bottom quarter," says Nelson. "Lo and behold, that's not even close to true. If we were to actually go through that initial plan and scale, we would be bankrupt almost overnight."

Despite its low cost, high prestige, and distinctive curricular and cocurricular structure, Minerva thus faces a challenge no different from many traditional private schools: to become sustainable, significant contributions from philanthropy will be needed to underwrite financial aid. Enrollment may also need to double or triple, and adjustments may have to be made to the mix of students paying full tuition and those receiving financial aid. Further adjustments such as increases in tuition and fees and new graduate programs may also be needed to create long-term viability for Minerva's business model. As Minerva considers these changes and challenges, it will have to contend with competition from traditional universities, who favor subject-matter proficiency over the kind of intellectual versatility that Minerva prizes. Minerva will also have to offer a value proposition that counters the tendency for faculty and students to be drawn to the often lavish physical campuses provided by competing peer institutions. Such campuses provide many opportunities for forging human and intellectual connections that are more difficult to achieve without a physical colocation of faculty and students.

Still, in less than a decade, Minerva has created a novel interdisciplinary curriculum built on an intentional taxonomy of core concepts that is distinctive in higher education. And it has developed robust practices of teaching and learning far beyond other institutions. Minerva has also dramatically lowered costs, thereby supporting social mobility among a truly international student body. The project that began with no funding, no faculty, and not a single line of code has established something genuinely new in the world of higher education.

For its part, Minerva Project seeks to shape higher education more broadly by building partnerships with other colleges and universities who want to pay to adopt and adapt its approach. To this end, in 2018 it began offering partners access to the main elements of the model in exchange for consultation fees and licensing agreements: curricular design, pedagogy, systematic assessment, and a virtual learning environment. Academic staff at the project collaborate with collegiate peers to develop customized programs for transforming learning. In the United States, partnerships have included the UC Berkeley School of Law, Paul Quinn College in Texas, Davidson College in North Carolina, Shenandoah University in Virginia, the University of Southern California, and the University of Miami. The collaboration with Shenandoah, a 150-year-old institution, focuses on reforming the general education requirements. The project with the University of Miami involves launching its New Century College, a conceptual incubator for educational ventures.

Globally, Minerva Project's collaborations have ranged from general education reform at Hong Kong University of Science & Technology to new degree programs in Spain. The Esade Business School in Barcelona has partnered with Minerva Project to provide general education courses and create a new bachelor's degree in transformational business and social impact. Other global partners include Zayed University, which established a partnership with Minerva Project to launch an interdisciplinary program of study across the entire institution, and the Universidad de la Libertad, a built-from-scratch venture in Mexico supported by business leader Ricardo Salinas Pliego.

At the end of the day, the aim is to establish a network of institutions that share Minerva's commitment to curricular coherence, learning science, and data-driven education. Collectively, the hope is that these schools will create an ecology that validates and continuously innovates in all these areas. The challenge will be to make Minerva Project's operations succeed as a business and to prove that the distinctive features of a Minerva education can thrive in cultures and contexts far different from a San Francisco start-up.

11

Essential Categories for Success in a Start-Up University

As organizations grow into maturity, they develop their own unique cultures. The first and most tangible level of culture includes what the organizational theorist Edgar Schein calls "visible artifacts"—not only physical facilities and written materials, but also organizational processes and practices, which are not always documented.[1] These artifacts are accompanied by a second level of culture—the framework of beliefs and values, which include the various norms and articulated strategies and philosophies that the group has developed to explain its operating principles. This chapter studies the Herculean task of establishing all of these essential categories that compose a new university in its most tangible form, along with the simultaneous building of a new start-up university culture.

Building the visible components or artifacts—business model, curriculum, physical campus, and faculty, for example—is the heavy lift needed to bring life to the new university. Each of these components also embodies the new values that the new university brings to higher education. There is a dynamic interplay between these values and the visible artifacts, such as curricular learning objectives, processes for hiring and retaining faculty, and mechanisms for communication and decision-making. Our stories in the previous chapters have conveyed the drama and complexity of these interactions, which operate simultaneously. It is helpful to separate the categories and consider how each has been shaped in each of our start-up universities, as well as how these categories have determined the level of success for each start-up. From our studies we have identified five key categories that make up a list of essential ingredients for a new university.

To successfully launch a new university, leaders need first to generate a sense of *prestige* to attract students and faculty in a challenging market, while also creating a sustainable business model to provide a sound financial footing. Recruiting the first faculty, admitting students, and establishing a vision that multiple stakeholders find compelling form part of the next phase, the *build and launch*. Like spacecraft missions, universities are most at risk in this launch phase and need careful planning to head off surprises. Simultaneously to *recruiting faculty* and students, the start-up university will need its *curriculum and accreditation*. To add to the challenge, it also needs to establish both a *physical campus* and a *virtual environment* to host emerging academic programs as they grow out of the improvised quarters from the launch phase.

In every case we examined in the previous chapters, the success or failure of the start-up academic institution depends on how well its leaders anticipate and manage this set of common issues. Shocks and setbacks can appear suddenly, catching the founding team by surprise—but these hurdles needn't come as entirely unexpected. Learning to predict and address challenges in these key areas can empower would-be founders and help ensure the survival and growth of new institutions.

More difficult to ascertain in analyzing start-ups are what Schein calls a third layer of underlying assumptions, which are truths that appear too obvious to the group to discuss or debate.[2] This deeper level of culture and belief often emerges from sustained interactions within the community. Mismatches between that culture and set of beliefs and various stakeholders within and outside the university lead to conflicts, which are a key part of the life of a start-up university. We examine the complexities of these emergent aspects of organizational culture in the next chapter.

Generating Prestige

Like it or not, building a prestigious brand has become essential for the survival of universities and colleges. Both global and US higher-education systems have created a status structure in which institutional prestige is considered a proxy for excellence. University rankings apply pressure on new institutions to imitate more-established universities, in particular by shifting faculty priorities toward research productivity and publication over teaching and service to the institution. This quest for prestige can even come at the expense of innovation and the quality of instruction. Any start-up university thus has a difficult task ahead: it must balance the need to create new models of education with the need for recognition and prestige generation.

Governments, professional organizations, and accrediting bodies further exert pressures for new institutions to conform to existing structures through requirements for certification or legal recognition. All these forces together push academic institutions toward imitation and dampen opportunities for differentiation and innovation. Importantly, these forces play different roles depending on the local context and saturation of the educational marketplace within a given country. Within highly saturated markets, such as the United States and Europe, differentiation through innovation takes on a premium, while prestige can be the dominant factor in other countries, such as Ghana and Vietnam, where higher educational offerings are more limited. Building prestige often requires brick-and-mortar construction: expensive facilities have come, rightly or wrongly, to signal institutional quality, as has the hiring of notably famous or prominent "star" faculty, factors much at play in the exploding costs for higher education globally. A new entrant to higher education thus faces the challenge of differentiating itself from competitors while also quickly developing a prestigious brand that will earn the trust of students and their families and bring employment to graduates.

Our case studies provide examples of how start-up universities have navigated these complex forces, surviving their initial turbulent launch and, in most cases, reaching stability and equilibrium as they approach something of a steady state. Yale-NUS College and NYU Abu Dhabi inherited much of the status and prestige of their founding institutions. Deft communications from the founding leadership conveyed both a continuation of the excellence of the parent institutions and a willingness to embrace innovation. Former Yale president Richard Levin described Yale-NUS as integral to Yale's future when he framed the formation of the new college as part of "the transformation of Yale, begun in the eighteenth century, from a local to a regional to a national and now to a truly international institution."[3] The presence of Yale's name in the new college's title, together with the placement of prominent Yale faculty in high-profile leadership positions, contributed to the new institution's prestige. In a comparable way, John Sexton, NYU's former president, would describe NYU Abu Dhabi and NYU as linked together in a larger effort to build a global network university. In Sexton's vision, global portal campuses such as NYU Abu Dhabi were "intricately connected with each other and anchored by NYU New York in a worldwide circulatory system."[4] These connections were strengthened by the fact that NYU Abu Dhabi granted an accredited NYU degree that carried the full prestige of the parent institution—something Yale-NUS did not offer its students. As Sexton put it, "whatever the academic standards are in New York, they should be in Abu Dhabi," a factor that may also have been important in sustaining strong ties to the founding NYU campus.

Most academic start-ups are not so fortunate, however. Fulbright University Vietnam (FUV), African Leadership University, Minerva University, Ashoka University, and Ashesi University all lacked the direct inherited prestige of established parent institutions and began with far less initial funding than NYU Abu Dhabi and Yale-NUS. Yet all five still leveraged connections with high-quality US institutions to build a prestigious reputation in their early days. FUV benefitted from its historic connections to Harvard, which had established the Fulbright Economics Teaching Program (FETP) in 1995, also known as the Harvard Vietnam Program.[5] The FETP was a joint program between Harvard University's Kennedy School of Government and Ho Chi Minh City University of Economics, and trained more than 40 percent of the current Vietnamese National Assembly members.[6] Similarly, in Ashoka's case, some of its founders were Ivy League alumni, and a direct messaging campaign depicting Ashoka as the "Yale of India" helped burnish its image—as did Ashoka's forerunner, the Young India Fellowship, which was tagged in the media as the "Rhodes Scholarship of India" and which garnered top graduates from the Indian Institutes of Technology (IITs) and Indian Institute of Management, creating an early and strong elite reputation. These early wins would create branding opportunities over time.

Ashesi University leveraged its partnerships in more subtle ways to bring prestige. Thanks to founder Patrick Awuah's ties, Ashesi built prestige from an advisory board that included top academics from UC Berkeley, Swarthmore, and the University of Washington. As Ashesi has built its reputation within Ghana and beyond, it has cultivated partnerships with additional prestigious institutions, most recently with the top-ranked Swiss Federal Institute of Technology (ETH) in Zurich, with which it offers a new joint master's degree in engineering.[7] African Leadership University, lacking a parent institution, was nonetheless able to leverage the prestige of the African Leadership Academy (ALA) in South Africa, which had a solid reputation for elite high-school education. ALU founder Fred Swaniker would frequently refer to his previous liberal arts education at Macalester College and his MBA at Stanford and would bring in talent from Silicon Valley, making an implicit connection between ALU and liberal arts and entrepreneurial culture in the United States.

Minerva University employed a novel strategy for building prestige from key founding intellectuals, including former Harvard president Larry Summers, who gave initial credibility to the ideas of its founder Ben Nelson, thus enabling the recruitment of top-flight academic leaders—Stephen Kosslyn from Harvard, Bob Kerrey from the New School, and Teri Cannon from the accrediting agency Western Association of Schools and Colleges (WASC). These new hires refined and amplified the founding vision and garnered additional media attention as educational thought leaders. In generating prestige, Minerva was remarkable for its rapid progress. A book-length exposition of the university, *Building the Intentional University*, was produced by Nelson and Kosslyn in 2017, years before Minerva University had graduated any students.

Minerva also built prestige with an innovative product launch reminiscent of Silicon Valley. To strengthen the experience and brand of their new university, Minerva staff members mailed a custom-made box to each student to announce that they were among the 2.7 percent of applicants selected to compose the first class. Minerva's Ayo Seligman and Robin Goldberg described what the students received:

> By creating "the box"—a hinged walnut case emblazoned with the word "curiosity" that was custom-built to house an Apple iPad Mini and its various components—and the sequence of interactive steps recipients were guided to follow, we sought to eliminate any doubt from the minds of these first pioneering students about attending Minerva. In the process, we exhibited the core principles that have come to define the organization.[8]

Olin College of Engineering took a middle path in its approach to building institutional prestige. Beginning with a core faculty with ties to MIT and Harvey Mudd College, Olin worked to build a unique presence and brand as a scrappy upstart working in rural Massachusetts to upend MIT as the best school for an undergraduate engineering education. By bringing top academics into the curriculum design process, and by attracting the best engineering students in the country with full scholarships, Olin established a solid reputation early in its launch. This reputation was further locked in place through the college's participation in the New Engineering Education Transformation (NEET) group, a consortium of top global engineering programs led by MIT, committed to assessing and modernizing engineering education. In 2018 NEET issued its report *The Global State of the Art in Engineering Education,* in which Olin tied with MIT as current leaders in engineering education in the world—less than twenty years after its founding.[9] Olin leaders had successfully engineered a brand that would catapult the new college into the elite rankings

In our analysis of prestige generation and innovation, the imperative for innovation varies depending on the market in which the new university is operating. In many cases, such as NYU Abu Dhabi, Yale-NUS, FUV, Ashesi, and Ashoka, the institutions to varying degrees enjoyed a monopoly on liberal arts in their region or country. This meant that they did not necessarily have to innovate to attract students. Instead, for those schools a premium was placed on prestige more than innovation. In cases with a nonsaturated liberal arts market, without an obvious competitor, start-up institutions will still innovate, however, not out of a desire for market share but out of necessity, due to unique challenges within their region. For example, Ashesi innovated by blending more vocational subjects with liberal arts and adjusted the liberal arts model for Africa. Additional innovations, including the leadership courses and the program in African studies, were all necessities to fine-tune the liberal arts for their region. One could argue that Ashesi would have attracted market share just by planting a copy of Swarthmore in Ghana, but other necessities, such as the need to reduce costs and provide a form of liberal arts that met the needs of Africa, required it to innovate. This leads to a second very important consideration—creating the business model.

Creating a Sustainable Business Model

Even when a start-up university manages to inherit or invent the mantle of prestige, it will not get far without a solid and sustainable business model. To achieve financial equilibrium, a start-up university needs robust initial funding, as well as a long-term plan for building a diverse network of supporters across many sectors. All of our start-up universities place a premium on providing the highest quality of education, which is an expensive proposition. Without the social capital and alumni base that established institutions enjoy, founders of start-ups need to be creative in rapidly building financial backing while rigorously containing costs. Our case studies suggest a variety of approaches to solving this problem.

Ashoka University created a group of over two hundred donors who share the title of founders, together creating India's largest shared philanthropic effort.[10] The founders have so far raised over Rs 1,500 crore (over US$200 million) to support their new university. This innovative support mechanism has had an impact on institutional governance, as we will explore in the next chapter.

Yale-NUS and NYU Abu Dhabi likewise benefitted from enormous resources granted to their founders, though their stories proved complicated. Yale-NUS College's operating budget was funded by a block grant from the Singaporean Ministry of Education and had the goal of raising a S$1 billion endowment after the start-up. By 2017, however, the college had reached just S$365 million (around US$220 million),[11] well short of this goal—and these funds had come primarily from donors contributing directly to NUS. NUS president Tan Eng Chye would cite this significant shortfall as one reason why the Yale-NUS financial model was unsustainable.[12]

NYU Abu Dhabi's finances have not been completely detailed, but we do know that the institution enjoys the full financial backing of Sheikh Mohamed bin Zayed al Nahyan, crown prince of Abu Dhabi. This funding provided benefits for the main NYU campus and provided NYU Abu Dhabi a sound business model—as long as Sheik Mohamed's support and resources would hold out. NYU's own reporting of the operating costs for the Abu Dhabi campus in 2019 showed that NYU was reimbursed costs for faculty expenses in the range of $21 million per year and received subsidies for faculty research at the level of $19 million per year,[13] with annual revenues from NYU Abu Dhabi in the range of $164 million.[14] With UAE's economy continuing to grow in the coming years, as it has for six of the past seven years, these revenues and NYU Abu Dhabi's business model seem secure for now.

FUV's business model was initially wholly dependent on both US and Vietnamese government support. US federal support totaled $60 million during the college's start-up phase (beginning in 2017) and included funds from USAID, the US State Department, and additional authorizations from Congress. An additional $37 million loan was approved in 2021 for helping Fulbright build its new campus on land donated from the Vietnamese government, using the US International Development Finance Corporation.[15] Fulbright placed itself at a higher price point than competing institutions within Vietnam, reasoning that the additional costs for tuition would signal prestige and value and would still be cheaper for families than educating their children in the United States or Europe. The FUV tuition generated enough revenue to enable the school to offer financial aid, a process that involved inventing an entirely new system to assess family income—a first for Vietnam.

ALU is part of an ecosystem of institutions that includes a nonprofit high school, a virtual career accelerator, and a global talent-matching system. These institutions have been collectively supported by almost $800 million from hundreds of philanthropists and foundations, who have provided long-term backing to help bring about massive changes to education in Africa. The greatest support has come from the MasterCard Foundation. In its early years, ALU was able to reduce the cost per student from an initial $30,000 for the high-school program in South Africa to $16,000 for the Mauritius campus and just $12,000 for the Kigali campus. Its new regional hub model of education has further driven costs down to $3,000 per student. The combined effect of aggressive fundraising and cost cutting strengthened ALU's business model while consciously pushing the envelope toward lower-cost experiential education and off-campus experiences. By leveraging peer instruction, reducing reliance on scarce PhD-holding academics within Africa, and keeping facilities costs to a minimum, ALU is offering the lowest-cost education of all our case studies. The university's prestige relies heavily on the results of its graduates, who, it is hoped, will soon occupy the commanding heights of African government and industry and create a powerful network to sustain ALU into the future.

From the earliest days of planning, Patrick Awuah and Nina Marini drove Ashesi toward a sustainable business model, building on their own business acumen and generating substantial backing from Silicon Valley and Microsoft. Their efforts also received fundraising support from an international Ashesi Foundation based in the United States. As Awuah and Marini worked on their business plan, they were frequently advised to plan on higher expenses than expected: their initial projection of $2 million in costs rose in a second business plan to $8.5 million and later rose even higher. The most recent (2020) financial statement shows the Ashesi Foundation with assets of $10.2 million, modest for a US-based university but sufficient to provide a solid financial footing in Ghana—and enough of a foundation to provide financial aid for students who cannot afford full tuition.

Jump-started by a $25 million investment from Benchmark Capital in 2012, Minerva began with strong financials and garnered additional investments in 2014 and 2019 that totaled more than $128 million. Such ample resources for an institution without a physical campus placed Minerva in an extraordinary financial position in its first years, alongside its unique corporate style that placed it apart from other start-up universities. Minerva founders focused their business model on offering a low price point, promising a $10,000 education that would surpass Harvard in quality and employing a distributed cadre of teaching faculty without the need for laboratories, start-up funding, or other research support. By choosing not to develop a physical campus, relying instead on rented apartments in a variety of world cultural centers for student residences, Minerva was able to further cut costs drastically. Over time, however, the design requirement of full-need financial aid for students from around the world made the university impossible to scale with its low price point.

Developing the business model for Olin was made much simpler by the initial outlay of more than $460 million from the F. W. Olin Foundation, one of the largest gifts ever made in higher education. This level of funding was itself a significant leap by the Olin Foundation and enabled development of an entire college campus and full scholarships for the initial student cohorts. Olin College has shown good stewardship of this endowment, pivoting away from the full scholarships for all students of the early days and moving toward a more conventional posture of need-based financial aid after the initial launch.

Each of the above approaches for building a business model has advantages and drawbacks. Even in cases with lavish funding sources, such as Yale-NUS College in Singapore, NYU Abu Dhabi, and Olin College, the institution can be vulnerable from its business model relying entirely on a single source of funding. Being entirely reliant on the Singaporean government or a wealthy sheikh does indeed provide abundant resources to start the new institution but runs risks of disruption if it loses this single source, as Yale-NUS College learned in its early demise. Maintaining the favor of the single supporter may also require additional compromises, which could compromise institutional autonomy in the long run. Fulbright Vietnam started with deep reliance on both US and Vietnamese government support for its business model, which created a potential threat if those governments had conflicting interests.

Ashoka University offers an excellent example of a decentralized philanthropic business model, using a network of founders to limit vulnerability to the whims of a single donor. Ashoka also very astutely limited its costs to be able to provide a sustainable university at a cost that is attainable by students in India. Fulbright University Vietnam has also diversified its support to include private philanthropy, and its most recent $40 million gift from eight philanthropists and their families is a step toward a more diversified and more sustainable business model. This is especially notable in the Vietnamese context, where seeking large-scale philanthropic gifts in support of universities is not a well-established practice. Olin College would seem to have an enviable business model, since it has absorbed the entire $450 million fortune of the Olin Foundation and therefore has a large endowment without the risk of influence from a single individual donor. However, even this magnificent gift has a downside, since while Olin is well endowed for its four-hundred-student size, it would need a comparably large gift to enable it to grow.

Build and Launch

Once the initial vision and a plan for generating prestige and building a business model are in place, the build-and-launch phase can commence. These first years for the new institution are extremely important. Among our case studies, we see a variety of strategies for this phase, including incubation years, codesign, and founding years—all periods prior to a full university or college opening in which the institution gains its footing. What are the benefits and drawbacks of the various approaches we've encountered?

In the partner or codesign year—demonstrated by Olin College of Engineering, Minerva University, and Fulbright University Vietnam—students, faculty, and staff work together before a campus launch to prototype and test the new curriculum and experiment with pedagogy. Olin was forced to use this technique because of delays in campus opening, but in hindsight, it turned out to be the best thing for the new college. "If we hadn't had what we called the Olin partner year, you wouldn't be talking to me today because it wouldn't matter," says Rick Miller, Olin's founding president. Olin's provost, Mark Somerville, points out that "none of us knew what we were doing in that year, neither students nor faculty."

This freedom of experimentation was crucial. An early article about Olin described how the student partners were put to work to "try out different learning methods, help professors design a curriculum, create a student government, and select a mascot." Olin was able to attract 664 applications for just thirty partner slots for this codesign year, even though the students were not compensated and had to stay and repeat their first year with the other incoming students later.[16] By enabling a rapid cycle of prototyping and testing of course modules, the codesign year mirrors some of the best practices of engineering. Rather than continuing down a path of faculty-designed curriculum, the codesign brings in student voices, optimizes the curriculum based on their interests, and immediately identifies problem areas with their help that might not be self-evident to faculty.

Minerva also made use of a codesign year, with twenty-eight initial students who worked closely with the founding team. They provided feedback on the first-year cornerstone courses and the overall Minerva experience, before rejoining as part of the inaugural class in 2015. This initial trial by students helped improve the signature Minerva cross-curricular Habits of Mind and Foundational Concepts, while also surfacing the need for a set of "Big Questions" that provide through lines in the curriculum.

Inspired by Olin's example, Fulbright University Vietnam also employed a partner year (naming it a codesign year). Leaders worked with fifty-five students and fifteen faculty during this phase, deploying techniques like design sprints to organize discussions. The pace of the effort was intense, with course protypes designed and tested within a timescale of a week. These short development cycles were followed by monthlong colearning modules where two to three faculty worked with twelve to fifteen students to help develop lessons and try out active learning techniques, new endeavors to most of the Vietnamese students. As Dinh Ngan, the first Fulbright dean, says,

> The teachers took the stage for the first half, and then the students became the teachers and taught the faculty, the foreign faculty, all kinds of things about Vietnam. And that was quite interesting. . . . [W]e were sitting down as students, and they were grading. They had such a great time fining us and scolding us and giving us Cs and things like that.

The exercise brought great insight to both the students and teachers, and similar dialogues throughout the codesign year set a standard at FUV for academic freedom. Within the Fulbright codesign year, students helped write initial drafts of the catalogue for the university and worked closely with faculty to develop a four-week intensive course on rhetoric that included both Vietnamese and Western approaches. During the codesign, students' initial feelings of vulnerability and frustration gave way to a deeper sense of ownership, satisfaction, and resilience.[17]

In the cases of both Olin and FUV, it is possible to see limitations as well as benefits in the codesign approach. Olin College, despite its partner year, still faced a crisis in its early days—all classes had to be stopped after students complained that the work level was far too difficult. At Fulbright, while the codesign year did give birth to successful curricular components, the process missed developing other key areas of the curriculum that the board had made a high priority, such as expertise in computer science. As a result, certain ideas from the codesign year wound up being set aside or joined with curriculum developed in the traditional way, without students. It is also worth noting that while the codesign experience typically proves valuable for students who participate, it can't be shared by the entire incoming class, thus generating unequal levels of experience and ownership of the curriculum among students after the first year.

But the benefits are also clear. For both FUV and Olin, the codesign or partnership year set the tone for a new institutional culture that is student centered and responsive to student input, generating a dynamic university ethos, a sense of the institution as a constant work in progress. This tone can bring durable value to a new institution. As Dinh Ngan says of the Fulbright codesign year, "We wanted to carry out this Co-Design spirit forever."

Not all of our case studies showcased codesign or partner years. Some commenced operations with a phased approach, testing things out with smaller cohorts of students before a full launch. Ashesi University, ALU, and (to some extent) Ashoka University all employed this model. Here, the earliest days of the institution offered an intense bonding experience for the faculty. The smaller size of the institution also enabled details of the curriculum, faculty governance, and student life to be worked out on a more intimate and personal scale before the institution reached full size. In Ashesi's case, eight faculty members, some of whom were visiting instructors, taught an initial cohort of twenty-seven students. The school opened in "two rented bungalows in Accra," recalls Marcia Grant, Ashesi's first provost, and "started with half the students that it had expected in the business plan." Breaking even financially took two years longer than planned.[18] This partial launch gave these first students a taste of a partner-year experience: they advocated for changes in the curriculum, such as shifting the content of the first mathematics course from pure calculus toward more algebra and other precalculus topics.

In a comparable manner, Ashoka University opened first with the Young India Fellowship (YIF) postgraduate program, bringing on board fifty-seven students selected from almost one thousand applicants who had just graduated from India's top universities. Like other first cohorts, these students were unique and self-selected. "They were people who thought differently," says Ashish Dhawan, one of Ashoka's principal founders, "who were frustrated with having been funneled down this narrow path and really had missed out on what they genuinely wanted to study." The YIF also enabled visiting academics to test out short courses in humanities and social sciences with talented Indian students before taking on positions at Ashoka as either visiting or permanent faculty. The extended development of the YIF with top recent graduates and prestigious visiting faculty gave their codesign effort a significant level of experience and maturity, propelling the YIF into a prestigious reputation that carried over to the new university.

ALU similarly began with a phased launch, starting with the ALA for students in their last two years of high school. Like the YIF, ALA and then ALU found their best students from across geographical regions and cultures, creating a strong reputation as they trained their initial cohorts. As ALU grew, its business model underwent dramatic evolution, with price reductions reverberating down through campuses. The latest version of ALU can be delivered for only $3,000 to students and builds on the lessons learned from earlier stages of the project. During each stage of the evolution of ALU, founding team members refined their approaches. This evolution included an effort to "maximize the role of the student as the key driver of their own learning," according to ALU founder Fred Swaniker, a move that also emphasized peer-to-peer learning opportunities. At each stage, ALU extended this reliance on peer learning, finding it a solid model for acquiring knowledge and actively using it. "If you as a young person have to explain something to someone else, it really means you have to learn it to be able to explain the thing," says Swaniker.

How did Yale-NUS College compare to these iterations? With temporary quarters within a New Haven office building adjacent to Yale University, the first Yale-NUS leaders worked for over a year without students on curriculum design before launching. The newly hired inaugural Yale-NUS faculty "had the great good fortune of having this incubation year," says founding Yale-NUS dean Charles Bailyn. During these months, faculty and administrators composed an extensive curriculum report, which documented the motivation and context for the new college and served as a blueprint for the more extensive curriculum development after launch.

Yet despite extensive planning, Yale-NUS College still missed potential problems, such as where to place history in the common curriculum and how to go about teaching interdisciplinary science. Bailyn notes that "one of the weird, weird things about that first year from the point of view of the dean was you had a faculty, 60 percent of whom were first year assistant professors. That's nuts." The limited experience of these inaugural faculty made it more challenging to design the curriculum. Still, the incubation year became a key part of faculty development, as young faculty members were able to interact extensively with scholars at Yale, make field trips to top liberal arts institutions in the United States, and advance research before jumping into the intense environment of the start-up university.

Like Yale-NUS, NYU Abu Dhabi had a substantial period of building before beginning to operate its undergraduate program. Like Ashoka, it began with a postgraduate program in a phased opening that allowed the new institution to gain experience and visibility before starting the undergraduate program. The NYU Abu Dhabi Institute and the Sheikh Mohamed Scholars Program were both led by women from the founding team. The Scholars Program, like the Ashoka YIF, provided a sample of the liberal arts approaches NYU Abu Dhabi planned to bring to UAE, and also communicated to Abu Dhabi the importance of empowering women at the new institution.

Either by accident or design, all of our institutions in the build-and-launch phase developed pilot versions of the institution and curriculum in temporary quarters with a small group of founders (and in many cases, students). These pilot and codesign efforts can be effective for prototyping and building a strong initial institutional culture. The codesign or partner year concept was especially effective for Olin College and Minerva, and the small and intense early phases of Yale-NUS, NYU Abu Dhabi, Ashesi, and Ashoka are all recalled fondly by their founders. The codesign in the case of FUV appears to have produced mixed results, since the remit for the founders and codesign students seems to have been altered after the founding year. We would advise other start-ups to give clear rules for the codesign process and the method for institutionalizing the results to assure stability and morale among the team. In all our cases, these early phases of incubation turned out to be crucibles where the ethos and creative capacities of the new institution all begin flowering.

For any new institution or company, these early days of launch are essential and even have a ritualistic dimension in which the new culture arises, forged from the great effort and shared risk among the founders. Benefits also arise from a delayed launch, which gives the institution more time to test and refine its approaches and to get to know the needs of its future students. In some cases, the extra time can offer opportunities for fundraising and refining the business model, such as with Ashoka University. In other cases, the prelaunch also allows for developing materials that effectively explain the institution to outside audiences, such the curriculum document of Yale-NUS College and the book edited by Kosslyn and Nelson about Minerva University.

Recruiting the Faculty

Part of any good build-and-launch phase is the recruitment of best-in-class faculty. In some cases, our start-up universities attracted top faculty based on the early prestige of the institution. Yale-NUS and NYU Abu Dhabi both benefitted from their parent institutions in recruiting early faculty. In the case of Yale-NUS College, the prestige of working at Yale University and connections to NUS, one of Asia's top-ranked universities, helped lure faculty into the fold. NYU offered a pathway to tenure and considered NYU Abu Dhabi as a school of NYU, and it also offered NYU Abu Dhabi faculty an integration semester or year teaching in New York, as well as sabbatical years at NYU or other NYU sites.

For NYU Abu Dhabi, tenure was essential to recruitment. "If we couldn't have tenure, we could forget about recruiting a top-quality faculty," says Westermann, current NYU Abu Dhabi president.[19] Yale-NUS similarly offered tenure, as well as the prospect of sabbaticals at Yale—these incentives doubtless helped with faculty recruitment and hiring. So did the promise of faculty involvement in curricular development, which was integral to the recruitment process. The initial interview process brought together batches of potential faculty, who would be asked to outline a new course and discuss pedagogy with one another and with the hiring team. Batch interviewing became an essential mechanism for meeting the goal to hire one hundred faculty in tenure-track jobs in the first few years and was ideal for assessing the teaching capacity and willingness to collaborate of potential faculty.

NYU Abu Dhabi leaders were uncertain how well their faculty recruitment would go, even after successfully recruiting many faculty for a global network of campuses. Newly hired Abu Dhabi faculty were to be blended in with NYU faculty in residence in Abu Dhabi. In the initial years, NYU faculty stepped in to fill the shortfall of faculty on site. Hilary Ballon, who served as deputy vice-chancellor during NYU Abu Dhabi's founding, recalls, "We did not have sufficient faculty at the outset to deliver all these majors." Some scrambling and relocating took place, as administrators "would bring over New York faculty to Abu Dhabi, and our Abu Dhabi students would have the opportunity to take two semesters in New York or another NYU site." The large number of faculty at NYU provided ample reserves for the new campus, and in the early years made up 75 percent of the NYU Abu Dhabi faculty, thus reducing pressure on the hiring. By bringing the best NYU faculty into Abu Dhabi in the initial years, the Abu Dhabi campus was eventually able to recruit large numbers of both junior and mid-career faculty. Jess Benhabib, who was senior vice-provost from 2005 to 2008, realized that "once there was something close to critical mass, we could turn to others beyond NYU and say, 'Would you like to come?'"[20] The development of this critical mass enabled NYU Abu Dhabi to begin to hire clusters of faculty in several fields and to develop considerable research capacity.

For other institutions, such as Ashesi University, faculty considering working at the new start-up were being invited into an entirely new academic environment—which might include an unfamiliar country or region or a curriculum well outside of the faculty member's own academic background, particularly for faculty educated in Ghana. When Asheshi's founders first tried to hire faculty from Ghana, for example, they had no applications. This led Ashesi to start with a mix of professors from the United Kingdom and the United States and with a part-time dean on loan from the University of Ghana. This group worked together on the initial launch. "It took us about a year to get enough credibility so that when we put out job applications we would get applications from Ghanaian faculty," says founder Patrick Awuah. As Marcia Clark put it in a 2007 interview, "Over the years, the faculty of Ashesi found the university, or the university found the faculty." In its first years, the majority of Ashesi faculty (twenty out of twenty-six) were from Ghana, and about half of these Ghanaians came with previous experience as a student in US higher education. Coming to Ashesi for many was a new experience but also attractive, because, according to Clark, "they need the freedom to teach in the new ways that Ashesi encourages."[21]

African Leadership University and Fulbright University Vietnam had similar issues recruiting faculty in the early days, partly because of the ways the new institutions challenged paradigms of teaching and learning in their respective countries. For ALU, shifting toward a more student-centered approach meant that the university and its faculty had to take a deliberately supportive or back-seat role. "We are not the most important people in this picture. We are part of it. We do matter, but we are not the only source of knowledge," says Swaniker. This paradigm shift involved thinking of ALU's graduates as "catalysts, not specialists," who would then "mobilize people to action to drive change in society." As Swaniker adds, for some faculty this shift was "a big threat to their identity."

FUV also had the challenge of offering a new teaching paradigm that made it difficult to recruit local faculty. This issue was compounded by the tight timeframe of the launch. Most of the early faculty were non-Vietnamese; over time, however, prospective faculty began to understand more about the goals of the new university. Most of the Vietnamese faculty who were approached were confused by the new university, until FUV recruited a few Vietnamese faculty who had received liberal arts degrees in the United States and who were successful. Like Yale-NUS College, FUV conducted group interviews for prospective faculty that might include four to six candidates from across disciplines. The schedule would include a two-day interview with an "impact talk" rather than a research seminar. Since Fulbright did not have students or faculty yet, the audience for the talks was a group of "Fulbright-sympathetic" young people. The team used Facebook to find these young people and several of them later applied to become students in the codesign year.

Olin College of Engineering began by hiring faculty in a conventional process, with individual faculty visiting campus, delivering a research talk, and discussing curriculum. Over the years, however, Olin changed things up, developing a batch-hiring approach that included a written interview to create a medium short list of about forty candidates, who would then go through video interviews. Once finalists had been selected, groups of candidates from a range of fields would visit campus and work in pairs to design and co-teach a course as part of the final interview.[22] This process gives hiring officials unique insights into candidates. It also effectively communicates the unique nature of Olin to potential faculty. As Somerville describes it, this process is "sending a pretty clear, cultural message around what kind of place this is and helping them make a decision about whether it's the kind of place they want to be."

Minerva University initially thought it might face challenges for faculty recruitment—in no small part because its environment differs dramatically from a conventional professorship. With its uniquely distributed faculty and shared repertoire of teaching practices, the Minerva model might have posed a puzzle for potential faculty. But its distinctiveness also worked strongly to its advantage. For faculty who are dedicated to teaching, Minerva's intense focus on student learning, reduced emphasis on research, and the absence of a high-stress tenure review have proved attractive. So, too, has the flexibility that comes with not having to relocate and to choose whether to work full-time or part-time without being treated as an adjunct instructor.

All start-up universities benefit from the excitement of building a new institution, which brings a certain cachet and brio to the initial set of faculty—who are often referred to as the founders of the institution. But with this excitement also comes risk. P. J. Henry, one of the first faculty hired for the new NYU campus in Abu Dhabi, put it in a way that could well apply to all faculty at these new start-up universities:

> A lot of us were really young. We shared a sense of adventure and a willingness to tolerate ambiguity and a lack of structure. It sounds very simple, but it's actually not. If you're just out of graduate school, you really need a structure in place, where there's a hierarchy and a way of doing things. So these people who signed on, especially the younger faculty, were taking an extraordinary risk.[23]

In addition to these risks, challenges also showed up in our start-up universities when they attempted to blend different cohorts of faculty hired at different stages of the build and launch—especially when the vision or business plan for the institution had shifted significantly since its founding. The most dramatic example of this would be ALU, which required a pivot in 2018 and a drastic retooling of its business model. This shift resulted in an even greater reliance on peer learning, online platforms, and other low-cost practices, triggering faculty resignations and ultimately resulting in half the ALU staff either being dismissed or quitting. A related lesson learned comes from the challenge of hiring many junior faculty in the first years, a move that can stress a new institution at multiple pressure points. "I think if I was giving advice to someone doing an academic startup," says Bailyn, "one of the things I would say is, be very careful about that huge wedge of first year assistant professors that you're inevitably going to end up with. Because you can't hire enough senior people into a startup at once to avoid that."

While the excitement of a start-up may attract some professors, any faculty member considering joining a new institution is taking considerable risk, and the start-up university needs to attract faculty using a variety of techniques that draw on the potential professor's interests for future advancement, job stability, or loyalty to the region or vision of the institution. NYU Abu Dhabi and Yale-NUS enjoyed strong connections to their prestigious parent institutions and could promise job stability through tenure. These considerable advantages were offset by the fact that many or most new faculty in both institutions had no prior connection or loyalty to either UAE or Singapore, which complicated the faculty recruitment and onboarding process. Institutions that are pioneering new approaches within a country can excite and attract expatriate faculty, who can also bring a familiarity and loyalty to the country that can boost the success of the new institution. Ashoka University, Ashesi University, and Fulbright Vietnam were able to attract both local faculty from India, Ghana, and Vietnam and a cadre of expatriate faculty who were strongly motivated to help their home country or region, and who made valuable contributions. Ashoka was particularly clever in using the Young India Fellowship to entice nonresident Indian academic talent to return to India through short course assignments that allowed them to test Ashoka's academic culture before committing to a full-time academic job in India.

How to consider the case of universities and colleges without prestigious parent institutions that lack a strong loyalty to a local culture and offer no promise of tenure? Three of our institutions, ALU, Minerva University, and Olin College all belong to this group, and all needed to innovate to attract faculty. ALU focused on a smaller cadre of faculty with advanced academic degrees and leveraged contacts among local entrepreneurs for its faculty. ALU was also able to leverage faculty interests in advancing Africa, even if it lacked a strong rooting in a single African culture. For Minerva University, the compelling mission of revolutionizing education coupled with the flexibility to work from anywhere proved to be a powerful draw. Olin College, by proclaiming its intention to re-engineer engineering education, was able to attract a certain type of academic motivated by the potential impact of the institution as a whole. In all these cases, our start-up institutions found new ways to respond to one of the key markets they are competing in—the market for faculty. A start-up university that lacks existing recognition must innovate and differentiate to appeal to these potential faculty. In all these cases, our start-up institutions experimented with new ways to conceptualize and structure faculty work in ways that established universities might learn from. For example, by expanding beyond conventional models of faculty primarily as exquisitely specialized researchers, ALU has made space for entrepreneurs, Olin for faculty interested in pioneering new models of curriculum, and Minerva for a distributed faculty forming collaborative teams.

Curriculum and Accreditation

One of the profound joys of the start-up university, which attracts some of the most dynamic, pioneering faculty and thought leaders, is the rare opportunity to design a curriculum from the ground up. Like an artist with a blank canvas, faculty and leaders building the new university can design entirely new structures in curriculum, freed from the constraints of tradition and the maxim of "we don't do things that way here" that constrain nearly all established universities. This process of creation is not *ex nihilo*, as each of the faculty at the table brings cherished ideas from former institutions, whether these ideas derive from their time as a student or as a faculty member. In most cases, designing the new curriculum is exhilarating and energizing, as groups of faculty (and in many cases students) gather together to combine ideas from a kaleidoscope of institutions and experiences. Design work can also be contentious, since each person has also imported assumptions about academia and its purposes, methods, and culture that can conflict with the assumptions of others and unsettle the emerging and fragile culture of the new institution.

With the benefit of the blank canvas, many of our case-study institutions have performed major remodels of the structures and architecture of academia. These break out of departmental boundaries and are also reflected in new curriculums and new areas of faculty research. Most have intentionally departed from the omnipresent general elective model of general education and, instead, have developed carefully designed common or core curricula, which provide a base of shared experience and interdisciplinary knowledge to all students that can be leveraged later in upper-level courses. One of the most extensive examples is the Yale-NUS common curriculum, which includes ten courses across the humanities, social sciences, and natural sciences. At Yale-NUS, students take all but one of their courses together during the first year of study—an embodiment of the institutional commitment to foster a community of scholars that serves "the common needs of the college and its students." Olin College has a similarly ambitious Foundations curriculum that emphasizes design projects and includes courses such as Design Nature, User-Oriented Collaborative Design, and Modeling and Simulation of the Physical World. Olin has succeeded so well in its approach that it has inspired other institutions to implement similar courses in their engineering schools. In most cases, the core or common curriculum is more than an academic introduction for students. Instead, many of the institutions view these curriculums as key components of their institutional identity, and a means toward essential reform of higher education as a whole.

By challenging the traditional disciplinary models of curriculum, Yale-NUS and Olin College both make a claim on the value of interdisciplinary education for faculty and students and as an essential foundation needed for twenty-first-century challenges. These claims all show up early within the start-ups' founding documents. For Yale-NUS, the common curriculum provides a "concrete centerpiece of deliberation for the faculty as a whole," which can demonstrate that "core courses need not be dismissed as musty remnants from previous centuries or outmoded surveys of irrelevant canons."[24] Olin's curriculum is designed to fundamentally reform engineering education with "hands-on projects involving the modeling, simulation and analysis of engineering systems" from the outset and featuring an interdisciplinary core curriculum "designed to build connections amongst fundamental science, mathematics and engineering; amongst different fields of engineering; amongst the arts, humanities and social sciences and technical disciplines; and amongst business, entrepreneurship and technology."[25] These innovations were key to Olin's view about the problem with engineering education, which "teaches students how to solve problems, but not how to find the right problems to solve, or how to get their solutions out of the lab and into the world."[26]

By building their interdisciplinary programs from the ground up, our start-ups were also able to integrate new perspectives from emerging fields of research and from industry. Examples here include the Yale-NUS scientific inquiry courses, which tackle interdisciplinary themes within science such as evolution and global climate change, or the NYU Abu Dhabi foundations of science courses, which look at cross-cutting topics such as "systems in flux" and "form and function." Olin College brings an emphasis on bio-inspired design, simulation, and modeling to its interdisciplinary curriculum, which helps students bridge multiple disciplines while pursuing solutions to intellectually interesting problems.

In a comparable manner, Minerva's curriculum has been described by Ben Nelson and Stephen Kosslyn as "a systematic rethinking of every aspect of the liberal arts curriculum," which in too many institutions offers "a completely unstructured curriculum in which nothing builds on anything else."[27] The Minerva cornerstone courses are built on a set of eighty core concepts, which are then scaffolded across the entire curriculum so that students continuously deepen their understanding of the concepts by applying them in different contexts and in progressively sophisticated ways. Taken together, the founding statements from Minerva, Olin, and Yale-NUS all offer curricular reform as an essential part of their identity—the desire to transform higher education as a whole and to acknowledge, increasingly, the global nature of the world their students are preparing to enter.

Why have these schools all arrived at such a similar end point? Though specific details vary, all share a deep commitment to an international, required core curriculum. It's worth asking what these institutions are reacting to within established universities when they make this move toward a shared or common core. At least two possibilities are worth considering. First, perhaps these start-ups are rejecting the current trend in traditional universities toward highly personalized and individualized distribution requirement options. By pushing for students to have a common set of courses and experiences, especially in their first year, the start-ups seem to be calling us back to an older model of shared knowledge, which can be applied and interrogated in new ways across disciplines. Second, it also seems possible that these newer institutions are simply responding to the global nature of their student bodies, stepping in to provide a common foundation of knowledge and experience for students who come from all over the world. In traditional universities where the default demographic is fairly homogeneous, common core requirements might not seem so essential: these students already have common ground because they tend to come from the same country. In the start-up environment, by way of contrast, commonality cannot be taken for granted: a shared language and shared reference points need to be built into the curriculum from the ground up.

Several institutions have developed shorter multicourse sequences focused on specific domains of knowledge instead of expansive common curricula. One example is the ALU leadership core, which emphasizes project management, entrepreneurial leadership, data and decisions, and communicating for impact. The goal? To "develop leaders who will change Africa" though "an entrepreneurial mindset" that trains students in "making judgements when faced with difficult dilemmas."[28] Ashesi University shares this intense focus on leadership, requiring all students to take its four-course leadership seminar sequence and a seminar during which students travel across Ghana to serve communities during their midsemester break.[29] The Ashesi leadership seminars are designed to "promote self-awareness among Ashesi's students and to expose them to the ideas of great historical thinkers and contemporary leaders."[30]

Fulbright Vietnam built a five-course core curriculum "designed and revised to be adaptable to trends and challenges in global higher education, while staying rooted in the Vietnamese context,"[31] with courses in global humanities and modern Vietnamese culture and society. FUV also offers interdisciplinary courses in quantitative reasoning, scientific inquiry, and design and systems thinking. Minerva University includes an intensive set of cornerstone courses that all students take in their first year, building skills in formal analysis, multimodal communications, empirical analysis, and complex systems. A novel assessment system at Minerva measures how students transfer their skills across a wide range of subjects in the curriculum and assigns a grade at the end of the four-year sequence.

Other examples can be found in the sciences, where several schools have invested heavily in multicourse sequences in integrated science, scientific inquiry, or foundations of science. Yale-NUS College developed multisemester sequences in all three of these areas, and the interdisciplinary science courses provided a significant investment of faculty staffing and represented a compelling part of the intellectual rationale for the new college. Indeed, the Yale-NUS "Curriculum Report" listed one of the overall goals for the new institution as to "redefine liberal arts and science education for a complex, interconnected world."[32] Science and math course sequences within the Yale-NUS common curriculum included a pair of scientific inquiry courses, a yearlong course on quantitative reasoning, and a sophomore science track that began with a choice between a yearlong foundations of science sequence (intended for nonmajors) or an intensive three-course integrated science sequence (intended for science majors).

All of these courses required intensive staffing, with five instructors team teaching in integrated science, ten instructors team teaching in scientific inquiry and quantitative reasoning and eight instructors team teaching in foundations of science. Integrated science began with "The Science of Water" as its theme, and utilized a "big-problem"-based learning strategy, with rigorous mathematics, computational science, biology, physics, and chemistry taught by instructors in all of those disciplines. The courses turned out to be difficult for the faculty to maintain—partly because of the breadth of interests within the student population, and partly owing to the challenges among science faculty in teaching outside their disciplinary expertise. One of the sequences, integrated science, was cancelled after two iterations; the foundations of science sequence was shortened to one semester and the scientific inquiry sequence was redesigned multiple times within the first few years of Yale-NUS. These frequent changes in the curriculum placed additional demands on faculty and perhaps also reflect some of the intrinsic difficulty in offering a truly interdisciplinary science course. Such courses are difficult to staff and teach even within an established institution, let alone a start-up university just staffed with fresh new faculty learning how to teach.

NYU Abu Dhabi, like Yale-NUS College, invested heavily in an interdisciplinary science sequence. Its Foundations of Science course is required for science and engineering students and initially consisted of six different courses taken during three semesters, which begins in the first semester of the first year for most of the science students. The sequence was designed to provide "a fundamental yet rigorous overview of science, focusing on the interrelationships among physics, chemistry, and biology."[33] The courses focus on interdisciplinary themes that include "energy and matter," "forces and interactions," "systems in flux," and "form and function."[34] These themes blend physics, chemistry, and biology in novel ways and the courses split course credits (and faculty teaching) between the different disciplinary departments. Like Yale-NUS, NYU Abu Dhabi has faced some challenges in training faculty to teach within an interdisciplinary environment, which requires expertise outside one's specialty. While the potential for innovation within interdisciplinary sciences is intellectually exciting, it has proven to be enormously challenging for a start-up institution to implement, and start-up institutions should be prepared with the necessary staffing and faculty support if they want to design a new interdisciplinary science program.

In addition to multicourse sequences, many start-up institutions have innovated by abandoning the conventional departmental major in favor of interdisciplinary degrees. ALU has moved furthest from the major by replacing fixed bundles of courses with a customized "mission" developed with faculty: this mission integrates work experience from internships, course work, and independent study. FUV offers eleven majors, including some that blend disciplines, such as an integrated science degree, and students are encouraged to build a customized course plan that includes one or two of the eleven majors as a "focus," much like a traditional minor. Minerva likewise offers its undergraduate degree in one of five colleges (Arts and Humanities, Business, Computational Sciences, Natural Sciences, and Social Sciences), but majors are not organized by discipline. Instead, students can major in areas such as designing societies; cognition, brain, and behavior; contemporary knowledge discovery; and scalable growth. And within a college, such as Arts and Humanities, a student might take three courses each in the areas of historical forces; philosophy, ethics, and law; and arts and literature.

The presence of such strikingly interdisciplinary degrees is an essential component of the start-up's claim to distinction. These degrees provide a channel for differentiation in an often-homogeneous educational marketplace. Bringing faculty from multiple academic disciplines together in teaching and research makes this interdisciplinary stance stand out and appeal to a range of stakeholders. Interdisciplinary and double majors encourage students to develop a broader range of interests and help them break out from the vocational mode of study that dominates higher education in most of the world—the same mode that students' parents often champion. Pramath Sinha, one of the founders of Ashoka University, notes that Ashoka's dual major in history and economics helped students "get the parental approval for studying history" by "throwing in the economics as a hedge." Other start-up institutions, too, clearly understand the multifaceted benefits of strategic interdisciplinarity.

Minerva University developed its curriculum in ways that mirror some aspects of product development in the high-tech sector, employing a cycle of development and refinement that has been shown useful for developing software and other tech products. As described by Minerva faculty Joshua Fost, Vicki Chandler, Kara Gardner, and Allison Gale:

> Syllabi, learning objectives, pedagogy, and assessment practices for the first-year cornerstone courses were developed and refined iteratively over a period of three years (indeed, refinement continues still) by a team that included the chief academic officer, deans of the four arts and sciences colleges, the associate dean of the faculty, the associate dean of institutional and educational research, the director of curriculum development, and a number of people who would later serve as development and instructional faculty.[35]

Engineered in this highly structured fashion, the Minerva curriculum intentionally signaled to the education world, prospective students, and investors that the new university was going to take a very different approach to education, focusing on efficiency, reproducibility, and interconnected units in its curriculum.[36]

Such an innovative curriculum can present challenges to accreditors. For Minerva, accreditation hurdles became one of the central through lines of its formation story. Its full accreditation, coming in July 2021 after ten years and four separate reviews, marked the successful culmination of this journey. Ben Nelson saw this accreditation as "absolute proof" that accreditors can appreciate programs that break tradition, and noted that "we didn't change a thing in the core offering of Minerva because of the demands of accreditors."[37] Yet as if proving a point about the tension between accreditation and innovation, WASC officials still cautioned Minerva about its culture of continuous educational innovation, which the association felt placed risks on the consistency of Minerva's program.

Ideally, a start-up needs to confer degrees that are not only innovative but widely recognizable outside of the new institution, capable of propelling students into graduate programs and strong employment. This constraint has prompted many of the start-up institutions to adopt more-conventional majors and degrees, which coexist alongside a novel general education or core curriculum. Ashesi offers a choice of six majors in largely vocational fields. Ashoka offers twelve majors in traditional academic disciplines, but with a number of additional interdisciplinary options that blend two or more fields. Yale-NUS similarly offered fourteen majors in academic disciplines, with some blending in majors. It also offered options for accelerated and dual-degree programs, such as concurrent degree programs with NUS and Yale in computing and public health, a dual degree in law and liberal arts, and more. Olin College degrees include very conventional degrees accredited by the Accreditation Board for Engineering and Technology in mechanical, electrical, and general engineering, but they also include innovative concentrations such as bioengineering, robotics, and sustainability. NYU Abu Dhabi, as a member of NYU's global network, can offer a vast array of degrees, including a choice of twenty-six undergraduate majors, and graduate programs offering PhDs in ten different fields.

The tension between innovation and convention is nowhere more visible than in the accreditation process. Accrediting agencies often look for conventional departments and curriculums, challenging innovative programs' attempts to depart from well-trodden pathways. Such tensions resulted in the frustrating yearlong delay for Ashesi University amid skepticism from Ghanaian accreditors. Awuah notes that while Ashesi was "coming from a very fast-paced place" where people "were allowed to take risks," it was being judged by public university officials who "didn't like taking that many risks." In a related way, ALU's unconventional "missions not majors" approach caused difficulties with its accreditation. According to Swaniker, "this notion of having students to declare their own mission and to curate their own learning" was "just anathema to most regulators." The solution was a Trojan horse approach, where ALU had to sneak innovation in under a conventional disguise. Degrees at ALU appear conventional and are offered in only two subjects—entrepreneurial leadership and computer science.

In some cases, government accreditors are required to authorize operation of the university. This was the case for Ashoka, which received authorization in 2014 by the Indian University Grant Commission. While Ashoka's initial accreditation went smoothly, the conservative BJP party and the new prime minister Narendra Modi changed the law suddenly to require all Indian undergraduate programs to conclude in only three years. Ashoka's solution was to reconfigure its undergraduate degree into one that technically can be completed in three years but can also be extended to four years if students opt for a postgraduate diploma in advanced studies and research. This solution enabled Ashoka to offer its full range of courses and to prepare students for graduate programs in countries that expect four-year undergraduate degrees.

One metaphor for accreditation is that of a troll on the road toward launch that is always there waiting to jump out and threaten a new start-up university. And it is indeed true that accrediting bodies have made things more complicated, delayed start-ups, and pushed institutions away from alternative models. Accreditors, like students and employers, prefer easily recognizable degrees to reduce the risks of students being unprepared for conventional employment. So, while the gatekeeping function of accreditation ideally is to assure quality, in some of our case studies it served to lock in outmoded and mediocre practices within academia. University founders have had to navigate past this obstacle. Some build strong partnerships with prestigious and well established institutions, others partially mimic some aspects of existing schools, and others are able to communicate the unique value proposition of their institution across their many audiences well enough to get past the troll of accreditation.

It is important to note that when given the unique chance to reinvent higher education, our start-ups in most cases decided to develop a common core with an original intellectual rationale for their courses that helped define the institution. We see many examples of pioneering intellectual achievement in these curriculums, which include the leadership seminars at Ashesi; Vietnamese studies at Fulbright; the core curriculum and foundations of science at NYU Abu Dhabi; the cornerstones at Minerva; Ashoka's nine foundational courses; the common curriculum at Yale-NUS; and the foundation, MODSIM, and design nature sequences at Olin. Along with the greater curricular coherence these courses offer, they also help students to have a shared interdisciplinary and intercultural understanding that also becomes a distinct feature of the new start-up university education. No doubt many existing universities would like to have similar course sequences, but the barriers to developing entirely new curriculums are great, and the start-up university provides an ideal laboratory to advance a new curriculum. These new institutions through their curriculums are also able to break through much of the stagnation and narrow overspecialization in traditional higher education, and move toward consilience, toward interdisciplinarity, and toward a curriculum that is more aligned with the complexities of the world's grand challenges.

Campus and Virtual Environment

For centuries, a college's or university's physical campus has served as the most tangible expression of that institution and its prestige, as well as the most expensive part of any start-up operation. More recently, new universities have questioned the value of this physical campus. Much as retailers in the brick-and-mortar realm have felt pressure from online retailers, so the physical campus has been described by some as an anachronism, destined to be displaced by lower cost and more agile online environments. Some contend that the campus is more than a luxury; it is a necessity for deep learning and for extended contact between students and between students and professors. For example, the historian Niall Ferguson, who is part of the group planning the new University of Austin, makes the case for a campus-based start-up university:

> Online learning is no substitute for learning on a campus, for reasons rooted in evolutionary psychology. We simply learn much better in relatively small groups in real time and space, not least because a good deal of what students learn in a well-functioning university comes from their informal discussions in the absence of professors. This explains the persistence of the university over a millennium, despite successive revolutions in information technology.[38]

The University of Southern New Hampshire enrolls ninety thousand online students and only three thousand on-campus students. President Paul Le Blanc acknowledges that online students miss out on the "coming of age" component, which "really requires a kind of intentional community that is a campus."[39]

Our case-study institutions span the range of thought on this issue. At one end of the spectrum, Yale-NUS College, NYU Abu Dhabi, and Olin College of Engineering boast some of the most beautiful and well-appointed campuses of any higher-education institution in the world. Each was designed with top architects, with buildings set in stone and brick, fostering interactions and the flow of people to facilitate conversation. On the campuses of Yale-NUS, Olin, and Fulbright University, faculty offices were intentionally mixed to encourage conversations and collaborations outside of traditional boundaries.

The campus for Yale-NUS, designed by renowned architects Pelli Clarke Pelli (who designed the Petronas towers in Kuala Lumpur), cost at least $240 million, and includes beautifully appointed residential towers as well as classrooms integrated into three residential colleges, which in turn are organized around separate common areas. Not just for show, this architecture was regarded as necessary for facilitating the "articulate conversation" so central to the Yale-NUS residential liberal arts education. As described in the Yale-NUS curriculum report:

The architecture of the residential colleges is designed to create a series of nested communities, one inside another. Students belong to a suite with roommates, to a block of suites sharing common space, to their residential college, to the College as a whole, to the much larger community of NUS and to the broader society of Singapore. This organization . . . provides an array of social interactions at different scales, offering a wide range of opportunities for personal development.[40]

NYU Abu Dhabi's lavish Saadiyat Island campus, designed and built by award-winning Rafael Vinoly Architects, includes a 450,000-square-meter (or forty-acre) footprint and a complex of academic buildings and laboratories. The total cost has been reported to exceed $1 billion.[41] Campus features include a library that has a swimming pool and basketball court integrated into the building, and a "high line" pathway helping connect buildings in a manner reminiscent of New York City. The combination of architectural elements in the NYU Abu Dhabi campus was designed "to reflect the University's three identities: Abu Dhabi, New York, and the world,"[42] with stunning facilities that embody the new institution's aspirations for world-class excellence. Hillary Ballon, a faculty member from NYU who led the planning of the campus from its beginnings in 2007, described the vision:

> We envisioned NYUAD as an open campus, with a seamless connection with the city. . . . To be prepared for that future stage of urbanism, the campus was designed with the latent potential to connect. Toward that end, every campus street is open; there are no gates. Visitors are welcome on campus; indeed, there is extensive programming—public lectures, art exhibitions, performances—to attract Abu Dhabi residents to the campus.[43]

With the initial gift of $450 million, Olin College was able to plan for an ambitious campus well before opening. The initial plan included eleven acres in eight new buildings, with the first four ready by the fall of 2002. The first four Olin buildings were the Olin Center, which contained faculty offices, administrative offices, a library, computer center, and auditorium; the Campus Center, with a dining hall; an academic center with twenty-seven classrooms; and a residence hall, which included 188 beds in double rooms.[44]

In all three of these well-appointed campuses, development included a preliminary stage of operating in more humble temporary quarters. For Yale-NUS College, the initial three years were spent in a borrowed NUS dormitory building known as RC4. Two floors of dormitory rooms were converted to faculty offices, and meeting rooms and classrooms were built within student common spaces, with the president's residence and offices squeezed into one of the residence floors. For NYU Abu Dhabi, the "downtown campus" was used for three to four years before the Saadhiyat Island campus was completed, and faculty recall some aspects of this first campus fondly. Despite being unable to provide science labs or student residence halls, NYU Abu Dhabi's downtown campus was "surrounded by Abu Dhabi buildings from the eighties and nineties" and was "in and of the city—it's perfect for us," recalled Ballon.[45] Olin College leaders and alumni often make reference to the farmhouses they occupied in their partner year while the campus was being built. The rough setting provided a dramatic base of operations for the maverick engineering faculty and intrepid students, who were taking on MIT. Rick Miller, Olin's president, jokes that the team was ready to say to MIT, "Excuse me. A few of us in a farmhouse out here fifteen miles [away] got the right answer. MIT's got it wrong."

In all three cases, the founding faculty, staff, and students recall affectionately how these more constrained quarters and younger and smaller institutions catalyzed creativity and interaction. Was the expansion to the larger and more lavish campuses entirely necessary for the long-term success of each institution—especially if budgetary conditions had been less favorable? Certainly, the need for science laboratory space and performing arts spaces requires the construction of larger facilities. And yet the degree to which each of these three institutions expanded its physical presence drove the costs of its start-up to levels that most other new institutions are unable to match—and at least in Yale-NUS's case, could have been a factor in the institution being deemed unsustainable from a financial perspective by NUS and the Singaporean government.

More intermediate costs for campuses can be found in three of the other start-up institutions, which are still expanding into larger facilities and are perhaps in an earlier stage of development. Ashoka University started as the YIF in a leafy, parklike setting in the south of New Delhi. This early campus had a peaceful and ethereal nature, with extensive landscaping, small fountains, and an oddly shaped building known as "the Treehouse," which looked out over the trees in the grounds and offered great views of the many birds making their homes there. This temporary campus was located closer to New Delhi than the ultimate permanent campus in Sonipat, a village one and a half hours outside of Delhi in the neighboring state of Haryana.

By contrast, the new campus was built in the Rajeev Gandhi Educational City, which allowed Ashoka to grow to the scale of the large university it aspired to become, with ample residence halls, laboratories, and common areas. Ashoka has just recently begun a new twenty-seven-acre campus adjacent to its current campus, which will allow it to nearly double, to be able to house six thousand students by 2027.[46] This expansion was made possible by its remote location in rural Haryana, where the state government acquired over two thousand acres of agricultural land for a "hub for higher learning and a centre for research," albeit with a trade-off for access to cultural and other opportunities in New Delhi for faculty and students.[47]

In the case of Ashesi University, its one-hundred-acre campus was built about an hour's drive away from Ghana's capital city of Accra. This location provides a spacious environment for students, with science laboratories, ample residential halls, and athletic fields. It was a marked upgrade from the two rented bungalows that composed Ashesi's facilities during its launch phase. Similarly, Fulbright University Vietnam began its operations in a launch-phase facility—in this case, a rented facility in downtown Ho Chi Minh City known as Bitexco Tower. With the university using donated office space, the entire team in these early days shared one large area, with the requisite crowding that invariably followed. After about a year and half, FUV moved to a building dedicated to the new university. Having a dedicated academic building proudly displaying the Fulbright logo was a big morale boost. Says FUV's first chief academic officer, Derby-Talbot:

> All of a sudden, now there was a big Fulbright University Vietnam sign displayed on the outside of the window. The great seal of the university, a tamarind tree, was also on display. There were banners. It was in a nice place and it looked grand. We had a groundbreaking ceremony. The ambassador and many VIPs came and gave talks, and that felt inspiring.

In coming years, FUV plans to expand still further, to a more remote location with a larger physical footprint.

African Leadership University and Minerva University have swung in a different direction, placing their bets on a minimal campus model. ALU has steadily moved away from a model that treats a campus as a central part of its operations. This shift has enabled it to radically drive down costs and, in doing so, to reach what it hopes will be many more students than the campus-based model can serve. ALU first built two campuses—one in Mauritius and one in Rwanda—but to scale ALU its leadership learned it would have to build a distributed model of regional learning hubs rather than full-blown campuses. Fred Swaniker, ALU's founder, plans to build thirty to fifty of these hubs across the continent of Africa and outside it. He describes the hubs as an alternative to a campus, a space that provides both internet access and electricity and embeds the students in a robust local community of mentors, employers, and fellow students, supplemented by visiting faculty. Students come to the Mauritius or Rwanda campus to start their college journey and then must cocreate their communal experience without the added cost and burden of significant travel.

Many of ALU's courses are online, and the university can provide this curriculum free of geographic constraints. As the core of an ALU education revolves around learning by doing—curating courses, exploring internships and gaining work experience—its leadership does not see the lack of a lavish campus as compromising its offerings, and would resist the characterization of ALU as "merely an online university." Indeed, Swaniker sees the regional hubs as facilitating more real-life experiences that contribute meaningfully to a student's education:

> You're spending time with your peers, with your mentors, with your coaches, you're doing. You're in the field, you're doing projects, you're doing conferences, you're shadowing professionals, you're doing research. . . . In the field, you're actually doing things. And you can also imagine now, in the hubs, we can have visiting faculty from all over the world. From Stanford, from Yale, from MIT, come and spend a month or half a month in one of these hubs, and have workshops and Master Classes. You can now have visiting professionals from the top companies in the world coming and doing residences in these hubs.

Minerva University likewise minimized its campus needs by relying on its technology platform for facilitating interactions between faculty and students. It even avoided building residence halls for students by placing them in rented apartment buildings located in a different global city each semester. Minerva's online platform is designed to promote mastery and active learning. It maximizes student engagement, delivers feedback to faculty about student engagement and understanding, and provides analytics to measure student participation on several levels. As described by Minerva's technology team: "The Active Learning Forum has no back row, no way for a student physically to hide or sit far away from the professor."[48] This platform was revolutionary when it was developed in 2014, and today it offers additional features and analytics that are not available to Zoom users. The ALF also measures faculty performance and can be used to train faculty to optimize student engagement. It has played a key role in binding faculty together in frequent meetings and reviews of student learning and curriculum.

The most vital function of a physical campus is to encourage serendipitous interactions between and among faculty and students. Many of our universities have adopted a solution in which faculty are based in a common area that is not segregated by discipline to foster more connections across disciplines and bridge narrow specializations. Most founders would opt for the enormous resources enjoyed by Olin, Yale-NUS, and NYU Abu Dhabi, which enabled construction of beautiful campuses in the first years of start-up. However, it is important to recognize that while such beautiful campuses do indeed convey prestige and provide wonderful environments for students, they also can inhibit the very flexibility and serendipity that was most prized in the start-up years. More than the heroic architecture or prize-winning architects, it is the quality of those conversations that ultimately will determine the institution's quality.

In the coming years, it remains to be seen whether students and their families will prefer the flexibility, mobility, and lower costs of an online experience that is coupled with in-person student living or regional hubs, rather than traditional physical campuses. So, too, we will see over time how the greater intentionality required by online education will compare to the established models of colocated students and faculty. Both types of instruction are increasingly likely to borrow from each other as education becomes more hybrid and blends the best of the in-person and online learning environments. Given the challenges of sustainability amid rising costs and the growth in hybrid forms of education, new start-ups should seriously consider leveraging technologies such as those at Minerva and ALU in their operations. And from a fiscal realism standpoint, new start-up institutions would do well to aim for more modest campuses. Lavish campuses used to signal affluence and prestige; today, what they signal appears to be changing. In a world where higher education is increasingly unaffordable, and with our world filled with inequalities, such campuses may instead signal a lack of concern for cost containment or for equal access.

12

Shared Governance and Global Aspirations

The early phases of building a new university are marked by creativity and informality, as the new institution struggles to confront and survive early crises. In this period, the strong relationships within a small group enable a transition into what appears to be a period of stability and growth. The increased scale of the organization itself then can produce new crises in identity and operations that have to be successfully managed. The USC business professor Larry Greiner, who charted this same process in the evolution of corporations from small start-ups, noticed that each phase of evolution requires new organizational practices, which "eventually sow the seeds of their own decay and lead to another period of revolution."[1] Some of our universities— NYU Abu Dhabi, Olin College of Engineering, and Ashesi University—have stood this test, by virtue of over a decade of successful operation since their inaugural class of students. Others—Fulbright University Vietnam, Minerva University, African Leadership University, and Ashoka University—are younger and still in transition phases as they work through issues of governance and growth. The other, Yale-NUS College, did not survive beyond the first decade—and provides us with some cautionary tales about how to structure leadership and vision in a way that builds a sustainable institutional culture.

In this chapter, we turn our attention to several cultural and political issues that proved especially challenging for our start-up universities to navigate and that, in many cases, their leadership will continue to wrestle with even as the schools become more established. We examine what the organizational theorist Edgar Schein calls the deep norms and assumptions that are often either hidden or so obvious to the group as to not warrant mention or debate. Arising out of sustained practices and norms within the community, this cultural layer fosters an implicit set of shared beliefs. In turn, gaps between those beliefs and various stakeholders within and outside the university lead to discord, a noteworthy part of the life of a start-up university.[2] This chapter focuses on two especially fraught areas that emerge from these different interactions, as well as the philosophical underpinnings of the institution. First, we examine the dynamic interplay between formal systems of governance and the informal culture that emerges over time in start-up institutions. Second, we explore the complex cultural and political dynamics underlying the aspiration many of these universities share: the establishment of a globally oriented institution simultaneously rooted in its distinctive local context.

Shared Governance in a Start-Up World

The system of shared governance common in US colleges and universities is both a source of strength and a barrier to innovation. This system disperses authority among faculty, administrative leaders, and board members, and gives special deference to faculty on matters of curriculum and pedagogy. Shared governance ideally fortifies institutional independence and improves overall quality while protecting academic freedom. These distinctive features of universities are difficult to establish in societies that are unfamiliar with, or hostile to, institutional autonomy and free expression.

Traditional shared governance models in established universities have also come in for considerable criticism. Former Princeton president William Bowen charged that shared governance produces inertia in the face of major challenges, such as runaway costs and insufficient access, and does little to prod faculty toward greater experimentation with new teaching methods or curricular structures.[3] Brian Rosenberg, former president of Macalester College and an advisor to ALU, puts the case directly:

> There is little about the governance structure or reward system in higher education that encourages substantial change. The careers of presidents and provosts are briefer, more tenuous, and more stressful than (maybe) ever before. About the best way for an academic leader to guarantee a tumultuous tenure is to try to shake things up. And it is the nature of

shared governance, faced with competing and argumentative constituencies to revert to the strategic plans and institutional priorities that will
be least offensive to the greatest number of people: unobjectionable and
uninteresting.[4]

Such inertia is often cited by the founders of new universities as a motivation
to work outside the established systems. For these schools, the fragmented
decision-making process attendant on shared governance can also make
it difficult to survive their early years, when a greater degree of flexibility
is often necessary. For all our new ventures, shared governance presents a
double-edged sword. If founders pay too much attention to the multiplicity of stakeholders involved—whether board members pressing for rapid
change or faculty defending the status quo—then the drive needed to achieve
lift-off in a start-up will dwindle. Conversely, it they pay too little attention
to shared governance, the school's academic character will be compromised,
and its legitimacy questioned by faculty, regulators, and the public.

At Fulbright University Vietnam, internal governance challenges
complicated the university's early years. The university churned through
several chief academic officers amid contending views over faculty governance, experimental education, the size and scope of the institution,
and how best to meet Vietnam's pressing needs. In its first years, FUV
favored younger faculty who loved teaching and mentoring students in
close relationships. Now the university faces challenges in transitioning
from a small, experimental undergraduate college to a more high-powered
research institution. In a related way, Olin College also struggled initially
with unclear and shifting expectations, especially about faculty promotion
and reappointment. In 2006, after Olin had graduated its first class, the
institution began to place more emphasis on research. This shift caused
some faculty to wonder if the administration was changing the rules of the
game and seeking to become a more conventional institution in which faculty research was central to promotion. The traditional metric of research
as the true sign of academic success continues to cast a powerful spell on
colleges and universities, even one like Olin, which was founded with the
specific intent to create a different kind of engineering graduate.

By 2010, Olin leaders had clarified that if the college's primary mission
was to change engineering education, then reappointment and promotion criteria needed to support that mission. This process of clarification
required an intentional effort to realign the culture with the institution's
highest priority: providing a high-quality and meaningful student experience.

Olin academic leaders had to consciously return to this touchstone and determine that the success of the institution required everything else at the school to reflect it, most especially the faculty experience and the system of rewards and recognitions.

Notably, Olin does not offer tenure to its faculty, a practice shared by African Leadership University, FUV, Ashesi University, and Minerva University. Instead, these schools offer various initial probationary contracts followed by multiyear contracts with an expectation of renewal. In cases such as FUV's, home-country regulations do not allow for tenure; for international faculty in particular, work visas must be renewed every two years and trump any other contractual commitments. In other cases, financial considerations weigh heavily on institutional hiring policies. ALU, FUV, Ashesi, and Minerva all began as bootstrapped start-ups without clear paths to financial stability. Under these conditions, the founders wanted to preserve financial flexibility, which a lifetime commitment to faculty would significantly reduce.

There's an even deeper reasoning at stake in some of these decisions. Many of these schools also elected not to offer traditional forms of tenure because planners feared that doing so would ultimately put the faculty's interests above those of the students. Since these institutions led with teaching and learning rather than research, they worried less about curbing research inquiry and more about ensuring that a commitment to students remained the faculty's highest priority.

Despite the absence of lifetime contracts, faculty at these institutions exert considerable influence on the institution. Most of them appear to have stable employment through a renewal process that is performance based. Yet there have been clear limits to this story in some cases, such as the dismissal of nearly half the faculty and staff at ALU in 2019, after a yearlong strategic planning process. More difficult to parse are whether the whims of management or the influence of external stakeholders is sometimes given freer rein in start-ups than at a traditional university. There is certainly less need for university leadership to consult faculty on core changes to the institution. Much, then, depends on the informal norms that evolve and the ways in which university leaders build processes that engage faculty. For the most part, our start-up universities that forgo tenure seem to have found ways to nurture strong faculty participation, even as they have clearly prioritized speed, flexibility, and coherence over shared governance.

By contrast, Ashoka, NYU-Abu Dhabi, and Yale-NUS College all offer traditional forms of tenure that include strong rewards for research productivity. By maintaining a dual focus on both research and teaching, these institutions have developed an institutional culture more like US research universities or the most elite liberal arts colleges. For these institutions, tenure protects academic freedom, induces performance in research, and aids faculty recruitment and retention. Of course, these very features have long been criticized for turning even the most radical faculty into narrow careerists who, by the time they receive tenure, have quietly become defenders of the institutional status quo. By adopting traditional US tenure standards, Ashoka, NYU-Abu Dhabi, and Yale-NUS also inherit a fundamental constraint on future innovation in teaching and learning, owing to the higher priority given to research. These constraints stand in marked contrast to the five other schools in our case studies, which have dispensed with traditional forms of tenure and concentrate fully on student learning.

At the moment of creation, schools that focus primarily on teaching and ones that combine research and teaching both elected to forgo conventional departmental configurations. Olin College, for instance, combined faculty into a single interdisciplinary group. "As an ever-evolving, dynamic college, we embrace a model of teaching and learning engineering that is forward-thinking, project-based, and centered on collaboration between faculty, and between faculty and students," a statement from the college reads. "We leave behind traditional structures like departments and tenured faculty with the goal of creating innovative, integrated learning experiences."[5] At Minerva, faculty are organized into five clusters. Yale-NUS divided its faculty into three divisions rather than erecting traditional academic departments. ALU, which offers "missions and not majors," places faculty in mission teams from multiple disciplines, mixed in with a large cadre of visiting practitioners and professors.

These schools share a strong commitment to robust general education requirements and nurture a culture in which all faculty have responsibilities for teaching these essential courses. A vital element here is the expectation that faculty are familiar with the core teaching across the institution and can make connections between disciplines across all four years. It is hard to overstate the radical nature of this expectation, which is simply not present at virtually any established school today, whether research university or liberal arts college. In our case studies, traditional departments and distributional requirements for general education were rejected for reducing the engagement of faculty in the larger collective enterprise. The architects of Yale-NUS explicitly pointed to a decay of effective faculty governance in American higher education as flowing, in part, from a curriculum and organizational structure that encourages faculty to think of themselves as free agents rather than members of a shared community. Instead, they, like the leadership at Minerva, Olin, and ALU, sought to create a curriculum that broke free from traditional departmental and disciplinary boundaries.

Internal challenges also emerge as a start-up institution traverses the distance between its initial founding vision and leadership and the dawn of new ideas and new leaders. This is especially the case when the founder comes from a background in business and has a strong view of the institution's purpose and defining characteristics. Ashesi's Patrick Awuah and ALU's Fred Swaniker completed professional degrees in business and first worked in corporate environments, Awuah at Microsoft and Swaniker at McKinsey & Company, and Minerva's Ben Nelson earned his undergraduate degree from the Wharton School at the University of Pennsylvania and worked in the private sector. Their sense of purpose, entrepreneurial energy, and corporate management style were essential to generating belief in the overall vision and attracting donors, staff, faculty, and students. Absent that drive and commitment, these schools would never have achieved lift-off or persevered through what often seemed like insurmountable challenges. As the institutions evolved, however, disputes arose over ways in which the founders could inhibit the growth of the same institutions they had created.

Minerva University navigated this territory through both formal and informal mechanisms. A set of legal agreements protects the university from control by the for-profit Minerva Project led by Nelson. Nelson was granted the status of chancellor of the university, an honorary role in which he presides over events, represents the university to the public as a thought leader, seeks philanthropic support, and offers advice to the leadership on keeping true to its mission. Over time, the other founding members of the leadership took on advisory roles or departed to take on new projects. One went on to start a two-year online college, another to lead product management for learning at YouTube, and a third retired and joined the board. Teri Cannon, the founding president, stepped down in 2022 to serve as an advisor to the next president of the university.

At Ashesi, Awuah's involvement in all aspects of the university led some members of the executive team to chafe at implicit restrictions on their autonomy to build the institution. Members of the executive team began to wonder if they had real remits and a mandate to lead. Over time, Awuah himself recognized that he had grown distant from many of the academic aspects of the university. He told cofounder Nina Marini he came to realize that "at one point, I [had] stopped talking to faculty about how things are going or walking through the halls asking 'What's this class look like? What are students getting excited about? What are they getting tripped up on?'" Faculty, too, asserted their right to speak publicly in support of students' rights to discuss openly controversial issues such as same sex relationships. Two factors enhanced Ashesi's ability to navigate this difficult terrain. The board and the university's executive leadership explicitly named the issue—they called it "founders' syndrome"—and consciously attended to instances where it threatened to undermine the institution's success. Equally important, Awuah himself came to recognize that he needed to strike a balance between leading the institution and enabling others to own it sufficiently so that authority became more dispersed.

At ALU, conflict between the founder and some staff and faculty led to mass resignations and firings. Frustrated by the pace and cost of building physical campuses across Africa, Swaniker doubled down both on his commitment to making a radical impact in Africa and beyond and on his philosophy of education, in which 70 percent of learning comes from hands-on practice in the field. He shifted from building brick-and-mortar campuses to creating coworking spaces across Africa that blend digital and experiential learning. Some faculty and staff, he argued, had misunderstood essential features of the institution's mission: the belief that educational quality improves as an institution becomes bigger, that creating problem-solvers requires dismantling academic disciplines and faculty-centered cultures, and that relying on government support or private donors both was unsustainable and would constrain innovation. This shift to regional hubs provoked a rebellion. Faculty and staff who were attracted to building the Harvard of Africa objected to the new strategy as diminishing ALU's educational goals, and they further criticized it as an indication that ALU was becoming too much like a corporation. Despite this conflict, ALU has seen new leaders come to the fore, as Swaniker has stepped back to build a global recruitment and outsourcing business, one that aims to ensure employment opportunities for graduates.

As two of the oldest of our start-ups, Olin College and NYU Abu Dhabi provide further examples of how to successfully navigate from a founding leader into an established and stable institution. Richard Miller was the first employee of Olin College in 1999; his successor, Gilda Barabino, arrived in 2020. An engineering dean based in Iowa, Miller drew up the blueprints and shaped the culture for the new college. Barabino, a member of the National Academy of Medicine and the former dean of engineering at the

City College of New York, faced a different kind of challenge: how to bring a fresh eye while staying true to the essence of the institution. The transition to a new leader after twenty years was made possible, in no small part, by Olin's underlying culture, seeded and nourished over time. Together with the shared vocabulary and institutional structures that reinforced it, this culture reflected a commitment to continuous reinvention and creativity in curriculum and in teaching and learning. Building a stable culture that is committed to change is something of a paradox, one that constantly risks destabilizing itself. Looking back, the institution's leaders recognized that this culture had evolved somewhat haphazardly—in a word, they got lucky. They advise others to be intentional about establishing the necessary culture from the beginning.

Launched in 2010, NYU Abu Dhabi managed its transition in leadership by bringing back as vice-chancellor the university's first provost, Mariet Westermann. In 2007, Westermann was part of NYU's advance team—"I was employee number 1," she says—and in that capacity she helped establish a temporary location; design curriculum; recruit students, faculty, and staff; and lay the plan for the new institution's full campus on Saadiyat Island. After three years, she departed to become vice-president at the Andrew Mellon Foundation in New York, and then returned almost a decade later as vice-chancellor. During her first stint in Abu Dhabi, Westermann was NYU's chief diplomat, shuttling between stakeholders representing Abu Dhabi, NYU, and NYU Abu Dhabi. When she returned in 2019, she carried the DNA from the early years of the institution—yet she also saw that it was entering a growth phase that would demand new insights, new skill sets, and new approaches. She stressed that the challenge NYU Abu Dhabi now faces is to mature into an enduring institution. In her first interview with the local media, she spoke forthrightly about the sensitive issue of academic freedom: "NYU Abu Dhabi enjoys the same academic freedom here that we do at NYU in New York and in our global network. It's a walkaway issue for us, of course—one needs a free spirit of inquiry to have a liberal arts education."[6]

Managing Conflict and Navigating Ambiguity

As Westermann's statement about academic freedom implies, educational founders must manage tensions between internal and external stakeholders. In addition to finance, regulation, and branding, categories that apply both to corporations and to nonprofits, university leaders operate in a unique environment at the interface of two governance systems—an internal system with faculty and an external system focused on the especially delicate relationship with political leaders. Successfully managing conflicts and navigating ambiguities that arise between these two systems requires founders to anticipate potential problems and communicate well with multiple audiences, though even the most adept leaders can find themselves struggling to do so in the glare of unwanted media attention.

Ashoka's founders managed to adroitly manage conflict in one area even as they struggled to do so in another. They identified and built a new kind of governance system for a university in India, one that simultaneously preserved the institution's independence and generated meaningful financial resources for it. Their simple but novel strategy was to avoid making the university subject to the control of a single donor by attracting a significant number of private supporters. The founders further enabled academic leaders to develop the curriculum, hire the faculty, and hammer out the overall intellectual culture of the institution without external interference. Founders Pramath Sinha and Ashish Dhawan listened to the input from their donors while socializing these benefactors in the Ashoka culture, nudging them toward an understanding that meddling with faculty recruitment or curriculum development wasn't in their best interest. "Business people need to unlearn, as they build a university, and learn what's different about a university versus a corporation," says Dhawan. At the same time, the founders brought a businesslike focus on setting strategic targets for institutional growth and tracking metrics of success. As a result, the university enjoyed both purposeful growth and freedom from undue pressure from donors—no small feat given the obstacles. In this way, Ashoka's founders adeptly managed conflicts between donors who came from the hierarchical corporate world and faculty accustomed to systems of shared governance in which they maintained ownership of academic matters.

The crises Ashoka faced arose from heated disagreements over academic freedom and dissent. These conflicts culminated in the resignation of the university's primary academic leader, following his ever-more-vocal criticisms of the Hindu nationalist government. His resignation, in turn, ignited an intense outburst of faculty criticism and student protest, prompting prominent international scholars to question whether Ashoka could survive as an intellectually independent institution. For Ashoka's founders, an outspoken academic leader had unnecessarily exposed the entire institution to significant risk at a time when its standing was far from assured. For faculty, political expediency had placed academic freedom at risk. The crisis exemplified how, even after setting up a system that works well at one level (donor management), piloting a safe course through the treacherous seas of academia and politics can at times be almost impossible. In Ashoka's case, university and academic leaders both felt they were put in an untenable situation. Such challenges are especially acute for start-ups in regions where ideological dissent is at risk and new universities cannot take for granted a centuries-long tradition of academic independence.

Fulbright University Vietnam was born amid concerns about whether the two very different governments of the United States and Vietnam would limit the new university's independence and sow ambiguity into the institution's core goals. Would US government funding influence what topics were taught and place FUV at odds with the Vietnamese government and Communist Party? As it turned out, neither US financial influence nor Party-enforced restrictions spawned major issues. FUV's leaders deftly steered around potential obstacles, winning ongoing buy-in from both the US and the Vietnamese side. Addressing potential ambiguity over the core goals of the institution proved more complicated. In its first five years, Fulbright wrestled with the meaning of being a deeply Vietnamese institution offering an American style of liberal arts education. For some of the founding faculty, the lack of clarity on how the Vietnamese and American features of the institution related to each other made for an opaque university identity. This opacity, in turn, hampered decision-making on key elements of the new venture.

The struggle over Fulbright's identity casts light on tensions that inevitably arise in audacious projects within the higher-education arena—particularly given the multiple interested parties involved. Creating a new university with academic freedom and institutional autonomy in a country under one-party rule is no small feat. Doing so in a way that attracts students and parents and meets international academic standards and local regulations adds an even higher degree of difficulty to the venture. The "blind men and the elephant" problem, in which every stakeholder imagines a different part of the institution as constituting the core of the entire university, characterizes Fulbright's early struggles. At the same time, taking on several large goals provided momentum and energy at Fulbright that might have been missing in a less aspirational venture. The daunting nature of the task got people's adrenaline going. In the process, the founders found themselves able to thwart the forces of inertia that otherwise could have prevented FUV from ever getting off the ground. Officials, investors, faculty, students, and other stakeholders could see enough of themselves in the project to commit to its success. Ambiguity, in other words, enabled buy-in.

As difficult as the governance challenges are within a single campus in a single country, some institutions must reconcile conflicts and contrasting institutional cultures among multiple sites separated by thousands of miles. These schools face thorny questions about intellectual freedom and institutional legitimacy, on the one hand, and cultural imperialism on the other. At NYU Abu Dhabi and Yale-NUS, tensions erupted from the onset of each venture. In New York, NYU faculty raised concerns about restrictions on free expression in the UAE, including prohibitions on insulting the royal families or Islam or engaging in homosexual relations, as well as denials of visas for specific individuals. Despite assurances of academic freedom, concerned faculty charged that scholars would necessarily self-censor what topics they address. In New Haven, Yale faculty raised similar fears about restrictions on protests and the lack of rights for gays and lesbians. Some faculty at both home campuses charged that merely by setting up shop in Abu Dhabi or Singapore, their institutions were legitimizing those repressive governments.[7]

At NYU Abu Dhabi and Yale-NUS, leaders insisted that academic freedom was a red line and that they would rather leave than see it compromised. More boldly, they argued that building campuses where debate and discussion could flourish might have a positive effect on the host society. Yale president Richard Levin, to take one example, advocated for deeper engagement with Singapore in the hope that greater mutual understanding and possibly even greater liberalization would result. In this context, proponents of the start-ups argue, there are many benefits to be gained when students from the host country as well as American students and their peers from around the world have a chance to learn about one another in a more open atmosphere than might otherwise be available.[8]

It seems important to note that sometimes these proponents suggest that the result of their work will be social change, yet at other times, and on occasion to different audiences, they assign few if any political or social implications to their institutional efforts. At NYU Abu Dhabi, for example, Mariet Westermann would explain that an education in the liberal arts did not mean adopting a Western lifestyle or political ideology. Instead, she would say, a liberal education is about freeing each student to develop their mind and maximize their potential. The question of what students might come to think or do as a result of such a liberating experience was carefully avoided. Such reticence to speculate on possible social or political outcomes offered a measure of ambiguity that allowed different audiences to interpret the aims of the university in ways each found reassuring.

A third line of argument occasionally appears as well—namely, that the perfect is the enemy of the good. Here, founders and other institutional proponents claim that it's better to make incremental progress in less-than-democratic countries than to hold out for perfection in matters of academic freedom before entering the fray with a new college. NYU's president, John Sexton, saw the benefits of building a more open and global dialogue in unlikely settings as outweighing the potential downsides. "Institutions, like people," he says, "are metaphoric victims of original sin, and we're not going to achieve perfection in this world." In 2013, concerns over the idea of a global network university constituted one factor leading to a vote of no confidence in Sexton by the faculty at the College of Arts and Sciences and several other academic units. Nonetheless, the NYU board backed Sexton, and NYU Abu Dhabi is now entering its twelfth year, even as some faculty and students in New York continue to express dismay over its existence.[9]

By contrast, Yale and Yale-NUS leaders were stunned to learn in 2021 that the new college would be closed and merged into NUS. The clashes among NUS, Yale, and Yale-NUS exemplify the problems that can arise when general agreement on the purpose of the institution can mask more fundamental differences. Singapore had wanted to unlock the kind of ingenuity that it saw driving technological invention and economic growth in the West. The iconic image of Steve Jobs speaking in front of two street signs—one labeled technology, and the other labeled liberal arts—captured the unique power of combining technical skills and human imagination. As Yale-NUS president Pericles Lewis wrote, "Steve Jobs . . . advocated for the value of a liberal arts education: 'We're not just a tech company. . . . [I]t's the marriage of technology plus the humanities and the liberal arts that distinguishes Apple.'"[10]

Over time, the experiment lost some of its luster for NUS leaders. Global attention elevated the college's Yale elements more than its Singaporean components, and doubts lingered among Singaporean leaders about potential intellectual and political ferment on campus. Building a new college "in Asia, for the world," came to be seen as too lofty and distant from the humbler task of meeting Singapore's economic needs and preparing more Singaporean students for employment at home. At the same time, the Yale faculty's reluctance to award a Yale degree to the school's graduates limited Yale's authority over its future. In this case, the ambiguity that enabled all parties to see what they were looking for in Yale-NUS contained the seeds of the university's eventual demise.

Ambiguity thus can both enable and undermine new multinational universities. By speaking carefully about the implications of an education that values debate and dissent, founders can secure sufficient support among their diverse backers and position a new venture to better manage the inevitable tensions. But not ensuring sufficient buy-in to foundational issues can also doom the institution when enough other conflicts among the parties arise. Of course, critics of the new global educational ventures regard any such ambiguity as not worth the risk. Their desire to protect intellectual freedom in places where it is clearly threatened is powerful and well warranted. But so, too, is the impulse of institution builders not to restrict the liberal arts to Western enclaves with their well-tended campuses and, instead, to protect new universities in their early years by managing rather than resolving ambiguities. There is something decidedly timid about the critics' refusal to take on the hard task of advancing intellectual freedom and human creativity in imperfect and fraught circumstances. In the end, there is no simple or clear way through this thicket. Perhaps there is even something of a moral division of labor here, in which proponents of unfettered academic freedom defend the garden walls and institution builders tend the new vines that must grow in inhospitable terrain. While the two may inevitably fall into discord, at times they may also be able to work in concert—thus achieving, in that moment at least, a productive balance between pragmatism and idealism.

Rooting Global Aspirations in the Local Context

Establishing universities in new global settings raises difficult questions about whether a liberal arts education is tethered to a set of Western cultural assumptions. Countries in the Middle East, Africa, and Asia that have thrown off the yoke of colonialism are, in many instances, still struggling to escape from educational systems inherited from Britain and other former powers. The philosophy undergirding those older systems seemed better designed to create workers who can function in a bureaucracy than entrepreneurs who can invent new companies or citizens who can advance democracy. By way of contrast, the new universities want to prepare students to roam widely and to succeed at home, to be leaders for the world and for Ghana, Vietnam, India, or Singapore. Yet preparing a student to be a top employee at Google in the United States may make that student a strange match for a government ministry in Vietnam—someone who asks too many questions, perhaps, or is impatient with the slower pace and bureaucratic structures of the public sector. The assumption that a student who is highly trained in implicitly American or Western habits of mind will naturally translate into a good fit in a very different culture might not be true.

There is some irony that countries like India and Singapore, steeped in older Western forms of colonial education, thus find themselves turning once again to a Western educational philosophy—here, the liberal arts as it has emerged most fully in the United States—in an effort to unleash greater creativity and innovation. This irony can itself spark tensions. Little controversy surrounds the straightforward adoption of American strategies for effective teaching, including the greater focus on individual student success. But questions do emerge about how well a liberal arts education fits different cultural contexts when it comes to the content of some courses, styles of learning that challenge traditional forms of authority, and the larger aspiration for students to think for themselves—and think *of* themselves as global citizens, rather than members of one particular nation. In some of our case studies, we see the challenges that arise when a distinctly Western and American approach to education clashes with local traditions and aspirations. In other cases, we see exciting new blends of cultures and philosophies taking shape.

NYU Abu Dhabi had to tackle an array of issues as a university committed to a global sensibility, formed in the US mold, and located in a culturally traditional and politically authoritarian Middle Eastern country. The university sought to address these complexities by blending Middle Eastern and Western perspectives in its curriculum and by offering options for mixed or gender-segregated halls in its residence halls, among other methods. At the same time, confusion persisted over what it meant to be global university. NYU's president, John Sexton, had articulated a quasi-theological vision of an "ecumenical university," which would push students to go beyond what he called "intellectual indifferentism" and engage with one another's differences. The goal was for them to argue and debate in ways that deepened understanding without assuming that there was one right answer or right way of thinking.

But NYU Abu Dhabi students struggled to understand what this ecumenical vision actually meant and worried about expressing views that might offend their peers. In the first years, students were more comfortable minimizing their differences. Over time, students have also described experiences of bias on campus. In 2020, the student newspaper the *Gazelle* reported that "more than a third of the student body signed a letter urging a renewed focus on combating institutional racism at NYUAD, citing 'an alarmingly skewed understanding of racism and how it manifests itself on our campus.'" The university's curriculum and hiring practices have come under criticism from students and faculty, who say that the curriculum is overwhelmingly Eurocentric and the faculty dominated by white Westerners. Awam Amkpa, dean of the arts and humanities, told the *Gazelle* that "decolonization is not an event. It's a permanent process of evaluation, restrategizing and addressing the themes of inequity and asymmetry." In response to these criticisms, the university has announced a series of initiatives that are strikingly similar to those seen on US campuses, such as mandatory training on diversity, equity, and inclusion for faculty, administrators, and staff, and required learning modules on the same topics for students.[11]

It is worth noting that this American-style rhetoric about decolonization and diversity is a feature of other multinational ventures in the Middle East and Asia. Georgetown University, for instance, established a campus in Qatar in 2005. Faculty there have observed the ways in which campus discussion is remarkably open about some topics that align with Western sensibilities. Ian Almond, a professor of world literature, writes that "here, on the other end of the planet, there are very similar arguments amongst our students about Black Lives Matter, trans rights, colonialism, and all the issues that get discussed on American campuses."[12]

It might seem strange if campuses constructed to engage the most profound questions in a global setting ended up as vanguards of a largely progressive, Western perspective. Yet such instances exemplify what sociologists of higher education have observed about the spread of universities: "The modern world is knit together by elites more schooled in a cosmopolitan world culture than in their own local ones, and linked more tightly to each other than to their own populations," Evan Shofer and John Meyer wrote in 2005. Universities, they continued, "reflect the themes—and the contradictions—of [this] world culture."[13]

Some global campuses can encourage debate or exploration that is even *more* open than on American campuses. Writing about his experience at another key node in NYU's global network, NYU Shanghai, law professor Rick Hills reports that he found intellectual debate more open in Shanghai than in New York City. He suggests that students raised in very different countries and cultures cannot help but undermine ideological orthodoxy:

> Coming from dozens of countries, [the students] are simply too unfamiliar with each other's mores and peeves to know whether and when to be offended. There are no longstanding family quarrels that we all know we must avoid to maintain a chilly peace. What is the consensus position on, say, the legality and morality of a ban on porn or a Muslim woman's entitlement to religious exemptions from a public school's uniform requirements

when the discussants are a Dutch atheist, a Pakistani Muslim, and a Chinese Communist Youth League kid?[14]

Discussions of democracy and free speech, he continues, take on a different tone when they occur inside a country governed by authoritarian leaders. The usual assumptions in a US classroom go out of the window when such different viewpoints on fundamental issues are present.[15]

Hills's classroom example is especially helpful, since what goes on there and in the hallways and common rooms is as important as the formal protections for academic freedom and free expression. It's also important to take note of what students and faculty don't say and do, as well as what they do. When does a professor decide not to assign a particular text out of concern that her visa might not be extended? What events are cancelled, or are never contemplated, out of an abundance of caution not to attract unwarranted attention? Are there taboo topics that students avoid discussing as a result of implicit peer pressure? A campus can be formally free and yet debate and dialogue hemmed in on multiple fronts, both seen and unseen. Of course, all campuses everywhere are subject to these same questions, most especially the implicit culture among students about what's acceptable to discuss and what's not. In both start-ups and established universities, the question is about the nature and extent of these constraints. Are they at the margins or are they so pervasive as to interfere with the core ideals of a liberal arts education?

Navigating these tensions in places like Shanghai, Singapore, Qatar, and Abu Dhabi can bring more depth and subtlety into student learning than is found on Western campuses. Students and faculty must be attentive to what is said on campus and what is said off campus. The academic freedom to choose books as a faculty member or a topic for a research paper as a student is not the same thing as posting an essay on social media intended to influence the public sphere. The latter is much more fraught and thinking through a decision like that is precisely what a liberal arts education should be preparing students to do. In this way, the local culture and political context aren't simply constraints; they are also spurs for students and faculty to become more adept cultural navigators than they otherwise might turn out. At the very least, these students are exposed to a different set of challenges than their peers who enjoy the comforts of formally unrestricted expression in New York or New Haven.

The more genuinely free-flowing and open discussions are on campus, the more they raise a deeper philosophical question: whether a liberal education itself presupposes the priority of secular over religious authority, tolerance for minority viewpoints, and the openness of a liberal society. For some observers, these underlying assumptions, together with the expectation that students will judge or evaluate texts and debate their peers and professors, remain fundamentally at odds with societies grounded in traditional forms of religious and communal authority. Writing about his experience teaching at the American University in Cairo, the historian David Blanks suggests that liberal education as practiced today in the West is tied to the notion that "limitless self-development is culturally desirable and beneficial."[16] In short, a true liberal education is thus not merely a method of analysis or pedagogy, but is itself a cultural and ideological conceit, one that, for Blanks, contradicts some Arab and Asian cultures that place greater emphasis on community and tradition. The risk, then, is that too-easy affirmations of the value of American-style liberal education will undermine local cultures and constitute a new form of cultural imperialism. As Kara Godwin, a scholar of comparative education, puts it: "If liberal education is to develop and sustain itself in a truly global context, then academic practices and curricula need to reflect the local and indigenous culture, economy, and society in which programs reside."[17]

If, however, localization entails significant deference to cultural taboos and explicit or implicit constraints on discussion, then it can sever the link between education and the *ars liberalis*, the practice of being free. A liberal education is meant to cultivate our capacities for reason, imagination, persuasion, and the various intellectual habits and dispositions thought to enable a person to govern themself, and therefore to be able to participate in governing others. This desire to create citizens who are well suited to democratic governance has been deeply embedded in the philosophy of liberal education, especially as it developed in the United States. On this view, students should learn to think for themselves not just as a matter of individual growth but as a prerequisite for democratic citizenship. As one of Yale-NUS's persistent critics, Jim Sleeper, writes, "a liberal capitalist republic has to rely on its citizens to uphold certain public virtues and beliefs—reasonableness, forbearance, a readiness to discover their larger self-interest in serving public interests—that neither markets nor the state do much to nourish or defend, and sometimes actually subvert. Good citizen-leaders must therefore be trained all the more intensively."[18] For Sleeper, as for many faculty in American universities, any attempt at teaching the liberal arts in illiberal societies will be insufficiently attentive to the demands of democratic citizenship. As a result, shorn of its Western and especially American context, the liberal arts will become a neutered form of education.

In his engaging book about his experiences teaching at Georgetown University's campus in Qatar, Gary Wasserman describes a more complex human dynamic at work. Faculty are broadly interested in promoting liberal values, while students are caught between their roots in Muslim and Arab cultural traditions and the pull of a globalist, consumer ethos. "For expatriate faculty," he writes, "motives were usually adapted from the old British imperial credo of 'God, gold, and glory' to suit the more secular goals of liberal scholars. Promoting interest in intellectual inquiry, religious tolerance, and an openness for dissent and debate—all while making a comfortable living in an exotic setting—covered quite a few of the likely motives." For the students, it was harder to determine whether the religious and regional traditions were the deeper substrata or their more secular, Westernized interests. "Although I often engage in the argument," he concludes, "I usually throw up my hands in the end. I have no idea." On the one hand, "some students upset by the numbers of expats in Doha as well as the perceived dominance of Western products and culture felt threatened by this foreign incursion." On the other, "exactly what the threat was and what the response should be got muddled whenever I heard it expressed." Wasserman's observations underscore ways in which the reality on the ground is always infinitely more multifaceted than abstract arguments for or against advancing the liberal arts in illiberal societies.[19]

Any honest accounting of the liberal arts in a global age nonetheless has to recognize a deep tension at work—a tension between core philosophical presuppositions that emerged in a particular culture and time and the many and varied cultures in which these presuppositions are now being put to the test. We see a global variation on the question of what commitments a liberal education presupposes in the case of Yale-NUS. When the venture first launched, critics questioned the assumption that Asian countries lacked their own tradition of liberal learning. Writing in 2016, Shun Kwong-loi, an eminent philosophy professor at UC Berkeley, took Yale president Rick Levin to task for the assumption that Yale was "bringing" a liberal education to Singapore:

> His perspective does not take into account the rich insights of the Confucian view of adult learning as a process of intellectual and moral transformation that involves the personalization of what has been learnt and the building of a broad world view. The Confucian model and the model of liberal education are different views of learning set in different cultural contexts, and each has important elements from which the other can benefit.[20]

In this view, the Western cultural narrative tends to prize the aggressive Socratic questioner, the gadfly and often alienated critic. In contrast, Confucian standards of moral and intellectual development give more emphasis to finding a balance between evaluating an idea's merits or faults and safeguarding harmony in society or relationships. (Confucianism, of course, also incorporates a multitude of traditions and interpretations within itself and is far from the only wellspring of values in Asian countries.)[21]

Kwong-loi's criticism suggests the possibility that new and more global liberal arts institutions might offer a more searching education than is currently available in the United States or elsewhere. Reason and critique, so central to Western universities, are supplemented in other traditions by concerns for character and community that have been eclipsed in the West. Global universities, which draw students and faculty from around the word, can thus more intentionally engage with the complex welter of issues at the intersection of wisdom traditions. Indeed, Levin himself argued that Yale had much to learn in Singapore: "Social norms, practices, and values differ widely across nation and cultures. We (our students and faculty) seek to embrace these differences and seek to understand them, as the first step toward building the cross-cultural understanding that must be the foundation of global citizenship and cooperation."[22] For its part, Yale-NUS ended up doing just this by building a curriculum in which students studied ancient Rome and the Ming dynasty and read both Homer's *Odyssey* and the Sanskrit epic *Ramayana*. They encountered Ibn Khaldun and Max Weber, Simone de Beauvoir and Saba Mahmood, the Buddhist monk Śāntideva and Shakespeare's *The Tempest*.

Yet even this global core curriculum raised thorny questions: What does "Asia" mean? Does it stretch from China to India, Southeast Asia to the Middle East? And however Asia is defined, how do the varied traditions, texts, politics, and cultures found there sit next to an equally varied Western tradition? Does the very formulation of "Asia" suggest a kind of Rudyard Kipling–like reification of East and West? Some students have felt that the curriculum places too much emphasis on China and India and is insufficiently attentive to the culture and traditions of Singapore and more locally rooted writers, thinkers, and communities.

These various disputes over culture and citizenship are challenging to resolve within a single curriculum for a heterogeneous student body. Yet they are also just the kind of disputes that fulfill the promise of the liberal arts in a global age. Is it better to offer a course on "Global Shakespeare," as Cyrus Patell does at NYU Abu Dhabi, one that examines a Western writer with whom writers around the world have had to engage? Or should a global university focus on an author like the Sudanese Tayeb Salih, as NYU Abu Dhabi student Tom Abi Samra argued, taking care to first require students to acquire the theoretical vocabulary of postcolonial studies?[23]

In a more global setting, a genuine exploration of competing and overlapping cultures and philosophical commitments could offer a fresh take on old debates. To do so, faculty and students will have to be willing to puncture lazy assumptions and ideological conceits inherited largely from US and European universities. But the promise is there, nonetheless. Most educational systems have been tied to both the economic aspirations and the underlying cultures and philosophies of a single nation-state. What's more, most universities are dominated by faculty and students from the countries in which they are located, which inevitably creates a set of default cultural assumptions and habits of engagement. New universities that draw students and faculty from around the world and that consciously engage with the messy issues at the juncture of the local and the global may well create better and more profound forms of education.

Rediscovered Heritages and Global Residents

Homegrown institutions like ALU, Ashesi, Ashoka, and FUV confronted challenges of their own: how to build stronger local connections that complemented their global outlook. At ALU, the relationship between global and local led to an intense debate over what it meant to be an African university. A key flashpoint focused on whether the curriculum offered was overly Western. Some faculty had been attracted to ALU's mission of building a new leadership cadre for Africa. They believed that the university needed to be built "by Africans, for Africans," and that it should offer African ways of thinking and doing. Fred Swaniker and Sidee Dlamini took a very different view. To their minds, being African meant that the university was created in Africa and that it prioritized strategies and solutions that would work within the constraints and needs of African students and countries, but these strategies and solutions didn't have to be African in origin: ALU should draw freely on the best ideas, regardless of origin, rather than relying solely on indigenous knowledge for its future.

At the same time, university leaders gradually learned that students had to be deeply embedded in the countries and cities from which they came if they were to tackle significant problems effectively and find employment in their communities. The importance of keeping students rooted in their local communities—and the financial unsustainability of building more campuses—caused the university to focus on experiential education supported by less expensive regional hubs across Africa. It saw this shift as a further indication of how its core approach would address the problems bedeviling higher education globally. ALU would pioneer a model that could work at scale while still delivering a higher-quality education than typically available to most students—a distributed university that emphasizes learning by doing, leverages technology, and offers a price point affordable around the globe.

In a manner similar to ALU, some faculty at Ashesi also argued that the curriculum was too Western oriented and that non-African content should be removed from the core curriculum. Texts and examples in the leadership seminars, for instance, should feature solely African exemplars and concentrate on problems that are relevant to Africa. Yet Ashesi consciously chose not to pursue this route. Instead, as the university evolved, it has given more consideration to African thought and local wisdom without diminishing a more broad-based education. There is also more attention given to balancing global and African examples to illustrate larger concepts in other courses. When Joseph Oduro-Frimpong, the director of the university's Center for African Popular Culture, first joined Ashesi, he says, it was common to hear, "'Oh, at Swarthmore, this is how it's done right,' and 'at Harvard, this is how it's done.' Now I've seen conscious efforts to see parallel examples drawn from here. I see the global and the local not existing in two separate spheres, but coming together."

Awuah, Ashesi's president, sees this blending as consistent with a vision of African futurism. He describes a sensibility that requires both the humility and the confidence to learn from everywhere in the world, while bringing African culture and content to the fore. "We should have this real spirit of the liberal arts of multiple perspectives coming to bear, and to do that requires confidence about who you are able to learn from," he says. "We can learn from the West, we can learn from the East, we can learn from Latin America and other places as they can learn from us." Like Swaniker at ALU, Awuah believes that to focus too heavily on African content would display a lack of faith in Africa. Instead, the goal is to ensure that the students are competent in both the global and the local.

Ashoka University also faced criticism that its liberal arts approach and branding as the "Yale of India" had made it an unwelcome Western import. This view came primarily from critics outside the university, who pointed to Ashoka's fees as an additional indicator of its preoccupation with educating elites in Western ways. Perhaps ironically, the university has developed a particularly strong emphasis on Indian culture, history, and thought. Some of this interest was stoked by the rise in nationalism in India and new conversations about what it meant to be part of India as a civilization. Students wanted to be able to engage traditional Indian texts such as the *Mahabharata* in sophisticated ways, as these texts increasingly served as reference points in public debates. Ashoka also found that it could attract leading scholars of India and South Asia from abroad, individuals who had become influential commentators on controversial issues at home, such as the rights and protections provided by the Indian Constitution.

FUV also wrestled with the tension between replicating an American-style liberal arts education for Vietnam and creating something new and distinctively Vietnamese. Over time, the university has embraced traditional disciplinary and applied forms of knowledge that can be of direct benefit to Vietnam. Fulbright's most distinctive educational efforts have come in its emphasis on Vietnamese art and culture, its incorporation of Vietnamese case studies through the curriculum, and its creation of a unique Vietnamese studies major. Debates erupted over how students could actively engage sensitive topics like the war with America or required courses in Ho Chi Minh thought and Marxism. Fulbright's answer, teaching Marx in the context of German thinkers and Ho Chi Minh thought in the context of Vietnamese history, and exposing students to American views of the war, encountered little pushback from authorities. For their part, students embraced the possibility that history allowed for different, even competing, interpretations. Western faculty did learn, however, that one discussion item was completely off limits: criticisms of the single-party system in Vietnam. And students implicitly seemed to understand that their ability to engage in free discussion on campus did not protect them from the repercussions of off-campus protest or political activity.

When universities such as FUV and Ashoka wrestle with the tension between the local and the global, the latter often appears in the form of Western and usually American ideas. Olin College and Minerva University are both located in the United States, and so find themselves operating squarely from an American context. At Olin, cultural issues have played out in terms of US discussions about diversity. From the beginning, the college has maintained a gender balance, unique among engineering schools. Half the student body receives some form of scholarship to attend. Fewer than 15 percent of students identify as underrepresented students of color. Barabino, the new Olin president, has made it a priority to further diversify the student body as well as the faculty and the board. She is also striving to foster a greater sense of belonging among all members of the community.

Minerva's geographic footprint shapes its approach to difficult conversations (seven sites on four continents), as does its wildly diverse student body (six hundred students from eighty countries) and its underlying philosophy. The university intentionally sends students to a major global metropolis like Seoul, where, just as they are beginning to settle in, they are uprooted and moved to Hyderabad. No one expects that students will become experts on Seoul or Hyderabad in four months. Instead, these locations should prompt them to practice what Minerva calls "critical wisdom," the ability to look at a problem they've never encountered before and apply their training to address it in systematic and thoughtful ways. As residents, rather than full citizens or mere tourists, students are expected to develop the capacity to observe and respond to the world's problems.

The challenge here is to guard against students proposing superficial solutions based more on abstract concepts than on genuine knowledge about local culture and history. In the wake of George Floyd's killing, for example, Minerva leaders found they needed to deepen students' grounding in the history and legacy of slavery in the United States and to sharpen their ability to analyze competing conceptions of identity and belonging. A global education spanning seven world cities with students from across the globe thus still had to ensure that students were sufficiently anchored in the history and politics of a specific locale before those students could begin placing interpretive judgments on events unfolding outside their doors.

Evolutionary Phases and Underlying Assumptions

The life of any start-up university, like a start-up corporation, goes through evolutionary phases. The management professor Mary-Ellen Boyle describes these phases as part of a complex system in which an initial and often chaotic phase of organizing gives way to "a period of tension and apparent resistance to change leading to a critical threshold, and emergence of a new configuration."[24] In telling the story of eight start-up universities, we have seen how some of their leaders found that a degree of ambiguity can be constructive in the dizzying and lean initial years. Sometimes they offered a capacious vision intentionally, as in the case of Yale-NUS and NYU Abu Dhabi; at other times, doing so reflected the reality that multiple stakeholders have different understandings of the larger project, as in the case of Fulbright University Vietnam. In either case, a measure of ambiguity offered enough room for stakeholders to see their interests advanced by the new university and so lend it their support. For others, clarity of vision proved crucial to attract supporters and overcome obstacles, as we saw in cases of ALU, Minerva, Olin, Ashoka, and Ashesi. In all cases, founders of truly innovative schools ultimately need both more strategic flexibility and more internal commitment to a shared vision than leaders of established universities can typically expect.

From those heady early years, a university will transition into an adolescent phase in which cohorts of students begin to graduate and newly hired faculty begin to outnumber the pioneering founding faculty. At some point, the turbulent launch phase settles into an equilibrium: new faculty and leaders take their place alongside the original founders, and together begin to reinvent and renew the energy and excitement of the new university. At this more adult phase of institutional life, a successful transition to new leadership must take place, one that allows both for greater stability and ongoing opportunities for invention. Some of the most challenging moments in this journey involve the founders' staying true to their own North Star—bringing forth a new and distinctive institution—without being so domineering that other leaders can't emerge to fix blind spots and navigate new territories. Without this transition, disaster awaits.

Throughout this evolution, the cultural and philosophical assumptions underlying the entire venture will be drawn out and tested. Schools advancing a global and cosmopolitan outlook in more traditional and less democratic settings must confront the degree to which their outlook represents an implicitly Western and usually American perspective. At the same time, we have seen how championing the global often leads to a renewed emphasis on the teaching of local traditions and cultures. At their best, all eight of our start-ups offer glimpses of a future in which students engage profoundly across traditions as well as explore more deeply within them. These glimpses are still heavily influenced by the past and, as such, may simply replicate existing views rather than breaking new ground. Yet compared with traditional universities tied to a single country, our start-ups are incubators of change in multinational settings. In an age where the local, the national, and the global jostle uneasily, they may yet offer the world a profoundly creative and generative form of education that is desperately needed.

13

Conclusion

LESSONS LEARNED AND PARTING THOUGHTS

Since we began work on this book in 2018, all eight of the universities we studied have experienced both steady evolution and dramatic change as they reached significant milestones. In August of 2019, Mariet Westermann, who had been NYU Abu Dhabi's first provost more than a decade earlier, returned to the United Arab Emirates as vice-chancellor to lead the university into its next phase of expansion. A very different story played out in Singapore. By 2021, Yale-NUS's founding president, Pericles Lewis, had returned to Yale to become vice-president for global strategy, and along with Yale president Peter Salovey, he was shocked to learn in August that the National University of Singapore would dissolve Yale-NUS as a separate institution and merge it with NUS's University Scholars Program.

Ashoka University, too, faced crises that called into question its institutional independence from larger political forces. In June 2021, the board of trustees moved to formally address this question by appointing former Indian Supreme Court judge Madan Lokur as its ombudsman. "Our aim is that through this and already existing processes we will be able to ensure that Ashoka lives up to its vision of being a space for free enquiry, free expression, intellectual honesty, respect for the dignity of all human beings and openness to constructive change," the board statement declared.[1] In the same year, Ashoka laid the foundation stone for an extension of its campus that, when complete, will more than double the university's footprint and enable it to expand enrollment significantly.

Meanwhile, across the Indian Ocean from Ashoka, on the island of Mauritius, Fred Swaniker and his colleagues in the African Leadership network of organizations were marking two milestones. In 2020, Swaniker secured a major investment in support of African Leadership University and the other key nodes in a network that today includes a nonprofit high school and a for-profit career accelerator and global talent-matching platform. Then, in 2022, Veda Sunassee, a native Mauritian and Princeton graduate, was appointed CEO of ALU, reflecting an important transition in leadership.

The year 2022 would prove especially auspicious for a number of our schools. Ashesi University was ranked first in Ghana, seventh in Africa, and among the world's top three hundred universities having the greatest impact, according to *Times Higher Education*. In February of the same year, Fulbright University Vietnam's founding president, Dam Bich Thuy, announced a commitment of $40 million from eight Vietnamese donors to support the creation of an expanded campus in Saigon High-Tech Park, one of the largest philanthropic gifts to a higher education institution in Vietnam. Dam remarked that "as the beneficiary of such generosity, it is Fulbright's responsibility to continue fostering impact not only in Vietnam but also in the world."[2]

The beginning of the third decade of the century also saw notable transitions and achievements in two more of our institutions. In July 2020, Gilda Barabino began her term as president of Olin College, and by February 2022 had also been named the new board chair of the American Association for the Advancement of Science. Olin has maintained its top standing in rankings of undergraduate engineering programs, an acknowledgement, Barabino says, "that we have one of the most innovative engineering programs in the country." In 2022, Minerva University also made a transition from its founding president, Teri Cannon, to Mike Magee, a leader in the K-12 world who joined the university with a remit to expand access for socioeconomically diverse students from around the globe. By 2022, Minerva had become a fully accredited independent institution and was ranked as the world's most innovative university, ahead of Arizona State University, MIT, and Stanford, as well as the top-ranked school globally for an education that teaches students how to translate their academic knowledge into practical results in the world.[3]

Starting a new university is a complex undertaking and, as these stories have demonstrated, can include noteworthy, rapid developments that require quick thinking. Being a founder is not for the faint of heart or for those used to a more predictable command and control operation. New universities must compete with institutions that have had as long as five hundred years to establish their position in a market more often defined by prestige than efficiency or customer satisfaction. Launching a new university requires leaping to the front of a race that has been in progress for centuries, while also fulfilling the multiple missions that higher education serves for a wide range of stakeholders.

The scholars Michael Cohen and James March have described universities as organized anarchies and characterized leadership in them as suffering from ambiguities of purpose, power, experience, and success. The university needs to challenge students to think deeply during a time of intense identity formation and individual maturation while also serving a larger goal—namely, to preserve historical and cultural memory while advancing scientific discovery and economic growth. Additional components of a university mission can include other overlapping and often contradictory goals. These include entertaining alumni and sports fans while solving social ills and preparing students for jobs, maintaining public support and financing while protecting free inquiry and faculty autonomy, and expanding campuses while pushing down costs.[4]

Given the complexity and difficulty of running a university, let alone launching a new one, it is remarkable that seven of our eight start-ups have survived into at least their young adult phase. The one institution that didn't survive, Yale-NUS College, was acquired by one of its parent bodies, the National University of Singapore. This is an astounding rate of success, as most start-up companies fail within the first five years.[5] More than surviving, many of these new institutions appear to be genuinely thriving in 2022. All of our start-ups receive strong applicant pools based on a growing local and global reputation. In several cases, such as at NYU Abu Dhabi, Minerva University, and Olin College of Engineering, they stand among the most selective institutions in higher education in the world. This success validates the vision of the founding leaders, embodying those original aspirations in dynamic and effective new institutions that promise to shape the lives of their graduates, their countries, and the world for decades to come. And yet, like start-ups in industry, the future of a new university is never assured. Each of these schools continues to face daunting challenges, ranging from ongoing financial pressures and challenges to maintaining its academic independence; perhaps a future account will tell us how well these universities were sustained as they navigated these obstacles.

For now, we conclude this book with a set of lessons learned for future founders of new universities, for current leaders and participants in established universities, and for all the doubters, disrupters, and defenders who care about preserving what's special about a liberal arts education while creating new ways for those values and precepts to live in the world. We offer three main takeaways: recognizing the necessity and the value of evolutionary adaptation, cultivating flexibility, and balancing centrifugal and centripetal forces. After reviewing these lessons, we offer our own individual reflections on what we discovered from our journey through the global landscape of early twenty-first-century start-up universities.

Adaptation and Succession

All of our university founders started with a powerful vision that drew in supporters and attracted attention from the larger academic world. Less visible but equally important, they had to recognize and react to key phases of development in their respective institutions and support the emergence of a new institutional culture. Organizational management scholar Larry Greiner identifies different phases of adaptation as organizations and groups increase in their size and formalization, each of which requires a different type of leadership and mode of interaction. These phases range from intense creativity to highly directive, and ultimately require a balance between control and autonomy.[6]

Among our start-ups, we often witnessed key inflection points, such as when Olin College had to bring out the "bouncy castles" usually seen at children's parties as a release valve for faculty and students overwhelmed by the demands of an overly ambitious curriculum. At Ashesi University, an important inflection point occurred when student elections demonstrated that the undergraduates tended to view leadership as a popularity contest, prompting academic leaders to develop a core set of courses focused on a deeper vision of the leadership Africa needed. In both cases, the founders recognized the need to consciously support and cultivate a new institutional culture. Future founders of universities will want to remain similarly agile and be willing to adapt their original vision or the means to accomplishing it.

Indeed, future founders must be adept not only at communicating their vision but also at listening and, when necessary, adjusting and refining their objectives and strategies. We can see examples of this nimbleness in our start-ups: recall, for instance, how Ashoka's founders made revisions and improvements to their plans through years of operating the Young India Fellowship, or how Yale-NUS leaders took in feedback from Singaporean parents and future students about the meaning and value of a liberal arts education, or how Ashesi's founders learned from focus groups with parents, employers, and government officials. Developing a successful university requires two-way communication with all of those different parties and participants.

Another key part of institutional development involves building a sustainable leadership model as the university grows. Founding teams, as well as founders, can struggle to let others contribute to what is an ongoing process of institutional and culture building. Yet to succeed, they must be willing to cede responsibilities and decision-making to newcomers—to "give away your Legos" if the institution wants to reach a broader scale, to invoke the title of an essay that Fred Swaniker circulated to his entire team at a crucial moment.[7] If a new institution can survive only because of the founders or the founding team, then it will eventually fail. Building an institution requires a clear and compelling vision *and* a willingness to actively make room for others, enabling a new generation of leaders.

So, too, local and regional cultures constitute powerful forces that founders ignore at their peril. To succeed, they will necessarily need to take account of the politics and mores of the region. At the same time, founders are seeking to bring about radical change, and it is imperative that they consistently remind their interlocutors that the goal is to build something genuinely new and valuable and not merely to mimic existing institutions. They must also resist leaning too heavily into their nostalgia or fondness for their own educational experiences, say from Yale or Swarthmore, as this can incline them toward replication of an existing form rather than firmly finding ways to renew old models or create new ones. What's needed is a delicate dance between vision and adaptation: new institutions require their own distinctive cultures, and a cut-and-paste model inevitably undermines their emergence.

We observed that university founders often have their best ideas in the early phases, but major change takes time. As Mariet Westermann told us, "The Polaroid is still developing." Founders of new universities need supporters who invest in their vision and critics who keep them honest. Most of all, they need partners committed to achieving the larger mission rather than only tracking quarterly metrics or pointing out where the new ventures are failing. It is much easier to point out shortcomings than to create solutions and build something new. Creating a new generation of leaders in Africa;

transforming East Asian, South Asian, and Middle Eastern higher education; redefining engineering education; and improving the quality of education globally while driving down costs—these are not small things. No one has yet fully figured out how to do them.

For all their human faults and strategic missteps, the founders of our start-ups have been willing to move beyond criticizing the world as it is; they have avoided the temptation to prognosticate about new worlds without taking on the hard task of bringing those worlds into being. While they need to be held accountable for their decisions, these founders also need the latitude to change course on how they fulfill their ultimate missions. Their partners should support them in navigating the winding road of their journey rather than keeping them to the straight and narrow path.

Cultivating Flexibility

You might imagine that for two people who just wrote a book about start-ups, we wouldn't attach much value to what goes on at long-standing or existing universities—but that wouldn't be true. There is much to admire in and learn from our established schools, ideas and practices that have shaped us and the founders of these new institutions. At the same time, many of the most exciting things start-up schools have been able to accomplish arise from taking a fresh start, from adopting an open-ended mind-set. Of course, incorporating some degree of open-endedness and possibility thinking is one of the most difficult things for established colleges and universities to achieve. Schools at the top of the leader board have few incentives to question the system, and those at the bottom often find themselves trying to emulate their better-resourced and better-known peers.

Yet there are examples of well-designed "skunk-works" programs—small, innovative undertakings run outside of normal research activities—in established universities, such as Georgetown's Red House (formally called the Center for New Designs in Learning and Scholarship), where the only rule is that any new project has to break at least one rule. Randy Bass and his colleagues at the Red House combine this fresh-look strategy with the patience to move incrementally by experimenting, iterating, and validating in ways that draw in their colleagues.[8] This combination of approaches has led to new ways that students can choose distinctive common core pathways, new experiential living and learning communities, and other novel programs on a campus that has been traditionally conservative when it comes to teaching and the curriculum.[9]

A host of other established schools are also creating academic incubators that merge teaching and learning centers with technology units in the hopes, as journalist Beth McMurtie writes, of "revamping large introductory courses, training professors in design thinking and active learning, and using analytics to improve retention and graduation rates."[10] Unfortunately, as Dartmouth's Joshua Kim and Georgetown's Edward Maloney observe, these centers and incubators can sometimes amount to little more than organizational theater, often involving consultants or coming from a new president's or provost's arrival but without an overall institutional strategy. In these circumstances, what most often results is "a snow globe reorg, with lots of shaking and movement, but almost always very little change in how teaching and learning occur once the snow settles."[11]

What's different about many of our start-ups is how they've integrated this sought-after flexibility, creativity, and continuous improvement into the core of their operating systems. These incubators aren't warehoused in a spare corner of campus; they *are* the campus. Olin College consciously sought to make it easy for faculty and students to experiment and iterate without requiring approval by the faculty senate at every turn. They encouraged prototyping, testing, and tinkering. "Startups are like gardens; you're really good at planting seeds, but you're not so good at weeding," says Provost Mark Somerville. "One of the ways that we've tried to navigate that is by basically being very flexible about the ways that people innovate by substitution, as opposed to innovation by addition." Minerva also places a premium on continuous iteration and improvement of individual courses, sequences, and majors, as well as the underlying learning taxonomy. An extended approval process isn't required to make changes, and this dynamism creates a culture in which faculty constantly talk about what's working and what's not.

At the end of the day, however, it doesn't require starting a new university to benefit from fresh thinking and a more open and iterative mind-set. What's crucial is creating a shared language and culture that connect artifacts, espoused values, and underlying assumptions; an institutional strategy that takes a deliberate and systematic approach; and systems and processes for change that aren't so gummed up or risk-averse that they deter faculty who want to experiment and innovate.

The global pandemic opened the door for just such widespread experimentation at established colleges and universities. Students, faculty, and staff all experienced rapid shifts in learning modalities, course calendars and schedules, and even the very places they live and learn. Yet at many schools the existing curriculum is still trapped in a set of dated systems and structures. As Fred Swaniker discovered as an undergraduate at Macalester College, in a traditional semester system he would receive only two years of education en route to earning a four-year degree. Might traditional colleges and universities imagine new possibilities to increase their efficiency and flexibility to facilitate deeper learning? Our start-ups offer several tantalizing examples. ALU has pioneered ways in which students can study asynchronously while being embedded in a local community and network where they are carrying out problem-based learning. Minerva's global rotation shows how a school can leverage synchronous online learning with in-person learning in cities around the globe. Such an approach might supplement or replace the traditional study-abroad model, thereby allowing schools both to serve more students and to strengthen the connection between immersive learning and academic learning.

There is, of course, a central factor that shapes what's possible at start-ups as well as established universities: the size of the fiscal envelope. Most of our existing universities develop their budgets through a "continuing resolution" that consists primarily of incremental change. The big political debates on campus revolve around who gets 2 percent more this year and who gets 1 percent less, with few opportunities to step back and consider whether an institution's mission, market, and margin are well aligned.[12] Start-ups, however, have the advantage of doing zero-based budgeting, at least in their formative launch period. Short of creating an entirely new institution, many existing universities might inject some of the same kind of dynamism if they undertook a complete strategic and fiscal review to generate the kind of entrepreneurial energy that we've seen drive our start-ups to great heights.

We are mindful of the considerable reasons why institutions don't undertake such an exercise: it's an enormous investment of time that can create a collegiate version of the Hunger Games, pitting the hard sciences against the humanities, athletics against the library, and students against faculty. Yet, particularly for institutions that can only envy the millions of dollars poured into ventures like NYU Abu Dhabi and Yale-NUS, there is enormous value in undertaking a process that asks: "How might we use what resources we have to differentiate ourselves rather than to mimic our more financially blessed peers? What if we thought like a start-up?" For these institutions, reinvention isn't a luxury but a necessity; and perhaps paradoxically, these same colleges and universities are the ones best suited to invent the future in ways similar to our start-ups.

Balancing Centrifugal and Centripetal Forces

At the other end of the spectrum from flexibility and modularity, our start-ups also offer established colleges and universities useful examples of shared citizenship and commitment to the commonweal of the institution. In the modern academy, as in much of modern life, centrifugal forces that push individuals away from the center are plentiful. Even in small liberal arts colleges, most faculty live their professional scholarly life with colleagues who are located outside their institution. They engage with them via e-mail, in journals, and at conferences; and their individual success, academic promotion, and social identity depend on the esteem in which they are held in these intellectual circles. Yet to fulfill the promise of a true community of teachers and learners, schools need to generate equally powerful centripetal forces that pull the faculty members inward, toward the center. Established universities might find inspiration in how our start-ups generate an ongoing sense of ownership and commitment to the institution—that is, in how they create true community.

Our start-ups all embrace a mission not simply to build their institution but to lead a broader reformation of the entire educator sector. While this social-reform objective points outward, it functions internally to tie adherents together. NYU Abu Dhabi and Yale-NUS promised to usher in a more truly global kind of education. Ashesi, Fulbright, and Ashoka drew faculty who wanted to transform their country and their region. ALU explicitly set as its goal the creation of a new leadership cadre for the whole of Africa and the building of a new educational model that is globally relevant—"a global solution that is African born," as ALU's Sidee Dlamini put it. Olin attracted faculty and students who wanted to create a new way of doing engineering education and serve as a beacon to others. Minerva casts itself as the vanguard of a social reformation to overturn the prevailing high-cost, low-quality system of education by demonstrating the value of imparting to students the critical wisdom they need for the sake of the world. Established colleges and universities also have broader missions, but they are harder to see after many years of being in business—and their missions often sound and appear interchangeable. Perhaps there is something in the more distinctive claims being advanced by our start-ups that can encourage venerable schools to look harder at what might differentiate them and, in so doing, draw their community more tightly together.

In all of our cases, faculty and students were especially attracted to the idea that teaching and learning would constitute the central activity of the institution and the central means to achieving its grand mission, rather than serving as a handmaiden to research. Some of our start-ups sought to plant versions of the liberal arts teacher-scholar model in new soil. Others went further in arguing that a truly transformative education required a more singular devotion to the science and the art of teaching. ALU has made space for entrepreneurs as instructors, Olin has attracted faculty who are passionate about hands-on learning, and Minerva has drawn faculty who value the chance to collaborate deeply while being able to live anywhere in the world. Across all our schools, faculty and students were more likely to find in each other compatriots deeply committed to the act of learning. This shared commitment, in turn, helped reinforce the centrality of common experiences in an age of increasing fragmentation.

So, too, our start-up universities understood in different ways the importance of having some common knowledge and experience shared among their students and faculty. This communal intellectual property provides a vital cohesiveness to the faculty and the institutional culture. A structured and shared curriculum for all students offers intellectual frameworks that enable the university as a whole to grapple with civilizational and technological change. Common reference points provide community members with a shared language, which deepens the quality of their interactions. For established universities confronting increasingly polarized campuses, where students often seem to regard one another as strangers, the different ways that our start-ups have constructed their common core might serve as helpful starting points. While they built their curriculums and shared experiences for highly diverse, global populations, our featured institutions here offer useful lessons for US campuses that have become more heterogeneous and are searching for ways to help students engage their differences productively.[13]

Many of our start-up universities also found new ways for faculty and students to make connections across the curriculum and the campus by wedding disciplinary knowledge to much more versatile interdisciplinary approaches. While many existing universities include interdisciplinary courses and even majors, interdisciplinary work is often considered experimental, or constrained by an institutional culture dominated by disciplines and departments. Many start-ups, in contrast, have abandoned these disciplinary departments and now structure their degree programs across multiple disciplines. Examples include Ashoka having nine pure majors and ten interdisciplinary majors, or Minerva creating a highly structured curriculum so that general education, majors, and electives are tightly linked by a set of underlying concepts that are applied across disciplines and contexts. In a few cases, such as at ALU, the major is considered more of a "mission," and the instruction includes a wide range of experiential and interdisciplinary courses.

All of our start-ups are responding to perceived needs from industry, from students, and from society for more intensive engagement across areas of knowledge. In these examples, interdisciplinarity, like innovation, is done not for its own sake but for the sake of fostering deeper understanding. The design process we learned about within many of these institutions included meetings with employers, codesign by students, and yearlong incubation periods that incorporated input from many voices. The new start-up curriculums approach complex phenomena such as global climate change, competing governance systems, and rapidly growing cities as central challenges that require the integration of knowledge and methods from different fields. These are also the challenges that faculty are increasingly organizing their research to address, thus weaving tighter connections between their scholarly interests and their teaching. While many established universities have also created majors that cross traditional disciplinary lines, our start-ups here offer examples of what a broader redefinition of existing categories might look like unconstrained by existing disciplinary fiefdoms.

Parting Thoughts

As our journey through the landscape of start-up colleges and universities comes to an end, we offer a few parting thoughts—what we found inspiring, what surprised us, and the questions with which we will continue to wrestle in the months and years ahead.

INSPIRATIONS

Noah: I was impressed by how all the founders we studied concentrated intensely on the deep needs of students while resisting simply catering to them as consumers. The overwhelming incentive in most colleges and universities is to prioritize research over teaching and learning. Focusing on the highest and best kind of education for students is difficult to accomplish in institutions that were not built to do that. At the same time, there are equally powerful forces that drive universities to offer what most students and parents think they want: narrow, vocational majors and the promise of a comfortable four years.

Our founders refused to make that bargain. They thought: "How do I build a university that will make students the most profoundly wise and the most capable of addressing major issues in the world?" even if doing so would be difficult and students would find that they were pressed to go well beyond their comfort zones. As the ALU injunction has it, many of the new universities both demanded and inspired students to "Do Hard Things."

The founders, too, embodied this trait. Each of them confronted what often seemed like insurmountable challenges on their journey. Many times, they simply didn't know what to do. Yet they exhibited a level of fearlessness and audacity that kept their dream alive and brought their teams along with them.

Fred Swaniker didn't know that financial exigencies would require him to ditch his 2014 vision to build twenty-five campuses across Africa. When he started out, Ben Nelson couldn't know that his commitment to the idea that talent is distributed equally would require a level of financial investment that would preclude scaling up Minerva. Even with significant support from both the Vietnamese and US governments, Dam Bich Thuy would have to discover that she needed to invent a culture of educational philanthropy in order for Fulbright University Vietnam to succeed. And as they waited to see if any students would apply to Ashoka's forerunner, the Young India Fellowship, Pramath Sinha and Ashish Dhawan genuinely did not know if their experiment in the liberal arts would work.

These and other founders had to invent new ways to achieve their underlying goal, sometimes at the very same time they were still building their prototypes. Like the cartoon character Wile E. Coyote, when they stepped off the cliff they could stay aloft only so long as they didn't look down. In some cases, that resistance to acknowledging everything that could go wrong could prove frustrating to the teams they had assembled. Tensions ran high when a founder almost willfully refused to address problems that others, often rightly, feared would dash the entire enterprise. And yet it's clear to me that there has to be someone who doesn't look down, someone who keeps the focus on the fundamental audacity of the larger venture.

It's equally clear to me that start-up universities succeed or fail to a significant degree based not on the founder but on the next level down of professional leadership. Think Tim Cook to Apple's Steve Jobs. I saw this up close in the case of launching Duke Kunshan University in China, where it required two successive provosts and their executive vice-provosts to drive the strategy and manage its implementation through innumerable blind curves and steep downhills. So, too, the success of the campus in China depended heavily on key academic hires from liberal arts colleges in the United States and the relationships they forged with Chinese counterparts. In *Empires of Ideas*, which tells the story of eight research universities across three centuries and three countries, William Kirby notes that while there are many books on presidential leadership, "much less is written about the individuals who run the universities day-to-day, with a long-term perspective on their future." Yet, he writes, "every great university has such individuals who do quietly transformative work outside the limelight of the presidency."[14]

In our case studies, we can see similar roles being played by Mariet Westermann, NYU's "diplomat plenipotentiary" and provost (now chancellor); Mark Somerville, the primary architect of Olin College's foundational year and later provost; and Dinh Ngan, a core leader in FUV's launch and now dean of undergraduate studies. As Somerville observes: "Most startups start off with a great sense of energy and . . . there's that initial phase of, 'This is going to be great. This is going to be awesome. We're going to change the world.' Then there's the valley of the shadow of death. And lots of startups don't make it through the valley of the shadow of death." The ultimate success of start-up universities owes much to leaders like Somerville, Dinh, and Westermann who secure safe passage through the valley.

Bryan: I'm inspired by the founders that we talked to, and it was a joy getting to know them during the pandemic, which ironically opened up the world to us by the fact that we were trapped in our offices for much of it. The book research enabled us to talk with leaders in India, in Vietnam, and in Ghana instantly, get to know them and their vision, and come away inspired by their future-oriented and selfless attempts to make something better in the world. These founders also were conducting this heroic work often while sacrificing their own self-interest for the sake of something larger that they believed in.

All of these founders could have perfectly happily gone on in conventional pathways and led more affluent and comfortable lives. But they knew that there was something better that they could help make. They stepped aside from a safe path into one of enormous risk, uncertainty, and in many cases hardship, to make a better future for the students of their new institution and to leave an impact on the world that could last for centuries, as many institutions do. I was inspired by that. It takes courage, it takes sacrifice, and it takes tenacity. These founders all have that.

The other thing that I was inspired by was their deep humanism. They were motivated almost to a person by a genuine concern for the people of their region, of their country, of the world. I found that very inspiring. They were motivated from a place of—you might call it spirituality. You might call it humanism, as well, just a very deep sense of the value of human beings and our shared future. That was inspiring to me.

I was also inspired by the fact that in all of these cases, the founders necessarily had to keep focused on the quality of the product they were delivering. The care of the students was central in each of these schools. I admired that greatly. In no cases would we find these schools being propped up as an instrument for making money or profit. They were genuinely interested from the beginning and throughout in producing the highest quality of education for their students. They worked diligently, as hard as they could, with their teams to make that happen. I found that inspiring, too, that single-minded and unwavering and brilliant approach.

SURPRISES

Noah: Even among eight start-up institutions around the world designed specifically to offer something new, I've been surprised by how powerful the pressures are to look and act like the old institutions. Some of these pressures are worth respecting, as they reflect the virtues of those colleges and universities that, over the centuries, have found ways to improve how faculty teach and how students learn.

But some of these pressures are worth resisting, or at least seeking to turn to one's advantage, in particular the ways in which the demand for prestige forces new institutions to emulate existing ones. It is hard to be truly innovative in a market in which colleges and universities succeed by looking more like the established brands than by differentiating from them. Take any campus tour in the United States and you will find that your tour guides have all converged on a set of talking points that are remarkably similar, despite the claims universities make to being distinctive.

Although I've been impressed by the tenacity of the prestige race, what truly surprised me is that the deepest constraints on innovation are internal rather than external. The simple truth is most of the people involved in building new institutions, and the faculty in particular, have been intensely shaped by the priorities of the institutions from which they came. Graduate education leaves an especially deep mark, as the guild-like ways in which most professors are minted ensure that those lucky few who successfully complete their PhD and secure a job are profoundly invested in the system that produced them.

Even in institutions that consciously sought to attract and select faculty who wanted to build something new, faculty were often still enamored of the lecture, tied to their disciplinary silos, and regarded themselves as free agents rather than citizens of the institutional commonweal. It's a testament to the universities we feature in this book that they were able to create new ways of educating students and stronger forms of community, as the modern organization of knowledge and rewards in higher education make this task enormously difficult.

Bryan: One of the surprises that changed the course of our writing is that I imagined I could take several different organizational theories from business and academia, overlay them on our case studies, and point out evidence that would support one or another theory. Instead, I found that in every individual case, there was no single theory of organizational change or business management or academic strategy that applied. That there is no single theory—which also speaks to another surprise that I encountered—is the complexity. That you can't think of a university just in terms of its components. While it is necessary to build each of those components to create a new university, all of them are interconnected and affect one another. This means that when you change one component, unexpected impacts can occur across the rest of the system. Since all of these different components are linked, as are all the different stakeholders, they all have to be addressed simultaneously. I was surprised by how many different moving parts there are in a university. I think that's something that surprised many of our founders as well, as they went into this work.

The other thing that surprised me was that, not only do you have diverse participants and engaged parties who have to be addressed simultaneously, but oftentimes these groups and individuals have divergent interests. Students, employers, parents, and financial backers often have different, competing interests in the institution, even as they all want the institution to succeed. Those differences can't be bridged by rhetoric, as often these diverse stakeholders have different definitions of success. Any university that you create is going to be a compromise that most closely meets the needs of all these different stakeholders. That's one reason why the utopian or idealistic visions within these start-ups will never be fully realized.

Maybe that's not a bug, but a feature—in other words, whenever you're trying to bring together thousands of people in a shared enterprise, you're never going to have a solution that's entirely satisfactory to all of them, but necessarily have to compromise.

From that compromise comes something else that also inspires me: a university is not the creation of any one person, any one department, but represents the wholeness of a collective enterprise, which, in its best examples, is far more than the sum of its parts. That collective dimension I find inspiring. Sometimes I've heard academics joke that they dream that their institution could approach the sum of its parts, but I think in many cases we've seen in these institutions examples where they exceed the sum of their parts and create something better, something that can exist only by the collective efforts of all who were involved. That surprised me and left me feeling energized about what's possible. I was surprised to see how important diverse leadership styles are for success in any university, and especially in a start-up university. We see in our studies that it is not a "founder" but several founders—with women playing an especially crucial role in our start-ups, with a vital capacity for navigating between conflicting stakeholders, and as diplomats and communicators with a capacity to listen and help the founding team adjust strategies based on hearing diverse voices. I was both surprised and delighted to learn about how the diverse leadership styles within the founding teams, which blended both charismatic and extroverted leaders with more quiet and thoughtful leaders who were great listeners, made for powerful results. This was a result we saw in founding teams at NYU Abu Dhabi, Ashesi, and ALU, and within the transfers of leadership to female presidents at Yale-NUS, Olin College, and NYU Abu Dhabi.

The other surprise that came to me is that when I began this whole odyssey working in Singapore, I believed in an imagined shared notion of what higher education was. I realize now that that everyone has a slightly different picture of what the purposes of academic institutions are, what higher education should be, and as a result, the values that they bring to the table are all different. Those values are shaped not just by which institutions you attended but also by your own country and by the country where the university is located. The cultures, past and present, national and academic, all play a central role in any global university.

Again, in just the same way that stakeholders will diverge in their interests, I think that cultures also diverge in ways that can't be papered over by clever documents or brilliant speeches. Sometimes one country simply wants to have better incomes for its students or better economic growth. All the lofty rhetoric that you might import from another side of the earth will not matter in this kind of environment. Their definition of success is rooted in their own local and national reality and will never waver from that. The tenacity of culture and regional interests always do seem to prevail and take precedence over more abstract and global concerns.

FURTHER QUESTIONS

Noah: I'm wrestling with two issues. One is the trade-off between pragmatism and idealism. We most often think of moral leaders as those who courageously stand up on the basis of their ideals. They follow their conscience heedless of the consequences. Yet seen from a different angle, those same leaders can be regarded as zealots who are unwilling to compromise. A more moderate or pragmatic temperament, by contrast, produces leaders who forge a middle way that honors competing principles in the hope of finding common ground. Such pragmatists, of course, risk giving away too much in what may be a vain effort to resolve unbridgeable differences.[15]

My view is that you need both kinds of leaders and that there can even be a kind of moral division of labor between the types. Someone, often outside the halls of power, needs to stand for a set of core principles in their purest form. And someone else needs to recognize that the world is a complex place and that the perfect can be the enemy of the good.[16]

When it comes to setting up new universities in undemocratic locales, I worry that the pragmatists may give away too much and that the sunk costs of setting up in a new country may prove difficult to overcome even if the situation warrants doing so. Yet I also find distasteful the view that if academic freedom and free inquiry are potentially at risk, then—full stop—that's it, time to go home. Such views often treat countries as if they are static, especially when it comes to Asian and Middle Eastern ones. In reality, debates over openness and control are often long-running and many-layered, and outsiders are often poorly positioned to understand whether they are seeing a single snapshot or an unfinished movie script.

I saw first-hand in China how one part of the government would issue condemnations of universities teaching "Western values" while another part encouraged liberal education initiatives. Certainly, the direction in recent years toward restricting debate and dissent is sobering, as the Party leans ever more heavily toward controlling what students learn. Still, the education business is a long game. In his recent book, *Empires of Ideas*, William Kirby notes that the modern university was born in Germany and managed, at times, to maintain a tradition of institutional and academic freedom even amid an illiberal polity.

I'm also reminded that free inquiry in the United States evolved against a historical backdrop that was hardly open to all ideas, much less to all members of society. Surely, though, we're glad that those schools were established and contributed over time to the opening up of American life. In congressional testimony, Jeffrey Lehman, the vice-chancellor at NYU Shanghai, pointed out that American universities were born in an imperfect country and that their presence mattered in making it less so:

> American universities were not established on a firmament of perfect respect for human dignity. Liberal education and academic inquiry are not fragile flowers that can survive only in perfect soil. To the contrary, America's best universities were established in a flawed land, one of whose greatest virtues was its commitment to improvement, to form a more perfect union. Precisely because those universities are hardy defenders of academic freedom and liberal education, they have been important contributors to America's progress.[17]

While hardly comparable to the current situation in China, I'm further mindful that American schools today are hardly bastions of open inquiry and debate, whatever formal protections are provided. Instead, they are threatened internally by faculty, administrators, and students who wish to reduce the chance of anyone being upset or challenged to debate competing principles, and externally by critics, state governments, and public governing boards who seek to shut down discussions of sensitive topics. To borrow a phrase from Michael Roth, the president of my own alma mater, Wesleyan University, we'd all be better off with "'safe enough spaces'— environments in which everyone is protected from harassment and intimidation but in which no one is protected from being offended or having their minds changed."[18]

Ironically, the hardest questions in these situations are often the easiest to answer. Were students truly unable to debate controversial issues or faculty impeded in their pursuit of sensitive lines of inquiry, then all those committed to the values of a free university should join in saying it's time to close up shop. Yet the greatest risk usually comes from the slow erosion of academic norms, and there's no formula for knowing exactly when we're seeing an erosion or just a temporary halt in the process of deposition in which those norms are being built up. I'm drawn to John Sexton's remark that "institutions, like people, are metaphoric victims of original sin, and we're not going to achieve perfection in this world." But I'm glad that there are also critics like Jim Sleeper at Yale, who asked the difficult questions and pressed the university to think hard about its aspirations and its guardrails.

In my own work developing a curriculum and hiring the faculty for Duke Kunshan University (DKU) in China, I often disagreed with colleagues who took an absolutist position and opposed the venture. But I learned from them every day, and I heard their voices in my mind every time I confronted what might turn into a challenging situation. In my work, I was most heartened when colleagues at Chinese universities would tell me to keep going, and that the more a foreign-joint-venture university with a major brand like Duke could push the envelope, the more that would open up maneuvering space for them.

The second issue I continue to wrestle with is closely connected to the first, although this time the tension emerges between the global and the local. I appreciate John Sexton's vision of a university in which students are invited to engage in profound explorations based on a deep understanding of the multiple traditions that have shaped them. But building the structures and culture to make this aspiration real is difficult, at home and abroad. In the United States, we are constrained both by a heightened concern to protect students from acute discomfort and, paradoxically, by the reality that many students in fact share many implicit views. For all the number of international students at selective American colleges and universities, these institutions are deeply and profoundly American. The discourse on campus is thus shaped by a predilection toward independent and autonomous individuals who make decisions on the basis of universal rules and rights-based thinking—what psychologists have called the hallmarks of Western, educated, industrialized, rich, and democratic (WEIRD) societies. Are we really encountering enough difference in these settings to permit Sexton's ideal of profound learning based on genuine multiplicity of thought?

Ironically, the challenge of meeting Sexton's aspiration in non-American settings is also shaped by the so-called WEIRD values. They are powerfully present among students and faculty at these institutions: wherever their origins, they nonetheless partake of an emerging global culture common at highly selective liberal arts colleges and universities. It's in this context that I find the term most often heard at new global start-ups—"global citizenship"—to be less than helpful. The term is often intended or understood to suggest a single universal conception of citizenship and belonging in which one's connection to humanity supersedes ties to family, kin, and nation. I find more compelling the concept of "rooted globalism," which we developed as part of seven animating principles at DKU. Here, rooted globalism means "to cultivate informed and engaged citizens who are knowledge-able about each other's histories, traditions of thought, and affiliations; and skilled in navigating among local, national, and global identities and commitments."[19]

In explaining this concept to students at DKU from China and forty other countries, I often told them that this concept replaced a vague aspiration with a difficult tension. It sought to draw students out of their more local and historical contexts without diminishing the value of the traditions and cultures that flourish there; at the same time, it invited students who came from more cosmopolitan backgrounds to engage with those contexts even as they proffered their claims to a more global community. Our students live in a world in which the push and pull of their multiple inheritances and aspirations will both define their own individual trajectory and shape the overlapping and competing levels of governance in which their stories will be written. We owe it to them to explain forthrightly that there are many individual and collective tensions with which they will have to wrestle, and that their challenge, and their opportunity, is to become fluent in navigating them.

Bryan: The thing I'm still wrestling with is the way that higher education, even in the cases of start-ups, often resists change. There are many valid reasons for emulating existing institutions. I think that's justified in some cases, but I'm wrestling with the fact that sometimes, in many cases, higher education becomes a performative ritual for young people so that they get a credential to then enter in a socially acceptable way into society. Sometimes the deeper learning and reflection that are the most lasting part of an educa-tion get lost in all of the tension surrounding the competitive admissions that dominate the lives of young people around the world.

I would like to see how we can break out of that mind-set and have the actual value of higher education be more evident and more visible to all—to the student, to the employer, to the faculty. But the learning and change that go on within a person are often invisible and hard to measure. This intangible quality of individual transformation means that a lot of what we do in higher education is lost, and too many stakeholders focus on the performative aspects, based on credentials and prestige that serve as proxies for quality but oftentimes only loosely correlate with it. I wrestle with that, and I wrestle with how to make learning and quality teaching more visible.

The other thing I wrestle with is this: As much as all these leaders have tried—and you can create an institution that's based on a collective shared sense of value and a better future and so forth (and we have seen those successes)—at the end of the day, human beings have egos and self-interest. And, just as a culture and region always prevail, to some extent in any human endeavor, ego and self-interest also prevail; and so how do we create institutions of higher education that ultimately don't cave in to egotistical demands of faculty, alumni, or administrators?

We've seen in these case studies how our institutions have successfully navigated around many of the obstacles that came from conflicting demands based on the self-interest of individual stakeholders, but I also am mindful of the fact that any human enterprise is imperfect. There are inherent tensions that come from the process of developing as a scholar that make it difficult to also respond to the collective needs of an academic community. The superb training required to become a faculty member requires decades to build the necessary expertise and credentials, which in most cases give faculty a well-earned sense of autonomy and self-worth. This process at the same time can also produce people who, by virtue of having those qualities, can find it very difficult to work cooperatively with others from different or competing academic fields. This is where leadership really matters, since the right kinds of leaders can bring people to a place where they are able to understand other points of view and feel a collective sense of value in their work. Too many leaders are selected, like students, more for their performative aspects and credentials and less for their ability to foster this kind of thoughtful reflection. I would like to understand how society can better celebrate and advance leaders who are operating less from a place of self-interest and more from a place of empathy and from genuine consideration of the larger and long-term interests of an institution, a region, and the world.

A final area I wrestle with is the way in which prestige has a performative aspect to it but also perpetuates injustice and inequity in the world. As well as all these institutions are doing in providing financial aid for students who can't afford their full fees, the cruel fact is that over 90 percent of humanity struggles with only limited resources and very marginal forms of education. I wrestle with the fact that despite the best efforts of all these schools and all the larger universities, only a tiny fraction of humanity will actually enjoy the benefits of a higher education. Many decades of experience of what were thought to be meritocratic approaches to admissions have made it clear that wealthy families who have access to the elaborate array of enrichment activities and test preparation services can tilt the playing field in their favor.

I would like to try to figure out whether it's possible for a larger percentage of our human family to receive quality education. This would include improving the admissions process to do a better job of providing access to the most deserving students, who would take full advantage of the intellectual and cultural riches of our universities. It would also include dramatically improving the efficiency of universities and colleges to reduce their cost and expand the numbers of students they can reach. At this point, I don't see how, because the highest quality of education does necessarily seem to be expensive and therefore will necessarily reach only a minority of students. The answer may lie in future start-up universities, which I hope will arise in the coming years and help find a solution to this problem.

I wrestle with the fact that there'll always be inequities, and I wrestle with the fact that, in many cases, higher education, instead of reducing those inequities, can accelerate and accentuate them. As our case studies have shown, however, these new institutions offer opportunities not only to break new ground in academics and research but also to pioneer new ways to advance their countries and offer new kinds of graduates to the world. Knowing that new institutions like those we have studied in our book are being developed to offer entirely new kinds of learning to previously unreached populations of students gives me a good deal of hope for our future.

NOTES

Chapter 1

1. Kuh, *High-Impact Educational Practices*.
2. Delbanco, *College*, 30.
3. Crow and Dabars, *New American University*, ch. 3; Christensen and Eyring, *Innovative University*; Staley, *Alternative Universities*, 30–31. John Lombardi captures succinctly the paradox of how competition among universities leads to similar rather than different offerings: "The similarity of college curricula comes from the twin power of competition and regulation," he writes. "Competition ensures that each college and university offers much the same curriculum to a common marketplace of students and parents seeking equivalent products. In competing for students, most institutions focus on minor forms of product differentiation, image and presentation. Regulation reinforces this standardization of content through accreditation, a process that encourages or coerces colleges and universities to deliver remarkably similar undergraduate programs" (Lombardi, *How Universities Work* [2013, 47], quoted in Staley, *Alternative Universities*, 273).
4. Kirby, *Empires of Ideas*, 234.

Chapter 2

1. Postiglione, Ma, and Te, "Institutionalizing Liberal Education." This paragraph and the next draw from the introduction to Godwin and Pickus's *Liberal Arts and Sciences Innovation in China*.
2. Godwin and Altbach, "Historical and Global Perspective," 9.
3. Ferrall, *Liberal Arts*.
4. Volk and Benedix, "Liberal Arts Colleges."
5. Ferall, *Liberal Arts at the Brink*.
6. Linshi, "10 CEOs."
7. Montgomery, "Famous Graduates."
8. Detweiler, "Evidence Liberal Arts Needs."
9. Anders, *You Can Do Anything*.
10. Quoted in Isaacson, *Steve Jobs*, introduction, para. 9.
11. Penprase, *STEM Education*. See also Hartley, *Fuzzy and the Techie*.
12. World Economic Forum, *Future of Jobs*, 22. See also Strada Institute, *Robot-Ready*.
13. Ellevate, "Skills You Need."
14. Delbanco, *College*, ch. 2. Delbanco notes that modern enthusiasm for how learning can be more active and collaborative draws on and vindicates this older idea of lateral learning—"a place in which students learn from their peers" (164).
15. Claremont McKenna College, "America's First Coed Colleges."
16. Mintz, "11 Lessons."

17. Cole, *More Perfect University*, 5. Michael Crow and William Dabars offer a more fine-grained analysis of the different waves of change in US higher education, in which they identify four different waves culminating in what they argue is the emergence today of a fifth wave that "has the potential to integrate world-class knowledge production and innovation with broad accessibility and thus conjoin in a single institutional platform the missions and objectives of the set of leading major research universities and liberal arts colleges—the sector in academic culture associated with elite higher education—with the egalitarian objectives inaugurated by the second and third waves" (*Fifth Wave*, 211–12).

18. D. Levine, *American College*; Penprase, *STEM Education*.

19. Cole, *More Perfect University*. See also Crow and Dabars, *Fifth Wave*.

20. Thurgood Marshall Fund, "History of HBCUs."

21. E. Levine and Rascoff, "Restoring Learning." See also E. Levine, *Allies and Rivals*.

22. For an analysis of the emerging landscape of the global higher-education marketplace, see Wildavsky's *The Great Brain Race*. For a historical and global analysis, see Kirby's *Empires of Ideas*.

23. For a recent survey of American schools abroad, see Purinton and Skaggs's *American Universities Abroad*. In his contribution to that volume, "Achieving Liberal Arts Education Transnationally," Richard A. Detweiler highlights the central role of US Christian missionaries in helping to found many of the early liberal arts schools abroad, including American University in Beirut, American College of Greece, and American University in Cairo. For a comparative analysis of liberal arts education today, see Kirby and Van der Wende's *Experiences in Liberal Arts and Science Education from America, Europe, and Asia*. For an overview of the liberal arts in East Asia, see Jung, Nishimura, and Sasao's *Liberal Arts Education and Colleges in East Asia*. For a historical, empirical, and philosophical assessment of the liberal-arts-abroad phenomena, see Marber and Araya's *Evolution of Liberal Arts in the Global Age*. Mary-Ellen Boyle provides an excellent summary and analysis of these books in "Liberal Education Unmoored?"

24. Godwin, "New Perspectives on Legitimacy."

25. Helfand, "Mucking About."

26. Technológico de Monterrey, "Modelo Tec21."

27. USFQ, "Por qué estudiar."

28. Nature Index, "2022 Tables."

29. Asian University for Women, "Who We Are."

30. Davis College Akilah, "Educating East Africa's Future."

31. Ash, "Belarus's University in Exile."

32. Ash.

33. Jaschik, "Bard College 'Undesirable.'"

34. Zaytuna College, "About."

35. Godwin and Altbach, "Historical and Global Perspective."

36. Kirby, "Liberal Education in China."

37. Li, "Significance and Practice."

38. Godwin and Pickus, *Liberal Arts*. See also Kirby, *Empires of Ideas*.

39. Van der Wende, "Trends towards Global Excellence." Mary-Ellen Boyle suggests that tangible factors such as the availability of funding, variation in government regulation and university autonomy, and the experiences and visions of different founders all contributed to where new schools have emerged—and where they have not. She writes: "Why have new schools espousing liberal education emerged in Singapore, China and Ghana (to name a few), but not in Thailand, South Africa, or Bahrain (considered an education hub)? Why are national policy changes that support liberal education being implemented in the Netherlands and Hong Kong, but not in France, Japan, or countries with similar economies and demographics?" ("Global Liberal Education," 232).

40. Godwin and Pickus, *Liberal Arts*, 6. See also Zhao, "Reinventing Liberal Arts Education"; Zha, "What Is Liberal Arts"; and Van der Wende, "Trends toward Global Excellence."

41. Godwin and Pickus, *Liberal Arts*.

42. Institute of Medicine, *Facilitating Interdisciplinary Research*, 2.

43. Nowotny, Scott, and Gibbons, *Re-thinking Science*.

44. In the US context, see Arnett's *Emerging Adulthood* and C. Smith and colleagues' *Lost in Translation*.

45. In the US context, see Deresiewicz's *Excellent Sheep* and Kronman's *Education's End*. For doubts about the role of elite colleges and universities in shoring up the social compact, see Sandel's *Tyranny of Merit* and Markovits's *Meritocracy Trap*.

46. Kerr, *Uses of the University*, 115.

47. On the distinction between sustaining innovation and disruptive innovation, see Christensen and Eyring's *Innovative University* (xxiv–xxvi). For a criticism of the kind of disruptive innovation that leads to the "unbundling" of education, see Crow and Dabars's *Fifth Wave* (81–82). On the value of rapid or radically incremental innovation, see Ebner and Pickus's "Right Kind of Innovation."

48. Crow and Dabars, *Fifth Wave*, 21.

49. Northeastern University, "Northeastern 2025." See also Aoun, *Robot-Proof*. For ASU: Crow and Dabars, *New American University*. For Georgetown: Groves and Bass, "Red House at Georgetown." For CUNY: Davidson, *New Education*.

50. Moner, Motely, and Pope-Ruark, *Redesigning Liberal Education*; Chopp, Frost, and Weiss, *Remaking College*; and Felten et al., *Undergraduate Experience*.

51. Kanelos, "We Can't Wait." See also Treadgold, *University We Need*.

52. Staley, *Alternative Universities*, 30.

Chapter 3

1. Wildavsky, *Great Brain Race*, 43 ("first movers" quote).

2. Sexton, *Standing for Reason*, 63.

3. Wildavsky, *Great Brain Race*, 44.

4. Sexton, *Standing for Reason*, 63.

5. Wildavsky, *Great Brain Race*, 45.

6. Flanagin, "Expensive Romance of NYU."

7. Sanderson, "I Cared for NYUAD."

8. Wildavsky, *Great Brain Race*, 52.

9. Panikkar, "Dialogical Dialogue."

10. Sexton, "Global Network University Reflection."

11. NYU Web Communications, "NYU to Open Campus."

12. Swarthmore College, "President Alfred H. Bloom."

13. NYU Abu Dhabi, "Global Education and Outreach."

14. Pennington, "Al Bloom Reflects."

15. Underwood, "NYU Abu Dhabi Student."

16. Lewin, "U.S. Universities Rush."

17. Global Media Insight, "UAE Population Statistics."

18. Eickelman and Abusharaf, *Higher Education Investment*, 11.

19. Bayles, *Through a Screen Darkly*, 219.

20. Lake, "NYU Abu Dhabi."

21. Lake.

22. Miller, "Emir's University."

23. NYU Abu Dhabi, "NYUAD Accountability Framework."

24. Trapman-O'Brien, "NYU Abu Dhabi."

25. Mills, "'Tabula Rasa.'"

26. Aviv, "Imperial Presidency."

27. Aviv.

28. Lindsey, "NYU Abu Dhabi."

29. Lindsey.

30. Kaminer and O'Driscoll, "Workers."

31. Hundley, "NYU Unveils Labor Guidelines."

32. Kaminer, "N.Y.U. Apologizes."

33. Kaminer, "Labor Conditions."

34. NYU Abu Dhabi, "NYU Abu Dhabi Celebrates."

35. *New York Times*, "Clinton Lauds N.Y.U. Graduates."

36. Free Library, "Set Aside All Differences."

37. Nardello and Co., "Report."

38. NYU Abu Dhabi, "Labor Compliance Update."

39. Osmandzikovic, "Core Curriculum."

40. Pearce, "Core Curriculum's Global Requirement."

41. Hawkins, "In Departure."

42. Bui, "Rethinking Curriculum."

43. NYU Abu Dhabi, "Core Curriculum—Expanding Horizons."

44. Cabal, "Timeline."

45. Quoted in Bothwell, "Universities' Focus on Careers."

46. Quoted in DeGeurin, "Hamilton Admits University Bungled."

47. DeGeurin, "Lack of Academic Freedom."

48. BBC News, "Matthew Hedges."

49. Quoted in Porcelli, "Academic Freedom at NYUAD."

50. NYU Web Communications, "Exchange of Letters."

51. Sexton, *Standing for Reason*, 106.

52. NYU Abu Dhabi, "NYU Abu Dhabi Welcomes."

53. NYU Abu Dhabi, *Life beyond Saadiyat*.

54. Hajee, "Unthinking Eurocentrism at NYUAD."

55. NYU Abu Dhabi, "NYUAD Accountability Framework."

56. NYU Abu Dhabi, "2018 NYU Abu Dhabi."

57. Abu Dhabi Office of Public and Cultural Diplomacy, "NYU Abu Dhabi."

Chapter 4

1. National University of Singapore, "Annual Report 2003."

2. International Monetary Fund, "World Economic Outlook Database."

3. Department of Statistics Singapore, "Economy."

4. Tucker, *Surpassing Shanghai*, 121.

5. Statista, "Singapore."

6. Shanmugaratnam, "Speech."

7. QS Top Universities, "QS World University Rankings."

8. National University of Singapore, "Annual Report 2001."

9. National University of Singapore, "Annual Report 2003."

10. Bain, *Super Courses*.

11. National University of Singapore, "Annual Report 2013."

12. Yale University Office of the President, "Archived Speeches."

13. International Alliance of Research Universities, "About IARU."

14. Yale University, "International Framework Yale's Agenda."

15. Quoted in Penprase, "Yale-NUS College," 123.

16. Branch, "Singapore Spinoff."

17. *Yale Daily News*, "News' View."

18. Saussy, "When Elihu Meets Confucius."

19. Quoted in Branch, "Singapore Spinoff."

20. Sleeper, "Innocents Abroad?"

21. Quoted in Branch, "Singapore Spinoff."

22. Quoted in Griswold and Henderson, "Academic Freedom Promised."

23. M. Smith, "Yale Faculty Resolution."

24. Quoted in Gideon and Woodford, "Faculty Approve."

25. Lewis, "About."

26. Lewis, *Cambridge Introduction to Modernism*, xvii.

27. Garsten et al., "Yale-NUS College," 37.

28. Griswold and Henderson, "Administrators Try out Ideas."

29. Garsten et al., "Yale-NUS College," 25.

30. Garsten et al., 33.

31. Garsten et al., 67.

32. Joraimi, "Yale-NUS."

33. Qing, "Yale-NUS Closure."

34. Yang, "Yale-NUS Experiment."

35. Yale University, "Statement."

36. Lewis, "Report on Cancellation."

37. Mahtani, "Yale's Venture in Singapore."

38. Jeyaretnam, "Up Close."

39. Quoted in Ross, "After Yale-NUS Divorce."

Chapter 5

1. American Society for Engineering Education, "Green Report"; Burns, "Olin College President."

2. Olin College of Engineering, "History."

3. American Society for Engineering Education, "Green Report," 2.

4. American Society for Engineering Education, 3.

5. American Society for Engineering Education, 1. See also Schwartz, "Re-engineering Engineering."

6. Marin, "NSF Update."

7. Schwartz, "Re-engineering Engineering."

8. Kerns, Miller, and Kerns, "Blank Slate."

9. Guizzo, "Olin Experiment."

10. Guizzo.

11. Somerville et al., "Olin Curriculum."

12. Olin College of Engineering, "Michael E. Moody Professorship."

13. Somerville et al., "Olin Curriculum," 199.

14. Olin College of Engineering, "Grand Challenges Scholars Program."

15. Somerville et al., "Olin Curriculum," 203.

16. Olin College of Engineering, "PInt at Olin."

17. Olin College of Engineering, "Olin College of Engineering Names Dr. Gilda Barabino."

18. Kurp, "No Longer on the Outside."

19. Olin College of Engineering, "Olin College of Engineering Names Dr. Gilda Barabino."

20. MIT School of Engineering, "Reimagining and Rethinking."

21. NAE, "Bernard M. Gordon Prize."

22. GBH Greater Boston Staff, "Olin College President."

23. Olin College of Engineering, "President Barabino's First Day."

24. Olin College of Engineering, "Olin College of Engineering Names Dr. Gilda Barabino."

25. Kerns, Miller, and Kerns, "Blank Slate."

26. Somerville et al., "Olin Curriculum."

27. Olin College of Engineering, "Consumer Information."

28. Olin College of Engineering, "Influencing Change."

29. Olin College of Engineering, "Consumer Information."

30. Olin College of Engineering, "Board of Trustees."

Chapter 6

1. Quoted in Thayer, "Obama's Visit to Vietnam."

2. Obama, "Remarks."

3. Marklein, "Expanding the Fulbright Legacy."

4. Marklein. See also Wasley, "Vietnamese Leaders."

5. Linh and Lam, "From a Bold Dream."

6. Linh and Lam.

7. Chirot and Wilkinson, "Intangibles of Excellence," 6.

8. Chirot and Wilkinson, 4.

9. Hoàng Tuy et al., "Proposal on Reforming and Modernizing Education" (2009), quoted in Chirot and Wilkinson, 9. Italics in original.

10. Hoàng Tuy et al., quoted in Chirot and Wilkinson, 17.

11. Hoàng Tuy et al., "Petition on Education" (2004), quoted in Chirot and Wilkinson, 8.

12. Chirot and Wilkinson, 18.

13. Quoted in Linh and Lam, "From a Bold Dream."

14. Fulbright University Vietnam, "Constructive Criticism."

15. Fulbright University Vietnam.

16. Taft, "U.S.-Backed University."

17. Linh and Lam, "From a Bold Dream."

18. Taft, "U.S.-Backed University."

19. Quoted in Taft.

20. Fulbright University Vietnam USA, "Fifth Anniversary."

21. Ninh, "Bob Kerrey in Vietnam."

22. Marklein, "Expanding the Fulbright Legacy."

23. Paddock, "Bob Kerrey's War Record"; V. T. Nguyen, "Bob Kerrey."

24. Quoted in Tran, "War Record."

25. Taft, "U.S.-Backed University."

26. Quoted in Linh and Lam, "From a Bold Dream."

27. Linh and Lam. The Boston Consulting Group was also hired to conduct interviews with students, parents, and companies in Vietnam (Pagano et al., "Lessons from Fulbright").

28. Pagano et al., "Lessons from Fulbright."

29. Tu, Student-Life archives.

30. Huong, "H'Mong School Dropout."

31. Huong.

32. N. Nguyen, "My Fellow-Vietnamese Students."

33. Fulbright University Vietnam, "Fulbright Welcomes Fifty-Six Students."

34. Kinho, "Co-designing a Rhetoric Course."

35. Marklein, "Expanding the Fulbright Legacy."

36. For an alternative view, see Mark Ashwill's "Coming to Terms."

37. Ashwill.

38. Derby-Talbot and Maguire, "Blessing and Curse."

39. Derby-Talbot and Maguire.

40. Ashwill, "US Institutions."

41. Fulbright University Vietnam USA, "Fifth Anniversary."

42. Vu, "Eight Philanthropists."

43. USDFC, "DFC Commits $37 Million."

44. Fulbright University Vietnam USA, "Fifth Anniversary."

Chapter 7

1. Choudhury, "Pramath Raj Sinha."

2. Nanda, "Only 2 Indian Varsities."

3. Kazmin, "Ashoka University."

4. McKenzie, "Indian Government Opens up Market."

5. Nandrajog, "Ashoka University."

6. Goyal, "Ashoka University."

7. Goyal. See also Mino, "Construyendo una tradición."

8. Kazmin, "Ashoka University." Dhawan was recognized in 2012 as the NextGen Leader in Philanthropy by *Forbes India* for his charitable work (Prasad, "Ashish Dhawan.")

9. Satya, "Ashoka University at Sonepat."

10. Reddy, "Two Young India Fellows." See also: Ashoka University, "ELM Impact Stories."

11. Goyal, "Ashoka University."

12. Finkel, "Penn Professors."

13. Sra, "India's New Ivy League."

14. Goyal, "Ashoka University."

15. Ashoka University, "Inclusion, Diversity & Belonging."

16. Quoted in Shyam, "Ashoka University."

17. Srinath Rao, "Ashoka University."

18. Srinath Rao.

19. Ashoka University, "Inclusion, Diversity & Belonging."

20. Ashoka University, Office of PR & Communications, "Ashoka's Nonconventional Interdisciplinary Approach." *Statesman* News Service, "Ashoka University's Economics Department."

21. Kazmin, "Ashoka University."

22. Kazmin.

23. Kazmin; personal communication from Ashish Dhawan, June 12, 2022.

24. Kazmin, "Ashoka University."

25. Kazmin.

26. Sengupta, "Statement against State Violence." Mukherjee quoted in Shriya Rao and Sai, "Breaking Down." See also Sharma, "Problem with Misuse."

27. Gautier, "Broadcast Message."

28. Quoted in Singh, "Ashoka University Slammed."

29. Quoted in Singh. See also Hazra, review of *A Gardener in the Wasteland*;

30. Mehta, "Dear Prime Minister."

31. Mehta, "2021 SSRC Fellow Lecture."

32. *Telegraph Online*, "Global Pressure."

33. Quoted in *Wire* Staff, "Ashoka University."

34. *Times of India*, "Ashoka University." See also Das, "Tale of Two Heroes."

35. Mattoo, "Which One"; *India Today* Web Desk, "QS Asia University Rankings"; Ashoka University, "Shaping the Leaders," 5. Across several cohorts, the top three industry placements for students included 26% in start-ups, 14% in the social sector or at think tanks, and 12% in education or educational technology.

36. Sharma, "With 131 New Institutions." Rishihood University, "Founders and Advisors." India has six categories of universities. Ashoka and similar schools are privately funded but regulated by the government and fall under the category of "state public university".

37. *HT* Correspondent, "UGC Releases Draft."

38. Kazmin, "Ashoka University."

39. *Express* News Service, "Ashoka University." See also Jebaraj, "Ashoka University."

Chapter 8

1. Awuah, "Path to a New Africa."

2. Sasu, "Share of Children."

3. Glavin, "Education Statistics in Ghana."

4. Sasu, "Tertiary Students Abroad."

5. *Times Higher Education*, "World University Rankings."

6. Gulati and De Lacvivier, "Ashesi University."

7. Mino, "Humanizing Higher Education."

8. Duthiers and Ellis, "Patrick Awuah."

9. Ashesi University, "Ashesi's Earliest Years."

10. Sasu, "Students in Public Universities."

11. Awuah, "Path to a New Africa."

12. Gulati and De Lacvivier, "Ashesi University."

13. Kigotho, "'Swarthmore' Grows in Ghana."

14. Ashesi University, "Our Mission."

15. Gulati and De Lacvivier, "Ashesi University."

16. Ashesi University, "Unlike Any Other."

17. Ashesi University, "Welcome to the Natembea."

18. Ashesi University, "Unlike Any Other."

19. Gulati and De Lacvivier, "Ashesi University."

20. Ashesi University, "Career Placement Record."

21. Ashesi University and Foundation, "2022 Strategic Priorities."

22. Ashesi University, "Teaching Skills."

23. Ashesi University, "Ashesi Way."

24. Ashesi University, "Our 8 Learning Goals."

25. Mino, "Humanizing Higher Education."

26. Ashesi University, "SDGs + Ashesi."

27. M. Grant, "Adapting the Liberal Arts."

28. Ashesi University External Relations Office, "Perfect Society."

29. Ashesi University, "Empowering African Women."

30. Seawright and Hodges, *Learning across Borders.*

31. Ashesi University, "SDGs + Ashesi."

32. Ashesi University, "Ashesi University's Entrepreneurship Center."

Chapter 9

1. Howell and Parke, "From Teenage Headmaster." See also Fast Company, "2019."

2. African Leadership Academy, "ALA Story." Swaniker's cofounders in launching ALA were Chris Bradford, an American who now serves as the school's chairman, and Acha Leke from Cameroon and Peter Mombaur, a German citizen and former classmate and mentor of Swaniker's, who provided the initial financial backing. Leke, now chairman of McKinsey's Africa region, is also a cofounder with Swaniker of the African Leadership Network, a group that convenes leaders. Mombaur is CEO of San Diego–based Terra Education, which focuses on experiential learning through trips and camps.

3. African Development Bank, *African Economic Outlook 2017*, cited in Panashe, "What Does Entrepreneurship Really Mean." See also Ireland, "Dynamic Africa"; UN Environment Programme, "Our Work in Africa"; "UNESCO, "263 Million Children"; Swaniker, "How to Unlock."

4. Baker, "It's Time."

5. Republic of Rwanda Ministry of Youth and ICT, "Smart Rwanda 2020."

6. Mitchell, "Rwanda Centres Innovation Drive."

7. MASS Design Group, "African Leadership University."

8. Swaniker, "Inspirational Toast."

9. African Leadership University, "Deep-Dive"; "Class Feature."

10. Cisse, "ALU #DoHardThings Series."

11. Muhire, "Young Leaders in Africa."

12. Rosenberg, "American Higher Education."

13. Center for Creative Leadership, "70-20-10 Rule."

14. Baker, "It's Time."

15. African Leadership University, "Annual Report," 9, 11. African Leadership University, "ALU Graduates Continue."

16. African Leadership University, "Two Alumni."

17. Graham, "'Give Away Your Legos.'"

18. McKie, "'Harvard of Africa.'"

19. Adegoke, "African Leadership University."

20. Swaniker, interviewed by Sara Custer for *PIE News*.

21. Students like Firdaus Salim, who was raised in a village off the coast of Africa, suggest the kind of student that ALX can reach. She is training to become a full stack software engineer and has interned with various start-ups. At ALX, she codes for a hundred hours a week for twelve months. Swaniker, "Most Inspiring Conversation."

22. Swaniker, "Five Reasons."

23. African Leadership University, "Excellence at Scale."

24. African Leadership University, "ALU Advantage."

25. African Leadership University.

26. Swaniker, interviewed by Sara Custer for *PIE News*.

27. Carnegie Foundation for the Advancement of Teaching, "Carnegie Foundation to Partner."

28. The Room, "About Us."

29. Chris Bradford, who cofounded ALA, is now the chairman of the board and Bilha Ndirangu, a Kenyan technology leader and MIT graduate, was appointed in 2021 as the institution's third CEO after Swaniker and Bradford. Cofounders Acha Leke and Peter Mombaur

serve on ALA's Global Advisory Council. After founding ALU and serving as its CEO until 2019, Swaniker returned temporarily in 2021 as CEO and now serves as chairman of the board with no executive role. Veda Sunassee, a native Mauritian and Princeton graduate, started at ALA in 2010, helped established ALU in Mauritius, served as the founding dean of ALU in Rwanda, and in 2022 was appointed CEO of ALU. He also hosts the podcast *In the Room*, where he interviews global leaders.

30. Both the high school and the university are nonprofit institutions, although the university began as a for-profit corporation and became a nonprofit in 2019. The career accelerator and talent match system are part of a legal entity called African Leadership International, a for-profit corporation led by Swaniker. ALA, ALU, and ALX are separate legal entities with separate boards of directors, CEOs, and advisory councils. All of these organizations are connected as part of an ecosystem under the heading of the African Leadership Group (ALG), which is headquartered in Nairobi. The ALG is not a legally independent body; it serves as a kind of coordinating body for all of these entities. ALG also includes in its network the African Leadership Network, which brings together leaders from across Africa, similarly to the Aspen Institute and the World Economic Forum. African Leadership Group, "We Are on a Mission."

31. SiliconANGLE theCUBE, "Sandy Carter."

Chapter 10

1. Nelson, El-Azar, and Seligman, "Creating a University." The development of Minerva's global rotation is a good example of the evolution, false starts, and course corrections that start-up universities all experience. While the concept of a global rotation was part of the original inspiration for Minerva, the specific cities changed significantly from what was originally envisioned. The original idea focused on San Francisco, New York, Mumbai, Hong Kong and other megapolises or financial capitals. During the beta-test year, the students complained that too many of the cities were too expensive and they wanted greater variety than the few cities that were originally offered. Over time, Minerva dropped New York, and substituted Hyderabad for Mumbai and Taipei for Hong Kong.

2. See, e.g., Kaminski, "Ben Nelson"; Shulevitz, "Future of College"; Clarke, "Future of Education"; Birzer, "Minerva University."

3. Vander Ark, "Minerva"; Peterson, "Minerva Delusion."

4. Quoted in Carey, "How to Raise."

5. Wood, "Future of College?"

6. Minerva Project, "Minerva Project Redefines."

7. TAL Education Group, "TAL Education Leads Consortium." See also Minerva Project, "Minerva Project Closes $57 Million."

8. WASC Senior College and University Commission, "Report."

9. Kosslyn and Nelson, *Building the Intentional University*.

10. Halpern and Hakel, "Applying the Science." Halpern later went on to serve as dean of social sciences at Minerva University in 2014 and 2015.

11. Fost, "New Look."

12. Fost. Also: Joshua W. Fost, pers. comm. "Knowledge Transfer," e-mail message to author, December 7, 2022.

13. Fost, "Quantifying Knowledge Transfer."

14. Chandler, Kosslyn, and Genone, "New Look at Majors."

15. Fost, "New Look."

16. Kosslyn, "Science of Learning"; Fost, Levitt, and Kosslyn, "Fully Active Learning."

17. McAllister, "Teacher's Guide."

18. Clarke, "Future of Education."

19. McAllister, "Teacher's Guide."

20. A regional accreditation team's report provides further support for this point:

> The review team was somewhat concerned before meeting with faculty and students that this comprehensive specification of program outcomes and use of pre-designed courses could constrain teaching and squeeze out serendipitous learning; however, the faculty reported that the extraordinary level of collaboration (both required and voluntary) actually enhanced their own teaching and the quality of the course content, after developing familiarity with the learning model. Several faculty members also offered that working with colleagues was a benefit that they had not experienced before in academia (suggesting that teaching had been a lonely endeavor). (WASC Senior College and University Commission, "Report," 19)

21. WASC Senior College and University Commission, 29.

22. Rousmaniere, "Fish out of Water."

23. Minerva University, "Consequent 2022."

24. Minerva University, "Pathbreaking Institution."

25. Minerva University, "Tuition & Fees."

26. Minerva University, "Pathbreaking Institution."

27. Minerva University.

28. Natural science, computational science, and business faculty in particular are more likely to be part time. This status enables the natural science faculty to maintain access to laboratory or field research, while business and computational faculty are more likely to be working for a company or consulting alongside their teaching.

29. WASC Senior College and University Commission, "Report," 28.

30. Over time, Minerva has developed policies and practices to support traditional research, including professional development funds for faculty to attend conferences and purchase materials. Some faculty publish in traditional research journals, and instructors can apply for grants and buy themselves out of teaching time so that they can pursue uninterrupted research. Minerva is especially supportive of research that incorporates students, and it provides stipends for undergraduates as research assistants. In 2021–22, more than 60 percent of faculty carried out some kind of creative or scholarly activity, including publishing books and articles and making academic presentations.

31. American Association for the Advancement of Science, *Vision and Change.*

32. Marsh and Hattie, "Research Productivity and Teaching."

33. Wieman, "Expertise in University Teaching."

34. An external accreditation review found that "faculty have the ability to modify, adjust and redirect the curriculum through Forum, and . . . [the] provost has academic authority and leadership in partnership with the faculty that is characteristic of other excellent institutions" (WASC Senior College and University Commission, "Report," 35).

35. These working groups also mine the extensive information generated from the online platform to investigate and disseminate the results of their analysis on key questions in teaching and learning, especially in online and hybrid environments. Research questions range from specific ones such as whether "cold calling" makes students prepare better for class to broad ones such as how to better quantify knowledge transfer across disciplines and contexts. Faculty regularly present their findings at research conferences on teaching and learning, and some have begun reaching even broader audiences. In 2021, Katie McAllister, the head of the College of Social Sciences at Minerva, published her book *Beyond the Lecture*, a guide for faculty who want to develop more active forms of teaching and learning both online and offline. Faculty and staff have also published an edited volume that provides a how-to guide to the construction of the university. The book, *Building the Intentional University*, "open-sources" their core

principles and practices and includes an appendix with a full list of their habits of mind and foundational concepts. See McAllister, *Beyond the Lecture*; Kosslyn and Nelson, *Building the Intentional University*.

36. WASC Senior College and University Commission, "Report," 44.
37. WASC Senior College and University Commission, 20.
38. WASC Senior College and University Commission, 7, 8, 10.

Chapter 11

1. Schein, *Organizational Culture and Leadership*, 56.
2. Schein.
3. Yale University Office of the President, "Archived Speeches."
4. Sexton, "Building the First Global Network."
5. Fulbright University Vietnam, "Origin Story."
6. Boston Consulting Group, "Learning Is Reimagined."
7. Ashesi University, "Ashesi to Start Engineering."
8. Seligman and Goldberg, "Building a New Brand," 256.
9. Olin College of Engineering, "Influencing the Global State."
10. BBC News, "Why India's Rich."
11. Pham, "Why Doesn't Yale-NUS."
12. Tan, "New NUS."
13. Dorph, "NYU's Global Strategy."
14. Porcelli, "What It Means."
15. USDFC, "DFC Commits $37 Million."
16. Mangan, "Students Arrive to Help."
17. Chan and Stacey, "Desirable Difficulties."
18. M. Grant, "Can Liberal Arts Education," 37.
19. NYU Abu Dhabi, *Origin Story*, 146.
20. NYU Abu Dhabi, 106, 144.
21. Seawright and Hodges, *Learning across Borders*, 42; see also M. Grant, "Can Liberal Arts Education."
22. June, "How One College Reinvented."
23. NYU Abu Dhabi, *Origin Story*, 166.
24. Garsten et al., "Yale-NUS College," 40.
25. Olin College of Engineering, "Overview."
26. Olin College of Engineering.
27. Kosslyn and Nelson, *Building the Intentional University*, 45.
28. African Leadership University, "8 Distinctive Things."
29. Ashesi University External Relations Office, "Learning to Serve."
30. Ashesi University, "Core Course Descriptions."
31. Fulbright University Vietnam, "Core Curriculum."
32. Garsten et al., "Yale-NUS College."
33. NYU Abu Dhabi, "Natural Science Minor."
34. NYU Abu Dhabi, "Courses: Requirements."
35. Fost, Chandler, Gardner, and Gale, "A New Team-Teaching Approach to Structured Learning," 179.
36. Kosslyn and Nelson.
37. Quoted in Lederman, "Minerva."
38. Ferguson, "I'm Helping."

39. Harvard Graduate School of Education, "HGSE's Leadership Series."

40. Garsten et al., "Yale-NUS College," 31.

41. Jimaa, "$1bn New York University."

42. NYU Abu Dhabi, "Campus."

43. Ballon, "Planning from Within," 159.

44. Kerns, Miller, and Kerns, "Blank Slate."

45. NYU Abu Dhabi, *Origin Story*, 173.

46. *Express* News Service, "Ashoka University."

47. Chowdhury, "'World Class' in Sonipat."

48. Katzman, Regan, and Bader-Natal, "The Active Learning Forum," 204.

Chapter 12

1. Greiner, "Evolution and Revolution."

2. Schein, *Organizational Culture and Leadership*.

3. Bowen and Tobin, *Locus of Authority*. For criticism of Bowen and Tobin's argument, see Ryan and Goldrick-Rab's "But What if the Shared Vision Is Myopic?"

4. Rosenberg, "Rigidness of Academic Routine," 2. See also Rosenberg, "Shared or Divided Governance?"

5. Olin College of Engineering, "About."

6. Sanderson, "NYU Abu Dhabi's First Provost."

7. For a critical look at the possibilities for academic freedom in the Middle East, see Noori's "Academic Freedom and the Liberal Arts in the Middle East."

8. See Lehman, "Testimony."

9. DeGeurin, "Lack of Academic Freedom"; Maharishi, "NYU and Professors."

10. Royster, "Steve Jobs on Technology"; Lewis, "Asia Invests in Liberal Arts."

11. Ibrahim et al., "Racism at NYU Abu Dhabi"; Hajee, "Unthinking Eurocentrism at NYUAD"; NYU Abu Dhabi, "NYUAD Accountability Framework."

12. Majumdar, "Honeymoon Period."

13. Shofer and Meyer, "Worldwide Expansion," 917.

14. Hills, "Academic Freedom."

15. Hills. See also Pickus, "Insider's View of DKU":

> Our class is the most global I've ever taught in twenty-five years. Half the students come from all over the world: Korea, Taiwan, Denmark, Serbia, Pakistan, and the Philippines, as well as from New York to North Carolina. And half the students come from Shanghai, Zhejiang, Beijing, Shandong, and a handful of other Chinese provinces. . . . "What would be the most controversial thing you could tell your parents about DKU?" I ask the students. "That I've become a Socialist," says Rachel, from New Rochelle, New York. "That I don't want to join the Party," offers Yue, whose home is in Huzhou.

16. Blanks, "Cultural Diversity," 32.

17. Godwin, "Counter Narrative," 240.

18. Sleeper, "Innocents Abroad?"

19. Wasserman, *Doha Experiment*, 105–7.

20. Kwong-loi, "Confucian Learning."

21. Parts of this paragraph come from previously published work. See Godwin and Pickus, *Liberal Arts*, 17.

22. Levin, "Presidential Statements." In an illuminating essay, Charlene Tan captures how the possibilities and constraints on cross-cultural understanding were evident in the disputes over academic freedom at Yale-NUS. One camp took an approach rooted in the belief that freedom

is unfettered and any restrictions on or off campus should be met with an adversarial stance, she writes. The other camp advanced a more conciliatory approach that gave greater respect to navigating tensions with local laws and cultures. See Tan, "Thinking Critically."

23. Samra, "Case for Theory"; Hajee, "Unthinking Eurocentrism at NYUAD."

24. Boyle, "Global Liberal Education," 240.

Chapter 13

1. *Times of India*, "Ashoka University."

2. Fulbright University Vietnam, "President of Fulbright."

3. World's Universities with Real Impact, "WURI Ranking 2022."

4. Cohen and March, *Leadership and Ambiguity*. See also Mintz, "11 Lessons."

5. Ward, "Is It True"; Eisenmann, "Why Startups Fail."

6. Greiner, "Evolution and Revolution."

7. Graham, "'Give Away Your Legos.'"

8. Bass, "Disrupting Ourselves." See also Blumenstyk, "From a Red House." On the value of incremental innovation, see Ebner and Pickus's "Right Kind of Innovation."

9. It's useful to contrast this approach with the one taken by NYU and Yale, which set up their global ventures as a kind of skunk-works project and found that the hard part wasn't innovating, it was bringing the new forms of teaching, curricular approaches, and cross-faculty interaction back to the home campus. (NYU did find that its decentralized and disconnected fiefdoms benefitted from having to work together to create more-integrated programs in Abu Dhabi.) This process of diffusion and reintegration is often the most difficult, as companies that have tried it can attest.

10. McMurtrie, "Hope and Hype." See also Bishop and Keehn, "Leading Academic Change."

11. Maloney and Kim, "How Universities Can Avoid." See also Kim and Maloney, *Learning Innovation*.

12. Staisloff, "How to Review."

13. For a discussion of the history of debates over general education in the United States, see chapter 1 of Menand's *Marketplace of Ideas*.

14. Kirby, *Empires of Ideas*, 387–88.

15. I draw this framing from Ruth Grant's insightful book, *Hypocrisy and Integrity: Machiavelli, Rousseau, and the Ethics of Politics*, pages 62–68 and 171–72.

16. I am grateful to Elizabeth Kiss for this formulation and for the insights that underlie it.

17. Lehman, "Testimony."

18. Roth, "Higher Ed's Role." See also Michael S. Roth, *Safe Enough Spaces*; Chemerinsky and Gillman, *Free Speech on Campus*.

19. Duke Kunshan University, "Undergraduate Curriculum." See also Stanford d.school, "Uncharted Territory," 108–23.

BIBLIOGRAPHY

Abu Dhabi Office of Public and Cultural Diplomacy. "NYU Abu Dhabi Launches Three Research Centres." Office of Public and Cultural Diplomacy, January 14, 2021. https://opcd.ae/nyuad-launches-3-research-centres/.

Adegoke, Yinka. "African Leadership University Has Raised $30 Million to Help Reinvent Graduate Education." *Quartz*, January 4, 2019. https://qz.com/africa/1515015/african-leadership-university-raises-30-million-series-b#.

African Development Bank. *African Economic Outlook 2017: Entrepreneurship and Industrialisation*. African Development Bank, Organisation for Economic Co-operation and Development, and United Nations Development Programme, 2017. https://www.afdb.org/fileadmin/uploads/afdb/Documents/Publications/AEO_2017_Report_Full_English.pdf.

African Leadership Academy. "The ALA Story." ALA, accessed March 17, 2023. https://www.africanleadershipacademy.org/about/our-story/.

African Leadership Group. "We Are on a Mission to Capture One of the 21st Century's Greatest Opportunities." ALG. Accessed January 1, 2022. https://algroup.org/.

African Leadership University. "Annual Report." 2021. ALU.

———. "The ALU Advantage." ALU. Accessed January 1, 2022. https://www.alueducation.com/home/the-alu-advantage/.

———. "ALU Graduates Continue to #dohardthings." *ALU News*, October 2, 2019. https://www.alueducation.com/alu-graduates-continue-to-dohardthings/.

———. "ALU Rwanda: Founding Class Reflections." YouTube, June 7, 2018. https://www.youtube.com/watch?v=svYwWaNv8rg.

———. "Class Feature: What Students Do in Projects." ALU, 2018 (page no longer available). https://www.alueducation.com/class-feature-what-students-do-in-projects/.

———. "Deep-Dive into the Entrepreneurial Leadership Course at ALU." ALU, 2019 (page no longer available). https://www.alueducation.com/deep-dive-into-the-entrepreneurial-leadership-course-at-alu/.

———. "8 Distinctive Things about ALU." *ALU News*, May 8, 2015. https://www.alueducation.com/8-distinctive-things-about-alu/.

———. "Excellence at Scale: African Leadership University." ALU, 2021. https://drive.google.com/file/d/1iVCF5O0leBkIF4_h5CDFY6QhLcTP6mAU/view.

———. "Two Alumni from ALU's Inaugural Class Named Schwarzman Scholars." ALU, 2021 (page no longer available). https://www.alueducation.com/two-alumni-from-alus-inaugural-class-named-schwarzman-scholars/.

Alexander, Brian. *Academia Next: The Futures of Higher Education*. Baltimore, MD: Johns Hopkins University Press, 2020.

American Association for the Advancement of Science. *Vision and Change in Undergraduate Biology Education: A Call to Action*. Washington, DC: AAAS, 2009. https://live-visionandchange.pantheonsite.io/wp-content/uploads/2011/03/VC-Brochure-V6-3.pdf.

American Society for Engineering Education. "The Green Report: Engineering Education for a Changing World." Washington, DC: ASEE, 2010. https://aseecmsduq.blob.core.windows.net/aseecmsdev/asee/media/content/member%20resources/pdfs/the-green-report_1.pdf.

Anders, George. *You Can Do Anything: The Surprising Power of a "Useless" Liberal Arts Education.* New York: Little, Brown, 2017.

Aoun, Joseph. *Robot-Proof: Higher Education in the Age of Artificial Intelligence.* Cambridge, MA: MIT Press, 2018.

Arnett, Jeffrey Jensen. *Emerging Adulthood: The Winding Road from the Late Teens through the Twenties.* New York: Oxford University Press, 2014.

Ash, Lucy. "Belarus's University in Exile." BBC News, April 24, 2013, https://www.bbc.com/news/magazine-22254545.

Ashesi University. "Ashesi's Earliest Years: Feasibility Study." Ashesi University, January 6, 2011. The Internet Archive. https://web.archive.org/web/20110106021317/http:/www.ashesi.edu.gh/NEWS/BULLETIN/EARLIEST_YEARS/FEASIBILITY_STUDY/feasibility_study.html.

———. "Ashesi University's Entrepreneurship Center." Seattle, WA: Ashesi University Foundation, 2021. https://www.ashesi.org/wp-content/uploads/2021/10/Ashesi-Entrepreneurship-Center.pdf.

———. "The Ashesi Way of Liberal Arts." Seattle, WA: Ashesi University Foundation, 2019. https://www.ashesi.org/wp-content/uploads/2019/09/2019-The-Ashesi-Way-Of-Liberal-Arts.pdf.

———. "Career Placement Record." Ashesi University, 2022. https://www.ashesi.edu.gh/academics/122-career-services/career-placement-record.html.

———. "Core Course Descriptions." Ashesi University, 2022. https://www.ashesi.edu.gh/about/11-academics/core-curriculum/37-liberal-arts-core-course-descriptions.html.

———. "Empowering African Women through Higher Education." Seattle, WA: Ashesi University Foundation, 2021. https://www.ashesi.org/wp-content/uploads/2022/01/2021-Empowering-Women-at-Ashesi.pdf.

———. "Our 8 Learning Goals." Ashesi University, 2022. https://www.ashesi.edu.gh/academics/learning-goals.html.

———. "Our Mission, Vision and History." Ashesi University, 2022. https://www.ashesi.edu.gh/about/at-a-glance/mission-history.html.

———. "SDGs + Ashesi: How Ashesi University Is Supporting the UN Sustainable Development Goals." Seattle, WA: Ashesi University Foundation, 2021. https://www.ashesi.org/wp-content/uploads/2021/03/SDGs-Ashesi.pdf.

———. "Teaching Skills That Last a Lifetime." Ashesi University, 2022. https://www.ashesi.edu.gh/academics/the-ashesi-education.html.

———. "Unlike Any Other in Africa." Ashesi University, 2022. https://www.ashesi.edu.gh/about/at-a-glance/quick-facts.html.

———. "Welcome to the Natembea Health Centre." Ashesi University, 2022. https://www.ashesi.edu.gh/academics/library/online-databases/176-academics/faculty-pages-arts-and-sciences-2/176-health-and-wellbeing.html.

Ashesi University and Foundation. "2022 Strategic Priorities." Ashesi University and Foundation, 2022. https://www.ashesi.org/wp-content/uploads/2022/02/2022_Ashesi-Strategic-Priorities.pdf.

Ashesi University Communications. "Ashesi to Start Engineering Master's Programme with Leading Swiss University ETH Zurich." Ashesi University, October 5, 2020. https://www.ashesi.edu.gh/stories-and-events/stories/3766-ashesi-to-begin-joint-engineering-master-s-programme-with-eth-zurich.html.

Ashesi University External Relations Office. "'Can We Create a Perfect Society?': Crafting a Social Honour Code." Ashesi University, December 3, 2018. https://www.ashesi.edu.gh/stories-and-events/stories/3309-can-we-create-a-perfect-society-forming-a-social-honour-code.html.

———. "Learning to Serve: Students Volunteer in Communities through Ghana." Ashesi University, October 30, 2016. https://www.ashesi.edu.gh/stories and-events/stories/2342-learning-to-serve-communities-beyond-students-go-into-the-field.html.

Ashoka University. "ELM Impact Stories, 2019–20." Ashoka University, 2020; accessed June 15, 2022. https://www.ashoka.edu.in/elm-impact-stories/.

———. "Inclusion, Diversity & Belonging Report, 2021–22." Ashoka University, 2022. https://www.ashoka.edu.in/wp-content/uploads/2022/02/2021-22_AU-Inclusion-Diversity-Belonging-Report-website-version.pdf.

———. "Shaping the Leaders of the Future: Placement Brochure 2021–22." Ashoka University, n.d. https://ashoka.edu.in/wp-content/uploads/2021/09/Ashoka-Placement-Brochure_2021.pdf.

Ashoka University, Office of PR & Communications. "Ashoka's Nonconventional Interdisciplinary Approach towards Natural Sciences: The Success of the Maiden Physics Batch." Ashoka University, August 6, 2021. https://www.ashoka.edu.in/ashokas-nonconventional-interdisciplinary-approach-towards-natural-sciences-the-success-of-the-maiden-physics-batch/.

Ashwill, Mark. "Coming to Terms with the Past by Honoring Historical Truth: The Case of Fulbright University Vietnam." CounterPunch, August 2, 2019. https://www.counterpunch.org/2019/08/02/coming-to-terms-with-the-past-by-honoring-historical-truth-the-case-of-fulbright-university-vietnam/.

———. "US Institutions Find Fertile Ground in Vietnam's Expanding Higher Education Market." International Higher Education, no. 44 (2015). https://doi.org/10.6017/ihe.2006.44.7914.

Asian University for Women. "Who We Are." Asian University for Women, accessed June 15, 2022. https://asian-university.org/who-we-are/.

Aviv, Rachel. "The Imperial Presidency." New Yorker, September 9, 2013. https://www.newyorker.com/magazine/2013/09/09/the-imperial-presidency.

Awuah, Patrick. "Path to a New Africa." Stanford Social Innovation Review, Summer 2012. https://ssir.org/articles/entry/path_to_a_new_africa.

Bain, Ken. Super Courses. Princeton, NJ: Princeton University Press, 2022.

Baker, Aryn. "'It's Time Africa Had Its Own Harvard.' Inside a University Training African Leaders to Solve African Problems." Time, June 11, 2019. https://time.com/5603886/african-leadership-university-mauritius-fred-swaniker/.

Ballon, Hilary. "Planning from Within: NYU Abu Dhabi." In The New Arab Urban: Gulf Cities of Wealth, Ambition, and Distress, edited by Harvey Luskin Molotch and Davide Ponzini, 147–71. New York: New York University Press, 2019.

Bass, Randy. "Disrupting Ourselves: The Problem of Learning in Higher Education." Educause Review, March 21, 2012. https://er.educause.edu/articles/2012/3/disrupting-ourselves-the-problem-of-learning-in-higher-education.

Bayles, Martha. Through a Screen Darkly: Popular Culture, Public Diplomacy, and America's Image Abroad. New Haven, CT: Yale University Press, 2014.

BBC News. "Matthew Hedges: British Academic Pardoned by UAE." BBC News, November 26, 2018. https://www.bbc.co.uk/news/uk-46341310.

———. "Why India's Rich Don't Give Their Money Away." BBC News, April 2, 2019. https://www.bbc.com/news/world-asia-india-47566542.

Birzer, Bradley J. "Minerva University vs. Liberal Learning." Imaginative Conservative, August 13, 2013. https://theimaginativeconservative.org/2013/08/minerva-university-vs-liberal-learning.html.

Bishop, M. J., and Anne Keehn. "Leading Academic Change: An Early Market Scan of Leading-Edge Postsecondary Academic Innovation Centers." William E. Kirwan Center for Academic Innovation, University System of Maryland, n.d. https://www.educause.edu/sites/default/files/library/presentations/E15/PS11/LeadingAcademicChangeProjectReport.pdf.

Blanks, D. R. "Cultural Diversity or Cultural Imperialism: Liberal Education in Egypt." *Liberal Education* 84 (1998): 30–35.

Blumenstyk, Goldie. "From a Red House Off Campus, Georgetown Tries to Reinvent Itself." *Chronicle of Higher Education*, January 19, 2016. https://www.chronicle.com/article/from-a-red-house-off-campus-georgetown-tries-to-reinvent-itself/.

Boston Consulting Group. "Learning Is Reimagined at Fulbright University in Vietnam." BCG, 2022, accessed June 19, 2021 (page no longer available). https://www.bcg.com/en-us/industries/education/reimagining-learning-experience-fulbright-university-vietnam.

Bothwell, Ellie. "Universities' Focus on Careers 'Fails to Address Global Division.'" *Times Higher Education*, August 26, 2017. https://www.timeshighereducation.com/news/universities-focus-on-careers-fails-to-address-global-division.

Bowen, William G., and Eugene M. Tobin. *Locus of Authority: The Evolution of Faculty Roles in the Governance of Higher Education*. New York: Ithaka; Princeton, NJ: Princeton University Press.

Boyle, Mary-Ellen. "Global Liberal Education: Theorizing Emergence and Variability." *Research in Comparative and International Education* 14, no. 2 (2019): 231–48. https://doi.org/10.1177/1745499919846010.

———. "Liberal Education Unmoored?" *Comparative Education Review* 63, no. 1 (2019): 127–31. https://doi.org/10.1086/701183.

Branch, Mark. "Singapore Spinoff." *Yale Alumni Magazine*, November/December 2010. https://yalealumnimagazine.org/articles/3022-singapore-spinoff.

Bui, Joey. "Rethinking Curriculum at Hack the Core." *Gazelle*, no. 69 (October 3, 2015). https://www.thegazelle.org/issue/69/news/hack.

Burns, Hilary. "Olin College President to Step Down in 2020." *Boston Business Journal*, July 12, 2019. https://www.bizjournals.com/boston/news/2019/07/12/olin-college-president-to-step-down-in-2020.html.

Cabal, Sebastian. "A Timeline of the Core Reform Process." *Gazelle*, no. 74 (November 14, 2015). https://www.thegazelle.org/issue/74/news/a-timeline-of-the-core-reform-process.

Carey, Kevin. "How to Raise a University's Profile: Pricing and Packaging." *New York Times*, February 6, 2015. https://www.nytimes.com/2015/02/08/education/edlife/how-to-raise-a-universitys-profile-pricing-and-packaging.html?smid=tw-share&_r=0.

Carnegie Foundation for the Advancement of Teaching. "Carnegie Foundation to Partner with the African Leadership University to Establish a Postsecondary Hub." News release, Carnegie Foundation for the Advancement of Teaching, December 1, 2021. https://www.carnegiefoundation.org/newsroom/news-releases/carnegie-foundation-to-partner-with-the-african-leadership-university-to-establish-a-postsecondary-hub/.

Center for Creative Leadership. "The 70-20-10 Rule for Leadership Development." Center for Creative Leadership, April 24, 2022. https://www.ccl.org/articles/leading-effectively-articles/70-20-10-rule/.

Chan, Kinho, and Pamela Stacey. "Desirable Difficulties and Student-Faculty Partnership." *Innovations in Education and Teaching International* 59, no. 3 (2022): 242–52. https://www.tandfonline.com/doi/full/10.1080/14703297.2020.1861964.

Chandler, Vicki, Stephen Kosslyn, and James Genone. "A New Look at Majors and Concentrations." In Kosslyn and Nelson, *Building the Intentional University*, 121–34.

Chemerinsky, Erwin, and Howard Gillman. *Free Speech on Campus*. New Haven, CT: Yale University Press, 2018.

Chirot, Laura, and Ben Wilkinson. "The Intangibles of Excellence: Governance and the Quest to Build a Vietnamese Apen University," White paper. New School, Harvard Kennedy School, and the Fulbright Economics Teaching Program, June 2009, revised January 2010. https://ash.harvard.edu/files/apex.pdf.

Chopp, Rebecca S., Susan Frost, and Daniel H Weiss. *Remaking College: Innovation and the Liberal Arts*. Baltimore, MD: Johns Hopkins University Press, 2016.

Choudhury, Sonya Dutta. "Pramath Raj Sinha: The Classroom Entrepreneur." *Mint*, January 20, 2017. https://lifestyle.livemint.com/news/talking-point/pramath-raj-sinha-the-classroom-entrepreneur-111646909433814.html.

Chowdhury, Shreya Roy. "'World Class' in Sonipat: How Privileged Private Universities Are Settling Down in Rural Haryana." Scroll.in, September 5, 2018. https://scroll.in/article/890578/world-class-in-sonipat-how-privileged-private-universities-are-settling-down-in-rural-haryana.

Christensen, Clayton M., and Henry J. Eyring. *The Innovative University: Changing the DNA of Higher Education from the Inside Out*. San Francisco: Jossey-Bass, 2011.

Cisse, Wasse. "ALU #DoHardThings Series: Wassa Cisse." African Leadership University, YouTube, July 31, 2020. https://www.youtube.com/watch?v=AuuuJ3SgleA.

Claremont McKenna College. "What Are America's First Coed Colleges?" *CMC Magazine*, Spring–Summer 2015. https://www.cmc.edu/magazine/spring-summer-2015/what-are-americas-first-coed-colleges.

Clarke, Bryony. "The Future of Education or Just Hype? The Rise of Minerva, the World's Most Selective University." *Guardian*, July 30, 2020. https://www.theguardian.com/education/2020/jul/30/the-future-of-education-or-just-hype-the-rise-of-minerva-the-worlds-most-selective-university.

Cohen, Michael D., and James G. March. *Leadership and Ambiguity: The American College President*. 2nd ed. Boston, MA: Harvard Business School Press, 1986.

Cole, Jonathan R. *Toward a More Perfect University*. New York: PublicAffairs, 2016.

Crow, Michael M., and William B. Dabars. *Designing the New American University*. Baltimore, MD: Johns Hopkins University Press, 2018.

———. *The Fifth Wave: The Evolution of American Higher Education*. Baltimore, MD: Johns Hopkins University Press.

Das, Gucharan. "A Tale of Two Heroes: An Ashoka University Donor on the Challenges of Doing Good in Today's World." *Times of India*, March 25, 2021. https://timesofindia.indiatimes.com/blogs/toi-edit-page/a-tale-of-two-heroes-tragedy-at-ashoka-university-shows-the-difficulty-of-doing-good-in-todays-world/.

Davidson, Cathy N. *The New Education: How to Revolutionize the University to Prepare Students for a World in Flux*. New York: Basic Books, 2017.

Davis College Akilah. "Educating East Africa's Future Leaders." Davis College Akilah, accessed June 15, 2022. https://akilah.org/.

DeGeurin, Mack. "Hamilton Admits University Bungled NYUAD Visa Denials." *Washington Square News*, February 11, 2018. https://nyunews.com/2018/02/11/2-12-news-abudhabi/.

———. "Lack of Academic Freedom Plagues NYU Abu Dhabi." *Washington Square News*, October 2, 2017. https://nyunews.com/2017/10/02/lack-of-academic-freedom-plagues-nyu-abu-dhabi/.

Delbanco, Andrew. *College: What It Was, Is, and Should Be*. Princeton, NJ: Princeton University Press, 2012. Kindle.

Department of Statistics Singapore. "Economy." Department of Statistics Singapore, 2022. https://www.singstat.gov.sg/find-data/search-by-theme/economy/labour-employment-wages-and-productivity/visualising-data.

Derby-Talbot, Ryan, and Andrew Maguire. "The Blessing and Curse of the Blank Slate." Medium, August 17, 2020. https://medium.com/@rderbytalbot/the-blessing-and-curse-of-the-blank-slate-8aa73a24860c.

Deresiewicz, William. *Excellent Sheep: The Miseducation of the American Elite and the Way to a Meaningful Life*. New York: Free Press, 2015.

Detweiler, Richard A. *The Evidence Liberal Arts Needs: Lives of Consequence, Inquiry, and Accomplishment*. Cambridge, MA: MIT Press, 2021.

Dorph, Martin. "NYU's Global Strategy: Financial Overview," New York University, November 2019. https://www.nyu.edu/content/dam/nyu/provost/documents/faculty-global-network/Global_Network_Finance_2019.pdf.

Duke Kunshan University. "Undergraduate Curriculum." DKU, accessed June 15, 2022. https://www.dukekunshan.edu.cn/about/the-liberal-arts-in-the-21st-century/.

Duthiers, Vladimir, and Jessica Ellis. "Patrick Awuah: Millionaire Who Quit Microsoft to Educate Future Leaders." CNN, May 1, 2013. https://www.cnn.com/2013/05/01/world/africa/patrick-awuah-ashesi-ghana/index.html.

Ebner, Kate, and Noah Pickus. "The Right Kind of Innovation." *Inside Higher Ed*, July 25, 2018. https://www.insidehighered.com/digital-learning/views/2018/07/25/yes-higher-ed-needs-innovation-it-should-be-right-kind-opinion.

Eickelman, Dale F., and Rogaia M. Abusharaf, eds. *Higher Education Investment in the Arab States of the Gulf: Strategies for Excellence and Diversity*. Berlin: Gerlach, 2017.

Eisenmann, Thomas R. "Why Startups Fail: It's Not Always the Horse or the Jockey." *Harvard Business Review*, May–June 2021. https://hbr.org/2021/05/why-start-ups-fail.

Ellevate. "The Skills You Need To Succeed In 2020." Forbes, August 6, 2018. https://www.forbes.com/sites/ellevate/2018/08/06/the-skills-you-need-to-succeed-in-2020/?sh=45c63911288a.

Express News Service. "Ashoka University to Build New Campus, Double Student Capacity." *Indian Express*, September 9, 2021. https://indianexpress.com/article/cities/delhi/ashoka-university-to-build-new-campus-double-student-capacity-7498028/.

Fast Company. "2019: The World's Most Innovative Companies." Fast Company, 2019; accessed June 15, 2022. https://www.fastcompany.com/most-innovative-companies/2019/sectors/africa.

Felten, Peter, John N. Gardner, Charles C. Schroeder, Leo M. Lambert, and Betsy O. Barefoot. *The Undergraduate Experience: Focusing Institutions on What Matters Most*. San Francisco: Jossey-Bass, 2016.

Ferguson, Niall. "I'm Helping to Start a New College because Higher Ed Is Broken." Bloomberg, November 8, 2021. https://www.bloomberg.com/opinion/articles/2021-11-08/niall-ferguson-america-s-woke-universities-need-to-be-replaced.

Ferrall, Victor E. *Liberal Arts at the Brink*. Cambridge, MA: Harvard University Press, 2011.

Finkel, Rachel. "Penn Professors to Join in Educating Students in India." *Daily Pennsylvanian*, February 18, 2011. https://www.thedp.com/article/2011/02/penn_professors_to_join_in_educating_students_in_india.

Flanagin, Jake. "The Expensive Romance of NYU." *Atlantic*, August 21, 2013.

Fost, Joshua. "A New Look at General Education." In Kosslyn and Nelson, *Building The Intentional University*, 57–72.

———. "Quantifying Knowledge Transfer of General Education Learning Outcomes." Unpublished MS, June 4, 2020, typescript.

Fost, Joshua, Vicki Chandler, Kara Gardner, and Allison Gale, "A New Team-Teaching Approach to Structured Learning." In Kosslyn and Nelson, *Building the Intentional University*, 179–92.

Fost, Joshua, Rena Levitt, and Stephen Kosslyn. "Fully Active Learning." In Kosslyn and Nelson, *Building the Intentional University*, 165–78.

Free Library. "Set Aside All Differences, Clinton Tells NYU Abu Dhabi Graduates." *Free Library*, 2014. https://www.thefreelibrary.com/Set+aside+all+differences%2c+Clinton+tells+NYU+Abu+Dhabi+graduates.-a0369213426.

Fulbright University Vietnam. "Constructive Criticism Is What Makes Fulbright Unique." FUV, April 29, 2020. https://fulbright.edu.vn/constructive-criticism-is-what-makes-fulbright-unique/.

———. "The Core Curriculum: A Unique Feature of Fulbright." FUV, February 18, 2022. https://fulbright.edu.vn/the-core-curriculum-a-unique-feature-of-fulbright/.

———. "Fulbright Welcomes Fifty-Six Students to the Co-design Year." FUV, May 28, 2018. https://fulbright.edu.vn/fulbright-welcomes-fifty-six-students-to-the-co-design-year/.

———. "Origin Story." FUV, November 2019. https://fulbright.edu.vn/origin-story/.

———. "President of Fulbright University Vietnam: 'It's Gratifying to See Liberal Arts Education Receive More Recognition in Vietnam.'" FUV, November 22, 2021. https://fulbright.edu.vn/dam-bich-thuy-president-fulbright-university-vietnam-liberal-arts-education-vietnam/.

Fulbright University Vietnam USA. "Fulbright University Vietnam Celebrates Its Fifth Anniversary." FUV USA. Accessed January 1, 2022. https://www.fuvusa.org/university/Fulbright-university-vietnam-celebrates-its-fifth-anniversary/.

Garsten, Bryan, Rajeev Patke, Charles Bailyn, Jane Jacobs, Hway Chuan Kang, and Bryan Penprase. "Yale-NUS College: A New Community of Learning." Curriculum Report. Yale-NUS College, April 2013. https://www.yale-nus.edu.sg/wp-content/uploads/2013/09/Yale-NUS-College-Curriculum-Report.pdf.

Gautier, Francois. "Broadcast Message." Facebook, December 10, 2018. https://www.facebook.com/francoisgautierofficial/posts/broadcast-message-ashoka-university-a-leading-university-for-liberal-arts-in-son/1962126927219515/.

Greater Boston Staff. "Olin College President Gilda Barabino on Forging Her Path as a Black Woman in Chemical Engineering." *GBH News*, August 5, 2020. https://www.wgbh.org/news/local-news/2020/08/05/olin-college-president-gilda-barabino-on-forging-her-path-as-a-black-woman-in-chemical-engineering.

Gideon, Gavan, and Antonia Woodford. "Faculty Approve Yale-NUS Resolution." *Yale Daily News*, April 6, 2012. https://yaledailynews.com/blog/2012/04/06/faculty-approve-yale-nus-resolution/.

Glavin, Chris. "Education Statistics in Ghana." K12 Academics, February 2017. https://www.k12academics.com/Education%20Worldwide/Education%20in%20Ghana/education-statistics-ghana.

Global Media Insight. "UAE Population Statistics in 2019." *Infographics* (blog), March 2022 (page since updated; 2019 statistics no longer available). https://www.globalmediainsight.com/blog/uae-population-statistics/.

Godwin, Kara A. "The Counter Narrative: Critical Analysis of Liberal Education in Global Context." *New Global Studies* 9, no. 3 (2015): 223–43. https://doi.org/10.1515/ngs-2015-0033.

———. "New Perspectives on Legitimacy for American and Liberal Education." In Purinton and Skaggs, *American Universities Abroad*, 311–24.

Godwin, Kara A., and Philip G. Altbach. "A Historical and Global Perspective on Liberal Arts Education." *International Journal of Chinese Education* 5 (2016): 9–11.

Godwin, Kara A., and Noah Pickus. *Liberal Arts and Sciences Innovation in China: Six Recommendations to Shape the Future.* CIHE Perspectives no. 8. Chestnut Hill, MA: Boston College Center for International Higher Education, 2017.

Goyal, Malini. "Ashoka University: India's Answer to the Ivy League, Promises 'World-Class' Liberal Arts Education." *Economic Times*, May 11, 2014. https://economictimes.indiatimes.com/industry/services/education/ashoka-university-indias-answer-to-the-ivy-league-promises-world-class-liberal-arts-education/articleshow/34936735.cms?from=mdr.

Graham, Molly. "'Give Away Your Legos' and Other Commandments for Scaling Startups." Interviewed by *First Round Review*. Accessed January 1, 2022. https://review.firstround.com/give-away-your-legos-and-other-commandments-for-scaling-startups.

Grant, Marcia. "Adapting the Liberal Arts Model to Create Ethical and Entrepreneurial Leaders for Africa: The Case of Ashesi University College, Ghana." In Purinton and Skaggs, *American Universities Abroad*, 229–42.

———. "Can Liberal Arts Education Have an Impact on Globalization in Africa? The Example of Ashesi University College." In Seawright and Hodges, *Learning across Borders*, 32–52.

Grant, Ruth W. *Hypocrisy and Integrity: Machiavelli, Rousseau, and the Ethics of Politics*. Chicago: University of Chicago Press, 1999.

Greiner, Larry E. "Evolution and Revolution as Organizations Grow." *Harvard Business Review*, May–June 1998. https://hbr.org/1998/05/evolution-and-revolution-as-organizations-grow.

Griswold, Alison, and Drew Henderson. "Academic Freedom Promised at Yale-NUS." *Yale Daily News*, April 1, 2011. https://yaledailynews.com/blog/2011/04/01/academic-freedom-promised-at-yale-nus/.

———. "Administrators Try Out Ideas at Yale-NUS." *Yale Daily News*, April 21, 2011. https://yaledailynews.com/blog/2011/04/21/administrators-try-out-ideas-at-yale-nus/.

Groves, Robert, and Randy Bass. "The Red House at Georgetown: Creating a Sustainable Future for Transformational Education." *Conversations on Jesuit Higher Education* 48 (2015): article 14. http://epublications.marquette.edu/conversations/vol48/iss1/.

Guizzo, Erico. "The Olin Experiment." *IEEE Spectrum*, May 1, 2006. https://spectrum.ieee.org/the-olin-experiment.

Gulati, Ranjay, and Caroline De Lacvivier. "Ashesi University: The Journey from Vision to Reality." Ashesi University Case Study, 2016. https://www.ashesi.org/wp-content/uploads/2017/05/Ashesi-University-Case-Study-FINAL-2.8.17.pdf.

Habib University. "Vision, Mission, Values and Learning Goals." Habib University, accessed March 30, 2023. https://habib.edu.pk/about-us/vision-values/.

Hajee, Kaashif. "Unthinking Eurocentrism at NYUAD: The Urgent Need to Decolonize the Curriculum." *Gazelle*, no. 193 (January 30, 2021). https://www.thegazelle.org/issue/193/features/unthinking-eurocentrism-nyuad-decolonize-curriculum.

Halpern, Diane F., and Milton D. Hakel. "Applying the Science of Learning to the University and Beyond: Teaching for Long-Term Retention and Transfer." *Change: The Magazine of Higher Learning* 35, no. 4 (2003): 36–41. https://doi.org/10.1080/00091380309604109.

Hartley, Scott. *The Fuzzy and the Techie: Why the Liberal Arts Will Rule the Digital World*. Boston: Mariner Books, 2018.

Harvard Graduate School of Education. "HGSE's Leadership Series: A Conversation with Paul LeBlanc, President, SNHU." YouTube, April 16, 2020. https://www.youtube.com/watch?v=A62BRhE3lzU.

Hawkins, Ari. "In Departure, Bryan Waterman Gives NYUAD Students His Applause." *Gazelle*, no. 228 (May 9, 2022). https://www.thegazelle.org/issue/228/features/bryan-waterman-profile.

Hazra, Indrajit. Review of *A Gardener In The Wasteland* by Srividya Natarajan. *Hindustan Times*, February 10, 2012. https://www.hindustantimes.com/books/review-a-gardener-in-the-wasteland/story-PPvTJtjRCXdmw28BFlA9pL.html.

Helfand, David J. "Mucking about in the Mess: Research-Based Education at Quest University Canada." *Council on Undergraduate Research Quarterly* 36, no. 3 (2016): 28.

Hills, Rick. "Academic Freedom in NYU-Shanghai versus NYU-NYC." *PrawfsBlawg* (blog), October 5, 2016. https://prawfsblawg.blogs.com/prawfsblawg/2016/10/last-week-the-gao-issued-a-report-on-academic-freedom-at-campuses-operated-by-american-universities-in-china-the-report-ha.html.

Howell, Robert, and Phoebe Park. "From Teenage Headmaster to Building the 'Harvard' of Africa." CNN, November 9, 2016. https://www.cnn.com/2016/09/06/africa/fred-swaniker -teacher-leadership-africa/index.html.

HT Correspondent. "UCG Releases Draft of Framework for 4-Year Undergraduate Courses." *Hindustan Times*, March 17, 2022. https://www.hindustantimes.com/india-news/ucg-releases -draft-of-framework-for-4-year-undergraduate-courses-101647540628376.html.

Hundley, Tom. "NYU Unveils Labor Guidelines for Abu Dhabi Campus." *World*, February 5, 2010; last updated May 30, 2010. https://theworld.org/stories/2010-02-05/nyu-unveils-labor -guidelines-abu-dhabi-campus.

Huong, To Lan. "The Journey of a H'Mong School Dropout to Fulbright University Vietnam." FUV, September 26, 2019. https://fulbright.edu.vn/the-journey-of-a-hmong-school-dropout -to-fulbright-university-vietnam/.

Ibrahim, Waad, Charles Kanyanta, Nour Ahmed, Yehowahi Sekan, and Mohammed Waseen Chaudry. "Racism at NYU Abu Dhabi: A Global Problem at a Global University." *Gazelle*, no. 180 (June 6, 2020). https://www.thegazelle.org/issue/180/features/racism-nyu-abu-dhabi -global-issue.

India Today Web Desk. "QS Asia University Rankings 2022: Ashoka University Ranks First in 'International Faculty' across All 118 Indian Varsities." *India Today*, November 5, 2021. https:// www.indiatoday.in/education-today/news/story/qs-asia-university-rankings-2022-ashoka -university-ranks-first-in-international-faculty-across-all-118-indian-varsities-p-1873420-2021 -11-05.

Institute of Medicine. *Facilitating Interdisciplinary Research*. Washington, DC: National Academies Press, 2005. https://nap.nationalacademies.org/download/11153#.

International Alliance of Research Universities. "About IARU." International Alliance of Research Universities, 2022. http://www.iaruni.org/about/about-iaru.

International Monetary Fund. "World Economic Outlook Database, April 2021." IMF, 2021. https://www.imf.org/en/Publications/WEO/weo-database/2021/April.

Ireland, Corydon. "Dynamic Africa." *Harvard Gazette*, March 13, 2013. https://news.harvard.edu /gazette/story/2013/03/dynamic-africa/.

Isaacson, Walter. *Steve Jobs*. New York: Simon and Schuster, 2011. Kindle.

Jaschik, Scott. "Russia Declares Bard College 'Undesirable.'" *Inside Higher Education*, June 22, 2021. https://www.insidehighered.com/quicktakes/2021/06/22/russia-declares-bard-college -%E2%80%98undesirable%E2%80%99.

Jebaraj, Priscilla. "Ashoka University to Double Capacity, Focus on Sciences." *Hindu*, September 9, 2021. https://www.thehindu.com/news/national/ashoka-university-to-double-capacity -focus-on-sciences/article36372095.ece.

Jeyaretnam, Miranda. "Up Close: 'The Narratives of Yale-NUS Were Not Shaped by Us.'" *Yale Daily News*, April 13, 2022. http://features.yaledailynews.com/blog/2022/04/13/up-close -the-narratives-of-yale-nus-were-not-shaped-by-us-the-history-and-unraveling-of-yale-nus/.

Jimaa, Heather. "$1bn New York University Abu Dhabi Construction Completed." *Gulf Business*, April 29, 2014. https://gulfbusiness.com/nyu-abu-dhabi-construction-completed.

Joraimi, Faris. "Yale-NUS in a Malay World: A Case for Decolonizing Our Common Curriculum." *Octant*, January 29, 2019. https://theoctant.org/edition/issue/allposts/opinion/yale-nus-in -a-malay-world-a-case-for-decolonizing-our-common-curriculum/.

June, Audrey. "How One College Reinvented Its Hiring Process to Better Test for 'Fit.'" *Chronicle of Higher Education*, July 6, 2018. https://www.chronicle.com/article/how-one-college -reinvented-its-hiring-process-to-better-test-for-fit/.

Jung, Insung, Mikiko Nishimura, and Toshiaki Sasao, eds. *Liberal Arts Education and Colleges in East Asia: Possibilities and Challenges in the Global Age*. Singapore: Springer, 2016.

Kaminer, Ariel. "Labor Conditions at N.Y.U.'s Abu Dhabi Campus to Be Investigated by U.S. Firm." *New York Times*, June 27, 2014. https://www.nytimes.com/2014/06/27/nyregion/nyu-abu -dhabi-investigation-middle-east-campus.html.

———. "N.Y.U. Apologizes to Any Workers Mistreated on Its Abu Dhabi Campus." *New York Times*, May 20, 2014. https://www.nytimes.com/2014/05/20/nyregion/nyu-apologizes-to -any-workers-mistreated-on-its-abu-dhabi-campus.html.

Kaminer, Ariel, and Sean O'Driscoll. "Workers at N.Y.U.'s Abu Dhabi Site Faced Harsh Conditions." *New York Times*, May 19, 2014. https://www.nytimes.com/2014/05/19/nyregion /workers-at-nyus-abu-dhabi-site-face-harsh-conditions.html.

Kaminski, Matthew. "Ben Nelson: The Man Who Would Overthrow Harvard." *Wall Street Journal*, August 9, 2013. https://www.wsj.com/articles/ben-nelson-the-man-who-would-overthrow -harvard-1376085938.

Kanelos, Pano. "We Can't Wait for Universities to Fix Themselves. So We're Starting a New One." *Free Press*, November 8, 2021. https://www.thefp.com/p/we-cant-wait-for-universities-to?s=r.

Katzman, Jonathan, Matt Regan, and Ari Bader-Natal, "The Active Learning Forum." In Kosslyn and Nelson, *Building the Intentional University*, 203–20.

Kazmin, Amy. "Ashoka University: Ivy League, Indian-Style." *Financial Times*, March 8, 2018. https://www.ft.com/content/b8fabc8c-1559-11e8-9c33-02f893d608c2.

Kerns, Sherra, Richard Miller, and David Kerns. "Designing from a Blank Slate: The Development of the Initial Olin College Curriculum." 1library.net, June 2004. https://1library.net/document /zl19x8ly-designing-blank-slate-development-initial-olin-college-curriculum.html.

Kerr, Clark. *The Uses of the University*. Cambridge, MA: Harvard University Press, 2001.

Kigotho, Wachira. "A 'Swarthmore' Grows in Ghana." *Chronicle of Higher Education*, November 5, 2004. https://www.chronicle.com/article/a-swarthmore-grows-in-ghana/.

Kim, Joshua, and Edward Maloney. *Learning Innovation and the Future of Higher Education*. Baltimore, MD: Johns Hopkins University Press, 2020.

Kinho, Chan. "Co-designing a Rhetoric Course at Fulbright University Vietnam." *Kinho Chan's blog*, December 2, 2018. https://kinhochan.home.blog/2018/12/02/the-journey-begins/.

Kirby, William C. *Empires of Ideas: Creating the Modern University from Germany to America to China*. Cambridge, MA: Belknap Press Of Harvard University Press, 2022.

———. "Liberal Education in China." In Godwin and Pickus, *Liberal Arts and Sciences*, 34–39.

Kirby, William C., and Marijk van der Wende, eds. *Experiences in Liberal Arts and Science Education from America, Europe, and Asia: A Dialogue across Continents*. New York: Palgrave Macmillan, 2016.

Kosslyn, Stephen. "The Science of Learning: Mechanisms and Principles." In Kosslyn and Nelson, *Building the Intentional University*, 149–64.

Kosslyn, Stephen, and Ben Nelson, eds. *Building the Intentional University: Minerva and the Future of Higher Education*. With a foreword by Senator Bob Kerrey. Cambridge, MA: MIT Press, 2017.

Kronman, Anthony T. *Education's End: Why Our Colleges and Universities Have Given Up on the Meaning of Life*. New Haven, CT: Yale University Press, 2008.

Kuh, George. *High-Impact Educational Practices: What They Are, Who Has Access to Them, and Why They Matter*. Washington, DC: American Association of Colleges and Universities, 2008. https://www.aacu.org/publication/high-impact-educational-practices-what-they-are-who -has-access-to-them-and-why-they-matter.

Kurp, Patrick. "No Longer on the Outside Looking In." Rice University, George R. Brown School of Engineering, October 12, 2020. https://engineering.rice.edu/news/no-longer-outside -looking.

Kwong-loi, Shun. "Confucian Learning and Liberal Education." *Journal of East West Thought* 2, no. 6 (2016). https://scholarworks.calstate.edu/concern/publications/td96k467j?locale=en.

Lake, Ed. "NYU Abu Dhabi: A Class Apart." *National*, September 24, 2010. https://www
.thenationalnews.com/arts/nyu-abu-dhabi-a-class-apart-1.565729.

Lederman, Doug. "Minerva, a Higher Ed Outsider, Is Now Fully Accredited." *Inside Higher Ed*,
July 22, 2021. https://www.insidehighered.com/news/2021/07/22/minerva-higher-education
-outsider-now-accredited-university.

Lehman, Jeffrey. "Testimony of Jeffrey S Lehman, Vice Chancellor of NYU Shanghai, before
the Subcommittee on Africa, Global Health, and Human Rights of the Committee on For-
eign Affairs of the United States House of Representatives at a Hearing on the Subject: 'Is
Academic Freedom Threatened by China's Influence on U.S. Universities?'" NYU Shanghai,
June 25, 2015. https://docs.house.gov/meetings/FA/FA16/20150625/103688/HHRG-114
-FA16-Wstate-LehmanJ-20150625.pdf.

Levin, Richard. "Presidential Statements Regarding Yale-NUS College." *YaleNews*, July 19, 2012.
https://news.yale.edu/2012/07/19/presidential-statements-regarding-yale-nus-college.

Levine, David O. *The American College and the Culture of Aspiration, 1915–1940*. Ithaca, NY: Cornell
University Press, 2019.

Levine, Emily J. *Allies and Rivals: German-American Exchange and the Rise of the Modern Research
University*. Chicago: University of Chicago Press, 2021.

Levine, Emily J., and Matthew Rascoff. "Restoring Learning, and the Humanities, to Higher Education's Center after the Crisis." *Inside Higher Ed*, April 15, 2020. https://www.insidehighered
.com/digital-learning/views/2020/04/15/restoring-learning-and-humanities-higher
-educations-center-after.

Lewin, Tamar. "U.S. Universities Rush to Set Up Outposts Abroad." *New York Times*, February 10,
2008. https://www.nytimes.com/2008/02/10/education/10global.html.

Lewis, Pericles. "About." Campus Press, Modernism Lab, 2012. https://campuspress.yale.edu
/modernismlab/about/.

———. "Asia Invests in Liberal Arts: U.S. Higher Education Expands Abroad." *Harvard International Review*, Summer 2013. https://campuspress.yale.edu/pericleslewis/asia-invests-in
-liberal-arts/.

———. *The Cambridge Introduction to Modernism*. Cambridge: Cambridge University Press,
2011.

———. "Report on Cancellation of LAB Module on 'Dialogue and Dissent.'" Yale Office of the
Vice President for Global Strategy, September 28, 2019. https://news.yale.edu/sites/default
/files/files/Pericles-Lewis-Yale-NUS-report.pdf.

Li, Can. "The Significance and Practice of General Education in China: The Case of Tsinghua
University." In Kirby and Van der Wende *Experiences in Liberal Arts*, 33–46.

Lindsey, Ursula. "NYU Abu Dhabi Behaves Like Careful Guest in Foreign Land." *Chronicle of
Higher Education*, June 3, 2012. https://www.chronicle.com/article/nyu-abu-dhabi-behaves
-like-careful-guest-in-foreign-land/.

Linh, Xuan, and Viet Lam. "From a Bold Dream to a Dynamic Reality." FUV, September 13, 2019.
https://fulbright.edu.vn/from-a-bold-dream-to-a-dynamic-reality/.

Linshi, Jack. "10 CEOs Who Prove Your Liberal Arts Degree Isn't Worthless." *Time*, July 23, 2015.
https://time.com/3964415/ceo-degree-liberal-arts/.

Maharishi, Meghna. "NYU and Professors Butt Heads over NYU Abu Dhabi." *Washington Square
News*, January 28, 2019. https://nyunews.com/2019/01/28/abudhabi-campus-university
-statement/.

Mahtani, Shibani. "At Yale's Venture in Singapore, a Canceled Course on Dissent Prompts Censor-
ship Claims." *Washington Post*, September 27, 2019. https://www.washingtonpost.com/world
/asia_pacific/at-yales-singapore-college-a-canceled-course-on-dissent-prompts-censorship
-claims/2019/09/26/692c9736-d946-11e9-a1a5-162b8a9c9ca2_story.html.

Majumdar, Saikat. "Is the Honeymoon Period Over for Liberal Arts in Asia?" *Times Higher Education*, November 25, 2021. https://www.timeshighereducation.com/depth/honeymoon-period-over-liberal-arts-asia.

Maloney, Edward J., and Joshua Kim. "How Universities Can Avoid Learning Innovation Theater." *Inside Higher Ed*, October 30, 2019. https://www.insidehighered.com/digital-learning/blogs/technology-and-learning/how-universities-can-avoid-learning-innovation.

Mangan, Katherine. "Students Arrive to Help Build 'College That Doesn't Exist.'" *Chronicle of Higher Education*, April 13, 2001. https://www.chronicle.com/article/students-arrive-to-help-build-college-that-doesnt-exist/.

Marber, Peter, and Daniel Araya. *The Evolution of Liberal Arts in the Global Age*. New York: Routledge, 2017.

Marin, Mark. "NSF Update: Investing in the Ideal University." *ASEE Prism*, November 1997, https://aseecmsduq.blob.core.windows.net/aseecmsdev/asee/media/content/member%20resources/pdfs/nsf-update-investing-in-the-ideal-university_1.pdf.

Marklein, Mary Beth. "Expanding the Fulbright Legacy in Vietnam." *Change: The Magazine of Higher Learning* 50, no. 1 (2018): 63–70. https://doi.org/10.1080/00091383.2018.1413909.

Markovits, Daniel. *The Meritocracy Trap: How America's Foundational Myth Feeds Inequality, Dismantles the Middle Class, and Devours the Elite*. New York: Penguin Books, 2020.

Marsh, Herbert, and John Hattie. "The Relation between Research Productivity and Teaching Effectiveness: Complementary, Antagonistic, or Independent Constructs?" *Journal of Higher Education* 73, no. 5 (2002): 603–41. Published online November 2016. https://doi.org/10.1080/00221546.2002.11777170.

MASS Design Group. "African Leadership University Opens Flagship Campus Designed by MASS Design Group." MASS Design Group, 2021; accessed June 15, 2022. https://massdesigngroup.org/african-leadership-university-opens-flagship-campus-designed-mass-design-group.

Mattoo, Shashank. "Which One Should I Choose, Ashoka University or DU?" Quora. Accessed January 1, 2022. https://www.quora.com/Which-one-should-I-choose-Ashoka-University-or-DU.

McAllister, Katie A. L. *Beyond the Lecture: Interacting with Students and Shaping the Classroom Dynamic*. Lanham, MD: Rowman and Littlefield, 2021.

———. "A Teacher's Guide: How to Use Data to Measure Student Engagement." *Minerva Project blog*, December 15, 2021. https://blog.minervaproject.com/a-teachers-guide-how-to-use-data-to-measure-student-engagement.

McKenzie, Lindsay. "Indian Government Opens Up Market for Online Higher Education." *Inside Higher Ed*, February 17, 2020. https://www.insidehighered.com/news/2020/02/17/indian-government-opens-market-online-higher-education.

McKie, Anna. "'Harvard of Africa' Now 'Not an Academic Institution.'" *Times Higher Education*, July 3, 2018. https://www.timeshighereducation.com/news/harvard-africa-now-not-academic-institution.

McMurtrie, Beth. "The Hope and Hype of the Academic Innovation Center." *Chronicle of Higher Education*, January 21, 2018. https://www.chronicle.com/article/the-hope-and-hype-of-the-academic-innovation-center/.

Mehta, Pratap Bhanu. "Dear Prime Minister." *Indian Express*, May 22, 2006. http://archive.indianexpress.com/news/dear-prime-minister/4916/.

———. "2021 SSRC Fellow Lecture." Social Science Research Council, November 3, 2021. https://www.ssrc.org/events/2021-ssrc-fellow-lecture/.

Menand, Louis. *The Marketplace of Ideas: Reform and Resistance in the American University*. New York: W. W. Norton, 2010.

Miller, Lisa. "The Emir's University." *New York Magazine*, May 3, 2013. https://nymag.com/news/intelligencer/nyu-abu-dhabi-2013-5/.

Mills, Andrew. "'Tabula Rasa' Attracts NYU Professors to New Abu Dhabi Campus." *Chronicle of Higher Education*, April 11, 2022. https://www.chronicle.com/article/tabula-rasa-attracts-nyu-professors-to-new-abu-dhabi-campus/.

Minerva Project. "Minerva Project Closes $57 Million in Series C Funding." Press release. PR Newswire, July 11, 2019. http://www.prnewswire.com/news-releases/minerva-project-closes-57-million-in-series-c-funding-300883338.html.

———. "Minerva Project Redefines Elite Education for Students Worldwide." Press release. Minerva Project, April 4, 2012. http://s3.minervaproject.com/press-releases/Minerva_Projects_Secures_25_Million_Release.pdf.

Minerva University. "Consequent 2022." Minerva University, accessed June 15, 2022. https://consequent.minerva.edu/.

———. "A Pathbreaking Institution of Higher Education." Minerva University, accessed June 15, 2022. https://www.minerva.edu/overview/.

———. "Tuition & Fees." Minerva University, accessed June 15, 2022. https://www.minerva.edu/undergraduate-program/tuition-aid/tuition-fees/.

Mino, Takako. "Construyendo una tradición de artes liberales en India." *Revista Española de educación comparada* 39 (July–December 2021): 123–37. https://doi.org/10.5944/reec.39.2021.30042.

———. "Humanizing Higher Education: Three Case Studies in Sub-Saharan Africa." *International Journal of African Higher Education* 7, no. 1 (2020). https://ejournals.bc.edu/index.php/ijahe/article/view/11249.

Mintz, Steven. "11 Lessons from the History of Higher Education." *Inside Higher Education*, May 7, 2017. https://www.insidehighered.com/blogs/higher-ed-gamma/11-lessons-history-higher-ed.

MIT School of Engineering. "Reimagining and Rethinking Engineering Education." *MIT News*, March 27, 2018. https://news.mit.edu/2018/reimagining-and-rethinking-engineering-education-0327.

Mitchell, Jason. "Rwanda Centres Innovation Drive on Kigali." *fDi Intelligence*, July 27, 2020. https://www.fdiintelligence.com/content/feature/rwanda-centres-innovation-drive-on-kigali-77769.

Moner, William, Phillip Motley, and Rebecca Pope-Ruark. *Redesigning Liberal Education: Innovative Design for a Twenty-First-Century Undergraduate Education*. Baltimore, MD: Johns Hopkins University Press, 2020.

Montgomery, Mark. "Famous Graduates of Liberal Arts Colleges." *Great College Advice* (blog), February 24, 2010. https://greatcollegeadvice.com/blog/famous-graduates-of-liberal-arts-colleges/.

Muhire, Frank. "Young Leaders in Africa." ALU, Vimeo, July 15, 2021. https://vimeo.com/showcase/young-leaders-at-alu.

NAE (National Academy of Engineering). "Recipients of the Bernard M. Gordon Prize for Innovation in Engineering and Technology Education." NAE, 2022. https://www.nae.edu/55293/GordonWinners#tabs.

Nanda, Prashant K. "Only 2 Indian Varsities among the World's Top 400: THE World University Rankings." *Mint*, September 2, 2020. https://www.livemint.com/education/news/only-2-indian-varsities-among-the-world-s-top-400-the-world-university-rankings-11599048715517.html.

Nandrajog, Simran. "Ashoka University Is Second Home for Me, But Things Started a Lot Differently." Youth Ki Awaaz, September 27, 2016. https://www.youthkiawaaz.com/2016/09/life-in-ashoka-university/.

Nardello and Co. "Report of the Independent Investigator into Allegations of Labor and Compliance Issues during the Construction of the NYU Abu Dhabi Campus on Saadiyat Island, United Arab Emirates." Nardello and Co., April 16, 2015. https://www.nardelloandco.com/wp-content/uploads/insights/pdf/nyu-abu-dhabi-campus-investigative-report.pdf.

National University of Singapore. "Annual Report 2001." NUS, 2001. https://www.nus.edu.sg/docs/default-source/annual-report/nus-annualreport-2001.pdf.

———. "Annual Report 2003." https://www.nus.edu.sg/docs/default-source/annual-report/nus-annualreport-2003.pdf. NUS, 2003. https://www.nus.edu.sg/docs/default-source/annual-report/nus-annualreport-2003.pdf.

———. "Annual Report 2013." NUS, 2013. https://www.nus.edu.sg/docs/default-source/annual-report/nus-annualreport-2013.pdf.

Nature Index. "2022 Tables: Institutions." Springer Nature, 2022. https://www.nature.com/nature-index/annual-tables/2022/institution/all/all/countries-Ecuador.

Nelson, Ben, Diana El-Azar, and Ayo Seligman. "Creating a University From Scratch." *Stanford Social Innovation Review*, May 11, 2020. https://ssir.org/articles/entry/creating_a_university_from_scratch#.

New York Times. "Clinton Lauds N.Y.U. Graduates, and Inquiry, in Speech." May 25, 2014. https://www.nytimes.com/2014/05/26/nyregion/clinton-lauds-nyu-graduates-and-inquiry-in-speech.html.

Nguyen Nam. "My Fellow-Vietnamese Students, In You I Trust." FUV, March 6, 2020. https://fulbright.edu.vn/my-fellow-vietnamese-students-in-you-i-trust/.

Nguyen, Viet Thanh. "Bob Kerrey and the 'American Tragedy' of Vietnam." *New York Times*, June 20, 2016. https://www.nytimes.com/2016/06/20/opinion/bob-kerrey-and-the-american-tragedy-of-vietnam.html.

Ninh, Ton Nu Thi. "Bob Kerrey in Vietnam." Letter to the editor. *New York Times*, June 7, 2016. https://www.nytimes.com/2016/06/08/opinion/bob-kerrey-in-vietnam.html.

Noori, Neema. "Academic Freedom and the Liberal Arts in the Middle East." In Marber and Araya, *Evolution of the Liberal Arts*, chap. 9.

Northeastern University. "Northeastern 2025: Our New Academic Plan." Northeastern University, accessed June 15, 2022. https://www.northeastern.edu/2025/.

Nowotny, Helga, Peter B. Scott, and Michael T. Gibbons. *Re-thinking Science: Knowledge and the Public in an Age of Uncertainty*. Hoboken, NJ: John Wiley & Sons, 2013.

NYU Abu Dhabi. "The Campus." NYU Abu Dhabi, 2022. https://nyuad.nyu.edu/en/about/nyuad-at-a-glance/the-campus.html.

———. "Core Curriculum—Expanding Horizons." NYU Abu Dhabi, 2022. https://nyuad.nyu.edu/en/academics/undergraduate/core-curriculum.html.

———. "Courses: Requirements." NYU Abu Dhabi, accessed March 29, 2023. https://nyuad.nyu.edu/en/academics/undergraduate/majors-and-minors/natural-science-minor/courses.html.

———. "Global Education and Outreach." NYU Abu Dhabi, 2022. https://nyuad.nyu.edu/en/about/leadership-and-administration/office-of-the-provost/global-education-and-outreach.html.

———. "Labor Compliance Update," NYU Abu Dhabi, October 2019. https://nyuad.nyu.edu/content/dam/nyuad/about/social-responsibility/compliance-monitoring-at-nyuad-report-october-2019.pdf.

———. *Life beyond Saadiyat: Where They Are Now, Aggregate Outcomes, Awards and Scholarships, Their Local and Global Impact*. Abu Dhabi: NYU Abu Dhabi Career Development Center, 2020. https://nyuad.nyu.edu/content/dam/nyuad/academics/undergraduate/career-development/life-beyond-saadiyat/report/life-beyond-saadiyat-2019.pdf.

———. "Natural Science Minor." NYU Abu Dhabi, accessed March 29, 2023. https://nyuad.nyu.edu/en/academics/undergraduate/majors-and-minors/natural-science-minor.html.

———. "NYU Abu Dhabi Celebrates Its First Graduating Class at Historic Commencement Ceremony." Press release. NYU Abu Dhabi, May 25, 2014. https://nyuad.nyu.edu/en/news /latest-news/community-life/2014/may/nyu-abu-dhabi-celebrates-its-first-graduating-class -at-historic-commencement-ceremony.html.

———. "NYU Abu Dhabi Welcomes 45 New Faculty Members." NYU Abu Dhabi, September 7, 2020. https://nyuad.nyu.edu/en/news/latest-news/community-life/2020/september/nyu -abu-dhabi-welcomes-45-new-faculty-members.html.

———. "NYUAD Accountability Framework: Fall 2020–Spring 2022." NYU Abu Dhabi, 2022. https://nyuad.nyu.edu/en/about/inclusion-diversity-belonging-and-equity/nyuad -accountability-framework.html.

———. *The Origin Story: An Oral History of the Founding of NYU Abu Dhabi 2005–2010*. Abu Dhabi: NYU Abu Dhabi Corporation, September 19, 2021. https://nyuad.nyu.edu/content /dam/nyuad/about/nyuad-at-a-glance/history/20210919-oral-history-digital-web.pdf.

———. "2018 NYU Abu Dhabi Research Conference Showcases Cutting-Edge Interdisciplinary Research." Abu Dhabi Education Guide, November 5, 2018. https://abudhabieduguide .com/2018-nyu-abu-dhabi-research-conference-showcases-cutting-edge-interdisciplinary -research/.

NYU Web Communications. "Exchange of Letters on Global Mobility at NYU Abu Dhabi (Journalism)." NYU, 2017. https://www.nyu.edu/about/leadership-university-administration /office-of-the-president/communications/exchange-of-letters-on-global-mobility-at-nyu -abu-dhabi-journalism.html.

———. "NYU to Open Campus in Abu Dhabi." NYU, October 12, 2007. https://www.nyu.edu /about/news-publications/news/2007/october/nyu_to_open_campus_in_abu.html.

Obama, Barack. "Remarks by President Obama in Address to the People of Vietnam." Obama White House Archives, May 24, 2016. https://obamawhitehouse.archives.gov/the-press-office /2016/05/24/remarks-president-obama-address-people-vietnam.

Olin College of Engineering. "About." Olin College of Engineering, accessed March 29, 2023. https://www.olin.edu/about.

———. "Board of Trustees." Olin College of Engineering, 2022. https://www.olin.edu/about /board-trustees/.

———. "Consumer Information." Olin College of Engineering, 2022. https://www.olin.edu/about /consumer-information.

———. "Grand Challenges Scholars Program." *Olin College of Engineering Catalog*, 2019–20. https://olin.smartcatalogiq.com/2019-20/Catalog/Programs-of-Study-and-Degree -Requirements/Other-Academic-Programs-and-Opportunities/Grand-Challenge-Scholars -Program.

———. "History." *Olin College of Engineering Catalog*, 2018–19. https://olin.smartcatalogiq.com /en/2018-19/Catalog/Information-about-Olin/History.

———. "Influencing Change: Annual Report 2019." Olin College of Engineering, November 25, 2019, last modified November 21, 2020. https://issuu.com/olincollege/docs/olin_2019 _annualreport_rev21november2020.

———. "Influencing the Global State of Engineering Education." Olin College of Engineering, January 20, 2021. https://www.olin.edu/articles/influencing-global-state-engineering -education.

———. "The Michael E. Moody Professorship—the Olin Art Gallery." Olin Art Gallery, 2022. https://art.olin.edu/about/moody-professorship/.

———. "Olin College of Engineering Names Dr. Gilda Barabino as Its Second President." Press release. Olin College of Engineering, March 26, 2020. https://www.olin.edu/news-events /2020/olin-college-engineering-names-dr-gilda-barabino-its-second-president-0.

———. "Overview." *Olin College of Engineering Catalog*, 2017–18. https://olin.smartcatalogiq.com/en/2017-18/Catalog/Programs-of-Study-and-Degree-Requirements/Curriculum-Goals-and-Outcomes/Overview.

———. "PInT at Olin." PInT, Olin College, 2022. http://pint.olin.edu.

———. "President Barabino's First Day." Olin College of Engineering, July 8, 2020. https://olincollege.exposure.co/president-barabinos-first-day.

Osmandzikovic, Emina. "Core Curriculum to Be Re-examined." *Gazelle*, no. 26 (February 1, 2014). https://www.thegazelle.org/issue/26/news/cores-4.

Paddock, Richard C. "Bob Kerrey's War Record Fuels Debate in Vietnam on His Role at New University." *New York Times*, June 2, 2016. https://www.nytimes.com/2016/06/03/world/asia/vietnam-fulbright-university-kerrey.html.

Pagano, Ernesto, Lane McBride, Ken Watari, and Nam Tran. "Lessons from Fulbright on Developing the University of the Future." Boston Consulting Group, April 2, 2020. https://www.bcg.com/industries/education/lessons-fulbright-developing-university-of-the-future.

Panashe, Patience. "What Does Entrepreneurship Really Mean in the African Context?" *Mail & Guardian*, December 19, 2021. https://mg.co.za/opinion/2021-12-19-what-does-entrepreneurship-really-mean-in-the-african-context/.

Panikkar, Raimon. "Dialogical Dialogue or Dialogal Dialogue." Raimon Panikkar's website. Accessed June 15, 2022. https://www.raimon-panikkar.org/english/gloss-dialogical.html.

Pearce, Connor. "Core Curriculum's Global Requirement Sees Mixed Success." *Gazelle*, no. 53 (December 6, 2014). https://www.thegazelle.org/issue/53/features/coresuccess.

Pennington, Roberta. "As He Readies for Retirement, Al Bloom Reflects on a Remarkable Decade at the Helm of NYUAD." *National*, April 1, 2018. https://www.thenationalnews.com/uae/as-he-readies-for-retirement-al-bloom-reflects-on-a-remarkable-decade-at-the-helm-of-nyuad-1.717427.

Penprase, Bryan. *STEM Education for the 21st Century*. Cham, Switzerland: Springer, 2020.

———. "Yale-NUS College." In *Envisioning the Asian New Flagship University: Its Past and Vital Future*, edited by John Aubrey Douglass and John N Hawkins. Berkeley, CA: Berkeley Public Policy, 2017, 187–200.

Peterson, Chris. "The Minerva Delusion." MIT Admissions, *Public Statements* (blog), April 6, 2012. https://mitadmissions.org/blogs/entry/the-minerva-delusion/.

Pham, Le Vi. "Why Doesn't Yale-NUS Release Its Financial Reports?" *Octant*, February 11, 2017. https://theoctant.org/edition/vi-2/allposts/news/yale-nus-release-financial-reports/.

Pickus, Noah. "An Insider's View of DKU." *Duke Magazine*, October 14, 2018. https://alumni.duke.edu/magazine/articles/insiders-view-dku.

Porcelli, Victor. "Faculty to Discuss Academic Freedom at NYUAD." *Washington Square News*, December 2, 2018. https://nyunews.com/2018/12/02/nyu-uae-connections-forum-with-faculty/.

———. "What It Means for NYUAD to Be Fully Funded by the UAE." *Washington Square News*, April 7, 2019. https://nyunews.com/news/04/08/nyu-abu-dhabi-tax-returns/.

Postiglione, Gerard, Ying Ma, and Alice Te. "Institutionalizing Liberal Education in China: Obstacles and Challenges." In Godwin and Pickus, *Liberal Arts and Sciences*, 49–59.

Prasad, Shishar. "Ashish Dhawan: Next Gen Leader In Philanthropy." Forbes India, December 4, 2012. https://www.forbesindia.com/article/philanthropy-awards-2012/ashish-dhawan-next-gen-leader-in-philanthropy/34241/1.

Purinton, Ted, and Jennifer Skaggs, eds. *American Universities Abroad: The Leadership of Independent Transnational Higher Education Institutions*. Cairo: American University in Cairo Press, 2017.

Qing, Ang. "Yale-NUS Closure: Employers Say Job Prospects of Graduates Remain Bright." *Straits Times*, September 5, 2021. https://www.straitstimes.com/singapore/parenting-education/employers-say-job-prospects-of-yale-nus-graduates-remain-bright.

QS Top Universities. "QS World University Rankings 2021." Quacquarelli Symonds, 2020. https://www.topuniversities.com/university-rankings/world-university-rankings/2021.

Rao, Shriya, and Harish Sai. "Breaking Down the Kashmir Petition: What You Need to Know." *Edict*, October 15, 2016. https://medium.com/the-edict/breaking-down-the-kashmir-petition-what-you-need-to-know-1f4ba4244d12.

Rao, Srinath. "Ashoka University: Of the Elite, for the Elite, by the Elite." *ArmChair Journal*, June 26, 2020. https://armchairjournal.com/ashoka-university-of-the-elite-for-the-elite-by-the-elite/.

Reddy, Krishna. "Led by Two Young India Fellows, This Mumbai-Based Organisation Aims to Transform Early Education." Social Story, October 9, 2019. https://yourstory.com/socialstory/2019/10/ashoka-university-barefoot-edu-foundation-teresa-fellows/amp.

Republic of Rwanda Ministry of Youth and ICT. "Smart Rwanda Master Plan." Ministry of Youth and ICT, December 2016. https://www.theigc.org/wp-content/uploads/2016/11/Session-4.2-SRMP_Mineacom.pdf.

Rishihood University. "Founders and Advisors." Accessed January 1, 2022. https://rishihood.edu.in/founders/.

The Room. "About Us." Accessed January 1, 2022. https://www.theroom.com/learning-about/.

Rosenberg, Brian C. "The Rigidness of Academic Routine." *Liberal Education* 104, no. 4 (2018).

———. "Shared or Divided Governance?" *Inside Higher Ed*, July 29, 2014. https://www.insidehighered.com/views/2014/07/29/essay-new-approach-shared-governance-higher-education.

———. "What American Higher Education Can Learn from Africa." *ALI Social Impact Review*, November 10, 2020. https://www.sir.advancedleadership.harvard.edu/articles/what-american-higher-education-can-learn-from-africa.

Ross, John. "After Yale-NUS Divorce, Can Liberal Arts Survive in Asia?" *Times Higher Education*, September 3, 2021. https://www.timeshighereducation.com/news/after-yale-nus-divorce-can-liberal-arts-survive-asia.

Roth, Michael S. "Higher Ed's Role in a Culture War." *Inside Higher Ed*, June 1, 2022. https://www.insidehighered.com/views/2022/06/01/contemplating-higher-eds-role-culture-war-opinion.

———. *Safe Enough Spaces: A Pragmatist's Approach to Inclusion, Free Speech, and Political Correctness on Campus*. New Haven, CT: Yale University Press, 2019.

Rousmaniere, Izzy. "Fish out of Water: Building Intercultural Competence and Consciousness at Minerva." Minerva Quest, October 1, 2020 (page no longer available). https://www.minervaquest.com/2020/10/01/fish-out-of-water-building-intercultural-competence-and-consciousness-at-minerva/.

Royster, David. "Steve Jobs on Technology and the Liberal Arts," *The Liberal Arts in Singapore: A Thought Space for the Yale-NUS College Community* (blog), November 29, 2012. https://yalenusblog.wordpress.com/2012/11/29/steve-jobs-on-technology-and-the-liberal-arts/.

Ryan, Dan, and Sara Goldrick-Rab. "But What if the Shared Vision Is Myopic?" *Chronicle of Higher Education*, January 12, 2015. https://www.chronicle.com/article/but-what-if-the-shared-vision-is-myopic/.

Samra, Tom Abi. "The Case for Theory: Approaching Difficult Texts in the Classroom." *Gazelle*, no. 192 (December 12, 2020). https://www.thegazelle.org/issue/192/opinion/difficult-texts-in-the-classroom.

Sandel, Michael J. *The Tyranny of Merit: What's Become of the Common Good?* New York: Farrar, Straus and Giroux, 2020.

Sanderson, Daniel. "'I Cared for NYUAD When It Was a Baby, Now I Will Help It Become an Adult.'" *National*, November 18, 2019. https://www.thenationalnews.com/uae/education/i-cared-for-nyuad-when-it-was-a-baby-now-i-will-help-it-become-an-adult-1.938775.

———. "NYU Abu Dhabi's First Provost Is Back to Oversee Expansion." *National*, November 18, 2019, Pressreader, https://www.pressreader.com/uae/the-national-news/20191118/281526522887846.

Sasu, Doris. "Ghana: Share of Children out of School in Ghana." Statista, November 2021. https://www.statista.com/statistics/1179610/share-of-children-out-of-school-in-ghana/.

———. "Ghana: Students in Public Universities 2019, by Program." Statista, November 2020. https://www.statista.com/statistics/1180668/students-in-public-universities-in-ghana-by-program-discipline/.

———. "Ghana: Tertiary Students Abroad 2010–2018." Statista, November 2021. https://www.statista.com/statistics/1185192/ghanaian-students-in-tertiary-education-abroad/.

Satya. "Ashoka University at Sonepat and the Young India Fellowship." *Education in India* (blog), November 19, 2011. https://prayatna.typepad.com/education/2011/11/ashoka-university-at-sonepat-and-the-young-india-fellowship.html.

Saussy, Haun. "Saussy: When Elihu Meets Confucius." *Yale Daily News*, September 14, 2010. https://yaledailynews.com/blog/2010/09/14/saussy-when-elihu-meets-confucius/.

Schein, Edgar H. *Organizational Culture and Leadership*. 5th ed. Hoboken, NJ: Wiley, 2010.

Schwartz, John. "Re-engineering Engineering." *New York Times*, September 30, 2007. https://www.nytimes.com/2007/09/30/magazine/30OLIN-t.html.

Seawright, Leslie, and Amy Hodges, eds. *Learning across Borders: Perspectives on International and Transnational Higher Education*. Newcastle-upon-Tyne, UK: Cambridge Scholars, 2016.

Seligman, Ayo and Robin Goldberg. "Building a New Brand." In Kosslyn and Nelson, *Building the Intentional University*, 255–64.

Sengupta, Shuddhabrata. "Statement against State Violence in Kashmir: Ashoka University Students and Alumni." Kafila, July 25, 2016; web.archive.org, 2019. https://web.archive.org/web/20190317133622/https://kafila.online/2016/07/25/statement-against-state-violence-in-kashmir-ashoka-university-students-and-alumni/.

Sexton, John. "Building the First Global Network University." In *Places of Engagement: Reflections on Higher Education in 2040—A Global Approach*, edited by Armand Heijnen and Rob van der Vaart, 95–100. Amsterdam: Amsterdam University Press, 2018.

———. "Global Network University Reflection." NYU, December 21, 2010. https://www.nyu.edu/about/leadership-university-administration/office-of-the-president-emeritus/communications/global-network-university-reflection.html.

———. *Standing for Reason: The University in a Dogmatic Age*. New Haven, CT: Yale University Press, 2019.

Shanmugaratnam, Tharman. "Speech by Mr. Tharman Shanmugaratnam, Minister for Education, at the MOE Work Plan Seminar 2005." Press release. Singapore Government, September 22, 2005. https://www.nas.gov.sg/archivesonline/data/pdfdoc/20050922991.htm.

Sharma, Kritika. "Ashoka University Says Problem with Misuse of University Name, Not Kashmir Petition." *DNA India*, March 27, 2017. https://www.dnaindia.com/india/report-ashoka-university-says-problem-with-misuse-of-university-name-not-kashmir-petition-2369645.

———. "With 131 New Institutions in 4 Years, It's Boom Time for Private Universities in India." *Print*, September 6, 2021. https://theprint.in/india/education/with-131-new-institutions-in-4-years-its-boom-time-for-private-universities-in-india/726908/.

Shofer, Evan, and John W. Meyer, "The Worldwide Expansion of Higher Education in the Twentieth Century." *American Sociological Review* 70, no. 6 (December 2005): 898–920. https://www.jstor.org/stable/4145399.

Shulevitz, Judith. "The Future of College Is Not as Bleak as You Think." *New Republic*, August 22, 2014. https://newrepublic.com/article/119165/atlantic-article-minerva-project-overstates-universitys-future.

Shyam, Sarath. "Ashoka University: Stimulating a Liberal Impulse." *Higher Education Digest*, May 3, 2019. https://www.highereducationdigest.com/ashoka-university-stimulating-a -liberal-impulse/.

SiliconANGLE theCUBE. "Sandy Carter, AWS & Fred Swaniker, The Room: AWS Re:Invent 2021." YouTube, December 2, 2021. https://www.youtube.com/watch?v=c5trRVK_ajU.

Singh, Nandita. "Ashoka University Slammed for Teaching 'Anti-Hindu, Anti-Brahmin' Book." *Print*, December 15, 2018. https://theprint.in/india/governance/ashoka-university-slammed -for-teaching-anti-hindu-anti-brahmin-book/164268/.

Sleeper, Jim. "Innocents Abroad? Liberal Educators in Illiberal Societies." *Ethics & International Affairs*, June 12, 2015. https://www.ethicsandinternationalaffairs.org/2015/innocents-abroad -liberal-educators-illiberal-societies/.

Smith, Christian, Kari M. Hojara, Hilary A. Davidson, and Patricia Snell Herzog. *Lost in Transition: The Dark Side of Emerging Adulthood*. New York: Oxford University Press, 2011.

Smith, Mitch. "Yale Faculty Resolution Expresses Concern about Singapore Campus." *Inside Higher Ed*, April 6, 2012. https://www.insidehighered.com/news/2012/04/06/yale-faculty -resoultion-expresses-concern-about-singapore-campus.

Somerville, M., D. Anderson, H. Berbeco, J. R. Bourne, J. Crisman, D. Dabby, H. Donis-Keller, et al. "The Olin Curriculum: Thinking Toward the Future." *IEEE Transactions on Education* 48 (February 2005): 198–205. https://doi.org/10.1109/te.2004.842905.

Sra, Gunjeet. "India's New Ivy League." *Open*, March 26, 2015. https://openthemagazine.com /features/india/indias-new-ivy-league/.

Staisloff, Rick. "How to Review Your Business Model: Some Best Practices." *Trusteeship*, March/ April 2013. https://www.etsu.edu/125-chapter-1/newbudgetprocess/documents/staisloff _ma_13.pdf.

Staley, David J. *Alternative Universities: Speculative Design for Innovation in Higher Education*. Baltimore, MD: Johns Hopkins University Press, 2019.

Stanford d.school. "Uncharted Territory: A Guide to Reimagining Higher Education." Stanford d.school. Accessed January 1, 2022. http://www.worldacademy.org/files/global_leadership /papers/Uncharted_Territory_A_Guide_to_Reimagining_Higher_Education.pdf.

Statesman News Service. "Ashoka University's Economics Department Ranked No. 1." *Statesman*, October 15, 2020. https://www.thestatesman.com/education/ashoka-universitys-economics -department-ranked-no-1-1502929648.html.

Statista. "Singapore: PISA Score by Subject." Statista, 2022. https://www.statista.com/statistics /1182289/singapore-pisa-score-by-subject/.

Strada Institute for the Future of Work. *Robot Ready: Human+ Skills for the Future of Work*. Strada Institute, January 16, 2019. https://stradaeducation.org/report/robot-ready/.

Swaniker, Fred. "Five Reasons Why You Should NOT Work at ALX." Linked In, August 25, 2019. https://www.linkedin.com/pulse/five-reasons-why-you-should-work-alx-fred -swaniker/.

———. "Fred Swaniker, African Leadership University." Interview by Sara Custer for *PIE News*, June 7, 2017. https://thepienews.com/pie-chat/fred-swaniker-africa-leadership -university/.

———. "Fred Swaniker Gives Inspirational Toast: 'Do Hard Things.'" *TIME*, YouTube, April 24, 2019. https://www.youtube.com/watch?v=88cdrM5XkMM.

———. "How to Unlock the Talents of Young Africans." *GatesNotes* (blog), September 12, 2018. https://www.gatesnotes.com/development/fred-swaniker-on-africas-next-generation.

———. "The Most Inspiring Conversation I've Had This Year." Linked In, November 4, 2021. https://www.linkedin.com/pulse/most-inspiring-conversation-ive-had-year-fred-swaniker /?trackingId=cyFYnNnKAvGDf6NO1aXPog%3D%3D.

Swarthmore College. "1992 13th President Alfred H. Bloom." Swarthmore College, June 2016. https://www.swarthmore.edu/a-brief-history/1992-13th-president-alfred-h-bloom.

Taft, Isabelle. "How a U.S.-Backed University in Vietnam Unleashed Old Demons." *Politico Magazine*, February 4, 2018. https://www.politico.com/magazine/story/2018/02/04/how-a-us-backed-university-in-vietnam-unleashed-old-demons-216528/.

TAL Education Group. "TAL Education Leads Consortium and Joins Benchmark Capital in Funding for Disruptive U.S. Higher Education Provider, Minerva Project." Press release. PR Newswire, October 15, 2014. https://www.prnewswire.com/news-releases/tal-education-leads-consortium-and-joins-benchmark-capital-in-funding-for-disruptive-us-higher-education-provider-minerva-project-279244992.html.

Tan, Charlene. "Thinking Critically about Liberal Arts Education: Yale-NUS College in Singapore." In Marber and Araya, *Evolution of the Liberal Arts*, chap. 8.

Tan, Eng Chye. "The New NUS: Amplifying the University Scholars Programme and Yale-NUS Story." *Straits Times*, September 11, 2021. https://www.straitstimes.com/opinion/the-new-nus-amplifying-the-university-scholars-programme-and-yale-nus-story.

Technológico de Monterrey. "Modelo Tec21." Technológico de Monterrey, accessed June 15, 2022. https://tec.mx/en/model-tec21#.

Telegraph Online. "Global Pressure Piles on Ashoka University." March 21, 2021, https://www.telegraphindia.com/india/global-pressure-piles-on-ashoka-university/cid/1810171.

Thayer, Carl. "Obama's Visit to Vietnam: A Turning Point?" *Diplomat*, May 31, 2016. https://thediplomat.com/2016/05/obamas-visit-to-vietnam-a-turning-point/.

Thurgood Marshall Fund. "History of HBCUs." Thurgood Marshall College Fund, accessed June 15, 2022. https://www.tmcf.org/history-of-hbcus/.

Times Higher Education. "World University Rankings 2022." *Times Higher Education*, August 2021. https://www.timeshighereducation.com/world-university-rankings/2022/world-ranking.

Times of India. "Ashoka University to Appoint Ombudsperson to Encourage Free Expression." March 22, 2021. https://timesofindia.indiatimes.com/india/ashoka-university-to-appoint-ombudsperson-to-encourage-free-expression/articleshow/81637374.cms.

Tran, Minh Van. "War Record of Vietnam University's U.S. Chairman Angers Some." *AP News*, June 14, 2016. https://apnews.com/article/d27ef16c4247472bb4b704d895f871e4.

Trapman-O'Brien, Yannick. "NYU Abu Dhabi: A Student's View." Al-Fanar Media, August 1, 2014. https://www.al-fanarmedia.org/2014/08/nyu-abu-dhabi-students-view/.

Treadgold, Warren. *The University We Need: Reforming American Higher Education*. New York: Encounter Books, 2018.

Tu, Ly Minh. Student-Life archives, FUV. 2019. https://fulbright.edu.vn/category/student-life/.

Tucker, Marc S., ed. *Surpassing Shanghai: An Agenda for American Education Built on the World's Leading Systems*. Cambridge, MA: Harvard Education Press, 2011.

Underwood, Stephen. "An NYU Abu Dhabi Student Dishes on Their Dorms, Swanky Lounges." *NYU Local* (blog), September 17, 2010. https://nyulocal.com/an-nyu-abu-dhabi-student-dishes-on-their-dorms-swanky-lounges-cef05f5b1b84.

UN Environment Programme. "Our Work in Africa." UN Environment Programme, accessed June 15, 2022. https://www.unep.org/regions/africa/our-work-africa.

UNESCO Institute for Statistics. "263 Million Children and Youth Are Out of School." UNESCO, July 15, 2016. http://uis.unesco.org/en/news/263-million-children-and-youth-are-out-school.

USDFC (US International Development Finance Corporation). "DFC Commits $37 Million for Fulbright University Vietnam's New Campus in Ho Chi Minh City, Expanding Economic Opportunity." USDFC, October 29, 2021. https://www.dfc.gov/media/press-releases/dfc-commits-37-million-fulbright-university-vietnams-new-campus-ho-chi-minh.

USFQ. "¿Por Qué Estudiar en la USFQ?" USFQ, 2022. https://www.usfq.edu.ec/es.

Vander Ark, Tom. "Minerva: Better & Cheaper HigherEd." *Getting Smart*, January 17, 2014. https://www.gettingsmart.com/2014/01/17/minerva-better-cheaper-highered/.

Van der Wende, Marijk. "Trends towards Global Excellence in Undergraduate Education: Taking the Liberal Arts Experience into the 21st Century." *International Journal of Chinese Education* 2, no. 2 (2014). 289–307. https://doi.org/10.1163/22125868-12340025.

Volk, Steve, and Beth Benedix. "Liberal Arts Colleges Must Rediscover Their Purpose: To Improve the World." *Times Higher Education*, November 12, 2020. https://www.timeshighereducation.com/features/liberal-arts-colleges-must-rediscover-their-purpose-improve-world.

Vu, Linh. "Eight Philanthropists and Their Families Commit $40 Million for Fulbright University Vietnam, Making the Largest Philanthropic Gift to an Educational Institution in Vietnam." Fulbright University Vietnam, February 25, 2022. https://fulbright.edu.vn/eight-philanthropists-and-their-families-commit-40-million-for-fulbright-university-vietnam/.

Ward, Patrick. "Is It True that 90% of Startups Fail?" NanoGlobals, June 29, 2021. https://nanoglobals.com/startup-failure-rate-myths-origin/.

WASC (Western Association of Schools and Colleges) Senior College and University Commission. "Report of the WSCUC Team Seeking Accreditation Visit 1." April 13–16, 2021. WASC, 2016. https://wascsenior.app.box.com/s/blxwvwu4s9qkj88ap4jsceibndtsp4fd.

Wasley, Paula. "Vietnamese Leaders Discuss Overall of Higher Education During U.S. Visit." *Chronicle of Higher Education*, June 29, 2007. https://www.chronicle.com/article/vietnamese-leaders-discuss-overhaul-of-higher-education-during-u-s-visit/.

Wasserman, Gary. *The Doha Experiment: Arab Kingdom, Catholic College, Jewish Teacher*. New York: Skyhorse, 2017. Kindle.

Wieman, Carl. "Expertise in University Teaching & the Implications for Teaching Effectiveness, Evaluation and Training." *Daedalus* 148, no. 4 (2019): 47–78. https://doi.org/10.1162/daed_a_01760.

Wildavsky, Ben. *The Great Brain Race: How Global Universities Are Reshaping the World*. Princeton, NJ: Princeton University Press, 2012.

Wire Staff. "Ashoka University Acknowledges 'Some Lapses' but Pratap Bhanu Mehta Insists on Moving On." *Wire*, March 21, 2021. https://thewire.in/education/ashoka-university-pratap-bhanu-mehta-lapses-protests.

Wood, Graeme. "The Future of College?" *Atlantic*, September 2014. https://www.theatlantic.com/magazine/archive/2014/09/the-future-of-college/375071/.

World Economic Forum. *The Future of Jobs: Employment, Skills and Workforce Strategy for the Fourth Industrial Revolution*. WEF, January 2016. https://www3.weforum.org/docs/WEF_Future_of_Jobs.pdf.

World's Universities with Real Impact. "WURI Ranking 2022." WURI, accessed June 15, 2022. https://www.wuri.world/%EB%B3%B5%EC%A0%9C-wuri-ranking-2021.

Yale Daily News. "News' View: Something to Talk About." Editorial, September 13, 2010. https://yaledailynews.com/blog/2010/09/13/news-view-something-to-talk-about/.

Yale University. "International Framework: Yale's Agenda for 2009 through 2012." Yale University, 2013. https://world.yale.edu/sites/default/files/files/Yale_International_Framework_2009-2012.pdf.

Yale University. "Statement Regarding the Cancellation of an Offering at Yale-NUS (National University of Singapore) College." *YaleNews*, September 14, 2019. https://news.yale.edu/2019/09/14/statement-regarding-cancellation-offering-yale-nus-college.

Yale University Office of the President. "Archived Speeches of Former President Levin." Office of the President, 1996. https://president.yale.edu/about/past-presidents/levin-speeches-archive.

Yang, Daryl. "Did the Yale-NUS Experiment Fail? No, but the New College Might." *Octant,* September 1, 2021. https://theoctant.org/edition/issue/allposts/opinion/did-the-yale-nus -experiment-fail-no-but-the-new-college-might/.

Zaytuna College. "About." Zaytuna College, accessed June 15, 2022. https://zaytuna.edu/about.

Zha, Qiang. "What Is Liberal Arts Education in the 21st Century? An Explanation Starts with Chinese Universities and Goes beyond China." In Godwin and Pickus, *Liberal Arts and Sciences,* 40–48.

Zhao, Yong. "Reinventing Liberal Arts Education in China in an Age of Smart Machines." In Godwin and Pickus, *Liberal Arts and Sciences,* 23–33.

INDEX

academic freedom: Ashoka, 134–36, 140, 249; Claremont faculty, 59; Fulbright University Vietnam, 96, 98, 102, 108, 115, 218, 250; new universities, 250–53, 256, 281; NYU Abu Dhabi, 32, 34, 42–45, 48–51, 248, 251, 252; US colleges and universities, 242, 245, 282; Yale-NUS, 61–63, 72–74, 251

accreditation: African Leadership University, 176; Ashesi, 141, 149–51, 161; Ashoka, 233; curriculum and, in start-up university, 226–34; external review, 297n34; Fulbright, 115–16; Minerva, 184, 186, 188, 204–5, 232; regional team report, 297n20; standardization of content, 287n3; start-up universities, 9, 14, 226–34; Yale-NUS, 54

Accreditation Board for Engineering and Technology, 78, 233

Africa: finding market for liberal arts in, 148–51; future of, and Ashesi University, 159–61; training ethical entrepreneurial leaders for, 154–57. *See also* African Leadership University (ALU); Ashesi University

African Leadership Academy (ALA), 164–65, 211

African Leadership Experience (ALX), discontent and emergence of, 175–77. *See also* African Leadership University (ALU)

African Leadership Group (ALG), 296n30

African Leadership International, 296n30

African Leadership Network, 295n2, 296n30

African Leadership University (ALU), 2, 3, 4; ALU 2.0 and The Room, 177–80; audacity and risk-taking, 180–82; campuses of, 238–39; codesign year, 219; curriculum, 168–70, 229, 231, 233; discontent and emergence of African Leadership Experience (ALX), 175–77; excellence at scale, 177–80; faculty without tenure, 244; from academy to university, 164–67; impact of,

11; interdisciplinary education, 275; lacking inherited prestige, 211; making it safe to innovate, 172–74; Mauritius, 14, 166, 167, 173, 174, 175, 178, 180, 215, 238–39; phased launch of, 220; recruiting faculty, 223, 225, 226; Rwanda, 14, 173, 174, 175, 178, 179, 180, 238–39; Rwanda campus, 166–67; School of Wildlife Conservation, 167; student experiences, 169–72; sustainable business model, 215; transition phase of, 241; turning university on its head, 167–72

African Renaissance, 148, 161

Alexander, Bryan, forecasting the future of higher education, 28

al Mawrid Arab Center for the Study of Art, 52

Almond, Ian, on global issues, 255

ALU. *See* African Leadership University (ALU)

Amazon Web Services, Swaniker and, 182

ambiguity, new universities and, 252–53

American Association for the Advancement of Science, 266

American Association of University Professors, Yale community, 62

American College of Greece, 288n23

American Society for Engineering Education, 78

American University: Beirut, 288n23; Cairo, 257, 288n23

Amherst, 72, 124, 173

Andersson, Bertil, Nanyang Technological University, 187

Andrew Mellon Foundation, 248

Ansah, Angela Owusa, education of Ashesi provost, 158

ANZ Bank, 97; Vietnam, 1

Aoun, Joseph, on intelligent machines, 28

Appiah, Kwame Anthony, *Cosmopolitanism*, 40

Apple, 147, 164, 177

Archimedes' lever, Ashoka University as, 137–40

A NOTE ON THE TYPE

This book has been composed in Adobe Text and Gotham.
Adobe Text, designed by Robert Slimbach for Adobe,
bridges the gap between fifteenth- and sixteenth-century
calligraphic and eighteenth-century Modern styles.
Gotham, inspired by New York street signs, was designed
by Tobias Frere-Jones for Hoefler & Co.